ALEX MacCORMICK is the author of five books, including *The Mammoth Book of Maneaters*. She is based in London but spends much of her time working and painting around the Mediterranean.

ROD GREEN is an author and editor who has written a number of books for Constable & Robinson, including *100 Military Inventions That Changed The World*. He lives in Surrey.

Recent Mammoth titles

The Mammoth Book of Weird News
The Mammoth Book of Undercover Cops
The Mammoth Book of Antarctic Journeys
The Mammoth Book of Muhammad Ali
The Mammoth Book of Best British Crime 9
The Mammoth Book of Conspiracies
The Mammoth Book of Lost Symbols
The Mammoth Book of Nebula Awards SF
The Mammoth Book of Steampunk
The Mammoth Book of New CSI
The Mammoth Book of Gangs
The Mammoth Book of SF Wars
The Mammoth Book of One-Liners
The Mammoth Book of Best New SF 25
The Mammoth Book of Jokes 2
The Mammoth Book of Street Art
The Mammoth Book of Ghost Stories by Women
The Mammoth Book of Irish Humour
The Mammoth Book of Unexplained Phenomena
The Mammoth Book of Best British Crime 10
The Mammoth Book of Combat
The Mammoth Book of Dark Magic
The Mammoth Book of Angels and Demons
The Mammoth Book of New Sudoku
The Mammoth Book of Zombies
The Mammoth Book of Covert Ops
The Mammoth Book of the Rolling Stones
The Mammoth Book of Prison Breaks
The Mammoth Book of Time Travel SF
The Mammoth Book of Westerns

THE MAMMOTH BOOK OF

SHARK ATTACKS

ALEX MacCORMICK and

ROD GREEN

ROBINSON

RUNNING PRESS
PHILADELPHIA · LONDON

Constable & Robinson Ltd.
55–56 Russell Square
London WC1B 4HP
www.constablerobinson.com

First published in the UK by Constable,
an imprint of Constable & Robinson Ltd., 1996

This revised edition published by Robinson,
an imprint of Constable & Robinson Ltd., 2013

UK ISBN: 978-1-47210-029-0 (paperback)
UK ISBN: 978-1-47210-030-6 (e-book)

1 3 5 7 9 10 8 6 4 2

First published in the United States in 2013 by Running Press Book Publishers,
A Member of the Perseus Books Group

Books published by Running Press are available at special discounts for bulk
purchases in the United States by corporations, institutions, and other organizations.
For more information, please contact the Special Markets Department at the Perseus
Books Group, 2300 Chestnut Street, Suite 200, Philadelphia, PA 19103, or call (800)
810-4145, ext. 5000, or e-mail special.markets@perseusbooks.com.

US ISBN: 978-0-7624-4433-5
US Library of Congress Control Number: 2012944615

9   8   7   6   5   4   3   2   1
Digit on the right indicates the number of this printing

Running Press Book Publishers
2300 Chestnut Street
Philadelphia, PA 19103-4371

Visit us on the web!
www.runningpress.com

Printed and bound by CPI Group (UK) Ltd, Croydon, CR0 4YY

Contents

Introduction

"Tonight the whole town is stirred by a personal feeling, a feeling which makes men and women regard the fish as they might a human being who had taken the lives of a boy and a youth and badly, perhaps mortally, injured another youngster. The one purpose in which everybody shares is to get the shark, kill it and to see its body drawn up on the shore, where all may look and be assured it will destroy no more."

Not much seems to have changed since that report of the first "modern" shark attacks in 1916. "Summer of the shark" shouted newspaper headlines in the USA and elsewhere in 2001 – "The man-eating monster must be destroyed". But are sharks – of which there are some 470 species in the world – really "man-eaters", stalking unwary paddlers, swimmers, surfers and divers? Do they lie in wait to gobble up carefree children, men and women?

Of course not. Many of us are nowadays much better informed, through television documentaries and the like, than perhaps we were even a few years ago. Many recognize that sharks are fascinating, beautiful creatures about which we still know too little. Indeed, we may even applaud the fact that, in several parts of the world, a number of species – including great whites – have been declared endangered and hunting them is forbidden. And yet most of us are still afraid of them – very, very afraid.

"I actually broke my own arm off in its mouth – I heard the snap of it. He was gnashing back and forth like in the *Jaws* movie. Now he's got a Timex in his belly," said the swimmer mauled off Alabama. His colleague recalled: "It came up under me and I looked down and saw him staring me right in the face. I thought: 'I'm going to die.'"

"The shark came at me out of the blue, totally unexpected, not even a chance … I didn't see anything, no fish around – just bam!" recalled a young surfer in Florida in 2001.

The honeymoon couple kayaking off Maui, the grandmother on a crowded US beach who was testing the knee-deep water for her grandchildren, the schoolboys rowing on an Australian river, the Italian father and son fishing off Rimini in 2001, the diver in California's Red Triangle, the Japanese surfer who lost both legs and an arm, the member of the British Royal Family in the Bahamas, the eleven-year-old paddling in South African surf, the British policemen shipwrecked in the Caribbean, the two teenage girls swimming in an ocean inlet, the Papuan villager gathering food, the holidaymaker on Malta, the Hong Kong lady taking her daily dip – all of them knew unimaginable fear, some met their deaths.

Well over half the attacks on human beings by sharks occur in water no more than five feet (1.5 metres) deep. Until relatively recently the majority of attacks were on swimmers, but nowadays it seems that surfers are becoming the chief victims. Yet, no matter whether we are water sports enthusiasts, paddling holidaymakers or earning our living from the seas, too many of us inadvertently take risks. Too few of us seem to know in which parts of the world attacks are most likely to occur.

How safe is it to go in the water at popular beach resorts around the coastlines of, for instance, the USA, South

Africa, Australia, the Caribbean islands or even Britain? Are the Gulf and Atlantic coasts of Florida as dangerous as California's Pacific waters? And are there any sharks patrolling the waters off the holiday beaches favoured by millions of people around the Mediterranean? We may all think we are well informed, but the answer to at least one of these questions will surprise many.

According to British shark specialist and biologist Ian Fergusson, there is a thriving population of one of the world's most feared creatures – the great white shark – living and breeding in the Mediterranean.

"A commonly held view by regional governments and the travel business is that there are no great whites in the Mediterranean. Concerns about shark attacks are obviously a problem, so strenuous efforts are made to cover them up," he told the *Guardian* in London. "On average there is an attack once every two years, although in the 1950s and 1960s it was more like five a year."

For most of us the thought of being attacked and eaten alive by an unseen creature that appears out of nowhere is a vivid, deep-seated fear – even though we try hard to dismiss it as irrational. Shark attacks occur elsewhere, we tell ourselves, far from where we swim, surf, dive or go kayaking. Then, just when we have finally managed to convince ourselves that it *is* safe to go in the water, *Jaws* reappears on our television screens and our worst nightmares are once more reawakened. But perhaps what we see in the film is merely Hollywood hype?

Unfortunately it is not completely fantasy.

There are, in reality, fearsome sharks up to twenty feet long and weighing as much as a truck which attack boats and humans. The three species generally agreed to be most dangerous in the world are:

- The great white or white pointer (*Carcharodon carcharias*) – of *Jaws* fame and thought to be responsible for between one-third and two-thirds of fatal attacks each year from both coasts of the USA and the Mediterranean to South Africa and Australia, even though it tends to bite once and let go.
- The tiger shark (*Galeocerdo cuvieri*) – feared as the most ferocious of sharks from Australia and the Torres Strait to India and Florida, it hunts close to shore and locks tenaciously on to its prey.
- The bull shark (*Carcharhinus leucas*) – also known as the ground shark and cub shark, attacks not only at sea and close to shore but also in freshwater rivers and lakes, hence such local names as Zambezi shark, Swan River whaler, Lake Nicaragua shark and Ganges shark. Found in and around North, Central and South America, Australia, Africa, Asia and the Indian subcontinent.

Of the 470 known species of shark only thirty or so have been definitely identified as having attacked humans. Although many victims and witnesses (if there are any) are too shocked to identify accurately what type of shark it was that attacked. Research does show, however, that over 80 per cent of shark species are under five feet long and rarely encounter human beings.

It may also prove comforting to recall that in response to a question concerning the Royal Navy's need during the Second World War for an effective shark repellent, the then Prime Minister, Winston Churchill, declared forcefully to the House of Commons that "the British Government is entirely *opposed* to sharks!"

While seafarers the world over have, since time immemorial, feared "the monsters of the deep," the first reliable written accounts of seamen being killed by sharks are not found until the sixteenth century. There is no suggestion, though, that such events were uncommon. In 1580 a sailor fell overboard from a storm-tossed sailing ship somewhere between Portugal and its destination in India. As the hapless man grasped the line thrown to him by his shipmates and was being hauled back towards the ship, a "large monster called tiburon" suddenly leapt from beneath the waves and "tore him to pieces before our very eyes". "That surely was a grievous death," added the writer.

Only fifteen years later it was reported that:

This fish doth great mischiefe and devoureth many men that fish for pearles ... As our ship lay in the River of Cochin [India] ... it happened that as we were to hang on [replace] our rutter [rudder] ... a saylor, being made fast with a corde to the ship, hung downe with halfe his body into the water to place the same [rudder] upon the hookes, and there came one of those Hayens [sharks] and bit one of his legs, to the middle of his thigh, cleane off at a bit[e], notwithstanding that the [ship's] Master stroke at him with an oare, and as the poor man was putting down his arms to feel his wound, the same Fish at the second time for another bite did bite off his hand and arme above the elbow, and also a peece of his buttocke.

Over subsequent centuries the perils of travelling by ship or in small vessels remained the same for seamen and passengers alike until the advent of the Second World War, when at last governments began to give serious consideration to the substantial loss of human life and the cost thereof. Between 1939 and 1945 thousands, perhaps hundreds of thousands, of men, women and children endured unimaginable horrors as they floated helplessly in the sea following the loss of their ship or plane owing to enemy action. The large number of such people lost to shark attacks and the dreadful experiences recounted by survivors eventually forced naval authorities to investigate the feasibility of developing shark repellents and other aids to survival.

Progress was slow, however. It was not until 1958 – prompted by memories of the awful losses suffered by such vessels as the USS *Indianapolis* in 1945 and the realization that no effective shark repellent was available – that the US Office of Naval Research decided to fund a research programme related to sharks. That same year a group of international scientists met in New Orleans to discuss the problems involved. This, in turn, gave rise to the establishment of a Shark Research Panel, which agreed to coordinate the work and reports by international researchers. In addition, the panel initiated the Shark Attack File, the first attempt to document comprehensively shark attacks on a global historical basis. After undergoing various changes over the years, the file evolved into what is now the International Shark Attack File, based at the University of Florida, under the auspices of the American Elasmobranch Society.

By 1995, under the directorship of ichthyologist George Burgess, the file had expanded to encompass 2,500 individual investigations of unprovoked shark attacks primarily in North America, Hawaii, Australia and South Africa. Its growing renown as a professional research archive and source of information for the media has led to the establishment of a number of regional shark attack files around the world.

Through these files, internet sites and media reports

more information is now available on sharks and on incidents involving humans. However, there are still relatively few substantial reports available to the general public on attacks around Africa (other than South Africa), South America (Brazil is one of the top three "black spots" for fatalities), the Indian subcontinent, Asia and the Mediterranean. There are several reasons for this. In some regions, attacks may be too commonplace to be worth reporting and even the most serious attacks may not be deemed newsworthy enough to be of interest to anyone outside the remote region where they occurred. In other areas, attempts are made to suppress stories about shark attacks for fear of damaging tourism, although the different arms of the media – press, TV, internet, radio and social media – make it increasingly difficult to block the spread of stories about shark attacks in the twenty-first century. Nevertheless, the presence of sharks off popular tourist beaches is something that many would rather not broadcast too widely. Attacks in the Mediterranean may be decreasing and large sharks may be in decline there – but surely the general public still has a right to know about them? When millions of holidaymakers leap into the azure waters off a beach in Italy, Greece, Israel or North Africa, for instance, shouldn't they be aware about whether there are likely to be great white or other large sharks in the vicinity?

Choosing to get in the water with sharks is an ever more popular option becoming available through commercial enterprises offering guided encounters. Is the growing popularity of such enterprises a sign of public awareness that a significant number of shark species are now in danger of becoming extinct – do people want to see them before they disappear forever? Overfishing and finning – the disgusting practice of hacking off fins for oriental dishes such as shark fin soup and then chucking the sharks back into the sea to die – have reduced some populations in the Pacific, Indian and Atlantic Oceans by up to 80 per cent. In December 2000 President Clinton signed the Shark Finning Prohibition Act, banning finning in the US Exclusive Economic Zone that extends 200 miles from shore. The act was chiefly aimed at Hawaii, where finning had increased 2,000 per cent from 1991 to 1998.

In the last decade of the twentieth century, despite considerable opposition from hunters, laws that forbid the killing of great whites were enacted in South Africa (1991), the USA and Australia (1997), and, in 1999, in Malta, the first Mediterranean country do so. In 2010 an agreement was signed by eleven states at the United Nations to declare seven species of shark as "protected species": the great white, basking shark, whale shark, porbeagle, spiny dogfish, shortfin and longfin mako sharks. Still greater efforts need to be made to maintain the oceans' shark populations and protect the delicate balance of our planet's most important ecosystem.

Although the number of unprovoked shark attacks increases year by year because more people go in and on the waters of the world, we should all try to remember that *we* are the most dangerous predators on Earth, not they.

In the following pages, readers will find not only many accounts of gruesome shark attacks but also much that will enlighten, surprise and move them. The courage of survivors and of those who have risked their lives to rescue victims is frequently awesome and inspiring. No other book offers such a large selection of significant first-hand accounts and news reports of unprovoked attacks around the world.

SHARK ATTACKS
1900–39

1906

UNITED KINGDOM, AUSTRALIA AND ADEN
(NOW YEMEN), 1906
Letters to the Editor of *The Times*, London
Sir – Eight years ago, writing from this port [Mevagissey, Cornwall], I ventured to warn those who bathe from yachts and small boats anywhere within the ten-mile limit against the risk of an encounter with the blue or porbeagle sharks well known to swim no further from the Cornish coast on hot summer days. Only four days ago some of the local mackerel crews saw a blue shark, seven or eight feet long, swimming within Chapel Point – that is to say, not more than a mile from the harbour. A little further back a large party of visitors were fishing for pollack five or six miles off. A brand new line was then essayed, with the result that the monster was finally captured. Its measurements were, I regret to say, not taken, but some idea may be formed of its weight when I mention that five men were unable to drag it with the aid of a rope from the quay to their lodgings not far distant.

Fresh as I am from the Florida shores of the Gulf of Mexico, where on one occasion I had the misfortune to hook a leopard shark fourteen feet long, these Cornish marauders seem very puny; but they might, for all that, prove unpleasant bathing companions at close quarters. It has admittedly never been demonstrated that they will attack a swimmer in daylight; on the other hand, it has yet to be proved that they will not; and it is against involuntary settling of this vexed question that I once more make bold to warn your readers.

The coves along this coast, in which the water is deep enough for diving and clear enough to satisfy the most fastidious, are too many and too beautiful for there to be the need of this foolhardy practice of bathing from yachts' dinghies outside the headlands. On the other hand, these large sharks afford most exciting sport, being the only really big game in our seas, and a tussle with one is always an attraction – at the further end of a line. Anyone who sounds such a warning at that conveyed in this letter runs the risk of being abused as a sensation-monger, but I imagine that most would be willing to take that risk in the hope of averting possible disaster.

Your obedient servant,

F. G. Aflalo

Mevagissey, 3 August 1906

Sir – The warning to bathers published in *The Times* recently is a repetition of history. Even a caution from the same source which appeared eight years ago was by no means the first of its kind, for as far back as the year 1876 another, dated from Hastings, was circulated in the London Press.

The presence of sharks in British seas, contested even today by ill-informed persons, is appreciated only by those who fish for either sport or their livelihood as a very real evil. The larger sharks, of the blue and porbeagle kinds, make their presence felt inshore only in the hottest July and August weather ...

It is, however with the two summer kinds that the bather is chiefly concerned, since not only is salt-water bathing confined for the most part to the summer months, but it is only in a high temperature that, mindful perhaps of their centre of distribution in tropical seas, these tyrants venture to attack man. The greatest of all sharks, the huge basking shark or sail-fish, which yachtsmen occasionally encounter off the Irish coast and even near the Land's End, is a perfectly harmless creature, feeding on entomostraca, and incapable of attacking even the feeblest human being. To this species, no doubt, belonged an example measuring thirty feet in length which was found entangled in seventeen nets at Hastings in the year 1810. It was purchased by Colonel Bothwell "for his friend Mr Home, the surgeon of Sackville Street, who intends to dissect it and place the skeleton in his museum". It is believed by some that this is the skeleton in the Natural History Museum, London.

Of bathers being seized by sharks on the British coast there is, it is true, no record. At the same time it is well to remember that it is exceedingly improbable that there would be. Sharks are notorious cowards ... Sharks, unless encouraged by numbers of their own kind or by the helplessness of a solitary swimmer, give man a wide berth. It is, therefore, only the lonely bather who has anything to fear from these cowardly animals, and bathing, at any rate along our coasts in summer time, is a gregarious exercise. One swimmer among many would run little or no risk.

One of the well-known diving boys at Aden, whose evolutions round anchored lines have recently been discontinued by order of the authorities, contrived for many years to attract much sympathy and baksheesh by the loss of one of his legs, reputedly by a shark bite. The present writer interrogated him on the subject many years ago, and from him had a circumstantial account of his adventure. It has, however, since transpired, possibly when the prohibition of diving put an end to the profits from this source, that his leg was taken off by the screw of a steamer, from which he was not able to get clear, and thus one of the few authentic cases of sharks attacking human beings disappears from the list.

A very small boy in the company of others was badly bitten by a shark in Sydney Harbour in the Australian winter of 1895, but the case was exceptional. The lad's cap had blown out into deeper water, out of the "white water" range to which Sydney swimmers are careful to keep, and it was in floundering after it that he met with his accident, which was said to have resulted in death the same night from haemorrhage.

So far, it must be admitted, the evidence of death from sharks in English seas is altogether negative, but it is an article of firm belief with many well acquainted with the ways of these creatures that many of the cases of drowning from alleged cramp, in which the victim disappears and the body is never found, are in reality cases of seizure, not by cramp, but by sharks. Obviously, the theory is a matter of opinion only and cannot be argued to a logical conclusion.

A very interesting and in many ways unique experience lately came under the writer's notice, in which, in the year 1876, a gentleman, who plainly remembers every detail and has the evidence of a long letter written to a relative at the time, was almost certainly as near death from this cause as any one could be and yet escape.

He was bathing alone from the beach between Hastings and Fairlight [Sussex, England], and had swum out to an anchored smack about 400 yards from the shore. Returning almost immediately, he was carried sideways by a strong ebb tide and, when about 100 yards from the smack, he felt something in contact with his left leg. He struck out wildly, and immediately his left arm rubbed along some kind of fish. At this he shouted and swam with all his might, and two or three times more the fish scraped alongside him, but he managed to attract the attention of two men in a small boat, and into this he almost vaulted in his anxiety to get out of such company. A large fish was seen swimming round the boat, undoubtedly a blue or porbeagle shark, and the fishermen of the district were unanimously of the opinion that it had been a very near thing.

Why, it may be asked, did the shark not seize him and have done with it? Those who have had much traffic with sharks will at once recognize in the episode their invariable behaviour with any kind of bait. They always swim round it half a dozen times, nosing it, rubbing their body against it, and then, if all is well, they seize it in their teeth. All was not well on the occasion referred to, for the bait behaved most uncommonly, throwing out its arms and legs, and shouting at the top of its voice, a performance more than enough to scare any shark in comparatively shallow water.

The recent warning, then, touching the foolishness of bathing at any considerable distance from the shore in summer weather might have been coupled with a rider indicating the yet greater risk of bathing alone. In company with others, who might, and probably would, make a great deal of noise and commotion in the water, the risk would be slight. On the other hand, a solitary swimmer, too faint-hearted to frighten off his pursuer, would almost certainly go under, first with cramp induced by the paralysis of fear, and then with the shark's teeth in his body. This would never be recovered, and there would be one more disappearance, with perhaps its sequel in the Probate Court some years later.

From a Correspondent

20 August 1906

Sir – In a long communication in your issue of yesterday your Correspondent takes up the cudgels on behalf of the shark as an innocent and harmless bathing companion. The most serious impropriety which he will impute to the shark is that occasionally, like the tiger in the children's rhyme, "he comes and snaggles with his nose". He dismisses as apocryphal all the stories of bathers seized by sharks, and on the strength of one of the Aden diving boys having had his leg taken off by a ship's propeller and not by a shark, he remarks, "thus one of the few authentic cases of sharks attacking human beings disappears from the list".

Now I am afraid that this is a case of protesting too much. I happened to be on board a vessel off Aden when one of those cases occurred. I did not see the shark, but I saw the boy dive and reappear almost immediately with his leg bitten off above the knee. My recollection is very distinct that the propeller was at rest at the time. Moreover, judging from the place where the boy dived and the short time he was below water, it would have been necessary for the propeller, in order to reach him, to have left its place at the stern, to have rushed with ferocious speed to a point more than half the length of the vessel and some distance out from the ship's side, and to have afterwards returned to its proper position and have fixed itself there without exciting notice.

I am afraid I must continue to believe, in spite of your Correspondent, that that boy's leg at any rate was bitten off. On another occasion I was cabin mate for some time with a man who had recently been for some days hanging in the rigging of a vessel wrecked in tropical waters, and his knowledge of sharks and their ways was, like Mr Weller's knowledge of London, extensive and peculiar. But, while I respectfully question your Correspondent's premises, I fully endorse his conclusions, and for the future shall forsake the seclusion of the solitary swimmer for the vulgar security of mixed bathing.

I am yours faithfully,

H. Whitbread

Seal, Sevenoaks, 21 August 1906

1910

WESTERN AUSTRALIA, AUSTRALIA, 1910

An account reached Plymouth, UK, yesterday of a ship's crew having been devoured by sharks. Theodore Anderson was engaged in a pearling schooner on the Australian coast, when, during a storm, the vessel drove ashore between Broome and Fremantle. All the men with the exception of Anderson and the captain put off in the ship's boats, which capsized one by one, the men being eaten by sharks. The captain tried to reach the shore, but was seized before the eyes of Anderson, who eventually swam ashore.

The Times, London, 24 December 1910

1916

NEW JERSEY, USA, 1916

Captain Thomas Cottrell, a retired sailor, caught a glimpse

of a dark gray shape swimming rapidly in the shallow waters of Matawan Creek this morning [12 July] as he crossed the trolley drawbridge a few hundred yards from town. So impressed was he, when he recalled the two swimmers killed by sharks on the New Jersey coast within two weeks, that he hurried back to town and spread the warning among the 2,000 residents that a shark had entered Matawan Creek.

Everywhere the Captain was laughed at. How could a shark get ten miles away from the ocean, swim through Raritan Bay, and enter the shallow creek with only seventeen feet of water at its deepest spot and nowhere more than thirty-five feet wide? So the townsfolk asked one another, and grown-ups and children flocked to the creek as usual for their daily dip.

But Captain Cottrell was right, and tonight the people are dynamiting the creek, hoping to bring to the surface the body of a small boy the shark dragged down. Elsewhere, in the Long Branch Memorial Hospital lies the body of a youth so terribly torn by the shark that he died of loss of blood, and in St Peter's Hospital in New Brunswick doctors are working late tonight to save the left leg of another lad whom the shark nipped as the big fish fled down the creek toward Raritan Bay.

The dynamiters hoped, when they brought their explosives to the creek, that, beside the body, they might bring up the shark where men, waiting with weapons, could kill it. Others hastened to the mouth of the creek where it empties into the bay a mile and a half from town and spread heavy wire netting.

The people of Matawan had been horrified by the tales of sharks which came to them from Spring Lake, Beach Haven, Asbury Park and the other coast resorts. They had been sympathetically affected by the reports of the death of Charles E. Vansant and Charles Bruder. But those places were far away and the tragedies had not touched them closely.

Tonight the whole town is stirred by a personal feeling, a feeling which makes men and women regard the fish as they might a human being who had taken the lives of a boy and a youth and badly, perhaps mortally, injured another youngster. The one purpose in which everybody shares is to get the shark, kill it and to see its body drawn up on the shore, where all may look and be assured it will destroy no more.

The death of the boy and youth, and the injury to the other youngster were due to the refusal of almost every one to believe that sharks could ever enter the shoal waters where clam-diggers work at low tide. As long ago as Sunday, Frank Slater saw the shark and told it everywhere. He stopped repeating the tale when everyone laughed him to scorn.

Then today came Captain Cottrell's warning, and with that Lester Stilwell, twelve years old, might have been the only victim had it not been for the unfortunate coincidence that the boy suffered from fits. It was supposed that an attack in the water had caused him to sink, and rescuers, with no notion that a shark had dragged him down, entered the water fearlessly.

It was while trying to bring young Stilwell's body ashore that Stanley G. Fisher, son of Captain W. H. Fisher, retired Commodore of the Savannah Line fleet, lost his life. The third victim, Joseph Dunn, twelve years old, was caught as he tried to leave the water, the alarm caused by Fisher's death at last having convinced the town that a shark really was in the creek.

Stilwell was the first to die. With several other boys, he had gone swimming off a disused steamboat pier at the edge of the town. He was a strong swimmer and so swam further out than his companions.

So it was that none could follow him, but several boys, instead, raced through the town calling that Stilwell had had a fit in the water and had gone down. They said the boy rose once after his first disappearance. He was screaming and yelling, and waving his arms wildly. His body was swirling round and round in the water. Fisher was one of the first to hear and immediately started for the creek.

"Remember what Captain Cottrell said!" exclaimed Miss May Anderson, a teacher in the local school, as Fisher passed her. "It may have been a shark."

"A shark here!" exclaimed Fisher incredulously. "I don't care anyway. I'm going after that boy."

He hurried to the shore and donned bathing tights. By the time he was attired many others had reached the spot, among them Stilwell's parents. Fisher dived into the creek and swam to midstream, where he dived once or twice in search of Stilwell's body. At last he came up and cried to the throng ashore: "I've got it!"

He was nearer the opposite shore and struck out in that direction, while Arthur Smith and Joseph Deulew put out in a motor boat to bring him back. Fisher was almost on the shore and, touching bottom, had risen to his feet, when the onlookers heard him utter a cry and throw up his arms. Stilwell's body slipped back into the stream and, with another cry, Fisher was dragged after it.

"The shark! The shark!" cried the crowd ashore, and other men sprang into other motor boats and started for the spot where Fisher had disappeared. Smith and Deulew were in the lead, but, before they overtook him, Fisher had risen and dragged himself to the bank, where he collapsed.

Those who reached him found the young man's right leg stripped of flesh from above the hip at the waist line to a point below the knee. It was as though the limb had been raked with heavy, dull knives. He was senseless from shock and pain, but was resuscitated by Dr G. L. Reynolds after Recorder Arthur Van Buskirk had made a tourniquet of rope and staunched the flow of blood from Fisher's frightful wound.

Fisher said it was a shark that had grabbed him. He had felt the nip of its teeth on his leg, and had looked down and seen the fish clinging to him. Others ashore said they had seen the white belly of the shark as it turned when it seized Fisher. Fisher said he wasn't in more than three or four feet of water when the fish grabbed him, and he had had no notion of sharks until that instant. If he had thought of them at all, he said, he had felt himself safe when he got his feet on the bottom.

Fisher was carried across the river and hurried in a motor car to the railroad station, where he was put aboard the 5.06 train for Long Branch. There he was transferred to the hospital, but died before he could be carried to the operating table.

At the creek, meantime, dynamite had been procured from the store of Asher P. Woolley and arrangements were being made to set it off when a motor boat raced up to the steamboat pier. At the wheel was J. R. Lefferts and in the craft lay young Dunn. With his brother William and several others, he had been swimming off the New Jersey Clay Company brickyards at Cliffwood, half a mile below the spot where Stilwell and Fisher were attacked.

News of the accident had just reached the boys and they had hurried from the water. Dunn was the last to leave and, as he drew himself up on the brick company's pier, with only his left leg trailing in the water, the shark struck at that. Its teeth shut over the leg above and below the knee and much of the flesh was torn away.

Apparently, however, the fish had struck this time in fright, for it loosed its grip on the boy at once, and his companions dragged him, yelling, up on to the pier.

He was taken to the J. Fisher bag factory near by, where Dr H. J. Cooley of Keyport dressed his wound, and then he was carried in a motor car to St Peter's Hospital in New Brunswick by E. H. Bomick. There it was said last night that the physicians hoped to save his leg if blood poisoning did not set in.

The youngster steadfastly refused to tell where he lived, for, he said, he did not want his mother to worry about him. From his relatives, however, it was learned that his home is at 124 East 128th Street, New York. He and his brother had been visiting an aunt in Cliffwood.

Fisher was the son of Commodore Watson H. Fisher, who for more than fifty years commanded boats of the Savannah Line up and down the coast. He retired from active service a few years ago. About ten days ago the father and mother went to Minneapolis to visit a daughter there, and they had intended to remain for another week, but, when word was sent this evening of the death of their son, they sent a message that they would leave for home immediately.

News of the tragedies here spread rapidly through neighboring towns, and from Morgan's Beach, a few miles away, came a report that two sharks had been killed there in the morning by lifeguards. One was said to be twelve feet long. Persons who saw the fish when it grabbed Fisher said they thought it was about nine feet long.

New York Times, 13 July 1916

1919

DEVON, UNITED KINGDOM, 1919
A shark which had made its appearance among women bathers at Croyde, North Devon, on Tuesday was the cause of considerable excitement. The bathers got safely ashore, and the shark was shot by Mr C. C. Cuff, assistant manager in the Great Western locomotive works, Swindon. It took five persons to drag ashore the shark, which measured 7 ft 6 in. in length.

The Times, London, 14 August 1919

1922

NEW SOUTH WALES, AUSTRALIA, 1922
Sir Walter Davidson, Governor of New South Wales, is sending an official report to the King [George V] of a gallant attempt by a returned soldier, Jack Chalmers, to rescue a boy named Coghlan from the jaws of a shark, with a recommendation that the Albert Medal be awarded to Chalmers, for whom a large sum of money has been collected locally.

The Times, London, 15 February 1922

1924

WEYMOUTH, UNITED KINGDOM, 1924
A man-eating shark twelve feet long was caught by Weymouth fishermen who were netting mackerel on Sunday. The shark broke two men's arms with its tail before it was hauled into the boat.

The Times, London, 15 July 1924

1925

PANAMA, CENTRAL AMERICA, 1925
In April of last year the New Zealand Shipping Company's steamer Dorset picked up a seaman who had fallen overboard from the American tank steamer *Fred W. Weller* twenty-two hours previously. Under the command of Captain C. R. Kettlewell, the Dorset was leaving the Panama Canal bound for Auckland, New Zealand, and at 2.30 a.m., when eighteen miles from land, a cry for help was heard from the water.

The captain turned the ship in a circle in the hope of locating the man, although the night was intensely dark. A lifebuoy was dropped with a flare attached, and the man was seen and rescued.

He turned out to be Cleomont L. Staden of Brooklyn and stated that he had been twenty-two hours in the water, supported by a lifebuoy which was thrown when he fell overboard during the night. He said that he was frequently attacked by sharks and that water snakes had repeatedly crawled over him. He had kept the sharks at bay by beating the water with a piece of driftwood, which he still held when rescued. Although much exhausted, he soon recovered ...

The Times, London, 13 October 1925

1927

NEW SOUTH WALES, AUSTRALIA, 1927
Stanley Gibbs, GC, who has died [1991] at Bondi, New South Wales, aged eighty-two, won the Albert Medal (subsequently exchanged for the George Cross) for gallantly attempting to save the life of a bather from a shark.

On 3 January 1927 at Port Hacking, near Sydney, New South Wales, a youth named Mervyn Allum was swimming a short distance from the shore when he was attacked by a large shark. It was at first thought that he was drowning, but Gibbs, standing on the nose of a launch, noticed the shark's attack.

He dived from the launch, fought the shark with his hands and feet, and eventually succeeded in extracting Allum from its jaws. He placed the victim in a rowing boat, but he died soon after.

Gibbs was invested with his Albert Medal at Sydney Town Hall on 28 March 1927 by the Duke of York [later King George VI].

Stanley Frederick Gibbs was born at Hunter's Hill, Sydney, on 2 January 1909. For most of his life he was employed by the Gas Light Company in Sydney. When the Second World War broke out, Gibbs was enlisted into the Army, joining 35th Battalion, and saw action in New Guinea. He retired in 1974.

Gibbs was awarded the Queen's Silver Jubilee Medal in 1977. His recreation was lawn bowls. He married, in 1948, Doris Mannix.

Daily Telegraph, London, 1991

1930

SOUTH AUSTRALIA, AUSTRALIA, 1930
Attacked by a shark off the end of the middle Brighton pier yesterday afternoon, Norman William Clark, aged nineteen years, of North Brighton, was mutilated and dragged to his death before assistance could be obtained.

Between 80 and 100 people saw Clark disappear. So sudden was the attack that few people realized what had happened until they saw the shark grip Clark in its jaws. It attacked him again and again, and eventually disappeared with the body fifty feet from the shore. Witnesses said that the shark was at least sixteen feet long.

Clark was treading water when the shark first attacked him. Suddenly he cried out and, throwing up one hand, disappeared under the surface. When he came up, the shark could be seen holding on to his leg. Clark appeared to be sitting across its nose and was punching it with his hands. Several women on the pier, including a girl in whose company Clark had been, fainted. Others tried to frighten the shark away with noise. It again disappeared and dragged Clark to the other side of the pier. When the youth came up again, he was still trying to beat off the shark, but his strength was fast ebbing.

The shark let him go, and then, with its fin and tail out of the water, made another rush at him. It almost lifted him from the water as it seized him around the chest in its jaws.

That was the last seen of Clark, who was dragged under by the shark and apparently carried away.

Experienced fishermen at Brighton claim that they have been warning people for weeks that there were sharks around the pier.

Sydney Morning Herald, 17 February 1930

1934

QUEENSLAND, AUSTRALIA, 1934
Roy Inman, 14, of Wordsworth Avenue, Concord, was taken by a shark at Horsefield Bay, Brisbane Water, about a mile from Woy Woy, before the eyes of his mother and two sisters yesterday afternoon.

The water was lashed to foam as the shark seized the boy, whose head appeared once above the surface. Then the shark returned to the attack and Inman was dragged beneath the water. His body has not been recovered.

The boy's twelve-year-old sister, Joyce, had a narrow escape. The shark brushed against her as it sped through the water, its fin wounding one of her legs.

The tragedy occurred a few seconds after the boy dived from a short jetty in front of the cottage in which he was staying. His older sister, Kathleen, 26, was standing at the door of the cottage, watching the children, and she saw the terrible tragedy. She made gallant attempts to rescue her brother after the initial attack, but reached the scene in a rowing boat too late to render him any assistance.

Throughout yesterday the boy and his two sisters, accompanied by others from nearby houses, had been swimming in the water and diving either from the front of the house or the jetty into the water, which is about ten feet deep. Shortly after lunch the Inman children decided to return to the water. Joyce and Roy arrived at the end of the jetty a few minutes before their elder sister, who changed into her swimming costume, intending to follow them immediately. While they were awaiting her arrival, they decided to hold a diving competition. Joyce dived from the jetty into the water. Roy applauded her effort, but said he could make less splash, and he plunged into the bay.

Just as he struck the water, Joyce screamed with terror. A huge black fin cut through the water towards her. She saw the shark when it was a few feet away. The shark apparently misjudged the location of its intended victim, for, as she kicked out, she felt it graze her leg and felt a sharp stinging pain in her calf. Then she saw her brother disappear in a swirl of foam, and she swam for the jetty a few feet away.

Mrs Inman was sitting on the verandah at the time and saw her son taken. She screamed out, "Shark," and saw Roy seized.

While the two children were diving, Kathleen arrived at the door of the house and stood watching them plunge into the water about twenty feet from her. Then she saw the shark racing towards the children. An instant later the boy's scream rang out, and the head of her brother was dragged down. With a cry of alarm, she ran to where a rowing boat was moored. She jumped into it and pushed off with an oar. She had almost reached her brother when the shark returned and, despite the struggles of the boy, dragged him down. Kathleen frantically searched the locality, pushing the oar down into the water in the hope that it would touch the shark and make it release its victim.

"Roy was seized by the monster and it dragged him down," Kathleen Inman said in telling the story of the tragedy. "Before I reached him the shark had grabbed him again and pulled him below the water. It was terrible. The boat was right over the shark and it was just covered with blood. It disappeared. I did not see it again. Other boats came over, but we could not find him."

In the meantime, Mr Inman arrived and the search was continued. Kathleen was taken ashore. Immediately she rushed to the house occupied by the Wasson family next door, and warned them against allowing their children to swim in the bay. Later in the evening, the Inmans returned to their home in Sydney.

During the afternoon the police at Woy Woy, which is about a mile from the bay, were notified of the tragedy, and Constable McKenzie hurried to the cottage. Sergeant Ravelli and a constable from the Newcastle Water Police joined McKenzie later, and they commenced dragging for the body. Their efforts had been unsuccessful when the search was abandoned at about eight o'clock.

For some weeks sharks have been seen in the bay and a warning had been issued to holidaymakers against bathing there. Local fishermen had spent considerable time in trying to catch the monsters.

Roy Inman was one of the most popular boys at the Concord public school. He was a diligent pupil. He took a keen interest in sport and was one of the best swimmers in the school.

Sydney Morning Herald, 24 December 1934

1935

NEW SOUTH WALES, AUSTRALIA, 1935

A youth of twenty, while swimming across the Georges River, near Sydney, was attacked by a shark and so severely injured in the leg that he died from loss of blood.

Three hours later a girl of thirteen was attacked and her right arm and left hand were practically severed. It is believed that a tiger shark about five feet in length was responsible for both attacks. The girl's condition is critical.

The Times, London, 1 January 1935

YUGOSLAVIA, 1935

At Susak, near Fiume [now known as Rijeka, Istria] on Monday a girl bather was killed by a shark.

The Times, London, 3 July 1935

1936

NOUMÉA, NEW CALEDONIA, 1936
At the Marine Board offices in Cardiff last week the
Lord Mayor of Cardiff, Alderman C. F. Evans, presented
the Bronze Medal and Certificate of the Royal Humane
Society to C. J. Butterworth, an apprentice of the
steamer *Great City*, owned by Messrs Sir W. R. Smith
& Sons, Cardiff, for diving into a shark-infested sea
at Nouméa and swimming round the ship in order to
rescue a seaman who had fallen overboard. The owners
also presented a cheque for £50 and a gold watch.

The captain of the steamer, in a letter to the owners,
stated that seven sharks were seen near the ship at the
time and they were kept at bay by coal flung at them
from the ship in order to disturb the water. Otherwise
the seaman and Butterworth would probably have been
attacked.

The Times, London, 9 July 1936

1937

SOUTH AUSTRALIA, AUSTRALIA, 1937
Having sailed home [Falmouth, England] from Port
Germein, Australia, by way of the Cape of Good Hope,
the Finnish fourmast barque *Penang* took 139 days to
complete the passage.

The captain relates that, while the vessel was at Port
Germein, bathers on the beach were horrified at seeing a
tiger shark rise out of the water with a man's body in its
mouth.

The body was that of one of the crew of the *Penang*,
who had been drowned on the previous night. Captain

Karlson manned a boat and chased the shark, firing several pistol shots at it, but it was not seen again. The body was, however, recovered.

On the previous night some members of the crew had overloaded a small boat when returning from a dance to the ship. The craft capsized in a rough sea and a seaman and the ship's carpenter were drowned. The other ten occupants of the boat were saved.

Captain Karlson said that the vessel made a very good start and had an average passage of ninety-six days to the Cape of Good Hope. The *Penang* sailed through the Azores, but lay in the doldrums for some time and failed to get the advantage of the trade wind. When approaching the English Channel, she encountered a heavy fog, which compelled Captain Karlson to remain on the bridge for forty-eight hours.

The Times, London, 13 July 1937

MAYO, IRELAND, 1937

A woman's shoe and what is thought to be a human bone were found in the maw of a thirty-foot shark that was caught after a great struggle at Keel Bay, Achill, Ireland, yesterday.

Hundreds of visitors watched the fight, which lasted for several hours, before the shark could be brought into shallow water and shot dead.

The Times, London, 5 August 1937

SCOTLAND, 1937

A large shark leapt out of the water in Carradale Bay, Kintyre, last night and holed a fishing boat, drowning three of the five occupants.

The victims were: Captain Angus Brown; his brother, Robert, a fisherman of Carradale; and his son Neil, aged ten. Captain Brown's twelve-year-old daughter and a local youth, Donald McDonald, were found clinging to the side of the sinking boat, the girl holding with one hand the body of her father.

Holidaymakers on the shore saw the shark leap high out of the water and the fishing boat disappear. The body of the boy, Neil, was found some distance from the boat, where it had been thrown by the charge of the shark. The bodies of Captain Brown and his son were taken to the pier. Meanwhile boats searched the bay for the body of Robert Brown, which had not been recovered at a late hour last night.

Large shoals of basking sharks, which measure up to thirty feet and weigh over six tons, have been in the Firth of Clyde for some days past and have been causing havoc among fishermen's nets. These sharks are generally considered harmless in that they do not normally attack human beings, but their weight and power when they leap out of the water make them a menace to fishing boats and other small craft.

The Times, London, 2 September 1937

SCOTLAND, 1937

A second attack by a basking shark on a fishing boat in the Firth of Clyde occurred early on Saturday when the *Lady Charlotte* of Campbeltown (twenty tons) was damaged off the Fallen Rocks, Arran.

The *Lady Charlotte*, which is owned by Messrs Neil McKenzie & Co., Campbeltown, had secured a catch of herrings off the Arran coast and was on her way to Ayr to market the fish when a member of the crew, who was near the stern, saw a huge shark charge at the boat. The shark struck the propeller a glancing blow. The stern of the boat was lifted three feet out of the water by the impact and came down again with a crash, fortunately on an even keel. The crew saw the shark pass underneath their keel at an angle and, as it disappeared, they were able by the gleam of the mast lights to follow its trail for some time.

Mr Colin McSporran, the skipper of the *Lady Charlotte*, said that if the shark had caught the boat a straight blow amidships, instead of merely a glancing blow on the propeller, the boat would have been sunk. The propeller shaft was smashed by the shark's charge and the engines thrown out of gear. It was with great difficulty that the vessel, after her catch had been dumped, was able to limp into Campbeltown harbour.

The previous attack by a basking shark was on the fishing boat Eagle, in Carradale Bay, Kintyre, last Wednesday, when three men were drowned.

The Times, London, 6 September 1937

SCOTLAND, 1937

Another incident indicating the manner in which navigation of the estuary of the Clyde by small vessels is being menaced by the presence of large numbers of basking sharks occurred last night. The pleasure steamer *Glen Sannox* was crossing from Ardrossan to Arran with many weekend holidaymakers when a shark struck the vessel. Two windows of the cabin were smashed. Some of the passengers were rather scared when they heard the crash, but beyond the damage to the windows no harm was done.

Fishermen in the Firth assert that the attacks on small vessels are being made by the blue predatory shark, which has not been seen in these waters for at least forty years, and not by basking sharks, which are harmless and are frequently seen in the Clyde.

The Times, London, 13 September 1937

QUEENSLAND, AUSTRALIA, 1937

Norman Girvan, 18, of Coolangatta, was killed by a shark while surfing at the main beach at Coolangatta this afternoon.

Jack Brinkley, a youth, of Coolangatta, was badly mauled and later had his left arm amputated in hospital.

Joe Doniger showed great heroism in going to the help of Brinkley and bringing him ashore.

This is the first shark tragedy at Coolangatta.

Six members of the surf life-saving club, including Girvan, Brinkley, Joe Doniger and Gordon Doniger, went for their usual swim after work. The surf was choppy and storm clouds obscured the sun. After some time in the water, Joe Doniger and two others returned to the beach, leaving Girvan, Brinkley and Gordon Doniger about one hundred yards out in the surf. Shortly after they reached the beach – about 5.25 p.m. – the shark attacked Girvan, inflicting terrible wounds.

Gordon Doniger swam towards Girvan to help him, but Girvan was then so badly torn by the shark that he was beyond aid, and Gordon Doniger and Brinkley swam as fast as they could for the shore.

When Brinkley, who was leading, was about seventy-five yards from the beach, the shark attacked him, tearing his left shoulder and one leg. He screamed for help and Joe Doniger dashed into the surf and swam quickly to Brinkley's side. "For God's sake hurry up," cried Brinkley, and collapsed. The shark was still cruising near by, but Doniger seized Brinkley and brought him to the shore, where he and the others applied a tourniquet to the torn arm.

Alf Kilburn, one of the party, then went out a short distance on a surf ski to find Girvan's body. At the first line of breakers he saw the shark circling near a patch of blood-stained water and he returned to the beach. By this time the surf club's boat had been manned and several surfers went out in it. They searched for half an hour for Girvan's body without success. They saw no sign of the shark.

The shark was about ten feet long and either a tiger or grey nurse. Girvan was a member of the Kirra Surf Life-Saving Club for years and was one of its most popular members.

Sydney Morning Herald, 28 October 1937

1938

HONG KONG, 1938

W. M. Baker, a sailor on HMS *Folkestone*, has died on board the warship *Tsingtao* after his leg had been bitten off by a shark while he was swimming near the vessel in the outer harbour.

The Times, London, 30 August 1938

A Shark is Born

Sharks have been around for a very long time – far longer than we mere humans have been walking the earth. The modern shark's predecessors date from around 420 million years ago while what might be regarded as our earliest ancestors didn't appear until 2.5 million years ago. There are around 470 species of shark that come in all shapes and sizes from the smallest dwarf-lantern shark at just 6 inches (15 cm) to the whale shark at a massive 41 feet (12.7 m) – the biggest fish in the sea. They all, of course, start life small, but in a surprising number of different ways.

Mother sharks can either be oviparous, meaning that they lay eggs without the embryo undergoing any significant development inside the mother at all; or ovoviparous, meaning that the embryos develop inside eggs but that the eggs are retained inside the mother's body until they are ready to hatch; or they can be viviparous, which is when the embryo grows inside the mother's body with a placental link, just as a baby does in a mammal.

Species like the bullhead or swell sharks lay eggs on the seabed. Bullhead shark eggs are a corkscrew shape in order that they can be jammed into gaps between rocks to keep them safe from predators while the shark embryos develop. Swell sharks lay eggs that have tendrils attached so that they can grip onto seaweed to anchor themselves to the ocean floor. The eggs of most sharks have a leather-like case rather than a hard shell and after the young shark has hatched, the case sometimes washes ashore where it is known as a "mermaid's purse".

Sharks that carry their young inside their bodies until they are ready to be born have the longest "gestation" periods of any creatures on the planet. The spiny dogfish carries its young for between eighteen and twenty-four months, which is longer than a whale or an elephant. Even the eggs that are laid on the sea-bed may take up to a year to hatch.

The long gestation period means that when the young sharks are born they are fully viable fish, able to hunt and look after themselves. The mother shark will have nothing more to do with her offspring once she has given birth and provides them with neither food nor protection. For the lemon shark, born in warm, shallow waters, often near mangroves, being able to fend for themselves doesn't extend to venturing out into the open ocean. The mother will give birth to as many as seventeen pups each around 3 feet (90 cm) long but they will double in size before they are ready to leave the shallows and that will take at least twelve years.

By then the mother will have given birth to another six litters of pups, producing one litter every other year. That sounds like a lot of lemon sharks, but not all of them will survive to maturity as, while they are still growing, they are not at the top of the food chain. Among their greatest natural predators are other, bigger, sharks. It is, in fact, something of a shark-eat-shark world for these fish. While still inside their mothers, the pups of many species, including great whites, will eat any unfertilised eggs they discover in the womb and, in the case of the sand tiger, the pups will turn completely cannibalistic, eating their brothers and sisters. This undoubtedly ensures the survival of the fittest, although some species go for strength in numbers, the blue shark having been known to give birth to more than 100 pups.

Even 100 pups, however, is nothing to the female whale shark, which can carry three times that number of young. She doesn't give birth to them all at once, the pups being at different stages of development, but produces them at a steady rate. She can afford to be patient, though, as whale sharks, like a number of other shark species, may live for up to a century.

SHARK ATTACKS
1940–49

1940

SOUTH AUSTRALIA, AUSTRALIA, 1940

Maxwell Arthur Farrin, 13, of Jacobson Avenue, Brighton, was killed by a shark while he was swimming about fifty yards from the shore at North Brighton yesterday morning. His left leg was severed and he suffered other injuries.

Although the shark, which is believed to be of the tiger species, remained in the vicinity, Mr Sydney Owen, 48, dashed into the sea and brought the boy ashore. The boy died almost immediately afterwards.

The last fatal shark attack on metropolitan beaches occurred when David Paton was taken at South Steyne in September 1936.

Farrin went to the beach opposite Bestic Street with Kenneth Moore, 12, also of Jacobson Avenue, and Harry Flower, 11, a cousin of Moore, of Melford Street, Hurlstone Park.

"We were paddling about on the edge of the beach while Max swam out about 50 yards," said Moore. "The sea was very calm. We heard a noise like a groan, and saw Max lying face downwards with blood all round him. We called to him, but he didn't answer."

"When a boy ran to me and said that another boy was covered in blood in the water, I ran into the sea," said Mr Robert Ambrose, of Frederick Street, St Peters. "I saw the fin of a large shark close to him and I ran over the sandhill to General Holmes Drive, where I stopped a lorry to get a length of rope to try and pull the boy in."

Mr Owen, whose home in General Holmes Drive faces the spot where Farrin had been swimming, said he heard shouts that a boy had been attacked by a shark. "I was watering my garden," he said, "but I dropped the hose, and in my shorts and a shirt I raced over the sandbank. I saw Farrin floating face downward, and, as I waded out towards him, someone on the beach shouted that the shark was still there.

"I waded out and splashed about until the sea was beyond my depth. Then I swam to the boy, who was floating in about twelve feet of water. When I caught hold of him, I could see that he had been shockingly injured.

"The shark was then not more than ten feet away. It seemed to be at least ten feet long. Luckily, it did not attack again. When I reached shallow water, others helped me carry the boy on to the sand."

The mother of the boy, who had rushed to the beach, collapsed as her son was brought ashore. The St George Ambulance wrapped the boy in blankets and rushed him to the St George Hospital, but he was then dead. His injuries, apart from the loss of his leg, were so severe that doctors expressed the opinion that he died as Mr Owen laid him on the beach.

The boy and his sister were the only children in the Farrin family. The boy attended the Hurstville Technical School and he showed great promise as a commercial artist. He had spent most of his school holidays drawing aeroplanes and motor cars for his school friends, and after his death yesterday they collected all his drawings and put them away for safe keeping. Farrin had won a lifesaving certificate ...

Mr W. A. Jackson, health inspector of the Rockdale Council, said that he saw the shark swimming about the spot where the boy was attacked for some time afterwards. "It is too risky for children to swim in the open sea as the bay is infested with sharks," he said. "While no swimmer has lost his life previously from a shark attack along the foreshore, the sharks frequently tear the nets of fishermen, and they snap at fishing baits. The Rockdale Council provides an enclosed bath where swimming is safe and children are admitted for a penny."

Sydney Morning Herald, 24 January 1940

1942

SYDNEY, AUSTRALIA, 1942

Zieta Steadman, 28, single, of Ashfield was killed by a shark while she was standing in shallow water in an upper part of Middle Harbour yesterday afternoon.

Miss Steadman was so shockingly mutilated that only the upper part of her body could be recovered. The remains were dragged from the jaws of the shark by Mr Frederick H. Bowes of Charlotte Street, Ashfield. Mr Bowes estimates that the shark was fourteen feet long.

Miss Steadman was a member of a picnic party, the other members of which were Mr and Mrs Bowes, and Mrs Reeve, the elderly mother of Mrs Bowes. They hired a motor launch from the boatshed of Mr J. H. West in Sailor's Bay at 1.30 p.m. and travelled up Middle Harbour until they were about three and a half miles above the

Spit Bridge. The boat was tied to a rock on the first point on the French's Forest shore, past Bantry Bay, a locality near the power works which is known to fishermen as Egg Rock. The picnic party then had lunch on the rocky ledge which lies between the water and the steep hill above the harbour.

Close to the shore the water is shallow. It falls away slightly for about twenty-five feet and then drops steeply to a depth of thirty feet. There is no beach, the bottom being of shells and rocks. The water is clear. Shortly before three o'clock Mr and Mrs Bowes and Miss Steadman entered the water to bathe, while Mrs Reeve watched them from an elevated position on the shore.

Mr and Mrs Bowes were standing together in water waist high. Miss Steadman was ten to twelve feet further out and in slightly deeper water. Mr Bowes called to her not to go so far, and she turned to come back. Suddenly she threw out her arms and cried in terror. Simultaneously Mrs Reeve saw the shark attacking her. Mrs Reeve immediately screamed out to her son-in-law.

Mr Bowes grabbed an oar from the boat and endeavoured to drive away the shark, which, in repeated attacks on Miss Steadman, was throwing itself out of the water and lashing the surface with its tail. The shark was so large that Mr Bowes could make no impression on it with the oar.

Gradually the shark drew its victim toward deeper water. Mr Bowes jumped into the boat, started the engine and steered the boat at the shark, every detail of which could be seen as it came to the surface, with the intention of ramming it. This plan failed. Mr Bowes then circled in the boat and, as he again came closer to the young woman, he left the tiller, jumped to the side of the boat and grabbed her by her long black hair. It was obvious, however, that she was dead.

Mr Bowes, a man of fifteen stone, had to use all his strength to free the upper portion of the body. So great was the force he had to exert that the young woman's hair bit into his hands. He saw the remainder of the body disappear into deep water. Mr Bowes then placed the remains of Miss Steadman, covered by a piece of canvas, in the bottom of the boat. When the party returned to the boat shed, the ambulance and police were called.

Mr West, owner of the boat shed, said last night that Mr Bowes had behaved with courage and great coolness in one of the most terrible situations in which any man could be placed. "There was no help available. The only other men in sight were fishing from another boat which was hundreds of yards away. When they came along the whole terrible affair was over."

Sydney Morning Herald, 5 January 1942

NEW SOUTH WALES, AUSTRALIA, 1942

Denise Rosemary Burch, 15, of Cliff Street, Manly was taken by a whaler shark in two feet of water in Middle Harbour on Saturday morning. She died before she was lifted from the water.

Miss Burch was one of a party of four girls and four boys, including the dead girl's elder sister, Pamela. They left the Spit at about 9 a.m. in two boats for a day's outing in Middle Harbour. The boys and girls, aged from fifteen to eighteen, rowed to Ironstone Point, near Bantry Bay, where they landed for lunch.

While one or two of the boys swam in deeper water, Miss Burch paddled in the shallow water. At about 10 a.m. the girl was standing in about two feet of water when the other members of the party heard her scream. One of the boys was swimming about fifteen or twenty yards away in deep water. Miss Burch was seized by the legs and dragged under the water by the shark. For a minute or two neither the girl nor the shark could be seen, but the water was stained with blood.

One of the boys grabbed an oar, with which he tried to drive off the shark. Other members of the party joined him, armed with sticks and stones. A few moments later Miss Burch appeared above water. She was taken ashore by her companions. She had suffered terrible injuries and she was dead before the party reached the shore. The body was taken to the Spit, and Sergeant van Wouwe and Constable C. Fenton of the Water Police met the party.

Mrs Burch and her two daughters were among those evacuated from Hong Kong about two years ago. Her husband, Mr R. J. Burch, and their son are prisoners of war in the hands of the Japanese.

Sydney Morning Herald, 28 December 1942

1945

PACIFIC OCEAN, 1945

On Monday 30 July 1945, at five minutes past midnight, four days after the USS *Indianapolis*, flagship of the massive Pacific Fifth Fleet, delivered the components of the Hiroshima bomb to Tinian, and just a few weeks before VJ Day, she was torpedoed by a Japanese submarine and sank within fifteen minutes. Of the 1,196 men on board, approximately 400 went down with the ship and 800 safely abandoned her. Of these 800 men in the water, only 316 survived. This was America's greatest wartime sea disaster; partly due to the secrecy surrounding her course, the US Navy left her crew drifting in shark-infested waters for four days. The following account is taken from *All the Drowned Sailors* by Raymond B. Lech, largely based on the first-hand accounts of survivors:

During this first day, a monstrous shark decided to investigate Captain McVay's raft and its edible cargo. The shark kept swimming under the raft. The dorsal fin was "almost white as a sheet of paper", while the body was a darker colour. The shark could therefore always be spotted because of the visibility of its white fin in the water. The frightened men attempted to catch some pilot fish by knocking them off with canoe paddles, but this was an exercise in futility. They also tried hitting the shark with paddles, but, when they occasionally did manage to do so, he swam away and returned a few minutes later. In the days to follow, this unwanted nuisance was to become a real menace.

During the entire time in the water, Captain McVay's wristwatch kept excellent time. At 1 p.m. a high-flying twin-engine bomber flew overhead in the direction of Leyte; at 3 p.m. either a B-24 or B-29 passed to the south of them, also heading for the Philippines ... After spotting two distant rafts, McVay and the others in his group assumed that they were the sole survivors of the ship and, all in all, figured no more than twenty-five or thirty men, including themselves, had made it off the ship. What they did not know at the time was that they had drifted seven to ten miles north of the main groups.

Stranded in the middle of the deep and seemingly never-ending Philippine Sea, the Captain understandably became very depressed. He daydreamed about taking a bath, drinking a cocktail and relaxing in comfort, and in the midst of such thoughts he wished to live, but soon reality broke in upon his fantasies ...

Two hours prior to the close of their first day a plane

flew overhead, its red-and-green running lights clearly visible. McVay fired one of the star shells skyward, but it went unnoticed ...

Most of the men [in a group out of sight of McVay] were unrecognisable since they were black from the heavy fuel oil blanketing the water. It burned their eyes, clogged their nostrils and choked their throats. Lieutenant McKissick was part of this group ...

Soon after the ship went down, there was an underwater explosion which was heard and felt by everyone. McKissick ordered the men around him to lie prone in order to raise their bodies as far out of the water as possible and lessen the concussion if there were any further blasts.

At approximately 1.30 a.m. [just over an hour after the ship sank] Quartermaster 1st Class Robert Gause spotted a fin. By estimating the distance between the dorsal and tail, he guessed the shark to be about twelve feet long.

Quite a few sailors in his group were critically wounded. There were a large number of severe flash burns of the face, arms and body, and some men had compound fractures of one sort or another. There were no medical supplies of any kind for the frustrated Dr Haynes, and many of the men with fractures and burns died from shock during the first few hours. After removing their life jackets, the dead were allowed to slip away. Before the boiling sun rose over the distant horizon that Monday morning about fifty of the original 400 were dead ...

By daybreak this mass of floating humanity had split into three subgroups. The largest group contained about 200 men, the second 100 and the smallest about 50. These subgroups were separated from each other by a distance of only several hundred yards at most. Leader of the group of 200 men was Captain Edward Parke, Commanding Officer of the Marine Detachment and holder of the Bronze Star for bravery on Guadalcanal ...

The main objective was for everyone to stay together. Captain Parke found a cork life ring with about 100 feet of attached line. To prevent drifting, he strung the line out and each man grabbed a piece of it and took up the slack. In this way they formed a long line which began to curl on itself, as a waggon train would circle against attack. The wounded were brought into the middle and tied to the life ring itself by the strings on their life jackets. There was no confusion and the men stayed well grouped together. If someone did drift off the line, Parke swam over to the man and herded him back in. On several occasions he gave his life jacket to a man without one and swam unsupported until he could find another ...

[During] the first day there was constant change among the three subgroups. They would merge for a short time, then break apart again. The wounded stayed in fairly good shape and only a few men died. In order to determine death, Dr Haynes would place his finger on the pupil of an eye and, if there was no reflex, it was assumed the man was dead. The jacket would be removed and the body allowed to drift away. In the background some of the men would recite the Lord's Prayer.

By noontime the sea became choppy again with large swells ... The survivors were beginning to see sharks in the area, but, so far, there were no major attacks. Giles McCoy of the Marine Detachment saw a shark attack a dead man. He believed that, because of the dead men in the water, so much food was available that the sharks were not inclined to bother with those still alive at this stage.

That, however, had been in the morning and

afternoon. By the time that the merciless sun began to set, large numbers of sharks had arrived on the scene, and the men were scared. Cuts were bleeding. When a shark approached a group, everyone would kick, punch and create a general racket. This often worked and the predator would leave. At other times, however, the shark "would have singled out his victim and no amount of shouts or pounding of the water would turn him away. There would be a piercing scream and the water would be churned red as the shark cut his victim to ribbons" ...

At dawn on the second day the isolated Redmayne group had about sixty men on rafts and another sixty to eighty in the water. Meanwhile, during the dark morning hours, some of the more seriously injured men had died.

The water breakers turned out to be a disappointment. Some of the casks were empty, while the others contained either salt or cruddy black water ... First-aid equipment was generally useless, since the containers were not watertight. Anything in tubes remained sealed, but there were not enough remedies to go around for burns and eye troubles caused by salt water and fuel oil. The food stayed in good condition, but, here again, there was a problem since the primary staple was Spam. Not only did this increase thirst because it was salty but also Spam draws sharks. The men discovered this when they opened a can of Spam and sharks gathered all around them.

The policy of the group was to put all men on rafts who were sick, injured or did not have life jackets or belts. The problem with this, however, was that men with belts or jackets began taking them off and allowing them to drift away in order to bqualify for the relative safety of a raft. This necessitated keeping a close watch on the men ...

As far as can be ascertained, there were no deaths in this group during the second day, and everyone appeared to be in fairly good shape ... The next day would be a different story ...

Even though total blackness surrounded them [during the night of Monday/Tuesday], because of the choppy sea the men [in Haynes's group] were having a very difficult time sleeping. In this inky isolation some of the weaker members of the crew, who could not face what they thought must be ahead of them, gave up all hope: they silently slipped out of their life jackets and committed suicide by drowning. Numerous deadly fights broke out over life jackets and about twenty-five men were killed by their shipmates. At dawn Dr Haynes saw that the general condition of the men was not good, and the group appeared to be smaller ...

During the latter part of Tuesday the sea grew calmer. The men's thirst, however, had become overpowering as the placid water became very clear. As the day wore on the men became more and more exhausted and complained of thirst. Dr Haynes noticed that the younger men, largely those without families, started to drink salt water first. As the hot sun continued to beat down on them, an increasing number of survivors were becoming delirious, talking incoherently and drinking tremendous amounts of salt water. They started becoming maniacal, thrashing around in the water and exhibiting considerable strength and energy compared to those who were exhausted but still sane ...

Haynes kept swimming from one huge huddle of sailors to another, desperately trying to help. All during this time people were getting discouraged and calling out for help, and he would be there to reassure and calm them down.

There were sharks in the area again. The clear water allowed the men to look down and see them. It seems that during this second day, however, the sharks were going after dead men, especially the bodies that were sinking down into the deeper ocean. They did not seem to bother the men on the surface.

Things became progressively worse from sundown on the second day. The men's stories become mixed up, and some accounts are totally incoherent, making it difficult to piece together what actually happened. Haynes remembered that shortly after sundown they all experienced severe chills, which lasted for at least an hour. These were followed by high fever, as most of the group became delirious and got out of control. The men fought with one another, thinking there were Japanese in the group, and disorganization and disintegration occurred rapidly ...

The Captain and the men with him were continuing to fare relatively well [by Wednesday, 1 August]. McVay still believed that his ship went down with all hands and that, at most, there would only be thirty survivors.

From the opening of this [the third] day the central thought on the minds of the men was to kill the shark; it was big, it kept circling closer and closer, and they were frightened. This monster could easily rip the raft apart with one swift motion of his enormous jaws. But the only weapon they had was a knife from the fishing kit with a one-inch blade, and there was no way they could tackle this massive creature with a blade that small. So the day passed with the men sitting and staring at the shark, annoyed that a larger weapon was not in the kit and further chafed that not one man had a sheath knife, an implement customarily carried by many of the sailors aboard ship.

Just before first light a plane flew over and two star shells were fired. Again at 1 p.m. a bomber, heading towards Leyte, passed above. They tried to attract this second plane with mirrors, yellow signal flags and splashing, but to no avail. They were becoming more and more depressed since it did not seem possible to them that somebody they could see so plainly could fail to see them ... Many aircraft flew close to the area where the ship sank. Each day planes were seen, but they all failed to spot the survivors. The glassy sea made it almost impossible to spot something as small as a man's head, and the chance of life rafts being picked up on radar was negligible unless the rafts were equipped with metal corner reflectors, which the rafts on the *Indianapolis* were not ...

Although the order had been given the day before to bring all food to the command raft, there was still a certain amount of hoarding going on. This morning, however, several more rafts handed their cached rations over to Redmayne. During the day one cracker, a malted milk tablet and a few drips of precious water were allocated to each man. Some survivors tried their luck at fishing, but, as with the McVay group, the numerous sharks in the area kept stealing the bait.

Not everyone realized there was safety in numbers. Some men swam away. Attempts to stop them failed and soon after leaving the security of the group these sailors were usually dragged beneath the surface by the sharks ...

Toward late afternoon some of the sailors started becoming delirious again. More and more men were drinking salt water. Chief Benton, Redmayne's assistant, attempted to talk to these half-crazed men in a calm, reassuring voice, but it was not much use. Fights broke out, men started swimming away and people committed suicide by drowning themselves ...

Dr Haynes's group disbanded again. Small groups were continually forming and breaking up. The night had been particularly difficult, and most of the men suffered from chills, fever and were delirious. These lonely people were now dying in droves and the helpless physician could only float and watch. By Thursday morning, 2 August, the condition of most of the men was critical. Many were in coma and could be aroused only with exceptional effort. The group no longer existed, with the men drifting off and dying one by one ...

At dawn, a sailor in a life jacket was seen bent over with his face in the water. Thinking him asleep, a shipmate swam over to waken the man. On attempting to rouse him, the body flipped over and from the waist down there was nothing. He had been sawed clean in half by a shark.

At 9 a.m., on Thursday 2 August, securely strapped in the pilot's seat, Lieutenant Wilbur C. Gwinn pushed the throttles forward, brought the motors of his twin-engine Ventura bomber to an ear-splitting roar and raced down the Peleliu runway. His mission was a regular day reconnaissance patrol of sector 19V258. The route for the outward leg of his journey just happened to have him flying directly over the heads of the dying men of the *Indianapolis* ...

At 11 a.m., about an hour and forty-five minutes out of Peleliu, Gwinn happened to look down from his 3,000-foot perch into the Philippine Sea. At that precise moment, he saw it. The thin line of oil could only have come from a leaking sub-marine, and the startled pilot rushed back to his left-hand seat and began flying the airplane.

At 11.18 a.m. he changed his course so as to follow the snake-like slick. Not being able to see very well, he brought the bomber down to 900 feet. Five miles later he saw wreckage and survivors. Dropping a liferaft and radio transmitter, Gwinn sent a message advising that there were many men in the water. All available aircraft and ships were ordered to head for the area to mount a rescue effort.

First to arrive was a PBY Catalina seaplane flown by Lieutenant R. Adrian Marks. Looking down at the bobbing mass of humanity, he knew they were in horrible shape, but also just as important – and maybe even more so – he saw the sharks. Therefore, at "about 16.30 I decided a landing would be necessary to gather in the single ones. This decision was based partly on the number of single survivors and the fact that they were bothered by sharks. We did observe bodies being eaten by sharks."

Contravening standing orders, Marks landed his plane on the open sea and began picking up lone swimmers. Before night fell Marks had picked up thirty people and crammed them into the body of his leaking seaplane. All were in bad shape, and they were immediately given water and first aid. Naturally, as soon as the first man was plucked from the sea, Lieutenant Marks learned that the *Indianapolis* had gone down. There was no way, however, that he was going to transmit this word in the clear, and "I was too busy to code a message of this nature". So it would not be until Friday 3 August that the US Navy finally learned that one of their heavy cruisers had been sunk just after midnight on 30 July ...

For miles around the sea carried corpses. The many destroyers on the scene served as funeral directors. Because the sharks had been at work, identification was next to impossible.

The search lasted six days, covering hundreds of square miles of ocean. The result was always the same – bodies, bodies and more bodies.

In his action report Commander A. F. Hollingsworth, Captain of the USS *Helm*, brought into stark reality how hideous the discovering of bodies really was:

"All bodies were in extremely bad condition and had been dead for an estimated four or five days. Some had life jackets and life belts, most had nothing. Most of the bodies were completely naked, and the others had just drawers or dungaree trousers on – only three of the twenty-eight bodies recovered had shirts on. Bodies were horribly bloated and decomposed – recognition of faces would have been impossible. About half of the bodies were shark-bitten, some to such a degree that they more nearly resembled skeletons. From one to four sharks were in the immediate area of the ship at all times. At one time two sharks were attacking a body not more than fifty yards from the ship and continued to do so until driven off by rifle fire. For the most part it was impossible to get fingerprints from the bodies as the skin had come off the hands or the hands had been lacerated by sharks ... There were still more bodies in the area when darkness brought a close to the gruesome operations for the day."

All the other ships of the scouting flotilla were performing the same revolting task as *Helm* ...

The sharks had been having a feast. When a boat reached a body, it was common to see a hand missing or foot gone, a part of the head ripped off, or a chunk of meat torn from the torso. It was also usual to find nothing but bones.

In two days the USS *French* examined twenty-nine bodies, but could not identify eighteen (sixty-two per cent) of them. The *French*'s report monotonously repeated over and over again: "Impossible to take fingerprints", "Body badly decomposed", "Very badly mutilated by sharks".

As the evening sun dropped over the western horizon on Wednesday 8 August 1945 the ships sailed for home, leaving in their wake the graveyard of the USS *Indianapolis* and the final burial ground of seventy-three per cent of her young crew.

1946

QUEENSLAND, AUSTRALIA, 1946

Before the horrified gaze of his wife and two young children, Philip South Collin, aged about thirty, was taken by a shark this afternoon at Ellis Beach, twenty miles from Cairns.

The shark, about twelve feet long, struck three times at the victim, whose body has not yet been recovered.

Collin was attending a picnic party of fellow employees of Cummins & Campbell Ltd.

More than thirty persons were in the water at the time of the attack. Collin had swum out beyond the bathers to retrieve a ball and was heard to shout, "Shark!"

The attack was so sudden that the others were unable to go to his assistance. Police are still searching for the body.

Sydney Morning Herald, 19 August 1946

1948

NEW SOUTH WALES, AUSTRALIA, 1948

A twelve-foot shark today attacked and killed Ronald Johnson, aged 16, of Stone Street, Stockton, fifty yards from shore at Stockton beach.

The shark attacked Johnson three times as he struggled towards a lifesaver, Albert Linich, aged 19, who went to his aid with a belt and line.

Johnson was brought to the beach suffering from injuries to the right leg, both thighs and his back. He died a few minutes later in the ambulance room at the lifesavers' pavilion.

The shark appeared a few yards from the shore shortly afterwards. A returned soldier had two shots at it with a rifle, but the bullets took no effect.

Harry Stephenson, who was on watch on the tower, said he saw the shark too late to warn Johnson. "Almost as I saw the fin Ron screamed and shouted, 'Shark – he's got me,'" said Stephenson. "I sounded the siren and Linich ran out of the pavilion and grabbed the lifebelt."

A few minutes before the attack Johnson had been swimming with about eight fellow members of the Stockton Surf Club. All but Johnson caught a shoot and returned to the beach. Johnson was about fifteen yards from other bathers when he was attacked.

When the siren sounded, there was a rush from the surf. Bathers who were nearest Johnson said they heard him cry, "Shark!" but did not know he had been attacked until they reached the beach.

After the attack Stockton Beach was closed for the day and baits attached to a buoy were set to catch the shark. Rod fishermen were fishing from the beach late tonight in the hope of landing it.

The Mayor said he would ask the City Council to support any move for recognition of Linich's act of heroism.

Johnson was the son of Mr Gilbert Johnson of the Public Works Department at Newcastle.

Sydney Morning Herald, 13 February 1948

QUEENSLAND, AUSTRALIA, 1948

A shark mauled and killed a lifesaver at King's Beach, Caloundra, about seventy miles north of Brisbane, today. The lifesaver was Eric Samuel Keys, twenty-eight, married, of Ashgrove, Brisbane. The attack occurred in five feet of water about 150 yards from the shore.

Keys was standing about thirty feet from Geoffrey Goadby, of Indooroopilly, Brisbane, waiting for a shoot. Suddenly Keys yelled out, "Shark!" twice.

Goadby said Keys seemed to struggle. Then Keys disappeared just as Goadby saw what looked like the tail of a shark.

Frederick Riddle, twenty-nine, of Reddiffe, saw Keys lying face down in the water. Riddle said: "I dived and brought Keys to the surface. When I turned him on his back, I saw that his left arm had been practically torn off his body."

Keys was also severely mauled about the left leg and the buttocks. He is believed to have died within a few seconds.

People on the beach saw a blood pool thirty feet wide soon after they heard the shark alarm. More than 200 surfers were in the water when Keys was attacked.

Sydney Morning Herald, 27 December 1948

1949

NEW SOUTH WALES, AUSTRALIA, 1949

A twenty-year-old youth was killed by a shark while he was taking part in a surf contest at Bar Beach, Newcastle, this afternoon. He was Ray Land, northern districts surf swimming champion.

His father and mother, Mr and Mrs Roy Land, of Young Street, Cook's Hill, saw the attack from the beach. He was their only child.

When the shark struck, Land was wearing a surf belt 120 yards from the beach, with the line firmly caught in rocks on the sea bed. Clubmates were swimming to help him free himself when he was flung out of the water by the shark's first attack.

He was dragged to the bottom and was under for about ten seconds before the shark released him. He was attacked again as he reached the surface.

A ski rider, Reg Trew, of Cook's Hill Surf Club, made a courageous attempt to rescue Land, at the same time exposing himself to attack.

Trew dragged Land across the craft and was kicking his way to the beach when the ski was overturned by a wave. He recovered the ski, placed Land across it straddlewise, and allowed half his own body to remain in the water so that he could control the ski and make quicker progress.

When Land was taken aboard a surf boat, it was found his left leg had been almost severed below the thigh. Flesh between the thigh and the knee had been torn away, and a deep wound extended from his knee to his ankle. He was dead when the ambulance reached Newcastle Hospital.

Sydney Morning Herald, 24 January 1949

QUEENSLAND, AUSTRALIA, 1949

While his parents watched, a thirteen-year-old schoolboy was killed by a twelve-foot shark in three feet of water near Cairns today.

The boy's father, driven frantic by his son's screams, plunged fully dressed into the water in a futile attempt to rescue him.

The victim was Richard Joseph Maguire of Tolga, about eighteen miles from Cairns. His left leg was severed near the hip and he died soon after he was carried ashore. The tragedy occurred at Ellis Beach, a popular resort about eighteen miles from Cairns.

Constable Edward Stockwell and Mr Leonard Hastie, both of Tolga, were about fifteen feet from the boy when the shark attacked. They dived to his help through bloodstained water and reached him seconds after the shark had mauled him.

A Cairns doctor, Dr C. H. Knott, who was further down the beach, was immediately called, but the boy was dead.

The boy's parents, Mr and Mrs C. J. Maguire, had formed a party at Tolga to spend the day at Ellis Beach. Richard, who was a boarder at the Marist Brothers' College, Cairns, joined them there.

Mr Maguire was the only member of the party who saw the shark. Ellis Beach is not patrolled by lifesavers.

The last shark tragedy near Cairns was also at Ellis Beach, where Philip Collin was fatally mauled by a twelve-foot shark on 18 August 1946.

Sydney Morning Herald, 18 April 1949

Blue Shark

Shark Facts

Length: 6 feet to 11 feet (1.8 m to 3.3 m)

Weight: 120 lb to 450 lb (55 kg to 204 kg)

Colouring: Deep blue upper with lighter sides and white belly

Diet: Squid, cuttlefish, shrimp, crab, fish, small sharks

Pups: May give birth to 100 or more pups, generally small in size

Status: Not under threat but numbers declining

Found in tropical and temperate waters from Norway to New Zealand, the blue shark is widely fished for its flesh which is either eaten or turned into fishmeal for pet food or fertiliser. Its skin is turned into leather, its liver used for oil and its fins for shark fin soup. They are also caught as game fish. When these fish venture into shallow coastal waters they come into contact with humans and there have been many attacks, including several fatalities, attributed to blue sharks.

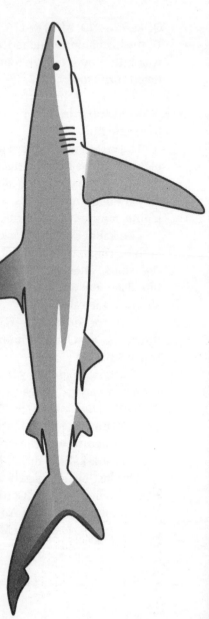

Blue Shark Range

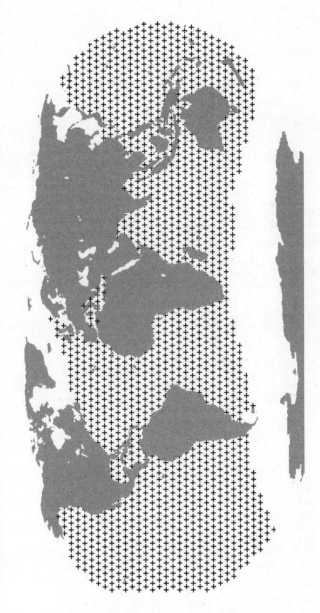

SHARK ATTACKS

1950–59

1951

QUEENSLAND, AUSTRALIA, 1951
The first shark casualty on the Queensland beaches this summer occurred on Saturday 20 October at Townsville, north Queensland, when a shark evaded the protective wire netting and fatally injured a swimmer.

The Times, London, 23 October 1951

NEW SOUTH WALES, AUSTRALIA, 1951
The horribly mauled body of Frank Okulich, 21, Australian surf ski champion, was washed into shallow water at Merewether Beach, Newcastle, at 4 p.m. today, an hour after a shark had dragged him under.

The shark took Okulich 100 yards from the shore, just after three other lifesavers swimming with him had caught a wave into the beach. Only a dark shadow, about eight feet long, was seen in the water when he was dragged under. His body disappeared.

The man who saw the attack from the beach, but who would not give his name, said: "There were four chaps swimming about 100 yards out at the southern end of the beach. Three chaps took a shoot in, but Okulich missed it. Then I saw a shadow in the crest of a big wave. It tugged the poor kid under, but he came up again waving his arms.

"I saw the shadow, which was bigger than a man, attack him again and again. Then his head just bobbed in the waves like a cork. After about four minutes I saw the shark have another go at him. Then his body disappeared. The sun was shining on the waves and you could almost see right through each breaker as it built up."

Okulich had been swimming with Merewether life-savers Bill Morgan, 24, of Ranclaude Street, John Blackett, 30, of Ridge Street, and James Robert Johns, 25, of Janet Street. Morgan and another Merewether lifesaver, Ron Galbraith, went out on surf skis immediately they heard Okulich was being attacked. They could not find his body.

Merewether beach inspector K. Ayton said: "I saw a big pool of blood on the water just after it happened."

Inspectors closed the beach. Two hundred girls from a Newcastle high school had left the water a few minutes before the tragedy.

Lifesavers at Newcastle Beach mauled a surf boat and surf skis and rowed to Merewether, about two miles away. They began a search for Okulich's body. A large crowd lined the promenade. At 4 p.m. a youth pointed to shallow water. A life-saver, Robert Mather, of Frederick Street, Merewether, dashed into the surf and recovered Okulich's mutilated body. The shark had mauled him on every part except his head.

Several women in the crowd wept when they saw his body carried out of the water.

Okulich belonged to the Dixon Park Lifesaving Club and lived with his widowed mother in Rose Street, Merewether. He had two sisters, Mrs Ielene [sic] Peterson, of Lambton, Newcastle, and Miss Renie Okulich, a schoolteacher at Lakemba. Okulich won the Australian single surf ski championship at Perth on 24 March. He joined the Dixon Park club as a young boy learning to swim.

His parents came from Poland before he was born and his father died when he was a baby.

The last shark fatality at Newcastle was in January 1949, when a Newcastle lifesaver, Ray Land, 20, was killed.

Sydney Morning Herald, 7 December 1951

1954

BERMUDA, 1954

Sub-Lieutenant E. M. Marks, aged twenty-two, who is serving with HMS *Sheffield*, was flown to London yesterday from Bermuda for emergency treatment for injuries received when a shark attacked him while bathing.

The condition of Sub-Lieutenant E. M. Marks, who was flown to London from Bermuda for emergency treatment after being attacked by a shark while bathing, is stated by Chatham Naval Hospital to be "quite satisfactory".

The Times, London, 10 and 12 July 1954

ITALY/CROATIA (YUGOSLAVIA), 1954

A large shark was seen in the sea close to Duino Castle, the residence at Trieste of General Winterton, the [post-war] zone commander, yesterday. Police launches patrolled the area and bathers were warned to keep near the shore. A few days ago a Hungarian refugee who swam to zone A from zone B reported that another refugee who had been swimming with him had been eaten by a shark.

The Times, London, 16 July 1954

SINGAPORE, 1954

A British sailor who was diving into the harbour at Singapore yesterday, helping the police to recover jettisoned packets of opium, was seized by a shark and has since died of his injuries.

The Times, London, 29 July 1954

HONG KONG, 1954
Able Seaman James Cook of HMS *Comus*, who lived in Highbury, London, has died from an attack by a shark in Junk Bay, Hong Kong. An unusual number of sharks and giant rays are reported in the colony waters this summer.

The Times, London, 17 September 1954

ISLE OF MAN, UNITED KINGDOM, 1954
The threshing tail of a twenty-foot shark, which was brought on board in the nets of a Fleetwood trawler off the Isle of Man, struck a deckhand and broke his arm.

The Times, London, 7 October 1954

1955

NEW SOUTH WALES, AUSTRALIA, 1955
A man was killed by a fourteen-foot tiger shark in Sugarloaf Bay, Castlecrag, yesterday afternoon.

The man, Bruno Aloysius Rautenberg, a twenty-five-year-old German migrant, was attacked twice in about fifteen feet of water between fifteen and twenty yards from the shore. The shark tore Rautenberg's legs to pieces. The flesh on the left leg was torn off between the knee and the foot. Large pieces of flesh were bitten on the right leg.

Yesterday's shark fatality, the second in Sydney in three weeks, occurred at about 2 p.m.

Rautenberg, a metalworker, boarded with Mr and Mrs K. Wood in Edinburgh Road, Castlecrag. He was cleaning himself in the bay after helping to clean out the Woods' swimming pool when the shark attacked. The attack was in a lonely part of Sugarloaf Bay, at the bottom of a high, sloping cliff.

Mr Wood, 37, a clerk, said that after he and Rautenberg cleaned out the pool, which is built of rock, Rautenberg said he would wash the mud off himself in the bay. "I warned him not to go out far, but he said he would try and recover an anchor we lost a few days ago. Suddenly I heard him give a piercing scream. He was a very good swimmer, but I thought he was in difficulties. I ran to the bank near him. There was blood in the water all around him. The shark was right beside him. I saw the shark grab him by the leg, drag him under and hang on.

"I didn't think the shark would let his leg go. Neither my wife nor I can swim. We were the only people around. I grabbed a piece of water pipe about fifteen foot long and threw it at the shark to try and drive it off. By this time Rautenberg was so weak he couldn't do anything.

"When he came to the surface again I waded out a little way from the rock, grasped his body and carried him up the bank. He was dead when I got him ashore. My wife called the police and ambulance."

Mr Wood said the shark seemed to have a pointed nose. It was black along the back. "It had a high triangular fin on its back," he said. "It was more than twice as long as Rautenberg. After the attack the shark swam around for more than two hours and I saw it six times during that time.

"Rautenberg migrated to Australia from Germany and had been boarding with us for about two months. He worked at Alexandria. He never spoke much about himself, but he told my wife he had a little girl, aged five, in Germany. He wanted the child and her mother to come to Australia and had been saving up for their fare. As far as we know, they were not very keen on coming out here."

Central District Ambulance officers and Dr E. Manuel of Castlecrag hurried to the scene soon after the attack, but Rautenberg was dead. Police said they thought he died within about two minutes of the first attack because he lost so much blood.

Police and ambulance men had to make their way down hundreds of steps, through thick bush, to reach the scene. They said the arteries had been torn out of Rautenberg's legs and it would have been impossible to save his life.

Police said that the risk of shark attacks was high at present because the water temperature along the coast was about 74°F. They said this high temperature was bringing scores of sharks and big game fish into the harbour.

On 13 January John Willis, 13, was killed by a twelve-foot grey nurse shark while spearfishing off Balmoral Beach. On 1 March last year a shark mauled a lifesaver swimming alone at The Entrance, near Gosford. The lifesaver died three days later. There have been more than thirty-two fatal shark attacks in New South Wales since 1919. Yesterday's fatality was the eighth in Sydney Harbour since that same year ... Six species of sharks in New South Wales waters are regarded as man-eaters: the tiger, grey nurse, blue pointer or mako, white shark, black or bronze whaler and the hammerhead.

Sydney Sun-Herald, 6 February 1955

ADEN (NOW YEMEN), 1955
Aden fisherman Mohammed Arecki ... armed with only an iron rod, replied to the screams of a woman swimmer [Mrs W. F. Dixon, wife of Wing Commander Dixon] being attacked by an eight-foot-long shark in Telegraph Bay, Aden.

The shark severed part of an arm and a leg, and ripped a gaping hole in the woman's back. With his arm round the victim, the fisherman fought off the shark with such determination that it was forced to release her mutilated body ...

The maddened fish then turned on the fisherman, jaws snapping, and tried to cause him to let go of its intended victim. Mohammed Arecki succeeded in struggling ashore with the woman and gave her first aid until an ambulance arrived. [Mrs Dixon subsequently died of her injuries.]

Baltimore Evening Sun, 27 September 1955

1956

VICTORIA, AUSTRALIA, 1956

A shark killed a twenty-seven-year-old lifesaver at Portsea, at the entrance of Port Phillip Bay, this afternoon.

The victim was John Patrick Wishart, a plumber, of Sorrento. His wife and seventeen-year-old sister were on the beach at the time.

Wishart was not seen again after the shark took him. The shark attacked while the lifesaver and five friends were swimming about 250 yards from the crowded beach.

Gregory Warland, 20, a sergeant in the College of Officer Cadets at Portsea, said after the attack, "Wishart was near me in the water, about five yards away. Hopper (a friend) was between us. Suddenly a shark about twelve feet long swam past Hopper. It hit him in the stomach with its tail, then swam towards Wishart.

"Suddenly there was a splash, and I could see the snout and the jaws of the shark above the surface of the water. Then it seemed to splash down on top of Wishart. It was about four yards away. There was a swirl in the water – and then nothing.

"Hopper and I tried to find Wishart. We realized it was useless, and swam madly for the shore. I reached the shore first and rushed up to the club house to see if I could see anything from there. Then I ran back to help Hopper ashore. I was so shocked I didn't even tell anybody at first. In the meantime the other three chaps had swum ashore."

Mrs G. Bell, of Aspendale, who saw the attack, said, "Suddenly one of the men threw up his arms and went under. We thought he was just playing about in the water, but then he began to thrash his arms about and we realized he was being attacked. Then we saw the shark's fin. The man struggled and seemed to be punching the shark, but then his struggles weakened and he disappeared."

Lifesavers tonight patrolled the beach in the hope of finding Wishart's body.

Sydney Morning Herald, 5 March 1956

MADEIRA, PORTUGAL, 1956
A shark attacked and sank a fishing boat, drowning a twenty-three-year-old fisherman, Manuel Pereira, off Funchal, Madeira.

The Times, London, 27 June 1956

VALETTA, MALTA, 1956
Mr Jack Smedley, a technical instructor at the British dockyard technical school, was killed by a shark today while he was swimming with a Maltese friend.

The Times, London, 21 July 1956

1957

NATAL, SOUTH AFRICA, 1957

A giant shark attacked and killed Allan Green, a fourteen-year-old Johannesburg schoolboy, while he was swimming less than thirty yards off shore at Uvongo Beach, South Coast, yesterday afternoon.

The tragedy, the second attack on the coast in forty-eight hours, took place in full view of a large crowd of bathers who looked on, horrified, as they heard Allan screaming and saw the shark's tail lashing the water before it pulled him along the surface and then let go. Within minutes bathers formed a human chain and recovered Allan's mutilated body from the blood-stained water.

Mr John De Gossely, a twenty-year-old Belgian visitor from Johannesburg, said last night that he had been swimming beside Allan just before he was attacked.

"We were about thirty yards off shore. I decided to catch a wave and swim back to the beach. On the way back I heard my father shouting, 'Shark, shark.' He was standing ashore.

"I looked round and saw a black tail lashing the water. It was about two to three feet wide. The shark grabbed Allan and pulled him along the top of the water. He screamed and the water was full of blood. I scrambled on to the beach and some people immediately formed a chain and pulled Allan out of the water. He was already dead and his body was badly mutilated." The right arm and side were torn away.

Mr De Gossely said that there were about forty people bathing in the small land-locked bay when the shark made its attack. He and Allan had been further out than any of the other bathers.

Allan was on holiday at Uvongo with his parents and

his younger brother. They had been staying at the Uvongo Hotel for three weeks and were due to return home on 5 January.

After the tragedy several people reported that they had seen a large shark cruising off shore and Sergeant Stan Cole, station commander of the Margate police, stationed a constable with a rifle on a rock. He stayed there until nightfall, but did not sight the shark.

The attack took place forty-eight hours after another youth, sixteen-year-old Robert Wherley, had his left leg bitten off by a shark at Karridene, about fifty miles from Uvongo. Robert, who lives at Aylesbury Flats, Amanzimtoti, was admitted to the African Explosives Hospital at Umbogintwini. Last night his condition was described as "much improved".

Mr Frank Shepard, an authority on angling, said last night that there was a danger that the shark might attack again, having tasted human blood. It was quite possible that the same shark was responsible for both attacks. It could easily have swum the distance from Karridene to Uvongo in that time. Judging by the size of the tail which was seen, Mr Shepard said the shark could have been a "ragged tooth" or a tiger shark. It could weigh between 400 and 500 lbs.

Cape Times, 21 December 1957

NATAL, SOUTH AFRICA, 1957

Four hours after his arrival in Margate yesterday, Vernon James Berry, 23, of Bulawayo [Rhodesia, now Zimbabwe] was taken by a shark and dragged sideways through the surf. He was rescued by two friends, but died on the way to Port Shepstone hospital.

Spectators of the attack, the second fatal one in the last week, said that the young Rhodesian and the shark turned grotesque somersaults in the water. Mr Berry was taken while he was swimming with a group of more than 200 bathers at a point almost in the centre of the bathing lagoon at Margate. He had arrived in Margate shortly after 1 p.m. on a five-day visit before going on to motorcycle races in the Cape, where he was to have taken part.

His two companions, Tommy Robinson and Fred Norman, both from Bulawayo, were the first to reach him after the attack and helped him to the beach.

It was thought that the shark had taken him from the side, as Mr Berry's left forearm was severed, his right arm badly mutilated, his lower abdomen, buttocks and right thigh were also badly mutilated. He was conscious when he was brought back to the beach, but soon lapsed into a coma.

Mr Robinson said that he was swimming a short distance from Mr Berry when he heard his cries for help. Someone had also shouted, "Shark!" He did not notice the shark, but saw only his friend floating on his back in a huge streak of blood. As he reached him, he called to their other companion, Fred Norman, who also swam to the mauled man.

They were helped in bringing in Mr Berry by Mr D. A. Saunders, of Benoni, who was also swimming near by. Mr Saunders said that, when Mr Berry was brought to the beach, he expressed horror at the sight of his own injuries before he lost consciousness. The scene was watched by hundreds of people who thronged the beach at Margate irrespective of the other fatal shark attack, at Uvongo, four miles away, only seventy-two hours before.

Mr T. J. Erasmus, of Roodepoort, said that he was sitting on the rocks, watching the bathers, when he saw the shark gliding through a breaker to the attack. He shouted, "Shark," but it was too late.

The shark was seen again a few minutes after the attack by Mr L. Band, of Johannesburg. He said that he saw it quite distinctly as it cruised parallel to the beach. At one point he could see its entire length as it swam along a breaking wave. He estimated its length to be more than ten feet.

The shark was first seen swimming past a group of Native bathers to the north of the main Margate beach. One of the Natives ran to the European beach to warn the lifesavers, but was beaten by the fast-swimming shark.

The Margate surf was deserted for the rest of the afternoon.

Cape Times, 24 December 1957

NATAL, SOUTH AFRICA, 1957

Doctors and nurses at Port Shepstone Hospital were still fighting early today to save the life of Julia Painting, a fourteen-year-old Bulawayo girl mauled by a shark as she bathed among hundreds of visitors at Margate yesterday. At midnight her condition was reported as "unchanged". Her left arm was torn off and flesh savaged from her body.

She murmured, "Let me die," as she was being taken to hospital. Julia was later reported to be still in a serious condition, but "there is a very slight improvement". She was operated on soon after the attack – the fourth since 19 December 1957 on the Natal South Coast. Her life hung in the balance when it was learnt that the hospital's blood bank was empty. Nurses and hospital staff immediately volunteered to be bled and, while two pints were being collected, an urgent call for ten pints of blood was sent to the hospital at Renishaw. It arrived in time.

The Margate Town Council banned all bathing off the beach until further notice at a special meeting held after the attack on Julia. Bathing will be allowed in the lagoon as soon as it has been deepened and the mouth sandbagged. The Council also decided to erect a shark net immediately.

A large crowd on the beach heard Julia's screams for help. They watched in horrified silence as the shark wrestled with her in clear, knee-deep water about thirty yards from the beach. Two men, Mr Paul Brokensha, 36, of Fort Victoria, Rhodesia, and a Margate lifesaver, Mr Aubrey Cowan, fought to free Julia from the shark's jaws. Eventually the shark let go and swam away.

Julia was standing in unclouded water on the fringe of hundreds of other bathers when the shark made its savage attack, taking away her left arm and leaving lacerations on her chest. A dumbfounded crowd of more than 2,000 on the beach heard the first frantic warning screams of "shark" and watched as the flurried water became blood red.

Lifesavers jumped to action and sounded a warning siren. Only moments previously a spotter aircraft of the shark patrol had passed over the area before wheeling back towards St Michael's.

Julia, her fifteen-year-old nephew Laurie, an uncle, Mr Arthur Painting, and Mr Brokensha were having a final dip before leaving the surf. Julia was due to return home today. She had been on holiday with her uncle and aunt for a month.

Mr Brokensha described how, standing only a few yards from Julia, he saw, simultaneously with her, the shark moving in to the first attack. It went straight for her without turning on its side. With a savage thrust it hit her and immediately mauled her side, before wheeling around for a second attack.

Mr Brokensha caught the shark's tail and tried to drag Julia away, but her costume came away in his hands. He started raining blows on the shark's back, but, in his own words, "It was like punching very solid leather and there was no 'give' at all."

The shark was so powerful that, with a flick of its tail, it threw him off. He immediately returned to the fray and hit the shark again. The shark let go, but not until it had severed the girl's arm at the shoulder and severely savaged her body.

The attack was so sudden and unexpected that the four life-savers realized that a shark was in the water only when they heard horrified screams and saw the water churning beneath flaying fins. Mr Frank Shephard, the Durban fishing authority, said that, from the description, the shark was undoubtedly a ragged-tooth shark – one of the most dangerous, and a cunning and quiet scavenger which creeps along the bottom towards the shore.

Cape Times, 31 December 1957

1958

NATAL, SOUTH AFRICA, 1958

As a wave of horror swept Natal's South Coast after a fresh shark killing yesterday, at least three families decided to pack up and leave. Some visitors said that the South Coast would become a "ghost resort" if immediate steps were not taken to make bathing safe.

The victim of the latest attack, Mr Derryet Garth Prinsloo, a forty-two-year-old farmer of Theunissen, Free State, was standing in about thirty inches of water a few yards from the shore and talking to a woman companion when he was taken by a lazy-grey shark at Scottburgh.

His frantic scream, "Help me, for God's sake help me," electrified the small crowd of early morning bathers as the shark, attacking from behind, ripped the flesh from both his legs and buttocks in a series of lightning attacks.

As three rescuers pulled him from the surf on to the beach, his sixteen-year-old son, Jacques, rushed from the water and, cradling the head of his dying father in his lap, cried, "Daddy, Daddy, don't leave me. I'm with you. Please speak to me."

Mr Prinsloo was taken to Renishaw Hospital in a station wagon, but was dead on arrival. An immediate ban was imposed by order of the Town Board on further bathing.

Mr A. Laing of Boksburg and his twelve-year-old son, Neville, had been standing alongside Mr Prinsloo only minutes before the attack. Mr Laing, feeling the debris of washed cane from the river stroking his legs in the murky surf, said to his son, "This is shark water, let's get out."

While walking out of the surf, he heard the screams for help and, looking round, saw the shark lashing its tail in a flurry of blood-stained water. He rushed back to help Mr J. Kelly of Ermelo and Mr J. A. C. Nieman of Virginia, who were pulling Mr Prinsloo by the arms away from the shark, which had knocked him on to his side. When they hauled him to the shore, both legs had been stripped of all flesh and the left leg was almost severed.

Mrs Nieman, who, with her husband and two children, had gone for an early morning bathe with Mr Prinsloo and his son, said she was standing right next to Mr Prinsloo when the attack occurred. "He was saying, 'This is what I like about the waves here – they're so beautifully even.' They were his last words. The next thing I knew he was screaming for help."

Mr D. Stamatis of Scottburgh, an experienced shark fisherman, sent home for a shotgun after the attack. He took up a position on the rocks, from where he saw a shark – which he believed was a five-foot, 200-lb lazy grey – make two more sorties into the shallow surf before 8.30 a.m.

Cape Times, 10 January 1958

Bull Shark

Shark Facts

Length: 7 feet 5 inches to 13 feet (2.25 m to 4 m)

Weight: 210 lb to 690 lb (95 kg to 315 kg)

Colouring: Grey upper with white belly

Diet: Sea birds, turtles, rays, dolphins, other sharks, crustaceans

Pups: Four to ten pups born up to 2 feet 4 inches (71 cm)

Status: Not endangered

Bull sharks are extremely aggressive and will attack other sharks that stray into their territory. As well as hunting in the shallows along the seashore, they will explore brackish river water and freshwater, having been reported as far up the Ohio River as Kentucky in the United States. They will leap rapids in rivers just like salmon. Also known as the Zambesi shark or Nicaragua shark it has been responsible for numerous attacks on humans, bull sharks having been blamed for a series of attacks along the coast of New Jersey in 1916 when four people were killed. The Jersey incidents are said to have inspired Peter Blenchley's novel *Jaws*.

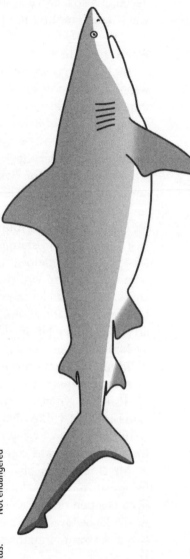

Bull Shark Range

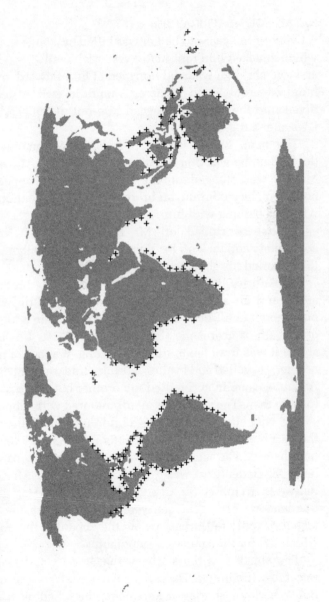

NATAL, SOUTH AFRICA, 1958

A twenty-nine-year-old bather was killed by a large shark which attacked him repeatedly yesterday while his wife and two children watched horrified at Port Edward, one hundred miles south of here. A middle-aged African dived into the surf and dragged him out of the shark's jaws after a tug-of-war.

The man, Mr Nicholas Francois Badenhorst, was dead when he was dragged to the beach by the African, Maseke, who plunged into the surf after frenzied appeals both from the victim and his brother, Andries Badenhorst, who was bathing with him.

The shark ripped off Mr Badenhorst's left arm completely and took off his right arm below the elbow. It then mauled his abdomen and one of his legs.

Mr Andries Badenhorst said last night: "My brother and I and an acquaintance were bathing a little way out – about chest-deep in the water. There were a lot of other bathers nearer the shore. Suddenly I saw this big shark. It was from ten to fifteen feet long. It attacked my brother. He yelled and I yelled. I think a line was sent out. A Native came in and pulled my brother out, but it was too late then. The water was all discoloured with blood."

Mr Nicholas Badenhorst's children, who were on the beach with their mother, are five years and twenty months old. The family was staying at a holiday camp here. Mr Badenhorst was a clerk on the South African Railways, living at Sir George Grey Avenue, Horison, Roodepoort. Arrangements were immediately made to take the family to Durban, where they boarded the train which left for the Transvaal last night.

The attack was the sixth on the South Coast since December. Before 18 December, when sixteen-year-old Bob Wherley lost a leg at Karridene, there had been no shark attacks in Natal waters since 1954. Then in quick succession came attacks at Uvongo beach, where Allan Green, 14, was killed only twenty-four hours after the attack on Wherley, at Margate, where Vernon Berry, aged twenty-three, was killed on 23 December, and fourteen-year-old Julia Painting lost her left arm and was mutilated a week later, and at Scottburgh, where Mr D. G. Prinsloo, 42, was killed on 9 January.

The mayors of three of the South Coast's premier holiday resorts, Mr Robert Barton (Margate), Mr Arthur Howes (Amanzimtoti) and Mr Les Payn (Scotsburgh) last night appealed to holidaymakers to obey the bathing instructions of lifesavers. Mr Barton said the tragedies indicated the danger of swimming outside safe-bathing enclosures. All three mayors pointed out that resort municipalities had spent thousands of pounds and many hours of deliberation in planning the safest form of bathing.

Cape Times, 4 April 1958

NATAL, SOUTH AFRICA, 1958
Efforts have been initiated to set up a statutory coordinating body to deal with the shark menace in South African coastal waters.

This move follows two more fatal attacks in shallow surf on Natal's south coast during the Easter holiday weekend. In one case a twenty-nine-year-old visitor, Mr N. F. Badenhorst, was attacked while bathing in full view of his wife and two children.

In the second case Mrs Fay Bester, 28, a widow with four young children, was attacked and killed in shallow surf. Three other bathers have been killed on this stretch of coast during the present summer season. An emergency meeting of the Natal Safety Bathing

Association is to be held tomorrow to form a plan for coordinating anti-shark measures.

The Times, London, 8 April 1958

1959

GULF OF MEXICO, 1959

The oil slick was four miles wide. Bodies and a life raft bobbed in it. Somewhere under it was the tomb of an undetermined number of persons on the National Air Line missing DC-7B. The big four-engine plane must have hit with a terrific impact. All of the clothing was torn from the bodies and the debris was in tiny pieces.

This reporter hitched a ride on a Coast Guard helicopter and arrived over the scene about 100 miles south-east of New Orleans at 11.30 a.m. yesterday. There were no large pieces of the plane and, even though the sea was very clear, we could not see it in the water. The first thing I spotted was a partially inflated, yellow life raft belonging to the missing plane. It bobbed in the oil slick, which was ever widening. Further on there was a smoke signal floating as well as several yellow dye markers, all dropped by other planes.

The first body I saw was an elderly, grey-haired man of heavy build with bruises on his back. His clothing was sort of purple and just hanging on him. Later we spotted another man. He was younger with blond hair and a good build, like an athlete. He was nude, but his body did not appear to be damaged externally. The next was a woman. Her blouse was up around her neck and that was all the clothing left on her. Before we left, the Coast Guard had recovered eight bodies and there appeared to be three more in sight.

Just as we turned to leave, we spotted the body of

another woman. Beneath it was something big and grey. At first I thought it was another body. But, no, it was a ten-foot shark.

I shouted to the crewman of the helicopter, and he confirmed it, to my horror. It was worrying the body, which appeared to be torn up. I saw one gaping hole in the back.

I have never seen anything like that. I was ready to head for home.

Searchers held slim hope late yesterday that any passengers would be found alive from the giant airliner which crashed into the Gulf of Mexico. Forty-two persons were aboard. Nine bodies in tattered remains of clothing and small pieces of plane debris were picked up by the searchers …

Searchers combed the oil-slicked Gulf throughout the day. A grey dense coat of fog hung over the current, pushed by a steady wind. The Coast Guard halted the search at nightfall, but left two vessels in the area. The crash site, the Coast Guard said, probably would be marked off to aid salvage operations, but it would be difficult because of the water's depth.

One searching ship came across mail and clothing. The wind spread the debris – pieces of foam rubber and other interior plane parts – over a three- or four-mile area. The Coast Guard estimated the plane was in fifty fathoms of water.

A ten-foot shark was the only sign of life spotted in the wreckage area.

New Orleans Times-Picayune, 17 November 1959

INDIAN OCEAN, 1959

A three-year-old child died and a woman was injured by sharks which attacked seventeen Maldivians who spent thirty-one days adrift in an open boat off the coast of Ceylon [Sri Lanka]. The islanders were rescued by the 20,500-ton Japanese tanker *Obminesan Maru*, which has reached Colombo.

The boat and its passengers were swept off course while crossing from one atoll to another in the Maldivian archipelago.

The Times, London, 14 December 1959

Saw Shark

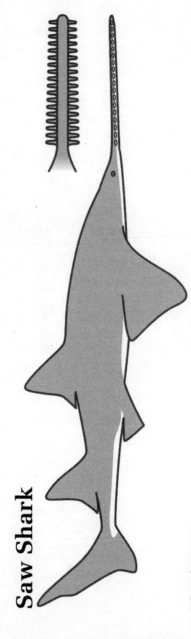

Shark Facts

Length: Up to 5 feet 7 inches (1.7 m)
Weight: Up to 40 lb (18 kg)
Colouring: Light brown/grey upper with lighter spots and with paler belly
Diet: Molluscs, crustaceans, small fish
Pups: Up to 22 pups born at around 1 foot 2 inches (34 cm)
Status: Not threatened

There are six different species of saw shark of varying sizes but all have the distinctive flattened snout with teeth along each side with which they slash their prey. Saw sharks swim along the bottom using two barbels that trail from their snouts to help locate their prey. Pups are born with their teeth folded back flush with their snout blades so that they don't hurt their mother. The saw shark is not thought to be a danger to humans and, because it is of no commercial value to fishermen, neither is it thought to be in any danger.

Saw Shark Range

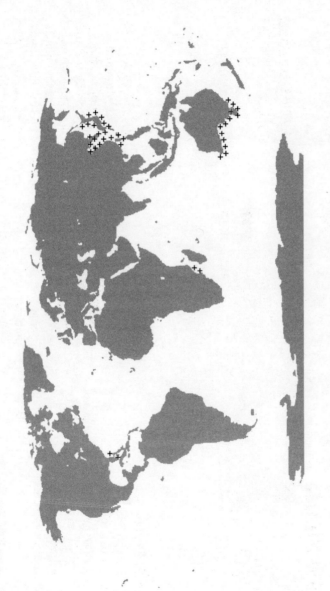

SHARK ATTACKS
1960–69

1960

NATAL, SOUTH AFRICA, 1960
By early today the Christmas weekend death toll in South Africa totalled forty-six from road accidents, drownings, assaults, faction fights, lightning and a shark attack at Margate on the Natal south coast …

An African, Serame Sithole, the servant of a Transvaal family on holiday at Margate, was killed by a shark in the surf on Christmas Eve. Both his legs were bitten off.

Cape Times, 27 December 1960

NATAL, SOUTH AFRICA, 1960
One of the largest sharks caught off the Natal south coast – a 352-lb ragged-tooth shark landed by Mr Dave Griesel after a three-hour struggle near Port Edward – contained human remains.

Nine bones were found in the stomach of the fish including a human kneecap with flesh attached. There was also a piece of black woollen material with a seam through the middle, which could have been part of a bathing costume.

Five teeth from the shark's bottom jaw were broken

off; and it is believed that this could be the shark that attacked and killed an African man [Serame Sithole] on Margate Beach on Christmas Eve. His legs were severed and two teeth were found in the stumps.

The human remains were removed by an unknown person at Palm Beach, and the Margate police were trying yesterday to trace this person as the remains will give valuable clues to the Oceanographic Research Institute in Durban. Thoughtless souvenir hunters carried away the head and body of the shark, also preventing valuable ichthyological study.

Mr Dave Griesel said that he caught the shark at 4 a.m. on Friday. It was cut for weighing and he then noticed the bones and flesh in its stomach. "When it was taken back to the beach, the souvenir hunters got busy. It was quite impossible to stop them and soon most of the shark had disappeared."

Cape Times, 3 January 1961

1961

CAPE PROVINCE, SOUTH AFRICA, 1961

Mr Peter Hendricks, aged twenty-eight, of Fourth Avenue, Elsie's River, is believed to have been bitten by a shark while swimming in chest-high water at Strandfontein, on the False Bay shore, at about 3.30 p.m. yesterday. He was helped from the water with a deep gash just above his left ankle.

Mr Hendricks told his helpers that he did not see a fish, but felt a jerk on his leg as he was waiting to take a breaker into the shore. He later told the staff at Victoria Hospital, Wynberg, that he saw a black shadow under the water. He was 75 to 100 yards out at the time.

He was treated for a three-inch long cut. It was stated by the hospital that it was probably a bite.

Mr Harold Burns, of Twinside, Lake Road, Grassy Park, who runs a beach café at Strandfontein, which is about four miles from Muizenberg, told a reporter: "At first Mr Hendricks thought his foot was entangled in weed. It was only when he got near the shore that he saw his left leg was bleeding profusely."

The injured swimmer was brought to him for attention before being taken to Victoria Hospital to have the wound treated.

"The sinews were showing through the gash," said Mr Burns. The shark apparently bit only once, for Mr Hendricks felt only one jerk, said Mr Burns.

There were between 2,000 and 3,000 holidaymakers on the Strandfontein beach when he was bitten, but only about 150 were in the water.

It was partly overcast at the time of the suspected attack – overcast conditions in summer are considered a danger time for sharks in Natal. The sea temperature in False Bay at 1.30 p.m. yesterday was 74 degrees – exceptionally high for this part of the coast, an official at the Muizenberg Pavilion said.

Two hammerhead sharks about four feet long were caught by trek fishermen about three-quarters of a mile off the Fish Hoek shore on New Year's Day, Mr Charles Home, the *Cape Times* angling correspondent, said last night. "Specimens this size could not have killed anyone – they could not have taken a big piece out of a limb."

The warm water in False Bay in the past week increases the danger of sharks. He thought it unlikely that a snoek had bitten Mr Hendricks as snoek are deep-water fish.

Cape Times, 4 January 1961

NATAL, SOUTH AFRICA, 1961
Eleven-year-old Michael Land, of Luanshya, Northern
Rhodesia, was attacked by a shark in three feet of
water about 100 yards from the edge of the surf near
Winkelspruit swimming baths at 7.30 last night.

Doctors reported his leg would have to be amputated,
probably below the knee.

He was swimming with four other youths when the
shark bit him just below the left ankle.

Hugh Gruddas, captain of the Winkelspruit Lifesaving Club, and Eddie Vincent, who is also a life-saver,
rushed to Michael and took him out of the surf, while
other life-savers called two doctors.

Michael was taken to Addington Hospital by
ambulance and there doctors performed an emergency
operation on his leg. Early this morning Michael's
condition was reported to be satisfactory.

Eddie Vincent said last night: "I heard screams and
rushed into the surf fully clothed while Hugh Gruddas
went to get a lifeline. Michael staggered towards me
screaming, 'My leg, my leg.'

"I grabbed hold of his hand and saw the fin of a shark
about ten yards behind us. The shark was about seven
feet long and it followed us before turning back.

"I put him on the beach. Michael hardly said a word and
was very brave. We told him that he had been scratched."

As Michael lay on the beach, two doctors arrived and
gave him morphine to ease the pain.

Cape Times, 7 January 1961

NATAL, SOUTH AFRICA, 1961
A grey shark, weighing between 300 and 400 lbs, attacked
a fifteen-year-old schoolboy, Michael Murphy, in six
feet of water about ten yards from an unprotected

stretch of beach at Amanzimtoti yesterday afternoon.

Michael was savaged in two places on the inside of his left leg. He was bathing only a few hundred yards from where the last attack occurred at Inyoni Rocks.

The lower inside thigh and the calf were bitten, and the femoral artery was severed. Surgeons were fighting at Addington Hospital last night to save the leg. Michael was taken from the beach by ambulance after spending the prescribed half-hour on the beach without moving.

The attack was watched by fifteen other young people, including his fourteen-year-old sister Diana. They had all spent the day together, boating on the Amanzimtoti River and picnicking on the beach.

Lifesavers and friends who attended him on the beach were full of praise last night for his magnificent courage. His first words on being taken from the water were, "Oh, hell," in a resigned voice. Once he realized the full import of the situation, however, he fainted on the sands. He recovered before being taken to hospital.

Experts have noted a similarity in the three attacks which have occurred on the South Coast this year. These are:

- the sharks are all believed to have belonged to the grey species;
- all the victims were swimming in or near a channel by the shore where the water was discoloured;
- the temperature has been around the 75°F mark.

The first inkling Michael's friends had that something was amiss was when he started shouting, "Shark! Shark!" They turned and saw him threshing in the water, but at first considered that he was playing the fool. Then blood appeared in the surf and three others in the water rushed to help him.

One of the friends, Gary Moore, aged seventeen, who was swimming near him, said yesterday: "He was trying to fight it off with his fists. He was lifting his leg and shouting. We went to help him and a wave came along and washed him to shore."

The local doctor put Michael in the prescribed position and administered morphine and saline. He was left on the beach for thirty-five minutes and was then taken to Addington Hospital slowly by ambulance.

Cape Times, 23 January 1961

QUEENSLAND, AUSTRALIA, 1961

Doctors are fighting desperately to save the life of eighteen-year-old Margaret Hobbs, a victim of yesterday's shark attack at Mackay.

Miss Hobbs has been receiving continuous transfusions of blood and saline solutions since she was admitted to the Mater Hospital, Mackay, at 3 p.m. yesterday. She is dangerously ill. Late tonight her condition was unchanged.

Miss Hobbs, a schoolteacher of Owen's Creek, near Mackay, and a friend, Martyn Steffens, 24, of Brisbane, were mauled by the shark as they stood in waist-deep water at Lambert's Beach.

Doctors in a two-hour emergency operation last night amputated Miss Hobbs' right leg near the hip. Her right arm was torn off at the shoulder and her left arm torn off above the wrist.

Steffens had his right hand and wrist mauled. Doctors amputated his hand above the wrist. His condition tonight was serious, but doctors consider his progress satisfactory.

Graham Jorgensen, 27, who saved the couple by driving the shark away, said today the couple had entered the water to wash sand off their bodies after playing on the beach. When the attack occurred, he was sitting on the beach with the rest of the party ...

Evidence of a growing shark menace in eastern Australian waters came with reports of shark sightings yesterday in many areas: a ten-foot shark surfaced near a fisherman while he was swimming to safety from a burning, sinking trawler off Southport, Queensland; a shark snapped a fish from a fisherman's line as he stood in shallow water near Murwillumbah; the body of a drowned man mauled by a shark was found yesterday floating in the Brisbane river; and a shark swam within ten feet of four adults and nine children at Northcliffe, south of Surfers Paradise, on Thursday.

Sydney Morning Herald, 30 December 1961

QUEENSLAND, AUSTRALIA, 1961

Margaret Hobbs, 18, the Mackay shark victim, died at 6.30 last night. Her death ended a grim round-the-clock battle by doctors and nurses since the attack. A sister at the Mater Hospital said, "Miss Hobbs fought courageously for her life."

Miss Hobbs lost consciousness in the afternoon and her parents were called to her bedside. Friends later took them home. "They couldn't stand it any longer," a hospital sister said. A doctor was called urgently in the late afternoon, but Miss Hobbs gradually sank.

A hospital sister who was with Miss Hobbs almost continually said tonight, "There was never any real hope. Margaret just held her own for the first twenty-four hours, but her condition deteriorated overnight and it was never good at any time today. She knew her parents this morning and was able to say 'yes', 'Mum' and 'Dad' – that's all. Margaret was very brave and she was fighting until the moment she lost consciousness."

Sisters at the hospital said that Martyn Steffens had been told during the day that Margaret's condition was deteriorating. His mother and her father were with him when the news of her death was broken to him at 7.15 pm. Friends of the couple said Steffens went to Mackay just before Christmas to meet the Hobbs family before announcing his engagement to Margaret.

More than twenty shark alarms along Queensland's central coast sent swimmers scattering from the water yesterday.

At Pacific Beach, near Surfers' Paradise, a group of fishermen digging for worms in ankle-deep water fled as a ten-foot shark cruised past in two feet of water less than ten feet away.

North Burleigh Beach lifesavers closed the beach three times in four hours when sharks nosed in close to swimmers. All life-saving clubs from the Gold Coast to the far north maintained doubled patrols, but many swimmers stayed out of the water or remained in the shallows. A privately owned spotting aircraft will keep a tight watch for sharks at the Yeppoon to Emu Park beaches. The aircraft's pilot today saw sharks up to ten feet long cruising within three yards of swimmers.

Sydney Sun-Herald, 31 December 1961

1962

SOUTH AUSTRALIA, AUSTRALIA, 1962
A sixteen-year-old spear fisherman was fatally mauled by a man-eating shark while competing in skindiving competitions near Normanville yesterday afternoon. It was the third fatality from shark attacks in South Australian waters in thirty-six years and it came

twenty-one months after another spear fisherman had been badly mauled at Aldinga Beach.

In a gallant rescue bid a fellow spear fisherman tied the injured youth to his surf ski and beat the shark off for ten minutes with a paddle before making it to the shore.

The dead youth was Geoffrey Martin Corner, son of Mr and Mrs A. M. Corner, of Nautilus Road, Elizabeth East, who were on the beach at the time of the attack.

The attack, one of the most vicious ever known in South Australian waters, occurred about 150 yards off shore from the Carrickalinga Beach, locally known as "the Gold Coast", two miles north of Normanville. The boy was attacked by the shark in twenty feet of water at 2.30 p.m. while taking part in the Underwater Skin Divers and Fishermen's Association in South Australia competitions.

The shark circled several of about sixteen other spear-fishermen within 200 yards of Mr Corner before lunging at him as he made his dive. The shark, believed to be a fourteen-foot bronze whaler, grabbed the boy's right leg between the calf and the thigh in its two-foot jaws and shook him violently before releasing him.

The attack was seen by fellow club member Allen Phillips, 27, of Reedle Street, Henley Beach, who was about ten yards away, towing a surf ski. Mr Phillips later told club members that the huge shark made a grab at the boy as his flippers were breaking the water in a dive.

Mr Phillips climbed on his surf ski and paddled over to the boy, whom he dragged from the blood-stained water. With the boy's body only half out of the water, he lashed it to the ski with a piece of plastic wire he was carrying, while at the same time beating off frenzied lunges by the shark. The battle lasted for ten minutes before Mr Phillips could make for the shore with the shark still following and circling him.

In the meantime, Murray Bampton, a member of the Knights of Neptune Underwater Club, who had just brought a man with cramp to the shore, saw the struggle and went out on his surf ski to help. Mr Bampton kept the shark away with his paddle, while Mr Phillips continued in. When in a few feet of water, the two men carried the boy on Mr Phillips' ski to the beach. Sister Heather Jones, who was on the beach, ran over to help.

Dr R. J. de N. Souter of Yankalilla, who was summoned to the scene, pronounced the youth dead. It is understood that the boy's injuries were such that he would have died within thirty seconds of the attack. The boy had suffered shocking injuries to his right leg, extending from the calf muscles to half way up the thigh, and gashes to his left leg, all of which are believed to have been made in the shark's only bite.

Adelaide Advertiser, 10 December 1962

1963

NEW SOUTH WALES, AUSTRALIA, 1963
Miss Marcia Hathaway, a well-known Sydney actress, was fatally mauled by a shark in Middle Harbour yesterday afternoon. The shark attacked her while she was standing in murky water only thirty inches deep and twenty feet from the shore in the northern arm of Sugarloaf Bay.

Seconds before she died, while friends were hurrying her to hospital, Miss Hathaway told her fiancé, "I am not in pain. Don't worry about me, dear. God will look after me."

Miss Hathaway, 32, of Greenway Flats, Milson's Point, was on a picnic trip with six friends in a motor cruiser.

When the shark attacked, her fiancé, who was

beside her, fought the shark with his hands and kicked it as it twisted in the blood-stained water, trying to drag its victim into deep water.

Miss Hathaway died twenty minutes later from her terrible injuries and shock. The shark almost tore off her right leg. Miss Hathaway's fiancé and two other friends were treated at the Mater Misericordiae Hospital for shock.

Miss Hathaway and her fiancé, Frederick Knight, 38, a journalist of Cook Street, Double Bay, were in the party of seven holidaying on the twenty-eight-foot cabin cruiser *Valeeta*.

Knight said later that Miss Hathaway at first thought she had been attacked by an octopus. "I have seen men die, but I have never seen anyone so brave as Marcia," he said. "I think the last words she said to me were, 'Don't worry about me, dear, God will look after me.' When I asked her if it hurt much, she said, 'No, I am not in pain.' She was a very religious girl. We were to announce our engagement formally on her birthday, Friday the 8th.

"I did not get a close look at the shark, I saw a fin and its girth as I straddled it. My legs were wide apart and its body touched both of them."

The *Valeeta* was anchored about twenty yards from where the shark attacked, which was close to shore. The attack occurred in a small bay with a small watercourse at its head. Several homes back on to the water about 700 yards away; they are not visible from the beach.

The other members of the party were David Mason, 28, a journalist, and Peter Cowden, 27, both of Balmain, who are joint owners of the cruiser, James Delmege, 39, of Potts Point, Alan Simpson, 21, of Auburn, and Sandra Hayden, 19, of Blacktown. Mason, Cowden and Simpson were on the *Valeeta*, Delmege and Miss Hayden were only about three or four feet from the shore gathering oysters from the rocks, while Knight and Miss Hathaway were standing in shallow water about twenty feet out.

Knight said, when the shark attacked, he was only a few feet away from Miss Hathaway. "I went to her and tried to drag her from the shark. It seemed like ten minutes to me while we struggled, but it could only have been a couple of minutes. The water was stained with blood and I never thought I would get her away from it. I think at one stage I had my foot in its mouth. It felt soft and spongy. I'm not too clear what happened. It happened so fast and I could not see much in the water. I tried to reassure her and told her that the shark had just brushed past her, but she knew a short time after that she was dying."

Delmege said he had his back to the couple when the shark attacked. Sandra Hayden was a few feet away from him. "I heard a scream, looked around and thought they were just skylarking. I continued looking for oysters," he said. "Then I heard a second scream and I turned, and saw the water bloodstained and foaming. I dashed in and helped Fred Knight to get Marcia away from the shark."

Knight said the shark apparently attacked Miss Hathaway below the calf on the right leg, then in a second lunge embedded its teeth into her upper right thigh near the hip. Her right leg was almost torn off.

Delmege and Knight carried Miss Hathaway to the sandy beach in the small cove. Mason said that, when he and Cowden saw the attack, they tore sheets off the cruiser's bunks for tourniquets, then rowed to shore in the dinghy. They applied tourniquets on the beach, lifted Miss Hathaway into the dinghy and rowed back to the *Valeeta*. They took the cruiser to a boatshed at the foot of Edinburgh Road, Castlecrag, where Knight dived overboard and swam about twenty yards to a house to get the occupants to phone for an ambulance.

He swam back to the cruiser and comforted his fiancée as they made for Mowbray Point, where they were met by ambulance officers Ray Wrightson and Robert Smith of Central District Ambulance. Miss Hathaway was unconscious. The ambulancemen used oxygen in an attempt to revive her.

They put her in an ambulance, but, because of the steep grade leading up from the water's edge and slippery surface, the ambulance clutch burnt out. Although about thirty people, including Knight, tried desperately to push the vehicle, the gradient was too steep. A reporter radioed his office and a second ambulance was sent.

Ambulance officers worked on Miss Hathaway continuously and doctors at the hospital also tried to revive her, but she was dead. Miss Hathaway's mother collapsed when told the news of her death and was taken by ambulance to a private hospital.

Mr Michael Vaux, the owner of the Castlecrag boat shed, where the *Valeeta* pulled in with Miss Hathaway, said he saw two large sharks earlier in the morning in the bay. "There were a couple of dogs taken by sharks in the area last week," he said.

Sydney Morning Herald, 29 January 1963

Adult Behaviour

Once a shark has outgrown its nursery and is ranging further afield, it may adopt the life of a lone hunter, or it may band together with others of its species. Dogfish are so called because they hunt in packs that can number hundreds or even thousands and other species, like the blue shark, live together in large groups segregated by size and sex.

Even sharks that tend to be solitary creatures, like the great white or the bull shark, will tolerate other sharks from time to time. The bull shark is not the most sociable of creatures and is very territorial. It will attack other sharks that venture into its feeding ground and pretty much any other animal that does, including humans, but these sharks have also been observed hunting and cruising in pairs. The great white is also known to tolerate company with small "clans" coming together that appear to observe a pecking order that constitutes a distinct social hierarchy. Males defer to females and smaller sharks defer to larger ones. The sharks may group together during their migration cycles, with Californian great whites migrating out into the Pacific to an area known as the White Shark Café, taking three months over spring to make the journey, with some then venturing on to Hawaii to spend the summer. It is believed that the migration is due to mating and feeding habits.

South African great whites, for many years thought to be a permanent presence off the coast, have also been discovered to migrate. Tagged sharks have been tracked by satellite making a mammoth journey from the southern tip of Africa to the northern shores of Australia. These migrations, alone or in groups, are impressive endeavours but not as awe inspiring as the mobile army of sharks that closed the beaches around Palm Beach in Florida in March 2013. The seasonal northward migration happened a month or so later in 2013 than in previous years and a lot closer to the shoreline. Many large sharks could clearly be seen from the beach, chasing fish in the surf, but when helicopters were used to observe the migration from above it was estimated the around 15,000 blacktip and spinner sharks were swimming just off the coast.

Sharks migrate, just as other fish do, to follow their prey or stay in water that is of a temperature to their liking. The Californian great whites that drift off into the Pacific return towards the end of the year to take advantage of the elephant seal breeding season – elephant seals being one of their favourite prey.

While hunting, sharks will often breach the surface, a consequence of attacking from below at great speed. A great white, targeting a seal and rising from the depths at around 25mph (40 km/h) can launch itself 10 feet (3 m) into the air. The mako shark is more than 10 mph (16 km/h) faster, leaping even higher. What the great white does that no other sharks seem to do is to stick its head out of the water to take a look around. The habit, called "spy-hopping" allows it to see what's going on on the surface without the distortion of the water but also lets it use its sense of smell, scents travelling far better through the air.

Aside from hunting to keep itself alive, the most important function of an adult shark is to mate. As with so many things that sharks do, this can be a violent affair. Smaller, more flexible sharks curl themselves around each other when mating but a large male shark, which is generally smaller than the female, has to hold the female steady in order to insert its clasper (a development of the pelvic fin that serves the same purpose as a penis) into its mate's oviduct. The only way to hold the female steady is to bite her and mature females bear a variety of mating battlescars, although their flesh is up to three times as thick as the males' in order to ensure that they come to no real harm from the male's brutal lovemaking.

SOUTH AUSTRALIA, AUSTRALIA, 1963

A twenty-three-year-old spear fisherman was badly mauled by a man-eating shark while competing in the State spear fishing championships at Aldinga Beach yesterday afternoon The attack was the third – one fatal – in South Australia in less than three years.

Surgeons at the Royal Adelaide Hospital battled for four hours yesterday afternoon in a dramatic attempt to save the man's life after a high-speed dash by car and ambulance from Aldinga Beach.

The injured man is Mr Rodney Fox, married, of Hammersmith Avenue, Edwardstown. He suffered severe chest injuries, a punctured lung, loss of blood, shock and badly gashed right hand. His condition last night was described as satisfactory.

The attack occurred at 12.45 p.m. in about fifteen feet of water about 200 yards north of the reef at Snapper Point, Aldina Beach. It was within a few hundred yards of the point where spear fisherman Mr Brian Rodgers of Woodville was badly mauled by a shark in March 1961. Mr Fox was wearing a full-length black rubber suit with yellow stripes down the sides of the jacket, and blue flippers. The attack came suddenly, a few minutes after Mr Fox had unloaded his catch of fish into a patrol boat. Spear fishermen said they had not seen any sharks in the area during the day.

"Rodney was swimming about twenty yards from my boat when it happened," skipper Mr J. B. Francis said afterwards. "Suddenly I saw him flipped over on his back. His goggles and snorkel came off, and blood started to colour the water. I didn't see the actual attack though."

Mr Francis said he raced his fourteen-foot fibreglass boat, which is powered by a forty-five-horse-power outboard motor, towards the scene. With him in the boat was Mr Brian Brawley from Henley.

"We had Rodney on board within a minute of the attack," Mr Francis said. "We picked up another competitor, Mr Bob Davis of Payneham, and raced for the reef. Brian and Bob assisted Rodney. They tried to hold him in a position so that he was leaning forward to keep the wounds closed. Rodney was bleeding badly from gaping wounds in his left side."

In the attack the shark drove its teeth through the left side of the thick rubber suit, ripping it from just above the armpit to the waist. The semi-circular imprint of the shark's teeth on the suit showed the size of its jaws. The shark is believed to have been a bronze whaler because spear fishermen said Mr Fox had gasped, "It was a bronzie."

The chairman of the South Australian Council of Underwater Activities, Mr J. Alexander, drove his car from the beach on to the reef to get as close to the boat as possible. "We didn't see anything from the beach. All we heard was someone shout, 'Shark attack.'" Mr Alexander then set out immediately for Adelaide. Four miles south of Noarlunga on the Yankalilla road he met the ambulance, which reached the hospital within an hour of receiving the call.

One of the team of surgeons who operated on Mr Fox said: "He's a very lucky lad, all things considered. His whole chest wall was badly shattered, the ribs crunched and part of the left lung punctured by the shark's teeth." The victim's right hand was considerably mauled – "It looked as though he'd tried to fend off the shark with his hand." At least two tendons had been seriously damaged and there was the further possibility of some damage to nerves. "But it looks as though he will not only keep his hand, but all of his fingers."

Mr Fox has been spear-fishing for about six years and is a member of the King Neptune Spearfishing Club. He won the South Australian championship last year and was placed third in yesterday's championship, which was halted after the attack. Three boats were patrolling the sea in the vicinity of the competition.

After the attack competitors were cleared from the area. Previous victim Mr Brian Rodgers said last night that the injuries to Mr Fox's right hand indicated he had indeed attempted to ward off the shark. He had experienced the same set of circumstances when he was attacked. Mr Rodgers said he was sitting on the reef at the time of yesterday's attack. He had got out of the water because he had had "a funny feeling": "I don't know whether it was a premonition or not, but there was quite a lot of blood in the water from speared fish."

The history of shark attacks in South Australian waters has followed a haphazard pattern. The first known fatal attack was in March 1926, when Mrs Primrose White died a few minutes after having been mauled at Brighton. Another person disappeared at West Beach in January 1936 after a shark had been seen to leap out of the water.

Adelaide Advertiser, 9 December 1963

1964

VICTORIA, AUSTRALIA, 1964

A twenty-nine-year-old skindiver lost his left leg in a shark attack while playing with a school of seals off Lady Julia Percy Island, near Port Fairy, 180 miles west of Melbourne. The diver, Henri Bource, of East Hawthorn, Melbourne, was in a serious condition in Warrnambool Hospital late last night.

The attack occurred when Bource and two other

Melbourne skindivers, Dietmar Kruppa, 24, of Fitzroy, and Fred Arndt, of St Kilda, were playing with the seals in thirty feet of water about fifty yards from their boat. The shark, an eight-foot tiger, charged at Bource, who was unarmed, from underneath the seals.

Kruppa and Arndt answered his screams for help. They fought off the shark with their spears as it circled Bource several times before swimming away.

Kruppa, a German-born motor mechanic, said, "We were diving down to tickle the seals. Suddenly there was a swirl in the water and clouds of blood. I heard Henri scream. Then I saw his leg floating in the water. It was the most horrifying sight of my life."

Kruppa said the three divers, wearing rubber suits, flippers, masks and snorkels, were about fifty yards from the boat when the shark attacked.

"We were having a lot of fun playing with the seals," he said. "Fred was with Henri and I was about ten yards away. Fred and I had short hand spears, but Henri was unarmed. The shark must have shot out from a pack of seals and caught Henri by surprise. He didn't stand a chance. Henri is more interested in underwater photography and quite often he does not carry a spear.

"Henri screamed: 'Save me, save me,' and we swam to him. Fred had seen the shark with a flipper in its mouth, but thought it was a seal. There was blood everywhere in the water and then I saw the shark circling Henri and coming in to attack again. He was a big brute – about eight feet.

"Henri was so brave. He kept calm as the shark circled again and again as Fred and I jabbed it away with our short spears. I don't think Henri was in great pain – he was too shocked – but he kept his head and yelled his blood group to the people in the boat." Kruppa said

Bource had been petting a dog on the beach and in the boat, and the shark may have been attracted by its scent.

Mr Wal Kelly, captain of the boat from which the men were diving, said he heard one of the men call out, "Help me, help me." When he reached the swimmers, Bource's girlfriend, Miss Jill Ratcliffe, of St Kilda, wearing skindiving gear, took a rope and jumped in. When Bource was aboard, Mr Kelly sent an urgent radio message appealing to anyone hearing it to get in touch with Port Fairy police. He requested that a doctor be at the wharf for a transfusion.

The boat returned to Port Fairy by about 4 p.m. Two doctors were waiting and immediately gave the transfusion.

The *Roma Kay* was being used by members of the Victorian Aqualung Club and a local club for diving with several underwater cameras.

Bource, a real estate agent and saxophonist leader of a Melbourne rock-and-roll band, is regarded as one of Victoria's best aqualung divers. Mr H. J. Bource said his son did not like spearfishing and had refused to enter the recent State aqualung championships. "He does not like killing fish. He would rather take underwater movies of them," he said.

Mr Bource added that Jill told him Henri had tried to free his leg by thrusting his arm down the shark's throat. He then gouged the shark's eyes to loosen its grip. "Jill was very brave. She had to be held back because she wanted to go straight back into the water and spear the shark."

Sydney Morning Herald, 30 November 1964

1966

NEW SOUTH WALES, AUSTRALIA, 1966

A shark which today mauled a thirteen-year-old boy at Coledale, forty miles south of Sydney, was dragged from the water with its teeth still clamped in the boy's leg. Lifesavers battered the eight-foot shark to death with surfboards as it lay on the beach. The boy is in serious condition in hospital.

The Times, London, 28 February 1966

NAPLES, ITALY, 1966

Bathers along the Gulf of Naples were warned today not to swim beyond 400 yards from the shore because of the danger of sharks. A Coast Guard cutter yesterday sighted a number of sharks in the gulf, a relatively rare event. Today fishermen and maritime police were patrolling the area.

The Times, London, 14 June 1966

DUKE OF YORK ISLANDS, NEW GUINEA, 1966

A school of sharks tore to pieces two young native girls swimming off a reef at the Duke of York Islands, fifteen miles north of Rabaul.

The upper half of one body was the only remains of the two girls which terrified village people recovered after the attack on Sunday.

One of the girls died when she jumped among the sharks in an attempt to rescue her school friend who had been attacked. A third girl tried to jump into the sea, but her father held her back.

The victims were school friends, Memilana Bokset, 13, and Loding Etwat, 9, from Butliwan Village. They were returning from Sunday school with other children and decided to go for a swim off the reef near their homes.

Loding was dragged under the surface by a school of sharks which swam down the edge of the reef. Memilana jumped in to help her, but the girls were torn to pieces in front of the children and adults standing on the reef.

Brisbane Courier Mail, 23 August 1966

QUEENSLAND, AUSTRALIA, 1966
A skin diver had his shoulder mauled by a seven-foot shark while he swam in forty feet of water about eleven miles from Heron Island. The attack took place off Broomfield Island at about 5 p.m. on Monday.

The diver is Barry Davidson, married, of New South Wales. He was taking underwater photographs when he saw the shark coming fast at him. He prodded it off with his speargun and saw it move towards a reef. The moment he turned, the shark was on him, but he frightened it off and surfaced.

He was taken by launch to Gladstone yesterday and will probably be flown to Sydney for a skin graft operation. Davidson said the shark had a fishing hook and part of a line caught in its mouth.

Brisbane Courier Mail, 28 September 1966

1967

GIBRALTAR, 1967
It is the lonely distinction of Mr Bernard Venables, a sixty-year-old fisherman and writer, to have had a tooth knocked out by a shark.

Off Gibraltar with two friends last month, he had a bite from a 143-lb shark and they managed, while he still held the rod, to get it into the boat. "It is very unwise", Mr Venables recalled ruefully, "to bring a shark of that size into a small boat – ours was only a twenty-four-footer." But they got it in.

"And then it suddenly became very active. The back end hit one of my friends on the leg, so that he had to go straight to hospital. The front end gave me a wallop on the head and knocked my pipe out of my mouth.

"At the time I was chiefly concerned that I was going to lose the pipe." (He recovered it.) "It was only when I got back and looked in the mirror that I realized I'd lost a tooth. Right in the middle, I'm afraid."

One of Mr Venables's many books is *The Gentle Art of Angling*.

The Times, London, 15 May 1967

MEDITERRANEAN, 1967

Dr P. H. Greenwood of the Natural History Museum, London, with whom this paper spoke yesterday about the report of sharks in the Bay of Naples, tells us that there are some 200 sorts of shark and that many of them live and breed in the Mediterranean. It is the comparatively cool temperature of the water which makes them mostly harmless. But attacks have been recorded at Valletta [see below], Fiume [see below], the Piraeus, Corfu and Genoa.

Little is known, as he says, about what makes a shark attack a man. It will single out a particular swimmer among a crowd and pursue him. Statistics show that sharks do not discriminate between sex or colour. It was thought at one time that sharks preferred Englishmen to Frenchmen because of some attractive odour emitted by the beefeating race which became apparent in the water, but modern records no longer support this theory!

The Times, London, 15 June 1967

WESTERN AUSTRALIA, AUSTRALIA, 1967

A shark bit a spearfisherman in half near Jurien Bay, one hundred miles north of Perth, at the weekend.

Robert Bartle, aged twenty-three, of Princess Road, Doubleview, Perth, died instantly. He had gone to Jurien Bay with seven other Perth skindivers for a spearing competition. Mr Bartle was swimming from the shore to a reef about 800 yards out to sea with another spearfisherman, Lee Warner, aged twenty-four, five times holder of the state spearfishing title, when he was attacked by the shark, believed to be a white pointer [great white].

Mr Warner said last night: "The shark came out of the blue like a rocket and grabbed him when we were about eight feet down. It moved so fast that by the time I looked back, it had Bob in its mouth and was shaking him like a leaf. I dived straight down. It was directly below me. I put a spear in the top of its head, but it had no effect. The shark broke Bob in half and rose up at me.

"I only had an empty five-foot gun and I tried to hit the shark in the eye. It began circling, keeping about eight feet away. Its body looked about five feet thick, and it was an enormous length.

"By now I was swimming in a cloud of blood. I realized I was helpless without a spear, so I got Bob's, which was only a few feet away below the surface. I tried to belt the spear into the shark's eye, but the spear went just over the top of his head. The shark continued circling and I could see its mouth was about two-and-a-half-feet wide. Its teeth stuck out past its nose.

"I was stuck in this big cloud of blood. I knew Bob was dead. A little bronze whaler shark came and began darting around. I swam backwards fast. The blood was obscuring my vision. After about ten yards I got out of the blood. From 150 yards I could look back and see the blood, and the shark moving around tangled in the lines and our fishing gear.

"I felt pretty helpless. I kept stopping and looking back, convincing myself the shark was back there. I was still frightened. When I got to the beach I ran for help. We later recovered what was left of Bob's body. The shark swam away into deep water."

The Australian, 21 August 1967

1969

WESTERN AUSTRALIA, AUSTRALIA, 1969

A fifteen-year-old Sea Scout who was attacked by a shark in seven feet of water in the Swan River yesterday said today he had used one foot to push the shark away after it had mauled his other leg.

"After I had been bitten I was scared that the shark might strike again," Graham Cartwright of Mettam Street, Trigg, said from his bed in the Royal Perth Hospital today. "He took two chomps and that was it. I felt his rough skin with my hands and one eye as I pushed him away with my good foot.

"I called out: 'Help, help – a shark's got me' during a 400-yard swim from the other side of the river. My best friend, Greg Hams, was nearly at the shore when he heard me call. He yelled out to John, who had just reached the river's edge."

John Brockmeulen, 14, of Mt Lawley, called out to some boys to get an ambulance and then swam out to Graham.

"He told me to turn over on to my back and towed me ashore. I was all right in the water, but could not bear to look at my leg once I was ashore," said Graham.

Graham was bleeding profusely from a four-inch deep tear in his left thigh as he was towed 100 yards to shore.

Pathologist Graeme Shute, a scoutmaster in the 1st Mt Lawley Sea Scouts, stemmed the flow of blood. The wound extended from the knee upwards and had opened the flesh on the inside of the boy's thigh. There were one-and-a-half-inch teeth marks in a nine-inch radius.

John Brockmeulen said he thought Graham had scared the shark away by sheer luck when he touched one of its sensitive eyes. "I was confident I would not be attacked by the shark because I had read that a second person was not usually attacked," he said.

Surgeons operated on Graham's mauled leg for five hours on Saturday night. They expect him to regain the full use of it. He should be in hospital for a week.

Graham, a Balcafta High School student and keen surfer, who was to have started his end-of-term examinations today, said he did not think he would swim in the river again. "But the ocean will be OK," he said.

The three boys were among a group of twenty Sea Scouts who had spent the afternoon sailing and scouting. The attack took place thirteen miles upstream.

Sydney Morning Herald, 1 December 1969

Bullhead Shark

Shark Facts

Length: Up to 5 feet 6 inches (1.68 m)

Weight: Up to 44 lb (20 kg)

Colouring: Varies from grey to yellow with dark spots

Diet: Mollusks, crustaceans, sea urchins

Young: Spiral formed eggs are laid in rock crevices,
            hatching up to a year later

Status: Not threatened

There are several different types of bullhead sharks, some with very prominent ridges above their eyes that rise up like horns on their heads. They vary in size from less than 2 feet (61 cm) to well over 5 feet (1.5 m) but even the largest specimens present no threat to humans. Their mouths tend to be beneath their heads, designed for scouring the seabed in search of shellfish which they crush with an extremely powerful bite for a fish of this size.

Bullhead Shark Range

SHARK ATTACKS

1970–79

1970

WESTERN PACIFIC, 1970
Fourteen passengers were devoured by sharks when a motor launch capsized 200 miles south-east of Manila in the Philippines, police reported. Only a honeymoon couple survived out of the twenty-two on board. Six were drowned.

The Times, London, 24 September 1970

1971

US VIRGIN ISLANDS, 1971
It happened twenty-five years ago, but the image of sharks savagely attacking his diving partner and dragging him to the hazy depths of the Caribbean is as vivid in Bret Gilliam's mind today, in 1996, as it was in the days after the attack in 1971.

Gilliam wishes he could forget. Telling the story in its entirety for the first time, in a chilling article written for *Scuba Times* magazine, he describes that fateful day in the US Virgin Islands.

Gilliam, now [in 1996] editor of the *Advanced Diving Journal* and president of Technical Diving International, was with Rod Temple and Robbie McIlvaine on a scientific expedition to recover samples for a research project being conducted at Cane Bay on the island of St Croix's north shore.

The plan was to inspect and to photograph the deepest project, at 210 feet, located on the wall of a steep drop-off. Temple was the dive leader and timekeeper, in charge of the paperwork and running the decompression schedule during the ascent.

But for him there would be no ascent.

"I watched his lifeless body drift into the abyss with the sharks still hitting him," Gilliam writes. And many believe that the hurried ascent made by Gilliam – from 400 feet with practically no air in his tanks – should have killed him.

Veterans of hundreds of deep dives, Gilliam, Temple and McIlvaine made their way down the wall at Cane Bay. They eventually reached the collection project – set during a previous dive – at 210 feet. As Gilliam and McIlvaine worked, Temple looked around. He spotted two white-tip sharks, one about twelve feet long and the other a bit bigger, swimming in the distance.

"This was nothing new to us, as we dove with sharks routinely," Gilliam says. "But it was rare to see these open-ocean species so close to shore."

After finishing their work, McIlvaine started up first. He spotted the sharks again, swimming over the coral and down a sandy chute. But the sharks didn't seem to be paying attention to the divers, which in itself Gilliam thought odd because he had had "nasty encounters" with white-tips before while diving farther offshore.

"Our plan called for Rod to be the last guy up," Gilliam writes. "I rendezvoused with Robbie at about 175 feet just over a ledge, and we both rested on the coral to wait for him to join us. He was late, and Robbie fidgeted, pointing to his pressure gauge, not wanting to run low on air.

"I shrugged and gave him a 'What am I supposed to do?' look, and we continued to wait. Suddenly Robbie dropped his extra gear and catapulted himself toward the wall, pointing at a mass of bubble exhaust coming from the deeper water.

"We both figured that Rod had had some sort of air failure ... Since my air consumption was lower, I decided to send Robbie up, and I would go see if Rod needed help. As I descended into the bubble cloud, Robbie gave me an anxious OK sign and started up.

"But when I reached Rod, things were about as bad as they could get."

A twelve-foot white-tip shark had bitten into Temple's left thigh and was tearing violently at his flesh. Clouds of blood mixed in with the bubbles. The second shark appeared and made a blinding strike, ripping into Temple's calf.

Gilliam grabbed Temple by his shoulder harness and tried to pull him free. Both divers beat at the sharks with their fists, and the sharks finally let go, but only briefly.

They returned, bypassing Gilliam and striking Temple's bleeding legs. Temple had lost lots of blood and Gilliam felt Temple's body go limp in his arms. But he held on, and the divers and the sharks tumbled downward until the sharks finally ripped Temple from Gilliam's grasp, leaving Gilliam 400 feet beneath the surface, in shock and practically out of air.

"My depth gauge was pegged at 325 feet, but I knew

we were far deeper than that," he recalls. "The grimness of my own situation forced itself on me through a fog of narcosis and exertion.

"That's when I ran out of air. I think that subconsciously I almost decided to stay there and die. It seemed so totally hopeless, and my strength was completely sapped. But I put my head back and put all my muscles into a wide, steady power kick for the surface.

"I forced all thoughts to maintaining that kick cycle and willed myself upward. After what seemed like an eternity, I sneaked a look at my depth gauge and it was still pegged at 325 feet. I sucked hard on the regulator and got a bit of a breath – not much, but it fueled my oxygen-starved brain a bit longer, and I prayed my legs would get me up shallow enough to get another breath before hypoxia (an abnormal condition caused by a decrease in oxygen to body tissue) shut down my systems for ever.

"There's really no way to describe what it's like to slowly starve the brain of oxygen in combination with adrenaline-induced survival instincts. But I remember thinking, if I could just concentrate on kicking, I could make it. After a while the sense of urgency faded, and I remember looking for the surface through a red haze that gradually closed down into a tunnel before I passed out. The panic was gone and I went to sleep, thinking, 'Damn, I almost made it.'"

Remarkably, Gilliam did make it. The small amount of air in his safety vest floated him to the surface.

"I woke up retching and expelling huge burps of air," he recalls. "But I still had to deal with an unknown amount of omitted decompression and the certainty that I was severely bent. Swimming to shore as fast as I could, I felt my legs going numb. By the time I reached the beach I could barely stand. A couple on their honeymoon waded out and dragged me up on the sand."

(McIlvaine, presuming both of his partners were dead, had already reached the beach and had gone to notify the authorities.)

"I gasped out instructions to get the oxygen unit from our van, and then I collapsed. In an incredible burst of good fortune, it turned out the wife was an [emergency room] nurse from Florida and understood the pathology of decompression sickness."

Gilliam, airlifted to a hospital in Puerto Rico, recovered and was released two days later, still numb in the legs and arms, and nearly blind in one eye. That blindness persists to this day, but in his mind he can still see – all too vividly – the sharks ripping his partner.

Los Angeles Times, 20 November 1996

1973

CAROLINE ISLANDS, PACIFIC, 1973

"It is probably the most basic human fear: getting attacked by a wild animal. When a grey reef shark tore open my left hand, I remember feeling as if I had been hit by a sledgehammer. Such was the shock that I do not recall the actual bite."

The incident took place in 1973 in a remote Micronesian lagoon in the Caroline Islands. Underwater photographer and diver Bill Curtsinger was swimming alone, ascending in a slow spiral after a dive, when he noticed the shark.

"It was twenty feet away and closing. I saw it sweeping its head back and forth; its back was arched like a cat's. The shark was 'speaking' to me, but at the time I didn't know the 'words'. The shark came at me like a rocket. I had time only to lift my hand, the shark ripping it with its teeth. As I swam frantically toward the boat, I saw that each dip of my hand left a cloud of blood in the water.

"The shark struck again, raking my right shoulder. At that moment a friend in a dinghy rescued me.

"The next day I posed with my bandaged wounds. Later I had minor surgery on my hand and shoulder. I was lucky, yes, but this defensive animal, I realized later, was not trying to eat me. It was, in fact, driving me away, quite possibly seeing me as a potential predator.

"Since then I have learned defensive behaviour myself. When photographing in Bikini Atoll, I sometimes donned a stainless steel mesh suit and slipped into a plastic 'shark scooter'."

National Geographic, January 1995

1974

AMANZIMTOTI, SOUTH AFRICA, 1974

Within seconds of being attacked by a shark in the bathing enclosure of Amanzimtoti yesterday afternoon, a professional lifesaver, Mr Les Pyper, 33, shouted to two of his colleagues who were swimming close by to clear the bathing area.

The attack took place soon after lunch and scores of bathers saw Mr Pyper being lifted out of the water as the shark grabbed his leg less than 100 metres from the shore.

Two teenagers, Clive de Witt, 16, and Richard Cuff, 17, who were surfing near by, heard his screams and went to his aid, pulling him to safety on a surfboard. Mr Pyper received severe lacerations to his right leg and was taken to Addington Hospital with a police escort for emergency treatment.

After hearing Mr Pyper shout at them to clear the bathing area, one lifesaver, Mr Brian Fouche, ordered the bathers out of the water, while lifesaver Mr Derek Fourie ran to their hut and sounded the siren.

A doctor holidaying in the area gave emergency treatment on the beach, while scores of shocked holidaymakers and bathers crowded in, hampering operations. The injured lifesaver was then taken to the hut, where Mr A. Cloete, a first aid gold medallist from Welkom, stemmed the flow of blood before tourniquets were applied.

Mr Pyper described later how he fought off the attack by a large lazy grey shark, punching it on the snout while it lifted him out of the water by his right leg. In a hurried interview as he was being pushed to the operating theatre for stitches, he told of the horror when the shark fastened its jaws around his knee.

"I was just swimming along when suddenly I felt the pain. I realized it was a shark and started screaming. I was pretty scared, but managed not to panic. He was very big – I reckon between 400 lbs and 500 lbs. When he lifted me out of the water – that'll give you an idea how big he was – I punched him on the snout. It must have been my lucky day because he let go and swam away, and I screamed to a nearby surfer for help."

Richard Cuff said he was only a few metres from Mr Pyper when he heard him shout and saw him being lifted out of the water. "He shouted that a shark had attacked him and I saw him struggling in the water."

Clive de Witt said: "I saw a black object beneath the surface and I realized he was not joking. We paddled towards him and helped him on to my board. Blood was streaming from his leg. He had bite marks above and below the knee, and I could see right through to the bone."

Richard Cuff said that, although Mr Pyper had been bitten, he appeared to be calm, and insisted that the bathers be cleared in a hurry. "He was more worried about the bathers than himself."

An Addington Hospital spokesman last night described Mr Pyper's condition as "fair".

Cape Times, 8 January 1974

AMANZIMTOTI, SOUTH AFRICA, 1974
A shark savaged two voluntary lifesavers who were swimming in the safe-bathing area at Amanzimtoti last night. This is the second attack at the beach this year. The lifesavers are Joe Kool, 19, and Damon Kendrick, 14, both members of the Amanzimtoti Surf Lifesaving Club.

Damon Kendrick's leg was last night amputated below the knee at Addington Hospital. His condition has been described as "satisfactory". Joe Kool was bitten in the right knee.

"We were all swimming after training on the beach," he said later at the hospital. "I was the farthest out and I felt something hit me in the side. I didn't know what it was. I then felt it grab me in the leg and I hit at whatever I could. It was too dark to see and it let me go.

"I shouted to the others to get back – swim, swim like mad – get back to the shore. I caught a wave to the beach and was running up the beach when I heard Damon shout. I turned round and saw him flung in the air and the blood in the water. I ran back and grabbed him out of the water."

Cape Times, 14 February 1974

CARIBBEAN SEA, GULF OF MEXICO, 1974

A mother whose life was devastated when sharks killed two of her children during a "perfect family holiday" in the Gulf of Mexico is still struggling twenty years later to come to terms with the tragedy.

She has not been able to stand on a beach since and her hatred of sharks has remained undiminished. Mrs Horne, an American who says she relives the appalling experience every day of her life, is, with the help of wildlife experts from the American National Wildlife Foundation, trying to overcome her hatred of sharks.

On 2 July 1974, Diane and her husband Ed set off in a forty-three-foot motor boat for a 300-mile trip with their five children – Diana, 14, Gerald, 12, Billy, 10, Melissa, 4, and three-year-old Tex. The weather bureau had predicted a dry night with calm seas. Yet, within two hours of leaving Florida Harbour in Panama, a sudden storm smashed their boat to pieces and they were forced to leap into rough seas in pitch darkness. They managed to rope themselves together and floated about for several hours.

Diane recalled: "We felt very alone, just out there in the water and the night seemed to go on for ever."

The family, cold and exhausted, drifting in and out of sleep, were overjoyed in the early morning by the sound of a spotter plane. In their excitement they untied the rope to spread out in the water and began shouting. It was probably their biggest mistake, because the noise and disturbance alerted the sharks.

"We saw a dorsal fin, but thought it was a dolphin. All of a sudden we saw a rescue boat and were hit by the sharks at the same time," recalled Diane.

The family and screaming children thrashed the water with their legs and arms in a frantic attempt to keep the sharks at bay.

One by one the twelve-foot animals went on the attack. Their first target was Billy. Spiked teeth closed on him and the sea coloured with blood as part of his arm was torn off. Diane was pushed out of the water and the shark grazed her skin. The pilot in the aircraft reported seeing masses of sharks circling the family.

The arrival of a Coast Guard vessel saved the rest of the family from certain death. Her ten-year-old son Billy was badly savaged. Diane held him in her right arm, trying to staunch the gaping wound in his right arm, but he bled to death. Three-year-old Tex later died from exposure.

In a moving postscript Mrs Horne said: "There is not a night that I have laid my head on the pillow that I haven't thought of this, but it wasn't until I got involved with the National Wildlife Foundation, which made me understand nature more, that I've been able to accept it. They weren't really out to kill someone. They were doing their thing and I was doing my thing, and the two worlds collided."

London Evening Standard, 6 September 1995

AMANZIMTOTI, SOUTH AFRICA, 1974
Anthony Baker, aged seventeen, the Amanzimtoti schoolboy attacked by a shark while surfing off Inyoni Rocks late yesterday, defied a bathing ban because, he said today, "I thought I'd be safe on a surfboard." And he revealed that officials of the Anti-Shark Measures Board had instructed him not to speak to the press "because it might scare holidaymakers away".

Anthony was attacked by a shark in the unprotected surfing area on the south side of Inyoni Rocks at 4.30 p.m., about half an hour after a "voluntary ban" was imposed on all bathing in Amanzimtoti by beach officials. It was the fourth attack off Amanzimtoti in three months.

On 21 March another surfer, Mr Jimmy Gurr, aged twenty-one, was attacked while sitting on his board in the water off the south side of Inyoni Rocks. Although his board was damaged, Mr Gurr was not injured.

Fourteen-year-old Damon Kendrick, a voluntary life-saver, and his companion Joe Kool were injured in an attack on 14 February, while swimming at Amanzimtoti. Damon's right leg had to be amputated below the knee.

On 7 January Mr Les Pyper, a professional lifesaver, was swimming in murky water when a shark grabbed his leg, injuring him seriously, exactly thirty-four years after the first of a spate of shark attacks off the Natal coast which led to the installation of protective nets.

There have been eleven attacks in the Amanzimtoti area, which includes Warner Beach and Inyoni Rocks.

Anthony, a matric pupil at Kingsway Senior High School in Amanzimtoti, said today he had defied the bathing ban because he felt his surfboard offered some protection. "I knew that, as long as I was on a surfboard, the shark couldn't take my side out or anything like that."

Anthony was attacked while he was pulling himself back on to the board after slipping off. "I felt a tug on my foot and I knew immediately that it was a shark. I shouted to my brother, Raymond, who was also surfing and went straight to shore on my board."

Anthony said his foot was bleeding "a little bit". He was taken to a local doctor by holidaymakers, and received fourteen stitches on the ankle and heel.

The attack yesterday has left him "more scared than ever", he said. "I'll always be scared of sharks now, and I was pretty scared of them before."

Durban Daily News, 5 April 1974

HONG KONG, 1974

Doctors were last night battling to save the life of an eighteen-year-old boy, a freedom swimmer whose left foot was almost completely torn off by killer sharks.

In a nearby bed at Queen Elizabeth Hospital, his nineteen-year-old friend was being treated for a broken arm and severe lacerations to the body – caused in the same attack. It is believed that a third swimmer in a party of eight, who made their freedom dash from Siu Mui Sha, was killed.

The attack came as the swimmers had almost completed their five-mile crossing to Kai Kung Tau, in Mirs Bay. About 100 yards from the shore at Kai Kung Tau, and with freedom and safety in sight, a pack of sharks slashed into the small group.

The five uninjured swimmers managed to drag the two youths to the shore, where for seven hours they fought to stem the bleeding. Luckily, a police launch arrived. A call went out to Marine Police headquarters, who immediately asked for an RAF helicopter to airlift the injured to hospital. One, with a doctor on board, was sent to Taipo, where it picked up the youths. Ten minutes later they were at the hospital.

The doctor, Flight Lieutenant Chris Ross, said that in most cases all they have to do was give first aid. "But in this case I had to fight for his life."

The two Chinese Yee Wing-ping and Ho Sin-ming are believed to be farm workers from the Fa-Yeun Commune near Canton. A Government spokesman said last night that Yee was in a "poor condition"; Ho's condition was "fair". The five uninjured refugees are being held at Marine Police headquarters.

South China Morning Post, 17 August 1974

1975

NATAL, SOUTH AFRICA, 1975

A shark yesterday savaged a sixteen-year-old surfer, Bretton Jones, at Amanzimtoti, completely severing his right foot.

Bretton and two friends, Steven van der Welde, 15, and Justin Philip, 17, were surfing in an area unprotected by shark nets at the time of the attack. Bretton is the sixth person to be attacked at Amanzimtoti [see chapter 1] since January 1974.

"I never saw the shark, I just felt something grab me on the leg and try to pull me off my board. When I resisted, it shook me like a dog," Bretton told helpers on the beach.

He underwent an emergency operation at Addington Hospital yesterday afternoon. Doctors removed about another eight centimetres of his leg to clean the wound. He was in a satisfactory condition last night. "We can only thank God that he was not injured more seriously. It was an accident and could have been much worse," Bretton's mother, Mrs D. I. Jones, said yesterday, shortly after returning from Addington Hospital. Bretton is a standard nine pupil at Kingsway High School. He is one of a family of four children.

"We were about fifty metres from the shore. Bretton and I were both sitting on our surfboards when he suddenly screamed, 'Shark, shark,' and started paddling back to the beach," said Steven van der Welde. "I looked up and saw a fin and knew that it had attacked Bretton by the amount of blood."

Yesterday's attack on Bretton carried the grim coincidence that it marked – almost to the day – the first anniversary of the attack that cost his schoolmate, Damon Kendrick, a leg last year.

Cape Times, 24 February 1975

INDIAN OCEAN, 1975

Mr Valery Kosyak, a mechanic in the Soviet Union's Black Sea merchant fleet, has survived a four-hour ordeal among sharks. Mr Kosyak, who is twenty-five and married with two children, was swept overboard from a cargo ship during a storm in the Indian Ocean 600 miles south of Sri Lanka, and found himself surrounded by a shoal of man-eaters.

"At first, when I felt something brushing at my legs, I thought it was driftwood," he said. "But then I was hit hard and turned over in the water. When I opened my eyes, I saw this pig-like snout sticking out of the sea in front of me. Then it dipped and disappeared."

The sharks, which surrounded him, were between nine and fifteen feet long. "They were diving in and out of the waves, and I tried to float flat on the water so they wouldn't go for my feet," Mr Kosyak said. "They kept circling about fifteen feet away from me. When I realized they weren't going to attack immediately, I began to think a bit more clearly.

"They moved with me. I didn't hurry because it was obvious I could never shake them off. I knew I just had to keep up my strength until the ship came back, as I knew it would."

As he swam, he found himself talking to the sharks. "I was swearing and then cooing at them. I was steering myself by the sun, although it was pretty difficult to keep on course because I was swimming into the waves. Still, it helped me forget the sharks."

Two hours went by before his shipmates noticed that he was missing. The ship immediately turned back and found him after another two hours.

When M. Jacques-Yves Cousteau, the French underwater explorer, was asked to comment on Mr Kosyak's ordeal, he said: "I have heard of people surviving an hour or two among sharks, but four hours – never."

The Times, London, 26 July 1975

1976

UNITED KINGDOM, 1976

Popular belief has it that British sharks are harmless. Tell that to the Scottish fisherman who was terribly mauled by a shark while he was fishing close inshore from his home port. Or the Devon skindiver who fought off a big Porbeagle shark that came into shallow water off Bee Sands in Devon. Or the parents of the two children who were playing in the shallows of a well-known south coast beach when they were knocked flying by an unprovoked attack from a pair of thresher sharks.

Fortunately for the bathing and boating public, the seas around our coasts have been rich enough in fish life to satisfy any shark. Times, however, are changing. The once prolific mackerel shoals that normally supply our sharks with the bulk of their food are being decimated so rapidly by commercial overfishing that the shark population is now being forced to look elsewhere for a readily available food supply.

The Times, London, 3 July 1976

Spiny Dogfish

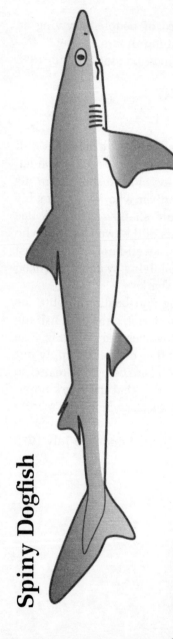

Shark Facts

Length: 3 feet 3 inches to 4 feet (99 cm to 1.21 m)

Weight: 10 lb to 21 lb (4.5 kg to 9.5 kg)

Colouring: Grey or grey/brown upper with pale grey belly

Diet: Bony fish, herring, mackerel, squid, smaller sharks and crabs

Pups: Six or seven live young are born at up to 1 foot 3 inches (33 cm)

Status: Listed as vulnerable and protected by fishing quotas

Once the most numerous shark species in the world, the spiny dogfish is under threat from overfishing due to its popularity on the dinner table as "rock salmon", "sea eel" or huss. It has also been widely used in fertiliser and pet food. It is, however, slow to reproduce with females maturing at around 21 years old and living to the age of 30. It uses the spines on its dorsal fins as a defence aid, arching its back when captured to try to stab its foe. The young spiny dogfish has white spots on its back which fade as it grows older.

Spiny Dogfish Range

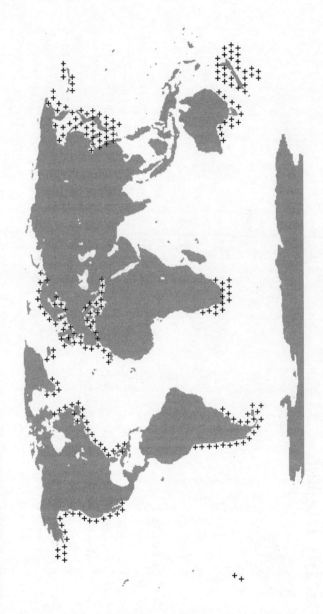

SHARK ATTACKS
1980–1989

1980

Many of the bodies recovered from the Gulf Stream twenty miles from Freeport, Grand Bahama, where a DC-3 crashed killing all thirty-four aboard, were mutilated in shark-infested waters, authorities said. The Coast Guard found sixteen bodies on Friday and Saturday, and suspended the search for more victims on Sunday. A Coast Guard spokesman said there was no chance any of the other eighteen people aboard survived.

Autopsies by assistant Broward County Medical Examiner Sashi Gore showed some of the victims had been mangled by sharks. Many apparently drowned and others died of multiple injuries. The plane was equipped with life preservers, but none of the passengers were wearing them.

A fisherman who reportedly witnessed the crash at 9 p.m. on Friday, told Federal Aviation Administration officials the plane was on fire and "flaming like a meteorite" when it crashed into fifty feet of water.

Two Coast Guard cutters and two helicopters conducted a ten-hour search in the Bahamian seas. The captain of the cutter *Current*, Lt Susan Moritz, 26, said the seas were four to six feet high and the wind was blowing out of the south-east at sixteen miles per hour.

The Florida Commuter Airlines plane crashed while making its final approach to Freeport in a violent thunderstorm. It was carrying passengers to Freeport casinos for a gambling excursion ...

New Orleans Times-Picayune, 15 September 1980

FLORIDA, USA, 1980

As darkness neared, sharks began circling the two scuba divers separated from their boat and one of them told himself, "This is the beginning of the end."

"It has already started," Greg EuDaly, 33, thought when he felt the first shark nudge him. But EuDaly and his companion, Chuck Castonguay, 38, were rescued when a third diver, Richard Schau, who stayed in the boat, radioed the Coast Guard and a Navy helicopter lifted them from the water on Sunday night as they fought the sharks off with their divers' knives.

"We were spearfishing in about ninety feet of water twenty-three miles off Jacksonville," EuDaly said in an interview on Thursday. "At that depth you always leave a man in the boat. Richard was in the boat and there was a current. It was pushing the boat one way and myself and Castonguay on the bottom of the ocean the other way."

When the two divers came to the surface, Schau was a mile away in the boat and could not see his companions. Trouble, thought EuDaly, we're in big trouble. "In the first few moments, I went into panic," he added. "I'd never been in this situation before." But EuDaly, a former Navy man, began to remember some of the things taught him in air-sea rescue.

He and Castonguay lashed themselves as best they could to their scuba flotation devices and empty air tanks. "The seas were getting rough and nasty," he said. "Eight-foot waves. We began rigging ourselves for a stay."

In the meantime Schau kept his position, radioed the Coast Guard and explained the situation. Within an hour a Navy helicopter had been dispatched from the Jacksonville Naval Air Station. The sharks, though, came before sundown. EuDaly said they liked him best.

"I was only wearing the top of a wet suit. Chuck was wearing a full wet suit. I had been in air-sea rescue in West Florida. I told Chuck about the night two guys over there were in the same trouble and they found them. I didn't tell him only one of them survived!"

EuDaly began striking at the sharks with his diving knife as they came close, adding, "I thought then our chances were nil, but I wasn't giving up."

Schau said he could hear the helicopter when it arrived, but the helicopter crew apparently could not see him. He found a flare and lit it. The helicopter then began searching the area for the divers. Castonguay had a small diving light and he waved it furiously. When the chopper moved toward them, EuDaly said, "It was the best sight I ever saw in my life."

Castonguay went up in the horse-collar hoist first. EuDaly thought he was home free, but, "Dog gone, if I didn't feel something at my legs. I looked down. It was a shark again. There is this halo above me with all the noise and the lights, and the rotors' spray – and the shark is at me." He stabbed at the shark's head and finally was hoisted out of reach.

New Orleans Times-Picayune, 3 October 1980

1981

ISLE OF WIGHT, UNITED KINGDOM, 1981

A 400-lb shark was killed yesterday as it leapt at a small fishing boat off the south coast. Two fishermen were injured and the boat was damaged when the shark landed across the deck.

The incident happened off the Isle of Wight. Mr Ross Staplehurst, a local fisherman, had taken a party of anglers for a day's fishing in his twenty-three-foot boat, the Albatross. They were fishing for tope and skate when the thresher shark, thirteen feet long, was sighted about fifty yards away.

Mr Staplehurst said: "It turned towards the boat and dived. Everything was quiet for a moment and we thought it had swum away. Then there was a great rushing noise and suddenly the shark came surging out of the water about five yards away.

"It landed across the boat, which is only nine feet wide, so its head and tail were sticking over each side. The impact nearly sank the boat and it killed the shark outright."

One of the fishermen was hit by the shark's tail and his nose was cut. Another had a bruised leg. The Albatross sailed back to Bembridge, Isle of Wight, where the shark is to be sold to fishmongers.

"I have fished these waters for ten years," said Mr Staplehurst, "but have never seen a shark act like that. It just went berserk. I'm convinced it was attacking the boat."

The Times, London, 15 June 1981

FLORIDA, USA, 1981

A wounded, six-foot-long mako shark "out for revenge" attacked the nineteen-year-old snorkeller who shot him on Monday, but the youth escaped with a relatively mild bite on the leg. Ted Best, a student at an auto mechanics school, was flown by helicopter to the Pensacola hospital, treated for "about a hundred" puncture wounds in his right leg and given a pair of crutches before he was released.

Best said he was snorkelling in twelve feet of water off the Gulf Island National Seashore Park when two sharks approached him while he was looking for shells about fifty yards off shore.

"They went off and I kept an eye on them," Best recalled. He said he surfaced for air and submerged again, and, "The next thing I knew – I guess it was a mako – he was right up on me. I hadn't provoked him. I hadn't shot a fish to make blood or anything. They've always minded their own business, but these two looked like they were out for revenge or something. They went by and then, before I knew it, he was right on me. I always carry a speargun and I shot him. I pulled the spear out of him, but, before I could get it back in the gun, he hit me. I was pretty scared because I knew what they can do to you. When he bit my leg, I didn't know how bad it was. I just remember looking at his eyes. He looked me in the eyes. I'll never forget that."

Best said the shark released his leg and moved away. He struck out for shore. One of the sharks followed him for a while and he saw "a black form" behind him in about seven feet of water, but then it disappeared. He scrambled ashore, breaking his face mask on a piling in the process, reached his car and drove himself to the ranger's station about half a mile from the beach. He was then flown in a helicopter to the Pensacola hospital.

New Orleans Times-Picayune, 25 August 1981

FLORIDA, USA, 1981

A man who bet a beer that he could swim three miles to a Gulf Coast island is the second person to die after a shark attack in Florida waters this year, officials say.

Manatee County authorities said Mark Meeker, 26, a Tampa bartender, drowned after a shark took an eight-inch piece out of his right leg.

Six weeks ago, a secretary died off the Atlantic Coast after being attacked by a shark.

Meeker disappeared on Tuesday afternoon after diving off Anna Maria City Pier, three miles across choppy waters and strong tidal currents in the mouth of Tampa Bay. His body was found on Wednesday morning, the drawstring of his bathing suit wrapped tightly around his right thigh as a makeshift tourniquet. Authorities said he drowned after either going into shock or becoming exhausted. Dr Stephen Pelham, Manatee's medical examiner, said that Meeker's wound was the result of a shark attack.

"The marks are consistent with a shark bite," he said. Since sharks have several rows of teeth, a wound left by a shark will generally show other cuts above and below the bite. Meeker's leg had such cuts, he said.

Manatee sheriff's deputy Mark Rominger said Meeker, Meeker's girl friend Angie Tucker and several other friends were on the pier on the south side of Tampa Bay when the bet was made. Rominger said the friends told him they became worried when they lost sight of Meeker after he was just a few hundred yards out. After trying to get a boat to go after him themselves, they alerted the Coast Guard.

On 10 August Christy Wapniarski died after being attacked by a shark while struggling to reach shore a few miles off Daytona Beach.

New Orleans Times-Picayune, 20 September 1981

FLORIDA, USA, 1981

"All I could see was teeth. I was so scared, I just started slapping him," Van Horn Ely, Florida's fifteenth reported shark attack victim of the year, recalled.

Ely, 19, underwent five hours of surgery on his left hand and arm, badly mauled in a shark attack which occurred only about thirty feet from shore in waist-deep water. The attack occurred on Monday, just three days after Robert Kiefling, 17, of Cocoa, was bitten on the left foot while surfing in the water off Cocoa Beach. Two earlier shark victims – Mark Meeker, 26, attacked in Tampa Bay, and Christy Wapniarski, 19, attacked off Ormond Beach – bled to death.

"I've swum from Maine to the Caribbean and a lot of places in between and never even known anyone who was bothered by sharks," said Ely, who moved to Jupiter Island four days ago from Cape May, New Jersey, to take a job as maintenance man at the Jupiter Island Beach Club.

Ely was attacked when he went for a swim in the Atlantic during his lunch break. He estimated the shark that seized his hand and forearm was six to eight feet in length. "It all happened in just a second or so," Ely said. "He bit down pretty hard. He pulled me, took me forward. I tried to slide my hand out of his mouth. His mouth was out of the water. All I could see was teeth. I was so scared, I just started slapping at him."

Somehow Ely managed to tug his hand free and turn and run through the water toward the shore. "I was most worried that he was going to come back and bite my leg. I didn't have much trouble running back to shore," he said.

As he ran to shore, he shouted to a youth on the beach in a golf cart, who stopped, picked him up and drove him to the Jupiter Island police station. Officers swathed his lacerated hand and arm in a towel and called an ambulance to take him to a hospital, where surgeons completed repair of his hand and arm after 5 a.m. on Tuesday.

The unusually high number of attacks this year has been blamed by some shark experts on the abnormal warmth of Atlantic waters. As a result, they say, schools of smelt fish, such as mullet, have been feeding close to shore and sharks, which prey on the schools, have been attracted closer than usual to Florida's beaches.

The experts say sharks have notoriously bad eyesight and most attacks on humans are cases of mistaken identity. They mistake a hand or foot for a fish, particularly if the swimmer is close to a school of bait fish.

New Orleans Times-Picayune, 21 October 1981

CALIFORNIA, USA, 1981
The shark-torn body of missing surfer Lewis Boren was pulled out of the surf near Pacific Grove on Thursday, ending the torment of uncertainty for his family in Torrance.

Monterey County Coroner Harvey Hillbun said the experienced twenty-four-year-old kneeboard surfer, a graduate of Torrance High School, was the victim of "a classic example of a shark bite".

Boren had been missing since last Saturday, and his surfboard found on Sunday, bearing teeth fragments and blood stains around an eighteen-inch gash. Hillbun said Boren was probably lying on the board waiting for a good wave just outside the breakers when the shark, believed to be a great white shark more than eighteen feet long and weighing at least two tons, moved in, "his mouth open, lunging toward his prey".

"When the shark bit, he had both the board and Lewis in his mouth," Hillbun said. "There's a large portion of his upper torso gone, from beneath the left armpit to just above the hip."

The body, clad in a dark wetsuit, was recovered from the surf by a park ranger. It was tentatively identified by a tattoo on the shoulder. Searchers had been scouring beaches and the coastal waters for a sign of Boren since discovering his chewed-up kneeboard, which is smaller than a regular surfboard and is ridden in the kneeling position.

Before the body was located, analysis had begun on blood samples found on the board, and officials of the Steinhart Aquarium in San Francisco started comparing the tooth marks with their extensive collection of shark jaws in hopes of discovering Boren's fate.

The victim's mother, Ella Boren, said Lewis began surfing in junior high school and was an accomplished surfer and water skier. He also enjoyed snow skiing, she said.

"Lewis was supposed to come down yesterday – we talked to him last Friday," Mrs Boren said as the family began gathering for a sad Christmas. "We had his presents all wrapped."

Before Monterey authorities called with news of the body, Mrs Boren said the family still held out hope. "It would be a miracle if he shows up, we know that. But not knowing, you can't help but hope."

Boren lived in a camper truck outside the Monterey engineering firm where he worked as a welder. He once attended El Camino Community College in Carson.

Experts have calculated that the shark was the largest known to prowl off the California coast and may have reached twenty-one feet. The largest great white ever captured measured twenty-one feet and was nabbed off Cuba. Sharks up to forty feet have been reported, but never captured. Surfers have been wary of the Monterey Bay waters since Boren vanished and a marine scientist said on Thursday that a rash of reported shark sightings was actually a school of about eighty large grey and white dolphins which entered the bay.

Los Angeles Times, 25 December 1981

1982

FLORIDA, USA, 1982

A ninety-foot government ocean-charting vessel was attacked by a sixteen-foot shark off the Florida coast last month and briefly disabled, the National Oceanic Survey said.

The Heck, headed for Key West with its sister ship Rude to search for and chart navigation hazards, sustained damaged oil seals and a burned out steering motor when the shark attacked the port propeller and rudder off Jacksonville, an agency spokesman said. The shark was killed instantly.

The ship's captain, Lt Cmdr Russell Arnold, reported that divers made temporary repairs and the vessel was able to make its way to Jacksonville, where a new steering motor was installed. "It's the first time to my knowledge that this has ever happened to one of the twenty-five charting vessels operated by the National Oceanic and Atmospheric Administration, a unit of the Commerce Department."

The ships, which docked on Thursday in Key West, search for navigation hazards by dragging a submerged wire between them. The findings are then noted on navigational charts issued by NOAA's ocean survey unit.

New Orleans Times-Picayune, 20 March 1982

CAPE PROVINCE, SOUTH AFRICA, 1982

Five surfers watched in horror as a Port Elizabeth student was dragged from his surfboard and under the water by a shark on the Transkei Wild Coast early yesterday morning.

Mr Alex Macun, 27, chairman of the Port Elizabeth Technikon Students Representative Council and well-known freelance surfing photo-journalist, was attacked and killed just after 9.30 a.m. at a secluded surfing spot, Ntlonyena, about thirty kilometres north of the Haven holiday resort.

Yesterday's attack is the second at Ntlonyena – notorious for its sharks – in just over a year. A Durban journalist, Mr Simon Hammerton, 24, lost a leg in an attack in May last year.

Mr Macun was a senior student at the Technikon's School of Art. His family lives in Cape Town and he is a SACS old boy.

A shocked witness to the attack, Mr John Luyt, of Port Elizabeth, telephoned his father, Mr Peter Luyt of Walmer, thirty minutes after the attack. "He was in a severe state of shock and told me he was surfing near by when a huge shark grabbed Alex ... and the shark just disappeared under the water with Alex in his jaws. It appeared as if there was nothing they could do. John was in such a state of shock that he called me first before informing the police," Mr Luyt said.

A Transkei police spokesman said: "From what we understand, the man did not appear again. His friends scattered and paddled for the safety of the beach. The surfers then raced to a trading store at Hobeni, where they informed the authorities and relatives."

Mr Harland Woods, who owns the trading store, said that the men were severely shocked. "My store is about ten kilometres from the beach where Mr Macun and his friends were surfing."

Police have been unable to recover Mr Macun's body, which was spotted in the small bay late yesterday afternoon.

Mr Macun's death happened on the eve of the start of South Africa's premier surfing event, the Gunston 500. The editor of a surfing magazine, Mr Paul Naude, said that Mr Macun was one of the best contributors to his publication.

The director of the Technikon, Professor P. D. Veldsman, said he was shocked by his SRC chairman's death. "He was an outstanding personality and a great thinker. Alex was an inspiration to everyone with whom he came in contact."

Mr Macun leaves his recently widowed mother, Mrs Bertha Macun, two brothers and a sister.

Mr Simon Hammerton, who was attacked at the same spot just over a year ago, said from his Durban home last night that he was terribly shocked to hear of the attack. He said the Wild Coast had become a notorious place for shark attacks and that it was not wise for people to surf at the same place where someone else had been attacked. "How many more people have to be attacked before they realize this?"

Cape Times, 30 June 1982

FLORIDA, USA, 1982
A fisherman on Saturday reeled in a 364-lb tiger shark stuffed with the complete leg of a man and a bone from another leg, authorities said.

Dr Ronald Wright, a medical examiner for Broward County, said a man's right leg with a sock and a tennis shoe, and an upper left thigh bone were found in the nine-and-a-half-foot shark, which had put up a four-hour fight with the fisherman. Wright said the shark's jaw measured fifteen inches in diameter.

Steve Cory, an investigator with the medical examiner's office, said that, when the fishermen brought the shark ashore and opened its mouth, "The leg popped out – literally."

Wright speculated that the victim was dead before encountering the shark.

"Now we're working on looking for traces of drugs and alcohol in the victim. That's a very important part of the puzzle," Wright said, adding that it might take several days to turn up such evidence. "In South Florida waters we just don't have sharks attack swimmers. For the last twenty plus years, the only ones we've ever seen are individuals who have drowned, usually because of intoxication, or killed by other means and dumped in the water."

Based on the size of the recovered bones, the unidentified victim was believed to have been about six feet tall, in his twenties and weighed about 190-lbs. Wright said the man probably had been dead from one to four days, based on what is known about the normal digestion time for tiger sharks. He said he thinks the attack took place within 100 miles of the spot where the shark was caught. Experts have told him that tiger sharks rarely travel more than twenty-five miles a day, he said.

"I've been on the phone with medical examiners in Hawaii, where there are lots of shark attacks," he said. "They told me their usual experience is to find the shark relatively close to where the event happened, not more than even a few miles."

Hollywood [Florida] police detective Ron Hickman said the shark was caught at 5.30 a.m. EDT about one and a quarter miles from Hollywood in the Atlantic Ocean. It was reeled in by Al Laurino, 36, a sport fisherman and custom fishing-rod manufacturer from Davie.

"I've been fishing for sharks for over fifteen years and I've caught a lot of sharks, cut them all open, and I've never run across anything like this," Laurino said. "Usually you just find a lot of fish inside them."

He agreed with Wright that the victim was dead before encountering the shark. "For one thing, there was a sneaker on the person, so you know he wasn't out diving. And another thing – tiger sharks mainly feed on the bottom. There's no doubt the body was laying on the bottom when the shark came along."

New Orleans Times-Picayune, 5 September 1982

CALIFORNIA, USA, 1982
When marine biologist Michael Herder felt a tug on his arm while diving for abalone, he thought he had become entangled in kelp. But the tug was from a great white shark. In a brief battle in fifteen feet of murky water 200 yards off the Mendocino County coast, Herder suffered wounds that required more than 100 stitches.

"I didn't have a whole lot of time to think," Herder, 28, said in a telephone interview from his home in McKinleyville. "About the time I realized there was any real fight, the shark had let me go."

Herder, who works for the state Department of Fish and Game, said he and two companions, Scott Sterner and Leo Millan, were diving in the chilly waters of Bear Harbor on 19 September.

The shark first seized Herder under his left armpit, leaving no marks on him, but puncturing his rubber wetsuit. Herder reached around and pushed at the shark's head. The great white, which he estimated at twelve to fourteen feet long and more than 800 lbs, then bit a second time, slashing into his buttocks and upper thigh with razor-sharp teeth.

"The shark released me then – let me go – and took off to the north," he said. "I headed back to the boat."

Herder says his wounds did not hurt for some time, probably because the cold water numbed him and stemmed the flow of blood. "When I got to shore was the first time I began to feel pain," he recalled. "I couldn't walk unassisted. It looks like I was real lucky. There are no nerves severed and no permanent muscle damage. I should regain full use of all my appendages. If the shark had bitten as hard on my upper body as he did on my butt, I would have been in serious trouble."

Herder's advice is never to dive when visibility is less than fifteen feet. "The visibility was so low, it might have mistaken me for a seal and let me go once it decided I wasn't what it wanted for lunch."

Los Angeles Times, 26 September 1982

1983

VIRGINIA, USA, 1983

A fourteen-year-old girl who had a chunk taken from her foot and leg while swimming in the Atlantic apparently was attacked by a sand shark, authorities said. Jill Redenbaugh was in satisfactory condition on Tuesday at a Virginia Beach hospital after undergoing surgery on Monday.

She was swimming in waist-deep water twenty to thirty feet from the shore when she was attacked, police said.

Jack Kownsend, who helped the girl, said "a two-inch chunk" of her left foot and Achilles tendon was taken out.

Kownsend and Ernest Singleton helped Redenbaugh out of the water. Singleton wrapped her foot and took her to the hospital. "She was a very brave young lady," Singleton said. "She held herself together very well. The emergency room physician thought it might have been a sand shark."

Harris Stewart Jr, director of the Center for Marine Studies at Old Dominion University, said sand sharks grow to six feet long and generally live in shallow water near sandy bottoms. "They terrify you, but the incidence of their giving you trouble are few and far between," Stewart said. "Usually you can scare a sand shark away by going 'Boo'."

It was only the third shark attack at Virginia Beach recorded in twenty-seven years. In 1973 a shark bit a seventeen-year-old boy crabbing at False Cape. In 1956 a fourteen-year-old girl was attacked by a shark while she was swimming.

New Orleans Times-Picayune, 17 August 1983

QUEENSLAND, AUSTRALIA, 1983

The skipper of a capsized shrimp boat said he watched helplessly as a shark dragged away his two crew members, one of them as he clutched her hand.

Ray Boundy, 28, skipper of the New Venture, told his tale a few hours after being rescued from Loaders Reef, forty-five miles north-east of Townsville. He had been in the sea off Australia's north-east coast for thirty-six hours.

Boundy said from his hospital bed that deckhand Dennis Patrick Murphy, 24, of Brisbane, and his cook Linda Anne Horton, 21, of Townsville, were attacked by a shark he estimated to be fifteen feet long as they clung to the capsized vessel. He said his boat capsized on Sunday night in heavy seas sixty miles out of Townsville.

"The deckie (Murphy) was on deck and jumped into the water, but Lindy and I were caught in the wheelhouse. We all ended up sitting on top of the upturned hull wondering what we were going to do," said Boundy. They clung to wreckage, which included a surfboard, a life ring and pieces of Styrofoam from shrimp boxes as the trawler sank.

Boundy said the shark approached on Monday night. "We weren't taking much notice of him, thinking that if we didn't antagonize him, he might leave us alone. He took a bite at my leg under the surfboard, so I kicked him with my other foot and he let go."

About ten minutes later the shark struck.

"He's got my leg, the bastard's got my leg," Boundy quoted Murphy as screaming.

"You're joking," I said. "But then I could see the blood coming to the surface through the water. I didn't know what to do. We'd been hanging together so well for so long ... pushed ourselves so hard. I just didn't know how to deal with it because we had no dinghy. We had nothing to use as a tourniquet, even if we stopped the bleeding. The shark was still going to come back and I just didn't know what to do.

"The shark came back and I said to Smurf (Murphy), 'What do you want to do?' and he said, 'You bolt. Gather in all the stuff. Leave me,' and he swam off about four or five paces.

"Everything seemed to be going all right for a couple of hours. I got Lindy to get her spirits back up and we seemed to be travelling along all right, and I knew we'd get to the reef some time in the morning," said Boundy.

At about 4 a.m. the shark struck again.

"Lindy was sitting in the sling of the lifebuoy when I saw him come along again. I was pretty sure he was the same shark this time. He came along as slow as you like beside me, then slewed around and grabbed Lindy around the arms and the chest.

"I was still holding her by the hand as he shook her about three or four times. She only let out one little squeal as soon as it hit and I knew almost instantly that she was dead."

New Orleans Times-Picayune, 27 September 1983

1984

FLORIDA, USA, 1984

Three men competing in a shark fishing tournament became bait themselves when a thunderstorm capsized their boat, tossing them into seas scattered with blood and fish to attract the undersea killers. The episode was "like a bad dream", William Anderson, 34, said on Monday. "It's hard to believe it happened."

Anderson, William McConnell, 30, and William E. Stevens, 34, survived on Sunday by pulling themselves into two five-foot-long coolers, where they bobbed in rough seas for five hours until being picked up by a passing boat whose captain heard their calls for help.

"The chests were bumped frequently by sharks just checking us out," said Anderson, owner of the eighteen-foot Boatem. "From the size of the dorsal fin we saw cutting through the water, the largest shark out there was well over ten feet long."

The three Orlando men were competing in the US Open Sharkfishing Tournament when the storm overturned their boat in the same waters where they had already tossed shark bait, a few miles off the north-east Florida coast.

"We didn't see many sharks, but we could see

the swirls and movements in the water around us," Anderson said. "We were using bonita as bait and that is a very bloody fish. All our efforts at attracting them were definitely beginning to pay off. We definitely saw them at a distance of fifteen to twenty feet."

The adventure began when the men were forced out to sea, trying to outrun a thunderstorm which walloped north-east Florida. The storm "chased us off shore for fifteen miles as we were running from it, trying to find a way through all that electricity," he said. Finally they found a way through the storm and anchored, settling down for some serious shark fishing in quest of the $4,700 first prize. But strong waves suddenly grabbed the stern around 6 p.m., capsizing the craft within two minutes.

"Then the hard part started," Anderson said. "We were caught by winds and current."

During the next half hour, the men struggled in three-foot waves, trying to climb into two large coolers which had held bait and sharks which had already been caught.

"I felt like something had rubbed up against my leg," McConnell said. "I've got very light scratches there, marks with equal distance between them. It appears to be from shark skin, either the tail or side of a shark."

The men were not in the coolers for long before more sharks drew closer, apparently following the scent of blood and fish oil.

New Orleans Times-Picayune, 3 July 1984

Dwarf-Lantern Shark

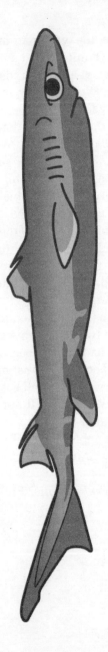

Shark Facts

Length: 6 inches to 8.3 inches (15 cm to 21 cm)

Weight: Half an ounce (14 grams)

Colouring: Dark brown with black markings

Diet: Krill, shrimp, small fish

Pups: Two or three born together, very small

Status: Not known

The dwarf-lantern shark is a member of the dogfish family and is one of the smallest sharks, tiny enough to be held in the palm of your hand. Seldom seen by humans, it lives at depths of up to 1,450 feet (439 metres) where there is very little light. As its name suggests, the dwarf-lantern shark can provide its own light, using glowing photophore cells as camouflage against light filtering down from the surface, protecting itself from predators attacking from below.

Dwarf-Lantern Shark Range

TEXAS, USA, 1984

A teenage girl's legs were mangled by bites from a shark while another girl required seventy stitches to close bite wounds, but city officials decided to keep their popular beaches open.

"We're probably taking more precautions than necessary," said city official Joe Rubio.

Carmen Gaytan, 18, attacked in the Gulf of Mexico by what rescuers said was a four-foot shark, was in guarded condition yesterday in the intensive care unit of Valley Community Hospital. She underwent extensive reconstructive surgery on her legs. "It's just wait and see," hospital spokeswoman Suzy Payne said of Gaytan's chances to recover without an amputation.

The second teenage girl was attacked just two and a half hours later in front of another luxury hotel three miles away and required stitches on many leg bites, authorities said.

City and tourism officials met and decided to keep the beaches open following the attacks, described as the first in the area in twenty-three years. The beaches were kept under surveillance by land, sea and air, said Rubio, a South Padre Island building department official who acts as city spokesman in emergencies. He said beaches in this South Padre Island resort at the southern tip of Texas would be evacuated if "any suspicious activity that can be confirmed as sharks" is spotted.

Gary Glick, who owns a deep-sea fishing charterboat in Port Isabel, said shifts in ocean currents moved sharks closer to the shore ...

Gaytan, of Mexico, was swimming in chest-deep water shortly after noon on Tuesday outside the South Padre Hotel when beachgoers heard her screams for help. "Help me, please, a fish is killing me," she cried, according to Cidonio Barron Leon, who helped pull her out. He said he saw a shark as he went to her aid.

The second attack, on a thirteen-year-old girl whose identity was not released yesterday, occurred near the Tiki Motel about two and a half hours later, officials said. The girl was treated at the Port Isabel Medical Center and was released, Dr Ralph Landberg said. "She had lots of teeth marks around her right foot up to her ankle. There were many lacerations," said Landberg, adding that the girl took seventy stitches. "I think she was very lucky."

However, Rubio said there was no evidence the second girl had been attacked by a shark. "We're not sure what happened," he said.

Mid-July is the height of the summer season for the high-rise hotels and condominiums on South Padre Island. No cancellations or early checkouts were reported by clerks at the two hotels where the attacks occurred.

New Orleans Times-Picayune, 26 July 1984

FLORIDA, USA, 1984

A twenty-three-year-old woman who was attacked by a shark while swimming just twenty feet off shore underwent surgery on Tuesday to repair a nine-inch gash in her right arm, a hospital official said.

Sunday's attack on Sandra Fletcher was the sixth to occur in a month along Florida's Atlantic coast.

Fletcher was in fair condition at Indian River Memorial Hospital before the operation, which was to reconnect severed nerves and tendons, and to stitch wounds made by the shark's double row of teeth.

"I knew what it was as soon as it grabbed me," she said on Monday from her hospital bed. "You always think it's something in the movies. You don't think it's going to happen to you."

Fletcher was attacked while body surfing with friends in waist-deep water three miles south of Sebastian Inlet in northern Indian River County. "I just saw all the blood in the water. I thought I was going to get it again. I was scared," the Clearwater teacher said.

Karen Kenney, 27, of Tampa, was with Fletcher and helped the injured woman pull herself free. "As soon as Sandy screamed, I saw blood in the wave behind her," Kenney said. "I ran out and tried to help pull her in. He just pulled her under – she had to fight to get loose. When she screamed, you could see a trail of blood in the water about five feet wide."

"She was very lucky that it didn't hit the major artery or she probably wouldn't have made it," Dr Peter Ciejek said. He described the gash on Fletcher's right forearm at nine to twelve inches long.

Six shark attacks have been reported in the past month between Stuart and Daytona Beach along Florida's east coast. Indian River County lifeguard Bruce Little said shark sightings are common at this time of year because "bait fish like mullet are migrating south now and the sharks follow them. It's dangerous to swimmers when the bait fish come too close to shore."

New Orleans Times-Picayune, 24 October 1984

1985

CAPE PROVINCE, SOUTH AFRICA, 1985
A Plumstead man is especially pleased to be helping at a neighbour's wedding today – he survived an attack by what he believes to have been a great white shark at Buffels Bay, near Cape Point, yesterday.

Mr Donald James was bitten in the ribs, the shark's

teeth piercing two wet-suits and puncturing his right side. He said that he felt as though someone had stood on his rib cage, but was obviously "pleased to be alive to tell the tale". He had been spearfishing with a friend, Mr Tullio Testa, about midday yesterday.

"We hadn't caught anything, so that dispels the myth that sharks attack when attracted by catches of fish," he asserted. "I felt something grab me and thought for a moment it might be Tullio playing a trick on me. When I turned round and saw the shark, my first, instantaneous thought was 'Dumb shark, what do you want me for?'

"It let go of me and swam away and circled around. I wasn't going to wait for it to come back, so I headed for the kelp, where I came up and called for Tullio. I saw that the shark had followed us to the kelp, which dispels the myth that sharks won't go into kelp."

Mr James ascribed his escape to the fact that he was wearing two wet-suits. Although both were punctured, the outer diving jacket had prevented blood from pumping into the water. He said he had checked the bite pattern against a reference book and thought the shark to be a great white. "I saw its eye, which was round and black, and that matches the description of a great white's eye," he said. He estimated the shark to have been about four metres long.

Cape Times, 5 January 1985

NATAL, SOUTH AFRICA, 1985
The hero of yesterday's shark attack on the south coast today described his horror when a shark two metres long "climbed on to the back" of his surfing friend.

The victim was top Natal surfer Bruce Eldridge, 18, who was savaged off an unprotected beach at Umbogintwini while surfing in conditions which the Natal Anti Shark

Measure Board warned today are ideal for shark attack.

Doctors were today optimistic that they had saved Bruce's foot. Bruce, who lives at Athlone Park, had a large portion of his right calf and foot bitten off. He was rushed to Kingsway Clinic and then to Durban's Addington Hospital, where he had a long operation to repair damaged tissue. He left the theatre at 3 a.m.

"It sounds hopeful that the foot will be saved," Dr Ralph McCarter, deputy medical superintendent at Addington Hospital, said today. But it was still too early to be sure. His condition was satisfactory, added Dr McCarter.

Bruce was surfing near murky water at the mouth of the Umbogintwini River with his friends, Eric Robinson, 24, a technikon student, and Mr Keith Lowes, late yesterday when the incident occurred.

Mr Robinson said a large chunk of the calf of Bruce's right leg was bitten out by the shark. His foot was also badly lacerated. He said the attack took place at about 6.30 p.m.

"We were paddling out for a wave, when Bruce started shouting. I turned to see what was happening and I saw him being pulled from the board into an upright position. Then he was down on the board and it looked as if the shark – it must have been more than two metres long – was climbing on to his back.

"The water suddenly went red with blood. I got a huge fright. I started paddling towards him – I didn't think about it at all. A wave came and, when it had passed, I saw that the shark had gone.

"Bruce and I paddled to the shore. I used a towel to make a tourniquet. Keith and I then carried Bruce to the car. He was very white, but I think he was still conscious. I don't think he saw his leg. He didn't look at it. I think his mind was wandering a bit. He was saying odd things: one time he asked if he was allowed to cry."

Mr Lowes said Bruce had not bled much as they rushed him to Kingsway Clinic and then to Addington Hospital: "He was very quiet. I kept asking him if he was still awake. I think he must have been in shock."

Mr Robinson said they had been surfing at the beach for about ten years and there had never been a shark attack there: "It had a reputation for being a safe beach even though it was unprotected. I'm certainly not going to do it again."

Bruce, a second-year student at the University of Natal in Durban, won the Southern Natal surfing trials at Greenpoint at the weekend and took part in the recent South African Surfing Championships.

Durban Daily News, 18 January 1985

SOUTH AUSTRALIA, AUSTRALIA, 1985
A massive hunt to track down and destroy a killer shark is due to start in Port Lincoln today. Divers in the area have described it as the biggest hunt of its kind mounted in the state.

It follows the horrific attack on Sunday on Port Lincoln housewife Shirley Ann Durdin, 33, who was torn in two and devoured by a six-metre white pointer [great white] shark.

A special meeting organized last night by the Port Lincoln Skin Diving Club and attended by abalone divers as well as members of the Port Lincoln Game Fishing Club, decided on the hunt. At least five vessels, including one from Adelaide, will take part in the hunt for the killer shark. The first boat is due to begin the search at about 10.30 a.m. Others will join later today.

Two large nine-metre search vessels will stay out at sea off Wiseman's Beach, north of Port Lincoln, where

Mrs Durdin was taken by the shark while diving for scallops on Sunday afternoon with her husband, Barry, and a friend. The others, smaller six-metre abalone boats, will resume the search each morning. The search vessels will fan out from a series of centre points off the coast in the Port Lincoln area in a bid to lure the giant shark into a specific area.

Whale oil and tuna blood will be poured into the sea from the search vessels to attract the shark. Special shark hooks will be baited and attached to floating drums, which will act as "positive anchors" if the shark takes the bait. The bow on each vessel will be armed with shotguns and high-velocity weapons to kill the shark if it is hooked. The fishermen, who are concerned for the safety of abalone divers operating in the area, are prepared to spend several days searching for the white pointer ...

Kevin Bruce Wiseman has lived almost half his life in a rudimentary tin shed in the idyllic setting of Peake Bay on the Eyre Peninsula. The fifty-eight-year-old retired fisherman has become such a familiar figure in the area that locals now refer to that stretch of white beach about thirty-five kilometres north of Port Lincoln as Wiseman's Beach. That was until Sunday, when the serenity of the picturesque bay was shattered by the shark attack which brought death in the afternoon to a mother of four young children.

Mrs Durdin of Lipson Place, Port Lincoln, was snorkelling for scallops with her husband of fifteen years, Barry, and a family friend when the six-metre shark struck in two-metre deep water as her three daughters and son watched from the shore 150 metres away.

"It will never be the same again," mourned Mr Wiseman. "I loved this place for its peace and quietness, but that's changed now, hasn't it? I've seen a helluva lot of sharks in my day, but I've never seen anything as big as that one. The awful thing was I could only stand there and watch and do absolutely nothing. And what is probably even worse is that that shark will be back again."

Veteran shark catcher Neville Osborn, 46, said: "This one now has the taste of human flesh and he'll be back." Osborn and his friend Colin Wood, 52, were fishing near Wiseman's Beach on Sunday afternoon when the great shark passed within metres of their boat. It was only hours after the shark had torn Mrs Durdin in two and devoured her. The two men are now planning to hunt the shark in what they believe is one of South Australia's few remaining long-line shark boats.

A specialist in diving medicine, Dr Carl Edmonds, said the return of the shark to the area was likely. He said the attack had been made for food or to protect the shark's territory. "The likelihood of shark attacks depends on two things: how many people are in the water and how many sharks are in the water," he said. "It is a worry when something like a white pointer, which is an open-ocean shark, comes into sheltered waters. It is certainly a cause for concern." Dr Edmonds added that sharks did not eat because they were hungry; they react to stimuli such as someone flapping around on the surface.

Mr and Mrs Durdin had only recently moved back to Port Lincoln after Mr Durdin, 35, suffered a number of allergies associated with work on his farm at Karkoo. Mrs Durdin had just completed a course in farm management at Port Lincoln's TAFE College. Her distraught mother-in-law said yesterday that Shirley had loved the water since childhood.

Mr Rob Kretschmer, who watched the attack from the shore, said he had to help restrain Mr Durdin from going back into the water after his wife. "The friends they had been snorkelling with had to hold him down on the rocks to stop him going back in. He was distraught and hysterical and kept saying over and over, 'My wife, she's gone, she's gone.'"

A police spokesman at Port Lincoln said that there were no immediate plans to issue a general warning to the public about the shark danger. Meanwhile, police combed the shoreline in search of remains of Mrs Durdin, while a local Department of Fisheries vessel searched the waters. But all that has been found is a single flipper and police have yet to ascertain whether it belonged to Mrs Durdin.

Adelaide Advertiser, 5 March 1985

SOUTH CAROLINA, USA, 1985

A Tifton girl was riding the last wave of the day with her father and a friend at Folly Beach, South Carolina, when a shark suddenly attacked and seriously injured the youngster.

Julie Steed, 10, who was bitten on the left leg last Friday by what is believed to have been an eight- to nine-foot-long tiger shark, is being transferred to Emory University Hospital from a hospital in Charleston. She could be admitted to Emory as early as next Tuesday, said Deborah Steed, the girl's mother. But Mrs Steed is still chilled by the irony that Julie, her father, David Steed, and friend Brittany Walker of Tifton had decided to call it a day just moments before the attack.

"They were actually coming in when she was bitten," said Julie's mother. "They had a two-man raft, and just wanted to ride that last little surf in."

Julie, who was admitted to Roper Hospital in Charleston, lost two-thirds of her calf muscle as a result of the attack, but doctors are confident that she will be able to walk, Mrs Steed said. The youngster, who had "too many stitches to count", will have to undergo extensive reconstructive and cosmetic surgery, her mother added.

Julie said she did not see the shark which bit her as she, her father and Brittany played in the surf only twenty feet from shore. "It was a total surprise, but I tried not to panic. I tried to stay calm," said Julie, who will be a fifth-grader in the fall. "The water was just a little bit above my knees, and, when a wave would come, to the bottom of my bathing suit."

John Jones, a spokesman for the Florida-based Cooperative Shark Attack Data Center [now the International Shark Attack File], said Julie most likely was attacked by a tiger shark eight or nine feet long, judging from the shark's biting pattern. The bite was about fourteen inches long, he said. Jones, who has been working with Folly Beach police and the Steed family to gather information about the attack, said Steed helped save his daughter's life by holding on to her when the shark struck.

"The shark apparently felt the resistance and let go. But he still dealt more damage than any attack I've dealt with up here," said Jones.

Sharks regularly go to shallow water to feed, but any number of things could have caused this particular shark to attack. "There are a lot of sandbars in the area. He could've gotten in and then felt trapped," said Jones.

Meanwhile, the eight-man police force in Folly Beach has been plagued with reports of shark sightings and swimmers being bumped, said Folly Beach Police Chief George Tittle. So far, no sharks have been found, he said.

Atlanta Journal-Constitution, 23 July 1985

CAPE PROVINCE, SOUTH AFRICA, 1985

A boogie-boarder's leg was gashed today when he was attacked by a shark while swimming at East London. The shark has been identified as a great white from a tooth extracted from the surfer's wound.

The attack happened at 8 a.m., when Mr Patrick Gee, 24, was swimming with a boogie-board on Eastern Beach. Mr Gee apparently saw the shark come at him and tried to fend it off with the board.

The shark evaded the board and bit Mr Gee on the right leg below the knee. He managed to reach the beach and was taken to the Frere Hospital by a motorist. He is reported to be in no danger.

The beach manager, Mr L. O. Branfield, immediately banned bathing on the beach.

Durban Daily News, 24 October 1985

1986

CALIFORNIA, USA, 1986

A twenty-seven-year-old scuba diver was critically injured on Saturday when he was attacked just off a beach near Carmel by what experts said was probably a great white shark.

Frank Gallo of San Jose suffered a punctured right lung and lacerations to his right shoulder, jaw, neck and forearm in the 10 a.m. attack off Carmel River State Beach, a spokesman for Community Hospital of the Monterey Peninsula said. Gallo underwent a four-hour operation by four surgeons beginning at noon.

"He's doing incredibly well considering what he went through," said Charles Bancroft, a ranger at Point Lobos State Park, who was on duty near the beach and went to the hospital later. "He's going to have quite a story to tell."

Bancroft said one of the doctors told him the size of the bite wounds made it likely a great white shark, at least twelve to fifteen feet long, was responsible. The ranger said he was aware of only two previous shark attacks in the last five years, both involving great whites.

The beach, known locally as Monastery Beach, was closed after the attack, said Claude Wilkerson, a park aide.

Bancroft said Gallo, a paramedic for the Morgan Hill Fire Department and a competition scuba diver, was diving with two friends and was about 150 yards off shore and thirty feet beneath the surface when the attack occurred. He came to the surface and waved that he was in trouble, then his friends carried him to shore on a diving mattress and called an ambulance, according to the park ranger.

"He was very alert and talking to medical people the whole time," said Bancroft. "He said he never saw the shark, but managed to brush it off and it didn't attack him again."

Los Angeles Times, 7 December 1986

CAPE PROVINCE, SOUTH AFRICA, 1986
A twenty-one-year-old Port Elizabeth student and son of a retired Cape educationist died on the way to George Provincial Hospital after being attacked by a shark near Great Brak River on Sunday. The Outeniqua Divisional Council was investigating the situation urgently to decide whether it will be necessary to close beaches.

Mr Wessel Olls, a final-year University of Port Elizabeth student, is believed to have been swimming off Eseistrand, between Great Brak River and Glentana Beach, when he was attacked late on Sunday afternoon. He was severely bitten on the left thigh. Some reports said Mr Olls's leg was bitten off. When asked what happened, his distraught brother, Mr Anton Olls, said he did not want "to have to go through the whole incident right now".

Mr Olls was rescued by two lifesavers and given immediate treatment by doctors on the beach.

The superintendent of George Provincial Hospital, Dr D. M. du Toit, said Mr Olls was dead when he was brought in at about 6.30 p.m. "He had very severe left thigh injuries. The customary police post mortem will be held, but at this stage it is not possible to say what kind of shark it was. The Natal Anti-Shark Measures Board has asked for photographs of the wound to try to establish that."

Mr Dawie de Vries, secretary of the Outeniqua Divisional Council, said the investigation would first establish precisely where the attack happened before a decision was made on closing beaches. "We can't simply close the beaches to tourists, and I doubt whether panic has set in at this stage. Durban shark authorities said it would be advisable to close the beaches only if the water was murky."

Johannesburg Star, 23 December 1986

1987

TEXAS, USA, 1987

A girl whose arm was bitten off by a shark remained hospitalized in a serious condition on Sunday, but officials said they will not close beaches to the thousands of Easter weekend visitors.

April Dawn Voglino, 16, of Kingsland, underwent surgery on Saturday at Memorial Medical Center in

Corpus Christi, and was in the intensive care unit, nursing supervisor D. Brown said.

The teenager was in chest-deep water near Mustang Island on Saturday when the shark attacked her. She was swimming with her father, who pounded on the shark and carried her ashore after the shark swam away. Her arm was severed about six to eight inches above the elbow.

Nueces County Commissioner J. P. Luby, whose precinct covers two and a half miles of beaches, said the attack probably was an isolated case and he would not order the beaches closed.

Luby said he planned to fly over the area with Coast Guard officials to make observations of any sharks. The flight was delayed because of mechanical problems with the Coast Guard helicopter.

"We'll take some action if we see a lot of sharks out there," Luby said. "We've had people bitten before, but nothing as major as this."

Andre Landry, a fish behaviour expert from Texas A & M University at Galveston, said there have been between thirteen and fifteen documented shark attacks along the Texas coast within the last hundred years. "We have one incident happening like this and this arouses the concern of bathers, but it's a freak occurrence, something that should not induce fear among the bathing populace," Landry said on Sunday.

Luby said Voglino and her parents were alone at an isolated beach near Aransas Beach about 6 p.m. on Saturday when the attack occurred. Robert Voglino, who was swimming with his daughter, was not hurt, Luby said.

"The father heard the daughter scream and, as he turned around, he saw the daughter and the shark," Nueces County Constable Deewayne Mathews said. "He then headed directly toward his daughter. He grabbed the daughter and started beating on the shark with his other hand. At that time the shark severed the girl's arm."

Voglino continued to beat the shark and yelled at his daughter to swim to the shore, Mathews added. When the shark swam away, the father carried his daughter to shore. They flagged down a motorist who had a citizens' band radio and called for help.

New Orleans Times-Picayune, 20 April 1987

CAPE PROVINCE, SOUTH PROVINCE, 1987
The sea "boiled with streaks of blood" when a massive shark savaged a Fish Hoek man surfing at Groot Jongersfontein, near Stilbaai, yesterday afternoon, an eyewitness told this paper.

Diver Mr Fanie Oosthuizen, who saw the attack on surfer Mr Peter John McCallum, 24, of Carmichael Road, said the surfer's board had saved him from an "almost certain death": "He was lying on his surfboard, which prevented the shark from biting him in half."

The attack occurred about 100 metres from the shore near a sandbank in water with a depth of a half to one and a half metres.

Mr McCallum's mother, Mrs Mary McCallum, said from Riversdale last night that her son was "fine" in Riversdale Hospital and was "resting quietly" after a two-hour operation, during which he received about 125 stitches. "We are extraordinarily fortunate: the shark's teeth must have slipped off the board." The shark had ripped "a large half-moon shaped" chunk out of the surfboard.

Her son sustained deep gashes to his right side, where the shark's jaws had gouged out pieces of flesh as it slipped on the board, Mrs McCallum said.

Mr Oosthuizen, a Groot Jongersfontein farmer, said he

was diving at about 11.30 a.m., when he heard "a piercing scream further out in the breakers".

"I heard him scream, 'Bite,' and thought he was warning me that a dog was attacking my little daughter on the beach. But, when I looked back again, I heard him scream, 'I've been bitten, I've been bitten.' Then I saw this huge tail about a metre long and realized he was being attacked by a shark."

Mr Oosthuizen then swam to one side to get a clearer view and saw a shark about three metres long – "then the water just boiled with blood".

"I swam up to him and he said, 'I don't want to die, I don't want to die.' Then he became calm and I said to him, 'Rascals don't die.'"

The two then swam to shore.

At the time of the attack Mr McCallum's girlfriend, Miss Jo-Anne Bosman, of Bergvliet, and another woman surfer were further out to sea. Another surfer went to help the two women and the three reached shore safely.

Mr Oosthuizen described Mr McCallum as "a big man about 1.95 metres tall with broad shoulders" and said the shark's teeth marks extended from his spine, around under his arm, along his side with a few gashes on his thigh. Some of the shark's teeth, which were longer than a centimetre, were stuck in the surfboard, Mr Oosthuizen added.

"He spoke to me when we got to shore and, despite his ribs showing from the shark bite and deep gashes on his side, he remained calm. He told me: 'I was lying on my board paddling out to catch a wave, when I noticed a large shark near me. I just lay still because they usually go away if you don't move. The next moment it went into a frenzy and attacked me.'"

Cape Times, 14 September 1987

Galapagos Shark

The Galapagos shark is found not only in the Galapagos region, but also further afield in the Pacific, Atlantic and Indian Oceans. It prefers the warm, shallow waters of tropical reefs and is known to be extremely inquisitive and aggressive, large groups reported as having attacked fishing boats, following the boats into water so shallow that the sharks could barely manoeuvre. Swimming or diving in water where these sharks are known to be present is highly dangerous.

Shark Facts

Length:	8 feet to 11 feet (2.4 m to 3.3 m)
Weight:	150 lb to 430 lb (68 kg to 195 kg)
Colouring:	Bronze/grey upper with white belly
Diet:	Eels, sea bass, squid, marine iguanas, seals, other sharks
Pups:	Up to 16 pups born at up to 2 feet 7 inches (78 cm)
Status:	Not under threat

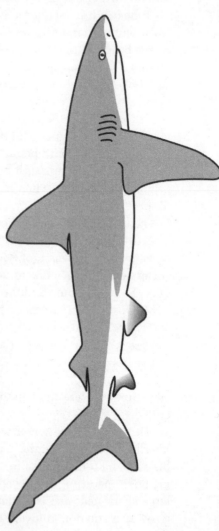

Galapagos Shark Range

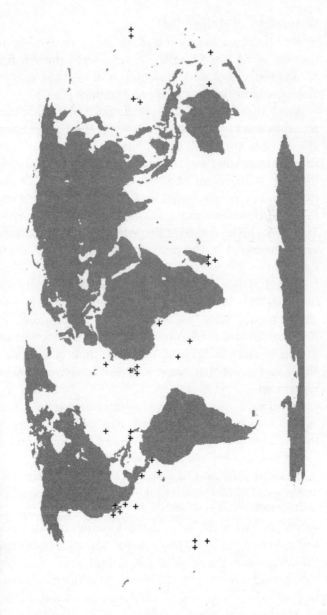

DOMINICAN REPUBLIC, 1987

Rescue workers on Wednesday began recovering the corpses of dozens of refugees who were thrown from a capsized vessel and drowned or were torn apart by sharks, authorities said in Santo Domingo.

More than 100 of the estimated 160 Dominicans, possibly attempting illegal entry into the United States, aboard the forty-foot boat bound east toward Puerto Rico were missing and presumed dead after the Tuesday disaster, said Eugenio Cabral, Dominican civil defence director. The overcrowded vessel left Nagua, about sixty miles north of the capital on the Atlantic coast, early on Tuesday. The boat caught fire when its motor exploded and it capsized in the tumult of attempts to douse the flames.

Five civil defence boats and several fishing boats resumed a search for survivors at daybreak on Wednesday. Three bodies were recovered, and Luis Rolon, civil defence director for San Juan, said eighteen women and four men were in hospital suffering from cuts, bruises, shock and burns. The remaining thirty-five were rescued unharmed.

Rolon said a female survivor interviewed by a radio station said the vessel's captain was intoxicated during the incident, and gas canisters aboard the boat spilled at the time of the explosion, spreading the flames.

Between forty and fifty sharks attacked the survivors as they clung to the wreckage or floated after currents pulled them twenty miles off shore, said Rolon, who accompanied Cabral on his flight. Rescuers in helicopters and fishermen in small boats pulled some survivors from the water amid the shark attack, Cabral said.

Ernesto Uribe, public affairs officer at the US Embassy in Santo Domingo, said he saw pictures of the accident

scene taken from a civil defence aircraft and that numerous sharks could be seen circling bodies and survivors.
"It was a big herd of sharks. It was an awful sight."

Many Dominicans attempt the ninety-mile crossing
of the treacherous Mona Passage to Puerto Rico. One
survivor told authorities that passengers had paid the
boat's operators from $200 to $600 to make the trip ...

Atlanta Journal-Constitution, 8 October 1987

ACAPULCO, MEXICO, 1980s

In the late 1980s, while avid American windsurfer Mike
Schecter was surfing with his buddies in Acapulco,
a decidedly irate shark, swimming at an alarming speed,
made its way towards the group.

Everyone quickly paddled for the beach, but the shark
popped up right beneath one fellow's board, chomping
and snapping. Following a dramatic struggle, the surfer
managed to catch a wave into the beach, followed by the
shark, which unsuccessfully chased him on to the sand.

Frustrated, the shark turned away and headed down
the coast, leaving the surfers with a premonition of bad
things to come. Sure enough, a Canadian tourist was
reportedly eaten later that day.

Windsurfing, September/October 1993

1988

SOUTH CAROLINA, USA, 1988

Diners at a Metairie restaurant which features a giant
aquarium got a real taste of deep-sea adventure when a
diver in the tank was attacked by a six-foot tiger shark.

Wiley Beevers was feeding fish on Friday night in
the tank in front of about fifty diners at Sharky's Reef

Restaurant, 3505 N. Hullen Avenue, when the 120-lb shark tore into his arm. Beevers left the aquarium under his own power and was taken to East Jefferson Hospital, where he received seventy-five stitches to close the shark wound, said Jack Dunn, one of the restaurant's owners. Beevers was released from the hospital later, officials said.

Dunn said that he and other divers routinely go into the 135,000-gallon aquarium to feed lettuce to the fish in the ninety-foot-long tank. The shark had never before bothered a diver feeding other fish, he said. "When he sees we have nothing but lettuce, he usually swims away."

Beevers, a Metairie lawyer, had been in the tank to feed the fish several times, Dunn said. Beevers could not be reached on Monday for comment.

The sharks are fed shad, mullet and other fish every three days by more experienced divers, Dunn said. He added that diners usually enjoy watching divers feed the fish, but they were alarmed when they saw the attack and Beevers' blood swirl to the surface.

"They got to see something a lot of people hope they'll never get to see," Dunn said. "They were concerned for the diver and were relieved to see he was OK."

New Orleans Times-Picayune, 23 August 1988

1989

NEW SOUTH WALES, AUSTRALIA, 1989
Adam McGuire can thank a school of dolphins for saving him from a shark which attacked him yesterday while he was surfing on the New South Wales north coast.

A local ambulance spokesman said that a group of dolphins chased off a shark which attacked Adam, 17, at

Half Tide Beach, near Ballina, leaving him with a severely lacerated abdomen, at about 5.15 p.m. Two companions managed to get him ashore and raise the alarm. Ambulance officers and a rescue helicopter were summoned to the beach. He was rushed to Lismore Base Hospital, where he was in a "satisfactory" condition last night.

Adam was on the second day of a holiday in the area with two companions, Brad Thompson and Jason Maloney, all from Newcastle. The three were riding 1.5-metre waves among a school of about fifteen or twenty dolphins. According to Brad Thompson, they noticed the dolphins start to get restless.

"All of a sudden, they started speeding up and swimming under us and we thought they were up to something," he said. "I looked over and saw Adam knocked off his board. I could see a hole in his board, and Adam in the water close to it. I saw the shark come up to him. He started hitting it in the head, trying to get it away from him. Then we didn't see it any more and we took Adam in to shore."

Police have asked Mr John Hajje, operations manager at Manly Underwater World, to identify the shark from a plaster cast of the bite on the surfboard.

"I can't be sure until I see the bite, but, from the description they gave me, it appears to have been quite a big one, about four metres, and in that area it's probably a tiger," Mr Hajje said. The bite was about thirty centimetres across with individual tooth marks measuring 6 cm × 4 cm.

He said Adam could probably thank his surfboard as much as the dolphins for his survival. "The police told me that, when the shark attacked, it took a chunk out of the board and he fell off," he said. "Rather than attack him, it kept on going for the board. It really just brushed him and didn't take much of a bite."

Sydney Morning Herald, 4 January 1989

NATAL, SOUTH AFRICA, 1989

A young Isipingo lifesaver was savaged by a shark while surfing at Isipingo Beach not far from the river mouth yesterday – the second victim of a shark attack there in nine months. And, by an amazing coincidence, the previous young shark victim was on the beach and ran for medical help.

The installation of shark nets at Isipingo has been a sore point for several years. Local lifesavers have made numerous pleas to the Isipingo Town Board, without success.

Mr Sudesh Hansraj, 19, a member of the Isipingo Lifesaving Club, was body-surfing about 100 metres from the Isipingo River mouth with two other club members when he was attacked just before 6 p.m. The trainee quantity surveyor was bitten twice on the left leg, once on the thigh and just below the knee.

Last night Mr Hansraj of Delta Road, Isipingo Beach, underwent emergency surgery at the R. H. Khan Hospital. A spokesman for the hospital described his condition as "stable".

An eyewitness, who did not want to be named, said Mr Hansraj and other members of the lifesaving club were about to start training for the forthcoming South African Surf Lifesaving Championships when the attack took place.

It was just before 6 p.m. when the shark attacked Mr Hansraj. Fortunately for him, two others, Mr Bahoo Jadwat and the club's vice captain, Mr Sherwin Stanley, were with him and brought him out of the water quickly.

"The last shark victim, Sastri Naidoo, was a seventeen-year-old schoolboy at the time. He ran to a doctor's home for help."

Two doctors soon arrived and Mr Hansraj was put on a drip before being taken to hospital.

Mr Graeme Charter, deputy director of the Natal Sharks Board, said it was too early to say what type of shark was involved. "The victim is very lucky. He has two deep wounds – one thirty centimetres in length and the other about twelve centimetres. We have taken photographs of the wounds and by Monday we should be able to say what species of shark attacked him."

Durban Daily News, 21 January 1989

NATAL, SOUTH AFRICA, 1989

Shark victim Sudesh Hansraj, speaking from his hospital bed in Chatsworth, where he is recovering after being attacked by a shark at Isipingo beach last Friday, said the incident would not stop him from going back into the sea: "It could have happened to anyone" ... Sudesh said he and other colleagues were waiting to catch a wave when he was attacked.

"The water was quite clear and I did not see it. I just felt a terrific blow on my left leg and, as I turned around, I saw the shark with its mouth wide open. I screamed for help and luckily for me my colleagues were near by and they brought me to shore. Had it not been for them, I might have been dead" ...

Durban Daily News, 23 January 1989

Scalloped Hammerhead Shark

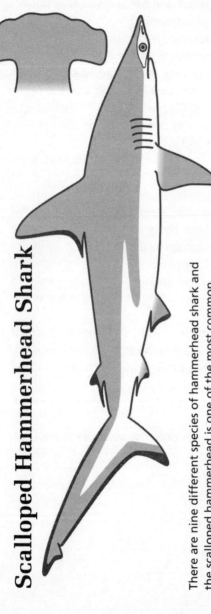

There are nine different species of hammerhead shark and the scalloped hammerhead is one of the most common. The highly distinctive flattened head of the hammerheads, with the eyes and nostrils located at the extremes of the shark's head, is believed to have evolved to enhance the shark's vision, allowing it to see above and below at the same time. The shark's electroreceptors are also spread along the hammer, providing a wider search pattern when hunting. The scalloped hammerhead has a more sculpted leading edge to its "hammer" and these fish have been known to gather in groups of up to 100.

Shark Facts

Length:	5 feet to 14 feet (1.5 m to 4.3 m)
Weight:	125 lb to 336 lb (57 kg to 153 kg)
Colouring:	Light greenish grey upper with white belly
Diet:	Sardines, herring, squid, mackerel, smaller sharks
Pups:	Up to 15 pups born at around 2 feet (60 cm)
Status:	Endangered due to overfishing and finning

Scalloped Hammerhead Shark Range

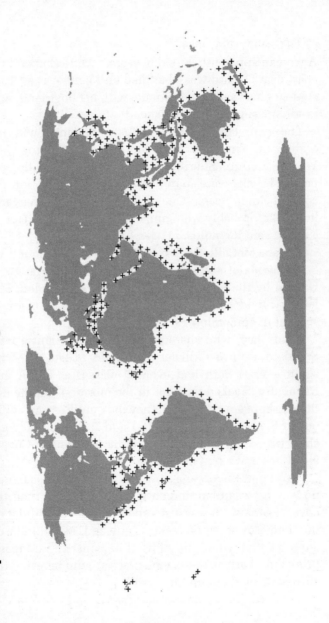

CALIFORNIA, USA, 1989

A woman apparently killed by a great white shark off the coast near Oxnard was identified on Monday as a UCLA student on a kayaking excursion with her boyfriend, who is still missing, authorities stated.

The two, both UCLA graduate students, had left Malibu on Thursday for a morning of kayaking, said Ventura County Sheriff Lt. Lary Reynolds. Both one-person kayaks were found on Friday five miles off the coast of Zuma Beach. One of the kayaks has three large holes that probably were punctures made by the teeth of a shark, said Reynolds.

Tamara McCallister, 24, of Mar Vista, was found on Saturday about six miles off Channel Island Harbor in Oxnard by the crew of a sailboat. Her companion, Roy Jeffrey Stoddard, 24, of Malibu, is a UCLA graduate student in epidemiology.

Randy Lee, who shared a Malibu beach house with Stoddard, said McCallister and Stoddard had dated for about a year. Both had evening classes at UCLA and frequently kayaked together in the morning. On the day they disappeared, Lee said, they took muffins and coffee out to the beach, had breakfast and then took off for a short trip. They planned to paddle to Paradise Cove – about one and a half miles away – and return.

"Roy knew there was a slow leak in his kayak, so there's no way he was planning on going any further than the cove," Lee said. "It was just a short trip and they did it all the time. Roy wasn't a reckless guy and he wouldn't do anything that would put himself in jeopardy. So I really think this shark business took place around here and the currents took them up the coast."

Stoddard "really knew the ocean", said Lee. He was

an experienced scuba diver and surfer, and had been kayaking more than five years. After graduating from Pepperdine University in 1987 with honours, Stoddard, whose family lives in San Jose, entered graduate school at UCLA. He had recently applied to medical school, Lee added, and had just received his first acceptance letter.

McCallister moved to Los Angeles from Portland, Oregon, in September to study for a master's degree in public health at UCLA, according to her mother, Linda McCallister. She had spent time in Africa and had wanted to go back there "to help people". The mother, who said she last saw Tamara at Christmas, called her daughter "an outdoors type". She said Tamara and Stoddard "took a liking to each other" because of their mutual interest in the outdoors.

Laverne Dye, who had rented a room to McCallister in her Mar Vista home, said she was an experienced kayaker, was extremely fit, and swam or ran every day …

Los Angeles Times, 31 January 1989

CALIFORNIA, USA, 1989
The search continued on Tuesday for the missing companion of Tamara McCallister, while news of her violent death stunned classmates and faculty members on the UCLA Westwood campus.

Members of Roy Stoddard's family were arriving at his Malibu home still hopeful that he would be found alive, even though it has been more than five days since he set out from Malibu on a short morning kayaking excursion. "My brother was an expert in the water and, if anybody can survive, he can," said Rod Stoddard, who said he planned to embark on his own boat to search for his older brother. "I'm going to find him."

Two Coast Guard boats and a helicopter are scouring

the coastline between Ventura and Malibu for signs of Stoddard, whose kayak was found on Friday about five miles off Point Mugu. The kayaks had been lashed together, a common practice when kayakers stop to rest or swim. One of the kayaks had three large holes, probably put there by the impact of a great white shark, authorities said.

McCallister's body, found on Saturday about six miles off the Ventura County coast, was identified on Monday. Authorities speculate that her body drifted north with the current ...

Rod Stoddard said that his brother Roy had taught him to surf when he was a child, coaching him to stay calm when the waves grew frightening. "We both have tremendous respect for the ocean and the environment. You can never underestimate the powers of the ocean."

Tom Myers, a friend and neighbour of Stoddard, described him as a careful and skilful outdoorsman who was as fit as a professional lifeguard. The shark attack, Myers said, had to have happened "within sight of shore. They wouldn't have gone outside the kelp beds. They're too smart for that."

He and Stoddard had gone scuba diving together, but had never been concerned about shark attacks, Myers said. "The possibility was always very remote. It's like going snow skiing and worrying about the wolves."

Los Angeles Times, 1 February 1989

TUSCANY, ITALY, 1989
The shark hunt is on. In the usually peaceful waters off the coast of Tuscany a small army of amateurs and professionals are searching for a twenty-foot killer shark that last week devoured a scuba diver, Luciano Costanzo, aged forty-seven.

The shark was seen by two people as it attacked its victim. They both identified it as a white shark, of the same family as the star of the film *Jaws*. Signor Costanzo was diving to examine undersea electricity cables in the Bay of Baratti, near Piombino. On a small motor-launch was his son, Luca, and Signor Paolo Bader, a friend. They say the shark attacked several times and then dragged its victim underwater. A search later found only small pieces of the body and torn fragments of his wet suit.

The actual hunt is without spectacular heroics. A police launch is searching with an underwater television camera, but it has a range of a couple of yards only.

Yesterday a shark cage was finally obtained and frogmen of the fire brigade are being slowly towed around in it. They also hope to find further remains of Signor Costanzo. His friends and colleagues have been trying to search for the shark themselves by diving normally, but have been stopped by the police.

Signor Carlo Gasparri, an expert diver who was once world spearfishing champion, is using a giant "mousetrap" baited with a dead sheep and claims that, if the shark is still around, it will not escape. He is also using huge steel fish-hooks with live fish as bait on a vertical line chained to anchored buoys.

As the hunt continues, the waterfront of the sleepy village of Baratti is becoming crowded with visitors. At the weekend small groups and families came with sandwiches and binoculars as the weather became unseasonably warm. There was not a single scuba diver to be seen.

The Times, London, 6 February 1989

TUSCANY, ITALY, 1989

Some of the anchored, baited hooks placed in the sea to catch the twenty-foot great white shark being hunted off the Tuscany coast have been torn from their moorings, it was discovered yesterday. In the hunt for the shark that killed a scuba diver last week, police divers have found the victim's air-tanks, his face mask and his ballast belt. The lead weights on his belt showed clearly the shark's teeth marks.

A number of residents along the coast between Piombino and San Vicenzo have claimed sightings of the man-eater before and since the attack.

The Times, London, 7 February 1989

TUSCANY, ITALY, 1989

The hunt for the man-eating great white shark off the coast of Tuscany has developed into a confused free-for-all involving the Italian Coast Guard, the Carabinieri, the fire brigade, a number of helicopters and amateur "avengers" who want to dive with anti-shark guns.

The normally placid waters of the Gulf of Baratti are being chopped up by hovering helicopters and cruising launches. The search for the remains of Luciano Costanzo was officially called off two days ago after recovering only some of the victim's equipment and a few small fragments of flesh. But the search for his killer, said to be twenty-five feet long, has begun in earnest. Until yesterday only baited hooks and a kind of giant steel mousetrap, using a dead sheep as bait, had been used so as not to obstruct the search for remains.

The official co-ordinator of the hunt is Signor Carlo Gasparri, an expert diver. "There is no need for helicopters," he said. "Sharks are hunted with baited hooks and that's all. The rest is all nonsense."

Clearly, however, several would-be shark killers do not agree and, as they hunt their quarry, curious onlookers can be seen all around the bay, keeping watch with binoculars, cameras and sandwiches. The authorities receive several reports of sightings every day from different points on the coast.

It seems the whole of Italy has suddenly become shark mad. Most newspapers have reporters permanently on the spot and print interviews with shark experts around the world. Each television news bulletin has the latest report on the situation, and it is not unusual to hear housewives, barmen, barbers and taxi drivers giving impromptu conferences on the migratory and feeding habits of Carcharodon carcharias, the lethal great white.

Off the Tunisian coast fishermen reportedly caught a twenty-one-foot thresher shark on Saturday. The species has not been seen there for thirteen years. The fishermen cut open their prize to see if it might have been the wanted fish, but found no such evidence.

The only people not enthralled by the great shark hunt are the inhabitants of resort villages around Piombino. They fear the affair is being overplayed and will ruin the tourist trade this summer.

The Times, London, 8 February 1989

LOUISIANA, USA, 1989

Carl Loe did not have to turn around to know what had happened. Nothing but a shark could clamp down on his leg with that kind of force. He turned anyway and watched as the six-foot sand tiger chomped and chomped again, then twisted its grip as if trying to tear off his right leg.

"When I turned and looked, there was nothing but teeth embedded in my leg," Loe said.

Loe, who was spearfishing on Saturday forty miles

off the coast of Cocodrie, Louisiana, suffered dozens of puncture wounds and lacerations on both legs, as well as muscle and tissue damage. The forty-five-year-old Slidell furniture retailer was rescued by helicopter and treated at Ochiner hospital. Doctors tell him he should make a full recovery, but they are watching out for infections. Survival did not seem so certain for a long fifteen seconds on Saturday on Loe's fourth dive of the morning.

Loe and his partner, Arthur Bukaskey, were more than one hundred feet under water near the floor of the Gulf of Mexico, swimming among the pipes of an oil rig. The pipes offered Loe and Bukaskey an edge in their battle with the swift and strong fish they were hunting. It was comforting to know, Loe said, that, if he speared a big barracuda or an angry amberjack, he could tether his line to one of the rig's pipes and win the tug-of-war with the fish.

Loe said they were not looking for sharks, but sometimes they hunt them as well. They had been under water less than a minute when Loe spotted a shark lurking in the murky water near the bottom. He swam away from it and let Bukaskey fire his custom-made fifty-six-inch spear. Bukaskey's shot was true, and the stunned shark fled. Bukaskey was pulled along for the ride. He did not panic, though. He knew the 150-lb shark would soon tire and he would tow it back to the surface. He got back safely with his prize.

Meanwhile, Loe turned and aimed at a small sheep's head. Seconds after he fired, he felt the clamp close on him. It was a second shark, one he never saw. Loe later theorized that the unseen attacker might have been responding to the distress signals of the speared shark.

He could feel the jaws opening and closing again, trying to get a better grip, mauling his right leg and poking a few stray teeth through his left leg. Using the butt of his speargun, he rammed the nose of the shark again and again.

"My only reaction was to punch him on the nose and get him off," Loe said. It worked. Loe, hoping the shark would not come back "for seconds", swam quickly to the surface, where his fifteen-year-old son, Carl Loe III, worked to stop the bleeding and called for help.

So on Monday, as he sat propped up in his hospital bed, his fishing cap on the nightstand, the life-threatening experience was already beginning to sound like a fisherman's story, with a touch of bravado. Loe stroked his bushy grey beard and considered his future in spear hunting.

"It's just a dangerous recreational sport," said Loe, who hunts most of the fish for food and kills an occasional shark for a trophy. "The statistics [of shark attacks] are so rare and so extreme that I don't think it's going to keep me from diving ... I may be quite a bit more cautious from now on though."

New Orleans Times-Picayune, 20 June 1989

CAPE PROVINCE, SOUTH AFRICA, 1989
A twenty-one-year-old surfer has described from his hospital bed how he survived a nightmare attack by a shark at Mossel Bay's popular surf spot, The Point.

Still badly shocked by his close shave with the jaws of death, Niko von Broembsen of Somerset West is in a serious but stable condition in the intensive care unit of the George Hospital after several hours of emergency surgery. The shark's teeth tore away muscle from Niko's left calf, left upper leg and thigh, and left forearm. The force of the bite exposed bone and broke his forearm.

He was attacked at about 10.45 a.m. yesterday by what is believed to be a great white shark while he and a friend, twenty-two-year-old Adam Harding of Gordon's Bay, were surfing the inside break at The Point.

"I did not see a thing before the attack. Suddenly I was clamped to my board and I could not move," he said. "But I was conscious the whole time. I felt no pain until I reached the hospital. I can remember clearly how it started pulling me under water. I suppose it wanted to take me down so it could eat me, and it let go once and bit again in the same area.

"I saw the shark's eyes and twisted my right arm around, pushing my fingers into an eye. I just kept pushing my fingers in and it let go of me eventually.

"I was close to the rocks at the beach and I moved towards them. There Adam and another man picked me up and carried me to the beach. I knew about everything that was going on around me – I kept on yelling at them to tie tourniquets around my arm and leg to stop the bleeding because I was bleeding badly."

Niko said that, as he was drifting to the rocks, the shark followed and he could see the big dorsal fin in the water behind him. "I was lucky, man. I could have been dead. Adam is my best buddy – if it wasn't for him, I would have been dead now."

Asked if he would surf again, he said: "No way. Well, I don't know. Yes, I'll probably go back into the water. That is, if I can ever walk properly again."

Meanwhile, there might soon be a price on the head of the shark. Mossel Bay Mayor Mr Johan Oosthuizen, said he would suggest his council should offer a reward for the fisherman who landed the huge great white thought to be responsible for this attack and others on ski-boats. However, he added: "I do not believe we should overreact because of the attack. In the past sixty years there have been only three attacks in the area from Little

Brak River to Hartenbos, and this one was the first in twenty to twenty-five years.

None the less the town is abuzz at this latest incident and local fishermen, already on the warpath against the shark because of recent attacks on ski-boats, have surrounded the area with baited buoys and line in the hope of catching the culprit.

Durban Daily News, 23 August 1989

CALIFORNIA, USA, 1989

Larry Stroup, a veteran diver on his first shark-filming expedition, was capturing what he hoped would be dramatic footage. The camera was rolling and a five-foot blue shark – a species not known for its aggressiveness – was banging its snout against the bubble-like lens. Moments later, Stroup was fighting for his life.

"I felt a tug on my arm, and I looked over and his mouth was around my arm," Stroup, 46, recalled on Monday, a day after surviving a rare shark attack off the Channel Islands about thirty-five miles off Santa Catalina Island. "He just wouldn't let go."

Stroup, an Albuquerque real estate developer, smiled cheerfully while recounting the harrowing incident at Harbor-UCLA Medical Center in Torrence, where he is recovering from emergency surgery late on Sunday after being bitten on both arms. Doctors said he may be hospitalized for a week and may suffer at least temporary loss of movement in his right arm, where the shark's teeth ripped through muscles and ligaments. But, as a happy Stroup was quick to point out, it could have been worse.

"Compared to the alternatives, it was a very good event," he quipped. "Right now I couldn't tell you if I will dive with sharks again."

From a wheelchair with an intravenous bottle hanging

above him, a refreshed, pyjama-clad Stroup told reporters there was no obvious reason that the shark turned on him. The attack occurred late on Sunday morning about ten miles north-west of Santa Barbara Island. Stroup was one of several divers aboard the sixty-foot Scuba Lover, a vessel hired out of Ventura Marina for a three-day recreational cruise aimed at observing and photographing the blue shark near a popular diving spot known as Lost Reef.

Members of the expedition – including an experienced shark diver and a veteran marine biologist – conducted many of their observations from within a ten-foot shark cage, but they also ventured outside the protective cage on several occasions to get a better look at the sharks, Stroup said. The practice is routine when viewing blue sharks if there are few of them and they are behaving passively, he added.

On Sunday, during a dive only a few feet below the surface, two senior divers left the shark cage in waters occupied by eight or ten blue sharks, Stroup recalled. At their signal that it was safe, Stroup also emerged from the cage, leaving one other diver behind. Almost immediately, he said, a shark approached him, bumping its nose repeatedly against his video camera. The behaviour was not unusual, so the amateur film-maker kept on shooting his adventurous home movie.

"I had just gotten out of the cage about fifteen seconds earlier," Stroup recalled, "there was nothing to warn us. It was butting its head against my camera, so I can't really say it snuck up on me. What surprised me was when he reached out and grabbed my arm."

Stroup did not feel any pain at first, only a strong tug, he said, but the shark held tight to his right arm. With his camera and his left arm, Stroup tried desperately to free himself from the shark's jaws as blood billowed out of his wet suit.

"All I could see was its snout," the diver said of the shark. "I saw its teeth. They weren't that big, but they looked sharp."

Los Angeles Times, 5 September 1989

CAPE PROVINCE, SOUTH AFRICA, 1989

A Table View diver narrowly escaped death when he was attacked by a shark while spearfishing in Smitswinkel Bay near the Cape Point Nature Reserve yesterday. The diver, twenty-nine-year-old Gert van Niekerk, suffered wounds to his chest and abdomen when the shark – believed to be a great white – attacked him about 250 metres from the beach yesterday afternoon.

Speaking from his False Bay hospital bed last night, Mr Van Niekerk said the force of the shark's attack ripped his diving goggles off his face. "I did not see the shark. The first thing I saw was the water turning brown."

He immediately started swimming to the beach, leaving his spear gun behind. On the beach bystanders applied emergency medical treatment and he was stabilized before being carried over a ridge to the road. "Four guys on the beach treated me and then carried me about 1.5 kilometres. They were very good," he said.

Mr Van Niekerk said he had been diving for the past five years, but yesterday's attack was his first brush with a shark. He had dived at the same spot previously without seeing any sharks. "I'm just glad the shark did not come back."

The attack was the third on divers in False Bay in six years. In October 1987 a Matie student was savaged by an enormous shark near Seal Island while spear fishing, and in 1983 a Springbok spear fisherman, Mr A. Louw, was attacked by a four-metre shark at the same spot. Both men survived the attacks.

Cape Times, 18 September 1989

TASMANIA, AUSTRALIA, 1989

A young Tasmanian surfer survived an attack by a big shark yesterday by jumping off his board seconds before it struck. But quick-thinking Steven Jillett, 17, had to survive almost ten terror-filled minutes in the surf while the 2.7-metre shark first circled him, then followed him to the beach after he had struggled back on to his board.

The attack occurred about eighty metres off the popular surfing beach at Shelly Point, about two kilometres north of Scamander on the east coast at about 2.20 p.m. The shark's teeth-marks on Steven's borrowed surfboard show how close he came to serious injury or death.

Last night, Steven, a boarder at Launceston's Scotch-Oakburn College, relived the minutes that turned a carefree afternoon in the surf with his mates into a fight for survival. Later he telephoned his shocked parents, who recently moved from Zeehan, where his father was a Renison Ltd metallurgist, to Geraldton in Western Australia.

Steven said he feared he would lose a leg or arm when he was floating almost helplessly in the water after the shark first struck.

He had started surfing at about 2.12 p.m. with seventeen-year-old twins Sean and Julian Larby, of nearby Beaumaris, with whose family he was staying. About six surfers were in the water when the shark appeared. Steven said he was lying on his surfboard preparing to catch a wave when he saw a dark shape move past him about one metre to his right and about thirty centimetres below the surface. He first thought it was a dolphin.

The shark circled in front of him, then moved to his left and behind him. It then moved about ten metres to his right before attacking.

"Its fin was up and it was a fair way out of the water," Steven said. "When it was about five metres away I jumped off the board and swam away. It sort of jumped out of the water, latched on to the board, thrashed it around a lot and then it must have turned it around a bit. Then it let go and I was yelling, 'Shark, shark,' at this time. The rest of the guys said, 'Quick get on your board, get on it, it's the safest place to be.'

"I had just been attacked so I wasn't too keen on that idea, but eventually I did. But, while I was in the water, it was just swimming around in between the board and me, just doing circles, and I was keeping as still as possible."

Hobart Mercury, 23 October 1989

WHAT IS A SHARK ATTACK?

That might sound like a fairly simple question with a very simple answer – a shark attack is when a shark bites somebody. Nobody could argue with that, although if we start to think about the nature of shark attacks in order to try to understand why they happen, which is surely the best way to work out how to avoid them, then it's worth thinking about the answer a little longer.

Most attacks on humans, some experts claim, are unintentional – if only to the extent that the shark didn't drift down to the local beach thinking, "I fancy a bite of surfer for lunch today." The shark, after all, has no idea what a surfer is and doesn't have much of a clue about the rest of the human race, either. It has no concept of life outside the ocean. It can't exist on the land. It can't walk; it can't ride a bike; it can't visit a restaurant (except on a plate); it can't even breathe our air. We don't expect to see sharks in our streets, parks or offices and sharks don't expect to see creatures like us in their ocean.

The difference, of course, is that we know what a shark is (albeit that a great deal more research needs to be undertaken for us to understand more about them) and sharks have no way of knowing what we are. Many shark attacks, therefore, may simply be the result of a shark trying to find out what we are and whether it would be wise to eat us. Such incidents are often said to be unintentional attacks on the part of the shark, but they are far from accidental. The shark attack is quite deliberate; only its purpose can be in doubt.

It is often said that a shark, attacking from below, can mistake the outline of a surfer paddling on a board, or a swimmer in the water, silhouetted against the light on the surface, for the outline of a seal. Although some sharks, such as river sharks used to hunting in murky waters, may not have particularly good eyesight, relying on their other senses to locate their prey, research has shown that other species have perfectly good eyesight. The lemon shark, for example, is thought to have far better sight than we do – good enough even to see by starlight. Most sharks are able to see quite clearly what's a seal and what's not but, even if the shark does recognize that you, on your surfboard, are not a seal, it won't necessarily cross you off its menu. Its priority will be to find out what you are and if you are good to eat.

Sharks are masters of survival, and to stay alive in the wild you have to use caution. Taking risks can mean sustaining an injury and the odds of an injured creature surviving in the wild are pretty slim. To determine whether you are a meal or a menace, the shark will use all of its senses. Watch a dog in the park. When it sees something that looks interesting or picks up the scent of something that smells intriguing, it closes in on the target to take a closer look. It might circle round, move in for a close-quarters sniff, then give it a quick lick. Finally, if all seems well, the dog picks up whatever it has found in its mouth and if it still feels no ill effects, all of its senses telling it that this is food, it will gobble it up. The shark isn't really so very different, but when it moves in to close quarters to take an investigative bite, the results can be catastrophic for its target.

If the shark gets a mouthful of boat rudder or kayak keel, it may well back off – such things do not make nutritious meals, even for sharks. If it gets a mouthful of you, the result might well be the same, with the shark retreating to a safe distance. It may want to consider whether what it has just tasted is proper food. Think about how you would react to tasting something out of the ordinary. Because you have been brought up eating cooked meat – beef, pork, lamb or chicken – taking a mouthful of raw venison or, although it is considered a delicacy in Greenland, decomposing fermented shark flesh will set off all of your natural alarm bells. Your senses will tell you to leave it well alone as it could be bad for you. When the shark gets a taste of you, it immediately recognises that you are not like a nice blubbery seal or an oily tuna. You won't provide it with much nutrition at all and you might even be bad to eat, so it leaves you alone. Unfortunately, that exploratory bite it has taken may have removed your leg or cut you in half. The fact that the shark has decided you are not worth eating explains why human remains and severed limbs are often washed ashore some time after an attack.

The shark may also leave you mortally wounded in the water because that is the way that it deals with its prey. A swordfish bitten by a shark has a serious weapon with which it can fight back if it gets the chance. Even though it has no hope of survival, it could cause the shark a nasty injury as it thrashes around in its death throes. The initial bite from a large shark may be fatal but the shark's tactics are to retreat to a safe distance, wait for the injured creature to grow weak enough that it no longer poses any kind of threat, then close in again for the kill.

There are no hard and fast rules, but the pattern of shark attacks on humans tends to suggest that the shark is either investigating potential prey or disabling its victim so that it can be devoured in safety shortly afterwards. Having no knowledge of human behaviour, the shark has no way of knowing that, while it waits to make sure that all the fight has gone out of us, we can escape by getting on to a boat and that our friends will help us to get out of the water. Tuna or even seals don't behave that way.

From the shark's point of view, therefore, there are a couple of different ways to explain the nature of shark attacks, but to answer the question "What is a shark attack?" we should also look at the way we categorize such attacks.

No city or holiday resort with a thriving beach culture or any kind of tourist trade helping to keep its economy afloat likes to admit that it has a shark problem. It's bad for business. Lots of people might want to come to see sharks in the water, but far more would rather be able to swim and play with their children in the sea without the thought of sharks nipping at their ankles. Sharks are there, however, to a greater or lesser degree, off the coast of every country in the world where it is warm enough for holidaymakers and watersports enthusiasts to want to get their feet wet. The authorities in such places can't deny the sharks' presence, but they can deny that they pose any risk to visitors using the beach. In most cases, they are probably right. Swimming off most popular holiday beaches you are in more danger from motor boats, jet skis or good old-fashioned cramp that leaves you helpless in the water than you are from a shark attack. Yet there are still around 100 shark attacks every year worldwide. Scores of shark attacks are listed in this book but, even in a book twice this size, you would not be able to record the details of all of the shark attacks that have ever been reported around the world. Some attacks – the ones which, on paper, appear to be less serious – have not been included. Historically, such "less serious" attacks may never have been recorded at all, but in recent times the global nature of news media with TV, radio, internet sites and social media combining to make any kind of news story available to a wider audience than ever before, means that anything that might be construed as a shark attack becomes a matter of record.

"Less serious", of course, is not a category into which anyone who has been the victim of a shark attack would choose to place themselves. Only they know the agony they felt when the shark shredded an ankle or took a chunk out of a calf. Only they know the terror they went through when they realized what was happening and struggled desperately to get back to the beach, leaving a red, cloudy trail in the water. Only they know the horror of looking round, dreading the sight of a fin slicing its way through the sea towards them. Then there is the trauma of medical care and surgery, the months of physiotherapy required to regain the use of an injured limb and the scars that, even after the wound has healed, will remain forever, a constant reminder of the day that a shark tried to decide whether they were good enough to eat. "Less serious" doesn't really do justice to their appalling experience.

To anyone charged with maintaining the prosperity of a beach resort that relies on the tourist trade, however, avoiding the stigma of being considered a shark-attack hot spot is a major priority. Dismissing a shark attack as not being "serious" is a huge temptation. Protecting local commerce is what *Jaws* was all about and it's not simply a fictional phenomenon. When an injured great white shark was washed ashore and died at Tossa de Mar in Spain in 1992, it was spirited away by the police in the dead of night and flung in an inland rubbish dump. It was later retrieved for study, but the incident demonstrates the depth of the shark paranoia that afflicts local authorities responsible for popular tourist resorts. In the unwavering spotlight of the twenty-first century's media cameras, that attitude may, perhaps, be changing.

When a great white was spotted off Savinosa beach a few miles down the Spanish coast at Tarragona in 2007, the police closed the beach until they were sure it was safe for holidaymakers to venture back in the water.

The two Spanish examples of extremely rare great white sightings in the Mediterranean hopefully demonstrate that the attitudes of local authorities are changing, but there is undoubtedly still an understandable tendency to play down shark attacks to try to quell any kind of panic. "Less serious" attacks will still be brushed aside as minor incidents and even fatalities have been downgraded to avoid the idea that killer sharks are lurking near popular beaches. Giving the idea that a swimmer has drowned is one way of dismissing the possibility of a shark having killed someone. Swimmers who have gone missing and whose bodies have later been discovered washed ashore or floating in the sea mutilated with bites from one or more sharks have been recorded as cases of "accidental drowning". There are ways for a post mortem examination to establish if wounds are inflicted before or after death but if a body has been in the water for a while, it can be difficult to tell whether it was scavenged by sharks after drowning or if the swimmer was attacked while still alive.

Al Brenneka is a good example of someone who, had there not been several witnesses who saw him being attacked by a shark, might have been classified as an "accidental drowning". Brenneka was surfing off Delray Beach in Florida in 1976 with a bunch of other surfers in the water around him. Having just caught a good wave, he was paddling back out to wait for another one when he felt something grab his right arm. An instant later, he was off his board and underwater. He could feel the sand beneath his feet and still had a fingertip grip of his board with his left hand, so he kicked off the bottom and wrapped his arm around the board. When he made it to the surface and gulped some air, he blinked the water out of his eyes and looked down to see a large lemon shark with its jaws around his arm.

The shark started "worrying" Brenneka's arm, thrashing this way and that, stripping the flesh down to the bone. Brenneka knew that if he let go of his board to thump the shark with his left hand, he'd be underwater again and would stand no chance, so he kicked out at it as hard as he could. When this had no effect, the nineteen-year-old wrapped his legs around the shark to try to stop it moving around as he was convinced it was going to tear off his whole arm. More by luck than judgement, he managed to clamp his knees across the shark's gills. At that point, the shark let go of his arm and disappeared.

Brenneka had not fought his brief battle in silence. He had been yelling "Shark!" and calling for help, but there was no one there to help him. All of the other surfers had already headed for shore, having spotted several sharks in the water. Lemon sharks are known to hunt in groups and the other surfers were screaming at Brenneka to get back on his board because there were sharks all around him. Sharks had been cruising beneath the other surfers while Brenneka battled to free his arm and one of the surfers had his board "butted". The sharks had followed the others almost all the way in to the beach.

Brenneka clambered back onto his board and started paddling with his left arm. Instinctively, he tried to use his right arm even though he thought the shark had taken it. When he looked down, he could see the arm was still attached, but he couldn't move it. Grabbing it with his left hand, he heaved it onto the board and could immediately see and hear the blood pulsing from a severed artery. Kicking with his feet and paddling with his good arm, he propelled himself towards the beach. A few small waves and the wind helped push him towards the shore but he could feel himself growing weaker by the second. Breathing was difficult and by the time he was within a few yards of the beach, he was losing consciousness. A couple of surfers dragged him onto the sand and within minutes a helicopter was on hand to whisk him to hospital. Al Brenneka was dead on arrival.

Dead he may have been, but Brenneka survived. He was resuscitated several times as the medical team fought to save his life and he spent the next three days in a coma. He underwent surgery, his arm being so badly damaged that it had to be amputated above the elbow, and had weeks of treatment to drain seawater from his lungs. There was, in fact, so much water in his lungs that, had he been in a more remote spot with no one else around and no chance of being resuscitated by a medical team, when his body was eventually recovered the cause of death would probably have been recorded as "accidental drowning". The fact that the water was in his lungs because the shark had dragged him under would not have been apparent if no one had seen it happen. Sharks scavenging on the body while it was in the water would have made it impossible to tell that he had been attacked while he was still alive. It follows that some cases of accidental drowning where it is assumed sharks have subsequently taken bites out of the body may actually have been shark attacks.

The other thing that should be considered when deciding what actually constitutes a shark attack is the idea that some attacks are provoked and some are unprovoked. If we take "unprovoked" to mean that the victim was simply wading, swimming or surfing, doing nothing to harass or deliberately attract the attention of a shark then, given that all normal, sensible precautions had been taken before entering the water, an unprovoked attack is difficult to avoid. If you don't know the shark is there and have done nothing to antagonize it, you can't be said to have provoked an attack and the only real way to avoid it would have been to stay out of the water altogether.

Provoked attacks, on the other hand, are entirely avoidable. You may not have intentionally provoked the shark. When Joel Bacud jumped into the water off the Philippines in 2008 to check his fishing nets, he did nothing to annoy the shark that attacked him except to have a net full of fish that had attracted the creature. Bacud was simply going about his daily business, but it cost him his life. If we are to be entirely objective, however, we have to regard this as a "provoked" attack. Similarly, Kydd Pollock, who was working on a conservation project at Palmyra Atoll in the Pacific in 2010 and trying to help free a reef shark from some nets, could not have been said to be provoking an attack. The shark bit him in the head and he was lucky to escape with his life. Yet, because he was interacting with the shark, we have to regard this as a provoked attack.

Many sharks are extremely territorial and will not tolerate another large creature, such as a spear fisherman, "poaching" their prey. Spear fishermen, whose catch inevitably wriggles about and bleeds after being shot, are creating exactly the right conditions to attract the attention of a shark. Whether they intended to or not, when the shark goes for them, they have provoked the attack. The most blatantly provoked attacks, however, are invited by shark-curious divers. Sharks are wild and dangerous creatures. It is extremely unwise to go looking for sharks just to get close to them in order to swim with them. Using bait in the water to attract them is surely asking for trouble and even when such underwater shark tours are conducted by experienced professionals, it is still a risky business. Dave Marcel found that out to his cost when introducing shark enthusiasts to some normally docile nurse sharks in Florida. An experienced diver and shark aficionado, Dave had learned that the nurse sharks actually enjoyed being petted and encouraged his scuba tourists to stroke them, hug them and even kiss them on the back. Things went horribly wrong for him in 2011 when he went to kiss a nurse shark on the lips and it bit him in the face. He needed cosmetic surgery to repair the damage to his lips in what must clearly be seen as a provoked attack.

Provoked or unprovoked; ignored as not "serious"; dismissed as a drowning; investigative or malicious – a shark attack can be many things but, when all is said and done, the answer to the question "What is a shark attack?" is still covered pretty well by the simplest, most straightforward response. A shark attack is when a shark bites somebody.

SHARK ATTACKS
1990–99

1990

FLORIDA, USA, 1990

Two sneaker-clad human feet were found in the stomach of a shark caught off the north-east coast of Florida, at Mayport.

The Times, London, 25 May 1990

CAPE PROVINCE, SOUTH AFRICA, 1990

A twenty-one-year-old Johannesburg woman died yesterday after being attacked by a shark while diving off Mossel Bay.

Miss Monique Price was diving with her fiancé, Mr Francois Suanepoel, and a friend when attacked about 500 metres from the shore at 4 p.m.

The three had intended to salvage an anchor from a boat and had been in the water only a few minutes when the shark attacked Miss Price about seventy metres from the boat.

She was rushed to hospital in Mossel Bay and died just before 6 p.m. She is reported to have suffered severe lacerations of her upper left thigh and to have lost a large amount of blood.

The last shark attack at Mossel Bay was only nine months ago, when a Cape Town surfer was badly bitten.

Cape Times, 25 June 1990

CALIFORNIA, USA, 1990

An abalone diver was recovering at home yesterday in Santa Rosa, wounded but undaunted after he was attacked by an immense shark in waters off Jenner.

Rodney Orr, 49, was attacked at about 1 p.m. on Saturday by what appeared to be a great white shark as he was diving near some isolated rocks at Russian Gulch Beach. Orr, an electrician and part-time commercial fisherman, said yesterday that he was sitting on a paddle board about twenty-five yards off shore when the shark rammed into the board and knocked him into the water.

Seconds later, Orr said, the shark had his head and neck in its jaws. "My head was in its mouth – I could see the teeth at an angle."

At that instant, recalled Orr, his response was guided by the primitive instinct for self-preservation: he clobbered it with his spear gun. "I resorted to being a cave man and clubbed it. I was beating on him something fierce. I wasn't going to take this sitting down."

The shark let go and Orr got on to his board and paddled twenty minutes back to shore. His only wounds were gashes to his face and neck.

"It was a really frightening experience," he said. "You think you know what is going to happen to you, but then you really don't."

He was flown from the beach by helicopter to Community Hospital in Santa Rosa, where he was treated for moderate cuts to his nose, cheek and neck. Orr speculated that his injuries could have been more serious if he had not been wearing his diving hood, which now has holes in it. He has been a fisherman for more than twenty years and said it was his second encounter with a shark: he barely escaped a similar attack in the 1960s.

San Francisco Chronicle, 10 September 1990

CALIFORNIA, USA, 1990
On a quiet day at the Farallon Islands a great white shark tried to eat scuba diver LeRoy French of Concord. "I could feel his mouth around my body and then he chomped me," French said. "When his teeth bit into my metal air tank, he let me go."

Last fall, also at the Farallons, a giant shark grabbed diver Mark Tiserand of San Francisco by the leg and dragged him off, as if looking for a quiet spot for a meal. "He was swimming off with me so fast I could feel the water rushing past," Tiserand recalled.

Last week, twenty-five yards off the beach near Jenner, Rodney Orr of Santa Rosa was knocked off his paddle board, then got a close look at some pearly whites. "My head was in its mouth, I could see the teeth."

Episodes like these are making the Bay Area coast the shark attack centre of the world. A search through this paper's files reveals there have been more than fifty shark incidents recorded off the Bay Area alone, though most receive little attention in the media. French, Tiserand and Orr all survived by fighting off their attacker. French and Tiserand had their lives saved when they were airlifted by helicopters to hospitals for emergency surgery. French ended up with a scar that runs four feet down his side, Tiserand with shark teeth souvenirs that doctors removed from his leg. Orr just about had his head bitten off, but escaped with big gashes around his left eye and neck. The shark lost interest when Orr clubbed him with his spear gun.

Waters off the Bay Area coast have sharks of mind-boggling size. In one fifty-minute period at the Farallon Islands, scientist Peter Klimely of Scripps Institute chummed up and tagged three different great whites that were all seventeen feet long. A few years back, at Ano Nuevo State Reserve in San Mateo County, a shark measuring nineteen feet and weighing an estimated 5,000 lbs washed up on the beach. That is as big as the one in the movie Jaws.

After a career of studying sharks, scientist John McCosker of the Steinhart Aquarium in San Francisco has identified the zone where the attacks are most common. "I call it the Red Triangle," said McCosker, who has travelled throughout the world to study man-eaters. The Triangle is bordered by Ano Nuevo to the south, the Farallon Islands twenty-five miles out to sea to the west and Tomales Bay to the north.

Both Ano Nuevo and the Farallons are breeding grounds for elephant seals, and the young 200-lb pups make perfect meals for the big sharks. The mouth of Tomales Bay, meanwhile, is believed to be a breeding ground for great whites.

Anywhere near the Triangle it may be foolish to spearfish, dive for abalone, surf, swim or kayak. Yet these sports remain popular because months can go by without an incident – and also because the history of danger is unpublicized. Yet the attacks just keep happening. In January a shark knocked surfer Sean Sullivan of Pacifica off his surfboard, leaving bite marks in the board. Sullivan reportedly escaped by getting back on his board and surfing into the beach with the shark chasing him.

I never gave the idea of a shark eating me any thought until a fall day about ten years ago. I had arrived at Pigeon

Point light-house, where there are a few secluded coves near by that are ideal for body surfing, but this time there was a crowd at the beach. It turned out that an abalone diver had just been bitten in half and killed at the exact spot I was planning to swim that day.

Since then there have been many other episodes. While fishing at the Farallon Islands with Abe Cuanang, the boat anchored, our depth finder was reading the bottom as 90 feet deep. Suddenly it was reading 65 feet, then 50 feet. It made no sense.

Then, all at once, it did make sense. "It's the Big Guy," Cuanang shouted. The Big Guy in this case was a great white so large under the boat that it was registering as the bottom of the ocean on the depth finder.

The same week Ski Ratto of Pacifica was fishing in his seventeen-foot Boston Whaler when he sensed "something was looking at me". Ratto looked behind him and a great white four feet across at the head, possibly longer than the boat, was on the surface, and it was indeed looking at him. "I started the engine and got the hell out of there."

Ever since these episodes I have not been one to dangle my legs over the side of the boat or body surf, abalone dive or anything else that means being in the water with the Big Guy. As long as other people do, it is inevitable that every once in a while someone will be attacked by a shark.

San Francisco Chronicle, 16 September 1990

1991

HONG KONG, 1991

Eight beaches in the Sai Kung area are expected to remain closed today after an elderly woman was killed yesterday by a shark. The attack, the first of its kind in twelve years, is believed to have been made by a tiger shark.

As a marine patrol launch combed Sai Kung waters yesterday looking for any unusual movement, there were two other reports of alleged shark sightings at the same beach. The gazetted beaches were closed by the Regional Services Department (RSD) after a "large tiger shark" allegedly savaged sixty-five-year-old Yeung Tam-ho while she was swimming off Silverstrand Beach.

Following the death, red flags were hoisted at the eight Sai Kung beaches and signs warning swimmers of shark-infested waters were put up.

The senior fisheries officer with the Agriculture and Fisheries Department, Dr Paul Mak Mo-shun, believes the attack may have been by a tiger shark more than three metres long. Dr Mak identified the species after studying photographs of the dead woman at Sai Kung police station.

"Judging from the photos, I cannot think of any other animal that could cause injuries like that," he said. "Her leg was cut off in one bite – it must have been a very big fish."

The woman, who also suffered serious abdominal injuries, disappeared while swimming with a friend outside the restricted area off Silverstrand Beach, near Hung Hau, in Port Shelter. She was a strong swimmer who used the beach regularly, friends said.

A police spokesman said her companion, a thirty-five-year-old man, saw a "large grey fish" swim past him at about 6 a.m. "He spotted the fish and thought it might be a shark and swam back to shore, but without warning his friend. On the way back to the shore his friend disappeared under the water without making a sound."

The man phoned rescue services and at 7.20 a.m.

a Marine Police launch discovered the woman's body. She was certified dead on arrival at United Christian Hospital in Kwun Tong.

South China Morning Post, 9 June 1991

HONG KONG, 1991
Closure of nearly half of Hong Kong's forty-one public beaches followed the recovery of a mainland Chinese fisherman's body, a government spokesman said on Saturday.

The body of the Chinese fisherman was found floating in the waters off Saikung, on the north-eastern Kowloon peninsula on Friday with his right arm severed from what is believed to be a shark, police stated.

An elderly woman died from a shark attack in the vicinity on 8 June. In addition to those local beaches, eleven other public beaches on the southern coast of Hong Kong island have been closed for the weekend with warning signals being hoisted after several sharks were sighted there.

Agence France-Presse, 29 June 1991

CALIFORNIA, USA, 1991
Two days after a great white shark bit him, a thirty-two-year-old surfer sat in a wheelchair and calmly described how he fought off the giant fish and swam to safety off the coast of Santa Cruz County.

"I vaguely recall trying to pry his jaws loose," a relaxed Eric Larsen said at Dominican Santa Cruz Hospital. "I hit him as hard as I could. The next thing I could feel was being pulled by the leash on my board. I got on my board and started to paddle for shore. I could sort of see a blood trail and I thought uh-oh, this isn't so good. I could see the blood spurting out on the left, so I clamped it."

Larsen was attacked on Monday morning while surfing with his brother Nick about eight and a half miles south of the Ano Nuevo State Reserve in Santa Cruz County.

After fighting off the shark, Larsen remembered first aid techniques he had learned while working on a ski patrol in Montana: he applied pressure to the artery on his arm to slow the bleeding. He had the strength to struggle to shore because he had been training for canoe races and had been paddling outrigger canoes every day this summer. As he approached the shore, a wave carried him on to the beach. He crawled out of the water and started yelling. The whole ordeal lasted about half an hour.

"It was so fast that I didn't get scared until I hit the beach," he said, with both arms and left leg bandaged. "It didn't feel all that painful."

Ben Burdette, a sixteen-year-old surfer, heard Larsen's cries, found him on the beach and phoned a bakery where he works to tell his boss to call for help.

Burdette's mother, Michelle Tummino, dashed to the beach. "Larsen told me where the main artery was and where to hold it," she said. "He told us his leg was getting cold and he told us to hold his foot up. We were joking and laughing to keep him conscious. I was afraid he would go under and I wouldn't know what to do."

San Francisco Chronicle, 4 July 1991

SANTA MARGHERITA LIGURE, ITALY, 1991
The Italian Riviera authorities have banned swimming at the height of the holiday season after a shark attacked a waterbed. Nobody was hurt. Greenpeace said the sighting had sparked unjusfified hysteria, leading to "a senseless monster hunt".

Reuters, 2 August 1991

TUSCANY, ITALY, 1991

Shark fever has taken hold of the beaches of southern Liguria and northern Tuscany after a woman was attacked on Tuesday, while paddling her canoe off Portofino.

Ivana Iacaccia, aged forty, was left frightened, but unhurt, after managing to swim ashore while the shark savaged her canoe. Subsequent sightings of sharks by the Coast Guard and tourists in small boats have, however, kept shark fever high.

A shark hunt, led by Antonio Alati, a rear admiral in the Coast Guard service, is now under way. "We will try to kill the shark with the weapons that equip our control boats," he announced. While Coast Guard launches and light aircraft patrol the water south of Genoa, dozens of would-be shark hunters are taking to the sea, armed with everything from makeshift harpoons to sophisticated fishing tackle. Those intercepted by the Coast Guard or the police are being advised to keep out of the way. The sightings – three on Tuesday and one on Thursday – report a shark between twelve and sixteen feet long, large by Mediterranean standards. Most beaches have put up red flags to warn swimmers, mothers are keeping an eye on their children, and bathers, sailors and windsurfers are scarce.

The national press has given ample space to the attack and hunt. The serious *La Stampa* newspaper of Turin even carried the report on its front page. This may, of course, be a reflection on the lack of substance in the recent, supposedly important rumblings in Italian politics.

Shark attacks in the Mediterranean are relatively rare. About thirty have been recorded this century [up to 1974], of which thirteen were fatal. Seven of these took place off Italy, and the most recent was in 1989 in the Gulf of Baratti, when a scuba diver was attacked. Marine biologists from Genoa University are examining the remains of Signora Iacaccia's canoe. Some believe the shark was a smeriglio, a native of the Mediterranean which rarely becomes aggressive.

The Times, London, 3 August 1991

SOUTH AUSTRALIA, AUSTRALIA, 1991

An experienced diver told yesterday how he heard a "thunderous roar" when his diving partner was taken by a shark off Aldinga Beach. Off-duty police officer Mr Dave Roberts watched in horror underwater as the shark he estimated was four metres in length careered past him thrashing its head about.

"I could not see him, but I knew the shark had my buddy," Mr Roberts said. "The thunderous noise was so loud I couldn't hear anything else."

A police spokesman said the dead man "had no warning. He was literally taken in one big grab."

The dead man, 19, of One Tree Hill, was a student at the University of Adelaide and was the ninth person to die in a shark attack in South Australian waters. Police have not released his name.

The shark, which Mr Roberts believes was a white pointer [great white], took the young diver about 350 metres off Snapper Point, the main look-out at Aldinga Beach, at about 3 p.m. yesterday. The man was diving with a group of other students and members of the Adelaide University Skindiving Club in eighteen metres of water at a popular skindiving spot called the Drop Off. Three other people, including Mr Roberts, were in the water in the vicinity of the tragedy, but no one else was attacked. Four others who had been part of the diving group had climbed aboard their boat minutes earlier.

By nightfall yesterday police had recovered the dead man's air tank, his diving finds and a small part of his body. The search was called off at dark, but will resume at first light today. The tank's rubber hose, which led to the mouthpiece, was severed.

Mr Roberts, a senior constable in the police prosecuting branch, said the group was on its second dive of the day and he and his "buddy" (a diving term for partner) were returning to their boat when the shark struck.

"We were heading back to the boat, which was not far ahead of us, when I looked back at him and everything was all right," Mr Roberts recalled. "I turned back and went down to have a look at this colourful rock, and then suddenly heard this thunderous noise. I turned again and saw the shark. It was close to me and it was thrashing its head around. The noise was very loud. It was like a boat crashing over waves on top of you. The whole bottom was dusted up. The shark kept thrashing from side to side. I couldn't make him out clearly, but I knew he was there. I hung around and took a defensive position behind the rock and it moved away. It came within one and a half feet of me as it went past. It didn't look at me. It just took my buddy first – just dragged him past me as I was behind the rock. It was totally unexpected – you just never see them out there. I don't know if I'll dive again – this scared the life out of me."

Yesterday's dive had lasted about twenty minutes before the attack and had followed fourteen other dives by about thirty club members who were spending the day at Aldinga Beach. Ben Petersen, 18, of Aldgate, was first back to the boat and had helped three others into it when he suddenly heard screaming. "It was Dave Roberts screaming out 'Shark', so I pulled the anchor up and we drove the boat over to him," Mr Petersen said.

"A tank, fins and other diving equipment floated by. We got Dave into the boat and he was saying a four-metre shark had come up and grabbed his mate."

Veteran Mr Rodney Fox recalled last night how he was attacked in the same place in 1963: "It's an interesting place to dive – lots of fish gather there near a big drop off the reef." Mr Fox had been defending his title as S. A. spear fishing champion when a white pointer hurled him through the water. He escaped after gouging its eyes and snout. Once he reached the surface he realized his chest was badly mutilated. Although he needed eighty-seven stitches, Mr Fox became fascinated with white pointers and continues to research them. Mr Fox continued with his sport and became involved in the making of several shark-attack movies, including Jaws, the Emmy-award-winning Mysteries of the Sea, and the South Australian Film Corporation's Caged in Fear television special. He is also a consultant to the Cousteau Society.

Adelaide Advertiser, 9 September 1991

CALIFORNIA, USA, 1991

With bandages hiding deep tooth marks, a lucky surfer yesterday talked about the horror of staring into the eye of the great white shark that had him captured in its jaws.

"It was only a split second, but it was very terrifying," said John Ferreira, a thirty-two-year-old machinist who was recuperating yesterday at Stanford Medical Center. Looking tense and grim, with his elbow swathed in bandages, Ferreira still mustered a few jokes as he told the story of the vicious encounter which could have cost him his life.

The attack occurred about 8.15 a.m. on Saturday as Ferreira was surfing 150 yards off the shore of Scott Creek, near Davenport, in Santa Cruz County. "I had just paddled into the line up, the take-off point on the waves," he said. "I was just about there and all of a sudden it felt like someone had dropped a Volkswagen on my back. The first thing I saw six or eight feet under water was its eyeball on the side of its face shaking in the furious manner they do."

Ferreira, of La Selva beach, Santa Cruz County, swam back to shore, where friends applied a tourniquet to his arm and stopped the bleeding by applying pressure to his back. He was flown by air ambulance to Stanford Medical Center.

The shark had apparently taken Ferreira and his surfboard in its mouth, the upper jaw closing down on Ferreira's arm and back, and the lower jaw closing upon his surfboard. "The surfboard saved my life," he said.

If it had not been for the surfboard, doctors believe that Ferreira would have lost his left arm and possibly suffered puncture wounds in his chest. Ferreira emerged from the incident with relatively slight injuries, suffering cuts and deep puncture wounds shaped like a crescent on his back. His wounds took an hour of surgery and about 100 stitches to close – far less time than the ten hours of surgery needed to repair the damage to another surfer, Eric Larsen, who was attacked in July also near Davenport. Unlike Larsen, who considered the attack a positive experience, Ferreira called it "the most negative experience of my life".

The attack appears typical of what some shark experts call the great white shark's "bite and spit" feeding strategy. John E. McCosker, director of San Francisco's Steinhart Aquarium, in Pacific Discovery magazine recently reviewed great white shark attacks and concluded that the huge fish usually inflict single, large wounds on prey such as seals and sea lions.

Ferreira does not blame the shark for mistaking him for a tasty seal because of his wet suit, but he said he is not ready to forgive the estimated fourteen- to eighteen-foot animal. "Last night I started thinking about it, and I woke up with a cold sweat and a tear in my eye," he said. "I could take a gun to his head and shoot him. It's an eye for an eye in this world."

San Francisco Chronicle, 9 October 1991

HAWAII, USA, 1991

A Vancouver doctor who was swimming with a friend while on vacation in Hawaii says that she tried to fight off a 4.5-metre Pacific tiger shark with a piece of driftwood minutes before her friend was attacked and killed.

Maui County police Sergeant Waldo Fujie said that Dr Luise Sourisseau, of West 14th Avenue, Vancouver, and her friend were swimming near Lahaina one morning last week when they noticed a shark which they said was the size of a car swim by. Sourisseau froze and was brushed by the shark, but her friend Martha Morrell, 41, of Lahaina, was attacked and killed after she panicked and started thrashing around in the water.

"When you splash in the water with any wild animal or predator, they could attack," Fujie said. He added that Sourisseau hit the shark with a piece of driftwood which she saw floating in the water, but was eventually forced to swim to safety while it was attacking Morrell.

The two women had been swimming in front of the Morrells' beach front home. A maid saw the attack and made the initial call to the emergency line.

Fujie said that sharks have been known to frequent that area for feeding during the night. Hawaiian police said that it was the first witnessed shark attack resulting in death in the last thirty-three years. "It is rare for this to happen. You could get into a car accident quicker than a shark attack."

The dead woman's body was recovered with limbs missing. Fujie said one shark was instrumental in the attack, but, since then, there have been reports of at least two or three in the area.

May Sourisseau said her daughter is still in Hawaii with friends, trying to recover from the attack. "It's been very upsetting for her." She added that her daughter, who did not want to be interviewed, said that she had initially thought the shark was a dolphin.

Vancouver Sun, 3 December 1991

1992

QUEENSLAND, AUSTRALIA, 1992

The father of shark attack victim Michael Docherty said last night he had warned his son to beware of killer sharks at Moreton Island. "My last words to him on Tuesday were to take care, to be careful of sharks," Mr Bill Docherty said last night as he battled to cope with the loss of his only son.

A massive white pointer [great white] shark savaged Docherty for twenty minutes before being forced to release the dead body in a horrifying attack off Moreton Island yesterday. Docherty, 28, of Palm Beach on the Gold Coast, died when the 4.2-metre shark rammed him and then towed him under water with his board – attached by a leg rope – often still visible above the waves.

His father said: "He was very much aware of the dangers. He told me he saw a bronze whaler shark down at Duranbah just last week." Mr Docherty and his wife Dell said that their son had fallen in love with surfing and fishing as a four-year-old boy. "He was very keen on sport, very outgoing and very healthy. He never smoked and hardly drank, if at all. He loved the outdoors."

Up to fifteen other surfers, including two of Docherty's close friends, watched helplessly from the North Point beach. The shark did not release its grip until Redcliffe police officer Sergeant Phil Sharpe and a holidaying school teacher rushed to the scene in a fishing boat. The two men shouted and revved the boat's engine to frighten the shark away.

Sergeant Sharpe said Docherty's two friends had raised the alarm at about 2.30 p.m., when they ran 150 metres to the tiny North Point settlement for help. When the boat caught up with the shark, the surfboard, with leg rope intact, was still being towed upright through the water.

Docherty had arrived only yesterday morning to begin the holiday with his friends. They had surfed at the same spot for more than ten years. Sergeant Sharpe said the water was clear and he was confident the shark was a white pointer. "It was bigger than the boat. He played with the body for about twenty minutes. I'd say the surfer would have drowned."

Docherty, who remained under water for much of the attack, had been paddling only about thirty metres from shore when knocked off his board. He had been wearing a black wetsuit. A dent was left in the board from the impact of the initial attack.

Twenty-one people have been killed by sharks and another four are presumed to have been taken since records have been kept in Queensland.

Palm Beach surfer Brett Provost, 25, likened the attacking shark to a fisherman "playing with a line". He said he took photographs from the beach as the board was towed through the surf.

Gold Coast surfer John Snip, 18, said he saw at least forty-five centimetres of the shark's dorsal fin above the water. Several times the board was towed backwards and under the water. He said there had been talk of a big white pointer off the point. "I've surfed here for seven or eight years and you see the sharks playing around, but, up until now, they have not been aggressive." He said the sharks seemed to be attracted to the area by the dumping of rubbish from trawlers which constantly lined the beach.

Brisbane Courier Mail, 2 October 1992

HAWAII, USA, 1992

It was little more than a year ago when Rick Gruzinsky, a construction worker from suburban Honolulu, was sitting on his surfboard at dawn at an offshore reef near Laniakea on Oahu's north shore. His friend had caught a small wave in. Gruzinsky was alone.

Or so he thought.

Lurking near by in the blue-green sea was a fourteen-foot tiger shark. It swirled beneath Gruzinsky, then crashed the surface and clamped down on the front of his surfboard, shaking its head and snapping off a large chunk. Gruzinsky vividly remembers seeing the chunk stuck in the shark's open mouth as the startled surfer climbed back on to his broken board and raced back to shore.

Reached the other day at his home in Hawaii Kai, Gruzinsky, 28, said he has not quit surfing, but he cannot shake the memory of that attack on 22 October 1992. Nor can anyone else in and even beyond the surfing community on Oahu.

Gruzinsky's was only the first of three confirmed attacks within a period of two months, including the fatal attack at Keaau Beach Park on body-boarder Aaron Romento, who bled to death after being bitten on the leg shortly after reaching shore screaming for help.

And then there was Gary Chun, who, like Gruzinsky, saw his board snatched and bitten by a large shark while Chun was waiting for a wave near Laniakea. He escaped with minor injuries.

Subsequent sightings and alleged sightings were reported by the dozens last winter as the situation bordered on hysteria, prompting a shark scare of unprecedented proportions and the first comprehensive shark hunts since the early 1970s ...

"According to my records, fifty-eight large tiger sharks were taken around Oahu, so I think we may have made a substantial dent in the population," said John Naughton, a National Marine Fisheries Service biologist and prominent member of the recently disbanded state shark task force. "Obviously there are still some around – but one thing, it seems to have really reduced the number of attacks around Oahu."

Some good seems to have come of the attacks and the subsequent scare. Surfers are more aware of their surroundings and for the most part are using better judgement, not paddling out near the mouths of rivers, where run-off carries dead animals and other debris that sharks feed on, and by not paddling out alone at dusk and dawn, particularly in murky waters, where tiger shark prefer to hunt.

A surfer suffered serious leg wounds after being attacked by a tiger shark last October off Kauai while surfing in murky water near the mouth of the Wallua River ...

Surfers, meanwhile, still are watching the horizon for more than the next set of waves, but are more comfortable knowing there are fewer sharks or "the guys in the grey suits" as they call them.

Los Angeles Times, 9 March 1994

GYOGO ISLAND, JAPAN, 1992

With one bite a shark wiped out this summer's tourist trade on the little Japanese island of Gyogo.

It attacked as Kazuta Harada was gathering shellfish on the ocean floor in his old-fashioned helmeted diving suit. He shouted, "Shark! Pull me up, pull me up!" but, by the time his crew could reel in the air line and intercom connection, there was nothing left. Just the gashed remains of his suit hung on the steel helmet.

Nobody saw the shark during the attack, although it had earlier bumped at the helmet of another diver, who feigned dead. Nobody saw it clearly after the attack either. One grainy photograph of a dorsal fin was the only firm evidence of its existence, but the fear was enough to destroy Gyogo's summer beach holiday business.

The people of Gyogo normally play host to thousands of visitors, who cross from the larger island of Shikoku and from the major cities hundreds of miles away to the north-east. This year nobody is coming, except a few morbid spectators hoping to be in on another kill. According to Japanese experts, the Gyogo attacker was probably a type of blue shark, a species which is found quite frequently off Britain's south-west coasts in September and October. It has never been known to kill anyone in British waters, although it has occasionally attacked boats, and the bad-tempered blue is certainly a confirmed man-eater elsewhere in its wide range.

The Times, London, 24 October 1992

Lemon Shark

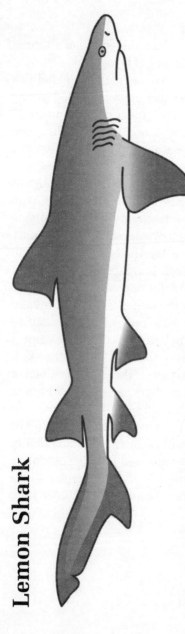

Lemon sharks are so called because of the yellow colouring on their skin which provides camouflage for the young sharks as they grow. Living in shallow water near mangroves until they are more than 12 years old, the yellow colouration helps them blend in with the sandy seabed. Researchers have trained lemon sharks to go through different coloured doors to find food, suggesting that they have good colour vision and tests have shown that their eyes are up to ten times more sensitive to light than ours, meaning that they can probably see by starlight.

Shark Facts

Length: 8 feet to 11 feet 4 inches (2.4 m to 3.4 m)

Weight: 200 lb to 405 lb (90 kg to 184 kg)

Colouring: Yellowish grey upper, white belly

Diet: Bony fish such as catfish or mullet, as well as crabs and crayfish

Pups: Up to 17 pups born every second year

Status: Not under threat

Lemon Shark Range

CALIFORNIA, USA, 1992

John Mark Regan believes that a six-foot Mako shark bit him on Sunday afternoon because it mistook him, in his all-black wetsuit, for a seal.

"In the animal kingdom there is no such thing as an experimental gourmet," Regan, aged thirty-one, a medical technician from Westminster, said three hours after the attack while limping on the boat ramp with his pants leg still bloody. "That shark took one bite and as soon as he realized I was not his usual prey took off."

Regan was not seriously injured in the attack, which occurred about 3.30 p.m. on Sunday 100 feet off the surf line near San Onofre as he snorkelled in fifteen feet of water while two friends fished from the trio's seventeen-foot aluminium skiff.

Earlier, he said, he had noticed something swimming in the water near the boat, but had mistakenly thought that it was a seal.

Suddenly, he said, he felt a pair of jaws grab his right calf from behind. "There was no pain at all. It was very fast and painless."

The shark attack left ten tiny puncture wounds, but Regan refused medical treatment.

Los Angeles Times, 30 November 1992

1993

CARIBBEAN SEA, GULF OF MEXICO, 1993

Two British brothers have arrived in Jamaica exhausted and starving after sharks attacked and damaged their canoe in the Caribbean, forcing them to abandon an attempt to become the first to paddle from Europe to mainland America.

Chris and Stuart Newman, from Middlesbrough, Cleveland, England, said yesterday that they clung to their capsized canoe for four hours in the middle of the night as sharks spun it round. By daylight the sharks had disappeared, but it was another five days before they came ashore on the sixty-eighth day of their attempt to cross from Portugal to Florida. The brothers are now recovering in hospital in Port Antonio, where they are being treated for malnutrition and salt-water boils.

Chris Newman, 32, said yesterday that the sharks were attracted by oil and blood seeping into the sea from a dolphin they caught south of the Dominican Republic on 4 January.

"We ran out of food on 23 December and the dolphin was to have been an excellent source of food. We butchered it and attached it to the canoe, but it attracted two white-tipped sharks," he said.

As one of the ten-foot sharks rubbed against the canoe, the brothers tried to scare it off by spearing it with a harpoon, but it dropped behind the canoe and was joined by another shark. They tore into the dolphin and damaged the canoe as they spun it round.

Stuart, 30, said: "We hung on for dear life. We could not right the canoe because that would have meant falling into the water again, so we waited for about four hours, for daylight, and by then the sharks were nowhere to be seen."

With no food and their navigation equipment destroyed, the brothers realized their record attempt was over. On Saturday they sighted Jamaica and early the next day they came ashore at Manchioneal, on the east of the island. But their ordeal did not end there. Chris said: "Starving and barely able to stand up, we found some coconuts to eat. When daylight came, a fisherman gave us some of his catch, but others tried to steal our equipment. But, since then, we have been well looked after in the hospital."

The brothers' canoe was so small, measuring 19 ft × 33 in. that they could not take enough food for the crossing and had planned to rely on fish, but fishing was so bad that, after their food ran out on 23 December, they radioed a passing vessel for supplies.

The brothers, who are both former oil-riggers, will still go into the record books for travelling the furthest distance across the sea in the smallest boat. However, Chris said he was disappointed not to have made the crossing: "We will try again. We know we can cope physically in the ocean, but we need bigger sponsors."

Members of the brothers' family were less happy to hear they were contemplating another attempt after the failure of their third transatlantic crossing. Stuart's wife, Amanda, said, "I cannot order him to stop, but I will urge him to change tack. He has given me such a fright, but thank God he is alive." Their mother, Ada, added: "They have always been an adventurous pair and I just hope this will calm them down."

The Times, London, 13 January 1993

TASMANIA, AUSTRALIA, 1993

Theresa Cartwright cannot have known what hit her. The keen diver and mother of five children, including quadruplets, died instantly when she was torn in half by a fifteen-foot great white shark off the coast of Tasmania on the weekend.

Terri's husband, Ian, and the couple's children watched in horror from a boat, unable to help, as she was brutally savaged. The family saw the sea turn red after the two-ton creature snatched her. Mrs Cartwright,

34, was last seen clamped in the shark's jaws. Part of her leg and a piece of wetsuit were found.

"The shark went at her like a train – she didn't stand a chance," said her husband, who was on a boat with the six-year-old quads – three boys and a girl – and the family's eleven-month-old baby.

The tragedy happened as Mrs Cartwright, who became a national celebrity when she had the quads, was studying seals at Tenth Island, a rocky outcrop off northern Tasmania. She dived in with two friends, who reached the sea bed without problems, but she appeared to have difficulty with her air supply and was slower to descend. Police said sharks and killer whales were known in the area and Mrs Cartwright was aware of the dangers.

Relatives of Mrs Cartwright, who was from Kent, England, said yesterday they were in shock after hearing of the attack … Mrs Cartwright and her husband emigrated to Australia in 1986. Bettine Cartwright, her mother-in-law, from Canterbury, said: "They were a wonderful couple, and I can't believe Terri has gone. It's just too terrible to think about."

Daily Mail, London, 7 June 1993

NEW SOUTH WALES, AUSTRALIA, 1993
A great white shark that killed an Australian newlywed diving north of Sydney rammed the fishing boat that had netted it on Wednesday and disgorged the remains of the man before breaking free.

John Ford – who had been diving near the tourist town of Byron Bay, about 350 miles north of Sydney – was grabbed by the sixteen-foot shark while under water, a police spokesman said.

The thirty-one-year-old victim's wife, Deborah, who was diving with her husband, was uninjured, but in shock, and swam to the surface, where she was pulled aboard the boat by friends.

Searchers later found the wetsuited torso with a weighted dive belt and a leg with a flipper attached in the sea near by, an ambulance service spokesman said.

The attack came only five days after another great white, called "white pointers" in Australia, killed a thirty-five-year-old mother of quadruplets who had been on a diving excursion off the southern island state of Tasmania.

Fishermen hooked the man's killer at sea, but the shark thrashed violently inside the netting and dragged the boat three and a half miles out to sea. It rammed the boat several times and disgorged human remains before tearing its way free.

Marine biologist and shark specialist Richard Fitzpatrick of Oceanworld marine park in Sydney said the two attacks were coincidental and not part of an emerging trend. He dismissed reports that overfishing had created a shortage of fish and caused sharks to seek other prey.

"White pointers feed on marine animals like dolphins and seals," Fitzpatrick said. "Divers with scuba gear don't look graceful. They would look to sharks more or less like an old or wounded seal, which is the shark's preferred victim."

Chicago Tribune, 9 June 1993

HONG KONG, 1993

Stories about man-eating sharks sell newspapers from Australia to Hong Kong, and the creature or creatures that have devoured two people here in two weeks, and another two years ago, are dominating the colony's front pages.

"We stalk the killer," the Standard, the livelier of Hong Kong's two English language daily newspapers, declared yesterday. The Standard is sponsoring the visit here of Vic Hislop, a tiny Australian who is one of the world's most famous shark hunters. Mr Hislop is a Crocodile Dundee-like character who wears a shark-tooth pendant, shorts and thongs. He has been busy for two days in his boat, flinging ducks and large fish into Silverstrand bay, where Kwong Konghing, a furniture dealer, had his leg and hand bitten off in waist-deep water last Friday by a shark said to be more than eighteen feet long.

The Times, London, 15 June 1993

CALIFORNIA, USA, 1993

A large great white shark attacked an abalone diver off the Mendocino County coast yesterday, half swallowing the man head first before spitting the struggling swimmer out.

David R. Miles, 38, of Eureka was hit as he and three friends were free snorkeling in thirty feet of water near the tiny coastal village of Westport, about four miles north of Fort Bragg.

"It swallowed him head first," a Coast Guard spokesman said in describing the near fatal encounter. "It happened so fast, he never knew what hit him." There was no estimate of the shark's size, but the spokesman added that any shark capable of half swallowing a man has to be considered large.

According to a spokesman at Mendocino Coast Hospital in Fort Bragg, Miles is in fair condition with bite wounds on his face, chest and back. He will be kept in the hospital overnight for observation.

The shark attacked shortly before 3 p.m. and either spit the diver out or loosened its bite enough for Miles to wriggle free. Miles then swam about thirty yards to the safety of rocks, where he was aided by his friends. A Coast Guard helicopter was used to lift Miles up a 200-foot bluff, where he was transferred to an ambulance and taken to the hospital.

Shark attacks are rare along that part of the north coast, according to Coast Guard officials. Most attacks have been further south. In Westport most of its one hundred or so residents were surprised by news of the shark attack. "We live off this ocean," said Marie Fostiak, who works at the Westport Community Store. "This whole town is talking about our shark. Not much else is getting done."

San Francisco Chronicle, 13 August 1993

CALIFORNIA, USA, 1993

A twenty-two-foot great white shark rammed a chartered fishing boat that was heading back from a Sunday outing to Santa Cruz Island.

No one was hurt in the incident, which happened when the shark, estimated to weigh about one ton, circled the vessel Seabiscuit and rammed it three times. "It was a very frightening experience," said one of the participants who wished to remain anonymous.

San Francisco Chronicle, 19 August 1993

HAWAII, USA, 1993

When Scott Shoemaker was attacked at Hookipa, the shark's motivation was probably territorial rather than a hankering for a tasty meal. Shoemaker was sailing at full speed, well away from the shore, when a sudden impact caused his board to spin out, leaving him dangling from his boom with a four- to five-foot reef shark attached to one thigh.

He let go of the boom, pushed the shark off with his hand and crawled on to his board to await the next attack. When none came, he mustered his nerve, jumped in the water, rearranged his rig, water-started and sailed to shore. His friends whisked him off to hospital.

Shoemaker says he felt no pain, but the look of terror in his eyes must have been quite a sight.

Windsurfing, September/October 1993

CALIFORNIA, USA, 1993

After being thrown from her kayak on to the body of a great white shark off the Sonoma coast last weekend, Rosemary Johnson has been taking life's little problems a bit less seriously. "I work in a restaurant where people get uptight if food is two minutes late," said Johnson, 34, who is a waitress in St Helena. "Now, I tell them, 'Hey, it's only soup – it's not even a matter of survival.'"

Johnson said she experienced a spiritual renaissance after a giant shark exploded through the water of Bodega Bay, south of Goat Rock, gripping her narrow vessel and launching her ten feet in the air in front of four other panicked kayakers.

"I thought I had hit some kind of sandy rock," said Johnson, whose feet landed on the shark as it swam underneath her. "Then my friends started screaming and shouting. They were so frightened, and I didn't understand why."

Friends screamed to Johnson to get back into the kayak, which kept tipping over. When Johnson understood a shark was near by, she began to go into shock.

"At first I was too confused to be afraid, but when I kept falling into the water over and over, then I have to say I was scared."

In a rescue which seemed miraculous, friends helped

Johnson get back into her kayak and to shore. The shark, which experts estimated from triangular teeth marks on the kayak to be fourteen to fifteen feet long and 1,000 to 1,500 lbs, never reappeared.

Johnson, who declined press interviews for several days after the attack, said she needed time to rethink her life. "I could have died. It changed my life. When I got back, I looked at my two kids and thought: wow, this is life, this is what's important – have fun, play."

Passing rangers from the Sonoma Coast State Beach checked Johnson for hypothermia, gave her a blanket and asked jokingly if she would like to buy them lottery tickets, she said.

A warning about the attack, the third along the Sonoma coast this year, has been posted for tomorrow along a ten-mile stretch of beach from the mouth of the Russian River to Bodega Head, said Brian Hickey, chief ranger for the Sonoma Coast State Beach.

Johnson said that she intends to continue kayaking and wind-surfing in the ocean, but that she will never again separate from her group. "What is the chance of me getting attacked twice? That would be pretty amazing."

San Francisco Chronicle, 15 October 1993

FLORIDA, USA, 1993

Most parents warn their children about sunburn and the hidden currents when at the beach, but MacIntyre Schaumann's swim turned into an amazing story. He survived a real-life Jaws attack – before he was even born.

Cradling her four-month-old baby son to her, Dawn Schaumann says, "MacIntyre William Shark Schaumaun is going to be a great surfer one day. And he'll have wild stories to tell his buddies."

The wildest happened in October 1993, before

Sharkey, as he is nicknamed, was even born. Dawn, a US champion in the flagracing – speed – division of lifeguarding, was at her lifeguard station on Treasure Shores Beach, Florida. Even though she was six months pregnant and had earlier hoisted red flags on the beach to warn swimmers of the danger of sharks, the twenty-six-year-old plunged into the sea.

She was only 100 yards out when a surge of pain ripped through her body. "A shark hit me so hard, it felt like a huge truck. The sea turned red around me and my first thought was: my time has come. Then I realized my husband Bill was going to lose me and our baby, all because I'd ignored his warnings of swimming that day. He'd seen bait fish close to the shore, a sign sharks were in the surf. I knew my only chance was to get out of that water pretty fast."

As she had been swimming freestyle, Dawn's left hand had covered her stomach and baby at the moment when the shark attacked. But its top jaw crushed her hand, severing tendons, while the bottom jaw bit into her left thigh, close to her femoral artery. Dawn was in incredible pain, but she says, "I swam faster than I'd ever swum before – amazingly, the shark didn't finish us off. I was losing a lot of blood and had to get help."

She rode on a wave and made it ashore, where an elderly couple alerted her lifeguard partner, Chris Henderson. He called an ambulance and her husband Bill, 39, a trained Emergency Medical Technician, rushed to the beach. He says, "I was the first EMT on the scene and took over the treatment from Chris. I shuddered when I saw the bone-deep bite on Dawn's thigh. Her pulse was weak and her heart was racing out of control."

Finally the ambulance arrived and took her to hospital. Barely conscious, Dawn told doctors, "I don't want anaesthetic if it's going to harm my baby." After being given painkillers which would not affect the baby, the jagged teeth marks were trimmed and then the thigh wound was closed layer after layer, needing almost 100 stitches.

For weeks it was touch and go for the baby. Dawn went into false labour many times, including an emergency just before Christmas, when she spent ten days in hospital. But, on 15 January, MacIntyre was born three weeks premature, weighing 71b 1 oz. Bill says, "It's a big relief to have such a healthy baby after all he's been through."

Dawn, who is still being treated for damaged hand tendons, adds, "I can't wait to take Sharkey swimming – I don't want him to develop any complexes about the ocean!"

News of the World, London, 29 June 1994

SOMALIA, EAST AFRICA, 1993

The United Nations yesterday unveiled what may go down as its only success in the Somali capital, Mogadishu – an anti-shark net installed at a cost of £40,000 to protect UN workers on the main beach.

Shark attacks on the beach next to the international airport were unknown when hundreds of US Marines cavorted in the Indian Ocean. But, since the UN took over command of the international force in Somalia last May, three foreigners – a French woman, an American and a Russian – have been killed by sharks attracted by effluent from ships close to the shore.

The French woman was killed when she swam well out to sea, but the last two victims were taken in waist-deep water. Since then the beach has been closed.

Farouk Mawlawi, the UN spokesman in Mogadishu,

yesterday defended the cost of the net and said it would
be left "for the use of the Somalis" when the UN leaves.

The Times, London, 25 November 1993

1994

CALIFORNIA, USA, 1994

A shark ripped open a man's arm in a night club four
miles from the ocean. Doctors needed 100 stitches to
close the wound.

Steve Rosenbloome was bitten on Monday as he tried
to move the four-foot lemon shark and another shark
from the sixteen-foot tank they had outgrown at the
Shark Club billiard hall. The animals were headed to the
Scripps Institute of Oceanography at La Jolla.

"I got bit by a land shark," joked the thirty-three-year-
old fish handler after arriving at the hospital emergency
room.

Associated Press, 9 March 1994

CALIFORNIA, USA, 1994

A young woman whose body was found floating off a San
Diego beach is believed to have been the victim of a shark
attack, lifeguard officials said.

"Large pieces of flesh were missing and we don't know
what else could have caused that type of wound," said
Lieutenant Brant Bass of the San Diego Lifeguard Service.
He said the right leg, most of the left leg and pieces of
muscle tissue were missing from the victim's body.

The victim, who was unidentified, is described as
white, between eighteen and twenty-four years of age,
with brown hair, brown eyes and a butterfly tattoo on her
right shoulder. The body was found in an area known as
Sunset Cliffs on Friday afternoon by a surfer who had

seen a seagull standing on an object in the water and had paddled out to find the mangled corpse.

The area is not generally frequented by swimmers, but its small sandy coves are sometimes used by sunbathers.

Bass said a shark expert called to the scene believed that a great white shark may have attacked the young woman. He said shark attacks were rare in the area, but suggested that those venturing into the waters should be "good swimmers".

Reuters, 16 April 1994

EASTERN CAPE, SOUTH AFRICA, 1994
It was a glorious hot Saturday and the rollers were good. Andrew Carter, one of South Africa's top professional surfers, was lying face down on his board, paddling hard, some 200 yards off East London's Indian Ocean shore, when he was hit from nowhere by the most powerful force he had felt in his thirty-one-year life.

Pinned to his surfboard, he twisted his neck and looked over his left shoulder. "I saw a big, black shiny head," he said. "Its teeth were embedded in my thigh and my board. We were gripped in its mouth like a big sandwich."

The mouth belonged to a great white shark, the marine beast of Jaws fame. Despite the horror of last month's attack, Carter survived, with terrible wounds to his buttock and thigh, which needed 400 stitches.

He was lucky: his friend and fellow surfing freak, twenty-two-year-old Bruce Corby, was attacked by the same shark and died. A third surfer, John Borne, was near both Carter and Corby as the great white first struck.

When Borne saw Carter in the jaws of the shark, he began paddling through the reddened sea towards him. As the shark released its grip to take another bite, Carter rolled off the board – just in time, because the shark clamped its jaws on the board and took a huge chunk out of it. As the great white dived, Carter grabbed the board again and caught a tow from a wave. Borne joined him on the same wave, and they were carried on to the shore.

"I began hollering, 'Shark attack,'" said Borne. "Then I saw Bruce (Corby) coming in and asked him if he had seen what happened. His words to me were, 'John, I've just lost my leg.'"

When Bruce Corby got to the shore, they could see the extent of his injuries. His right leg had been severed at the knee by the great white. His injury was severe, though survivable – but soon afterwards he stopped breathing. Fellow surfers pumped his lungs and tied an emergency tourniquet. But Corby never regained full consciousness and died in hospital several hours later.

Corby was the first person to die from a great white attack in South Africa since the country took steps three years ago to protect the shark from their only predator – man. Anyone who kills a great white in South African waters faces a fine of £10,000 or six years' imprisonment. Neither Corby's death nor Carter's injuries are doing much to slow the march of the great white fan club. Shark expert Craig Ferreira plans to visit Britain next month [August 1994], for instance, to canvass support for great white conservation.

"You can't talk about 'man-eating' white sharks," said Ferreira, who is field officer of Cape Town's White Shark Research Project (WSRP). "White shark attacks on humans are very rare and, when it happens, there's nothing personal about it. It's just doing what nature designed it for and, if you go surfing or diving, you have to accept that you're invading its space."

He will try to persuade diving clubs around Britain to visit South Africa for practical courses on the shark. At the same time, he hopes to persuade groups of enthusiasts and businesses to adopt individual great whites at £1,000 a time – a scheme already successful in Sweden to help finance the work of the WSRP. The project was launched in 1990 by Craig's father, Theo Ferreira, who was once the most renowned white shark hunter in southern Africa. He turned conservationist several years ago, when a fifteen-foot monster he had caught and towed into harbour refused to die despite being stabbed through the gill plates six times and having five bullets pumped into it.

"I realized for the first time, after mutilating it until the whole sea turned red, that we were dealing with a magnificent creature with a mighty will to live. I felt embarrassment and remorse, and I haven't hunted the great white since."

Craig and Theo now spend many weeks of each year on the waves helping research into great whites by tagging them so that individual animals can be tracked.

"No two white sharks ever behave in the same way," said Theo. "You can get very attached to a particular creature. We pat some of them on their heads like big puppy dogs. But you must be aware all the time that you're dealing with the King of the Heap who can destroy your life in one foul blow."

White sharks are extremely rare with only up to 2,000 around South Africa's 1,850-mile coastline. The conservation laws were introduced when scientists realized there were very few breeding adults left – as a result of big-game anglers taking trophy fish whose jaws sell for substantial amounts on the American market.

"In four or five years this legislation will ensure that our great white numbers begin recovering," said Theo Ferreira. "Meanwhile, I'm getting great pleasure and satisfaction in helping counteract shark abuse. You can't wipe out a species just because it occasionally comes in contact with humans."

Andrew Carter, reflecting on his lucky escape, reluctantly agrees. "It would be senseless to go on a hunting spree for that thing, as many people in East London wanted to do. But I obviously feel hostile and angry towards that particular shark. It killed my friend and, whatever the Ferreiras say, they haven't proved that a great white might not get a taste for man."

Sunday Telegraph, London, 31 July 1994

EASTERN CAPE, SOUTH AFRICA, 1994
When it comes to killer sharks Andrew Carter is probably the world's leading human guinea pig. He is the only man to have survived a double attack by a great white shark, which left him seconds from death. In the horrific encounter off the coast of South Africa, Andrew's right leg was bitten to the bone from hip to knee. His best friend died from massive injuries inflicted by the same shark.

The attack was twelve months ago, but in the next month Andrew will attempt to overcome his fear by returning to surf in the same waters in which he was attacked.

The memories of what happened are still vivid. "There was a fabulous clear blue sky and I'd been out surfing for about half an hour with my friend Bruce Corby," he remembers. "Suddenly, I felt this huge bang from behind. I realized straight away it was a shark. The first three seconds were the worst, sheer terror like I could never have imagined.

"I remember its power. It was the most helpless feeling because it had its jaws clamped round my leg and my surfboard, pulling me down into the water. I felt like my bones were being crushed. Its jaws alone were about four or five feet long. I looked down into its face. I think its eyes were probably closed.

"I could feel it was biting me, but I didn't feel much pain because my adrenalin was racing. It was just a crushing sensation and fear of dying because I was so far off shore, about 200 metres, where you're totally helpless, in the shark's domain.

"The guy who was closest to me said I let out one piercing scream. He said he thought the shark was biting me in half because its jaw was right over my leg, and the water all around me just flowed red. He turned round and paddled for dear life and I can understand why. You can't help someone escape from a shark that size."

Carter thought that he was being eaten alive. "It was a feeling of such unbelievable horror. I was holding on to my surfboard with all my might. Then for some reason the shark opened its mouth, probably to get a bigger bite. It went back into the water and leapt forward again. Because I was holding my board so tight, it twisted round and jammed in the shark's mouth, and I started to swim a few strokes away.

"I kept looking back because I was terrified it would come at me from behind. Then I saw it let go of the board and disappear. I knew then that it was coming after me.

"I was too far from shore and losing an enormous amount of blood, so I knew I was minutes away from passing out. In desperation I clawed my way back to my surfboard and, as I grabbed it, I caught the luckiest wave of my life, which carried me in to shore."

He saw two girls sunbathing on the beach and started shouting for help. One girl tore off her clothes, tied them round his leg and packed them into the massive wound.

"She was holding my hand all the time. I was very cold and could feel the warmth from her body flowing into me. It was then that I thought I would die and started to see my life flowing past my eyes. My vision went, I could barely hear, but I realized I had no fear of death and was completely at ease with myself."

Andrew's friend, Bruce, was further out and had to come through Carter's blood to escape. None of the witnesses realized he was the shark's second victim until they saw him dying.

"A guy on the beach saw Bruce coming in on a wave," Carter says. "He shouted, 'Get out of the water. Andrew's been attacked.' Bruce said, 'I've been attacked too,' but apparently he seemed very normal. Only then did the guy look down at him and see that he didn't have a leg. He grabbed Bruce and pulled him out of the water, and Bruce became totally hysterical. He went into shock and within about two minutes he'd stopped breathing. They gave him artificial respiration on the beach and revived him, but he was brain dead from that moment on and died forty-eight hours later."

Carter had a five-hour operation involving around 2,000 stitches. Every muscle and tendon had to be painstakingly sewed back together.

The champion surfer who has won South African and European titles remembers that only about two inches of flesh held his leg on to his torso. "The attack changed me a great deal," he says now. "It was a big thing to realize I have no fear of death when it comes to it. I used to get very uptight waiting for people when they were late or hanging about for a plane, whereas now I sit back and relax. I feel as though I'm living on borrowed time ...

"Now I have to go back to the place I was attacked to overcome my fear forever. I've been surfing for twenty-two years and only been attacked once. If anything, I think I'm kind of invincible now because I can get away from the buggers."

Independent, London, 29 September 1995

Mako Shark

There are two types of mako shark, the short fin and the long fin. The long fin mako is the larger of the two and is darker in colour. These large sharks are extremely agile, swimming at up to 37 mph (60 km/h) and leaping 25 feet (7.6 m) in the air. Although not as frequently involved in incidents with humans as other sharks, makos have been identified in a number of shark attacks over the years and their size makes them extremely dangerous.

Shark Facts

Length:	9 feet to 15 feet (2.5 m to 4.5 m)
Weight:	10 lb to 350 lb (4.5 kg to 159 kg)
Colouring:	Metallic blue or blue/black upper with white belly
Diet:	Cuttlefish, squid, mackerel, tuna, swordfish
Pups:	Two pups (longfin) at 4 feet (1.2 m) or eighteen pups (shortfin) at 2 feet 4 inches (70cm)
Status:	Both types listed as vulnerable and are protected species

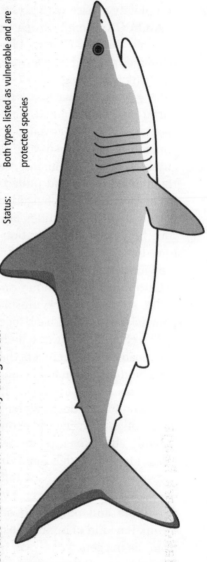

Mako Shark Range

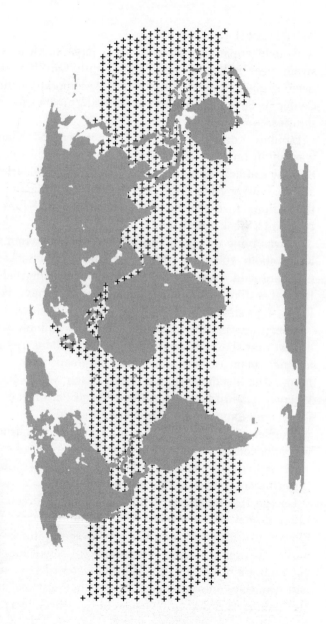

SOUTH CAROLINA, USA, 1994

A woman apparently attacked by a large shark as she swam near Hilton Head Island, South Carolina, was listed in good condition on Monday at Memorial Medical Center in Savannah, where she is being treated for her injuries.

Lioubov Kozarinova, 30, of Gaithersberg, Maryland, was bitten on her right abdomen and left hand during Sunday's attack off North Forest Beach, said her friend and co-worker Alex Grinberg. The two are biologists at the National Institute of Health, who arrived on Saturday to spend a week with friends, he said.

"I was lying on shore and my friend was swimming alone about 200 yards out when the shark attacked," Grinberg said. "She said there was no warning before it hit her like a torpedo." The shark may have been following a shrimp boat working near by, he added.

Kozarinova swam for shore, stunned and unaware at first that she had been bitten, said Grinberg. He and another man rushed into shoulder-deep water and helped the bleeding woman to the beach, where Ralph Wagner, head of the Hilton Head Beach Patrol, radioed for an ambulance and administered first aid.

Wagner said he could not confirm that Kozarinova was attacked by a shark. "I assume it was a fish of some sort, but I've never seen a shark bite," he said, describing Kozarinova's injuries as "severe lacerations".

George H. Burgess, an ichthyologist who directs the International Shark Attack File at the University of Florida in Gainesville, said non-fatal shark attacks are fairly common in Florida, where ten to fifteen occur each year, but are rarer in South Carolina waters. "They have had twenty-two unprovoked attacks, the most recent in 1987, since record-keeping began in the 1800s," he said.

The last thing you might ever see – a great white shark coming straight towards you. This photo was taken by a diver in a protective cage off Dyer Island, Western Cape, South Africa.

This 1778 oil painting by John Singleton Copely shows 14-year-old cabin boy Brook Watson being attacked by a shark while swimming in Havana Harbour in 1749. The shark removed the flesh from Watson's leg before biting off his right foot. Watson survived and went on to become Sir Brook Watson, a successful merchant and politician. He died in 1803 at the age of 72.

Sharks are not normally fussy eaters but this baby bamboo shark at the National Sea Life Centre in Birmingham, England, would only eat tiny mysis shrimps offered to it by hand.

This tiger shark caught in Kaneohe Bay, Oahu, Hawaii in 1966 measured 14 feet (4.3 metres) and weighed 1200 lbs (544 kg).

Surfer Bethany Hamilton lost her left arm to a tiger shark in Hawaii in 2003 when she was just 13 years old, but went on to achieve her ambition of becoming a professional surfer.

The strange and beautiful hammerhead shark swimming off Cocos Island, Costa Rica.

One of the few large sharks to be kept successfully for any length of time in captivity is the whale shark, as seen here at the Georgia Aquarium in Atlanta. The aquarium's whale sharks were caught in Taiwan and would have been eaten if the aquarium had not bought them to exhibit in a huge 6.3 million gallon tank.

A great white shark 'breaches' – leaps out of the water – to take bait on a fishing line in False Bay, South Africa.

The grey reef shark's sense of smell is so finely tuned that it can detect a single drop of tuna extract in 10 billion times the amount of sea water.

A great white showing its sleek, powerful shape, swimming in shallow water off Isla Guadalupe, Mexico.

Burgess said five unprovoked attacks, all non-fatal, have been recorded in Georgia waters since 1917. The most recent occurred in the surf of state-owned Jekyll Island in 1962.

Atlanta Journal-Constitution, 27 September 1994

TASMANIA, AUSTRALIA, 1994
A fisheries lecturer who witnessed a shark take an Exeter mother of five off Tenth Island told a coroner in Launceston, Tasmania, yesterday he did not believe anything could have been done to avoid the fatal attack.

At the inquest into the death of Mrs Therese Yvonne Cartwright, aged 35, Mr Stephen Ayers told the coroner Mr Zygmunt Szramka he did not believe there were defensive measures against shark attack.

He did not know if diving near seals or diving apart from a group increased the risk.

The coroner was told that eight adults and six children left Inspection Head on the Australian Maritime College vessel Riveresco. When the group reached the Barrenjoey fur seal colony, Mr Ayers, another experienced diver Josephine Osborne and Mrs Cartwright, who had not dived for eighteen months, left the boat.

Mr Ayers said in an affidavit that he was asked by Mrs Cartwright's husband to take special care of his wife.

"I still wasn't on the bottom when I looked around the second time and the (four-metre) shark was there," he said.

CSIRO shark biologist John Stevens said in his affidavit that white sharks, particularly ones over three metres long, fed on seals and were known to frequent seal colonies.

The officer-in-charge of George Town police, Senior Sergeant Graham Galloway, who headed the search for Mrs Cartwright and was a police diver for eighteen years, said in an affidavit that, in general, a diver would be most vulnerable diving in waters off a seal colony and particularly as the dive party was on the surface preparing to dive for anything up to five minutes.

The coroner will hand down his finding next Monday.

The Mercury, Tasmania, 11 October 1994

CALIFORNIA, USA, 1994

A shark, apparently a great white, killed a commercial diver in the water off San Miguel Island on Friday – the state's first confirmed death from a shark attack in nearly six years.

Santa Barbara resident James Robinson, 42, was treading water near his boat when the shark swooped in for a swift, brutal attack. He had just finished a routine dive to scout for sea urchins and had deposited his equipment aboard his boat. His two crew members were putting away the equipment when they heard Robinson scream – and whirled around to see him drifting unconscious in a gush of blood.

"His right leg was nearly severed and his left leg had puncture wounds on it," said Francis Oliver, a diver who came to Robinson's aid after hearing his crewmates' distress call. "It was pretty gruesome."

A veteran diver, Robinson was attacked at about 9.45 a.m., half a mile off the coast of San Miguel Island, which lies about forty miles west of Santa Barbara. Crew members on Robinson's boat, the Florentia Marie, tried to revive him, but could not find a pulse. A Coast Guard helicopter rushed Robinson to Goleta Valley Community Hospital, where he was pronounced dead of massive trauma at 11.15 a.m.

Neither of the crew members saw the attack, but Coast

Guard officials said they believe Robinson was targeted by a great white shark, a keen-eyed predator that can grow up to twenty feet in length and can sink its serrated teeth through a surfer and surfboard with one swift bite. "They say it's like a bullet – you never see the one that bit you," urchin diver Jeffery Gunning said. "I just hope it went quick for Jimmy."

Before entering the sea urchin business, Robinson had worked for years as a deep-sea diver for an offshore oil rig in the North Sea, near the English Channel. After settling in Santa Barbara, he quickly absorbed the California lifestyle. Deeply tanned with blond curly hair and an athletic build, Robinson loved surfing and diving – any activities which would keep him in the sun or in the water. Gracious and vivacious, Robinson was popular both in the harbour and in the neighbourhood. "You always hear about the good dying young and, golly, this guy was just one of the best," long-time diver Steve Rebuck said. "He will really be missed."

Most professional divers realize that great white sharks haunt the waters around San Miguel Island, where they feast on seals and sea lions, but their lurking presence has not deterred divers from prowling the ocean floor for valuable sea urchins, abalone and lobsters. It is a threat most divers take in their stride. "If you're frightened by it, you have no business being in the business," Rebuck said. "More people are killed by lightning and bee stings than by shark attacks."

Although great white sharks bump, bite and scare several people a year in California, fatalities are rare. No deadly attacks have been confirmed since UCLA graduate student Tamara McCallister was killed by a great white off Malibu in February 1989 ... In a more recent incident, a woman's shark-bitten body was found off the San Diego coast last April, but the county coroner said the victim may already have been dead when the great white gnawed at her body.

To protect themselves from attack, veteran divers usually descend to the ocean floor as quickly as possible. Once on the bottom, they can hide among rocks and shadows. Eventually, however, they must rise to the surface, where their wet-suited bodies are vulnerable. "It's one of the risks of diving," Gunning said. "We become part of the food chain when we enter the water." As a precaution, several divers in northern California have begun to tuck plastic pistols in their wet suits before jumping into shark-infested waters, Rebuck said. But most locals rely on more low-tech survival techniques – when face to face with a great white, they "say three Hail Marys and four Our Fathers," diver Matt Barnes said.

In the waters around San Miguel Island divers have learned to check for sharks by studying the behaviour of the sea lions and seals which carpet the beaches. If the animals look spooked or if any appear mauled, the divers know to stay away. Even the best precautions, however, are not fail safe. Sharks sometimes attack humans out of pure curiosity, marine biologist Gary Davis said, and they sometimes confuse divers in wet suits for sleek seals.

"They spend a lot of time bumping things on the surface and seeing if anything falls off," Davis said. "If it does, they taste it to see if it's something good to eat."

Divers are willing to face such risks in part because the sea urchin business can be quite lucrative. Sea urchin roe is a delicacy in Japan, prized for its rarity, freshness and delicate taste.

Los Angeles Times, 10 December 1994

1995

CALIFORNIA, USA, 1995

A Santa Cruz windsurfer escaped injury when he was attacked by a shark just off Davenport Landing on Friday.

The surfer involved in the 5.30 p.m. attack just north of Davenport, identified as Mike Sullivan, could not be reached for comment on Saturday, but Matt Haut, who works at Haut Surf and Sail in Santa Cruz, said he witnessed the incident, which he termed "pretty hairy".

"I saw this real thrashing, lots of white water spray everywhere," said Haut, who was windsurfing thirty or forty feet from the spot of the attack. "I saw his board being carried upwind and I saw him swimming frantically away from his gear. I knew something was wrong and I sailed up between him and his board. I saw death in his eyes, he was really, really scared."

Although the attacked surfer managed to swim ashore and was not hurt, Haut said, his board was pocked with teeth marks. Ben Christi, who also witnessed the accident, said, "There were teeth marks on both rails of the board, on one side between his rear and front straps, and on the other side near the fin – a span of maybe two feet – that's the mouth span."

"It's definitely a shark bite," said Sean Van Sommeran, executive director of the Pelagic Shark Research Foundation in Santa Cruz, who examined the bitten board and talked with several witnesses. He estimated the animal's size at twelve to sixteen feet.

San Jose Mercury News, 10 January 1995

Oceanic White Tip Shark

Known for the distinctive white tips on its fins, the oceanic white tip is a large, slow-moving shark that has been fished extensively throughout its range with its flesh being eaten either fresh, dried or smoked, its skin being used as leather and its long fins prized for shark fin soup. Although it does not tend to venture close to shore, it is known to have attacked humans who have been involved in shipwrecks, most notably the crew of the USS *Indianapolis* which was torpedoed by a Japanese submarine in the Philippine Sea in 1945 (see Shark Attacks 1940–49).

Shark Facts

Length:	10 feet to 13 feet (3 m to 4 m)
Weight:	125 lb to 370 lb (57 kg to 13.6 kg)
Colouring:	Bronze or bluish grey upper with yellowish white belly
Diet:	Barracuda, marlin, tuna, squid, mackerel
Pups:	Up to 15 pups born at around 2 feet (60 cm)
Status:	Vulnerable due to overfishing and finning

Oceanic White Tip Shark Range

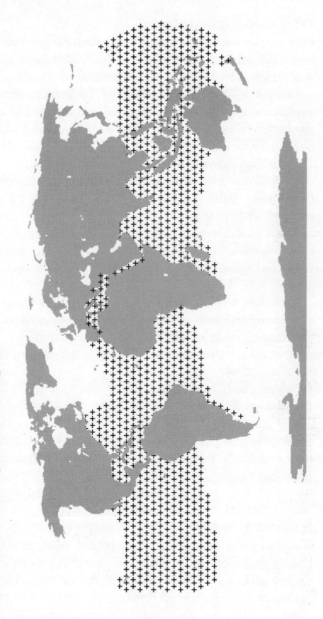

TASMANIA, AUSTRALIA, 1995

Police have warned people to take extreme care in the water off Bridport, in the state's north-east, after a dog was attacked by a shark yesterday morning.

Constable Tony Grundgeiger of Launceston Police said the dog's owner had reported the attack. He said the incident happened at the mouth of the Brid River at about 8.30 a.m.

"The man saw a three- to four-metre shark attack his dog while it was swimming in shallow water," Constable Grundgeiger said. "It was fairly low tide, and the dog escaped without injury."

The Constable said Anderson's Bay at Bridport was a notorious area for sharks and police often received reports of shark sightings from pilots who flew over the area.

Yesterday's attack follows two incidents in water off Weymouth and Bellingham on the north coast, just before Christmas, involving a five-metre great white shark.

The Mercury, Tasmania, 3 February 1995

LONDON, UNITED KINGDOM, 1995

A mother and her three children were treated by ambulance men ... after inhaling fumes from a dead shark. The one-foot fish, kept in formaldehyde and other toxic chemicals, had been left at their home in Brentford, London.

People, London, 16 April 1995

HONG KONG, 1995

A second man has died in a suspected shark attack in Hong Kong, sparking fears that a killer shark was stalking the annual Dragon Boat Festival which drew huge crowds to the colony's beaches on Friday.

A police spokeswoman said that the latest victim, identified as Herman Lo Cheuk-Yuet, was swimming with friends off Sheung Sze Wan beach in the New Territories when he was dragged under and mauled. "He was attacked by a giant fish about six to seven feet long," said the spokeswoman, declining to call it a shark. "The right leg was eaten by the fish. The left leg was wounded."

Lo, 29, was helped to shore by friends and rushed to hospital, but was dead on arrival. He was the second victim in two days, and shark experts think the same shark could be responsible for this and other fatal attacks in the same area this time every year.

On Thursday Tso Kam-Sun, 44, who once represented Hong Kong in swimming at the Asian Games, was found dead in his diving suit off nearby Sai Kung beach with his right leg cleanly severed. Police could not confirm that Tso was killed by a shark.

Australian shark expert Vic Hislop, who came to Hong Kong two years ago after a number of fatal shark attacks, said the shark was a repeat killer and warned of more attacks on the way. "Every year it's been the same," Hislop told government radio. "This time we are awake to it and we've been notified on the 1st of June of the first attack ... so you've probably got about three weeks that shark will be in your area. Something could be done about it."

The Government recently installed shark-proof nets at a number of key beaches.

The latest attack came as huge crowds came out to the beaches on Friday, a local holiday, many to participate in the annual Dragon Boat races, a traditional festival which celebrates a legendary sea rescue. According to the legend, a minister expelled from high office tried to commit suicide by throwing himself into a river; fishermen had to beat the water furiously with their paddles to prevent him from being eaten by fish.

Reuters, 2 June 1995

HONG KONG, 1995

Hong Kong has suddenly found its attention turned from fears of the impending Chinese takeover to something even more terrifying – a spate of shark attacks.

The latest attack, the third in two weeks, occurred yesterday at Clearwater Bay, an exclusive beachfront area of the city. Lifeguards pulled a forty-five-year-old woman out of shallow water where she had been swimming with fifty other people. Witnesses said one leg and one arm had been ripped off. She died before reaching hospital.

The attacks have confounded the politically correct view of sharks, that they are an unnecessarily victimized, environmentally friendly fish. Even Peter Benchley, author of Jaws, the man who did more than any other to besmirch the shark's reputation, has joined the revisionists. The post-modern, post-Jaws battle cry is: "Man eats more sharks than sharks eat man." But this argument is unlikely to find many adherents in Hong Kong just now.

A middle-aged swimmer said she heard the victim shouting for help with her hands raised above her. The woman then disappeared. "A pool of blood spilled out in the water, which was only up to her chest," the witness said.

The death of the woman – the third shark attack victim in a fortnight – was attributed to a possible feeding frenzy by a pack of sharks. No single species has yet been named as a suspect. But many people fear the beaches are being stalked by a large, lone killer with a taste for human flesh not too different from Mr Benchley's celebrated protagonist.

Local experts think the same shark could be responsible for this year's attacks and other fatal attacks in recent years. In June 1993 a hair salon owner was killed while swimming in the same vicinity. Two weeks later another swimmer was killed.

Man may be ultimately responsible. Hong Kong beaches are notorious for their pollution. Garbage and sewage have been known to attract sharks. When the pollution clears, the garbage is replaced by tasty bathers.

Independent, London, 14 June 1995

CALIFORNIA, USA, 1995

The following report is an account of a shark attack on myself, Marco Flagg. It details the sequence of events to the best of my knowledge and experience ...

Location of incident: outside Bluefish Cove, St Lobos State Park, Monterey, California ... Time of incident: approximately 5.30 p.m. on 30 June 1995. Weather: flat calm, minimal wind, no swell, reduced ambient surface light due to low clouds and relatively late time of day ... About myself: I am a thirty-one-year-old diver, certified in 1988. I hold both a PADI Advanced Open Water and a NOAA working diver certification ... By profession I am an electronics engineer ...

I had been invited to some pleasure diving at Pt Lobos by two friends, Steve and Marcie. We intended to make use of the good diving conditions which had lately been reported. After some engine trouble with the Zodiac inflatable early in the day, we finally started our first dive at about 2.55 p.m. The dive lasted about forty minutes and my maximum depth was ninety-eight feet. The visibility was about ten feet at the surface and improving to about thirty feet at the bottom. After the first dive we left our dive site marker buoy in place and headed for shore for a late lunch and a surface interval.

At about 5.20 p.m. we started the second dive of the day. I was trying out Steve's diver propulsion vehicle [scooter] and, propelled by it, was descending through the water at an angle of about twenty degrees. After maybe two minutes and at a depth of about fifty feet, I looked to my right and saw the massive pectoral fin attached to the end of the torpedo shape of a large fish, which was about twenty feet away, at the edge of the range of visibility. Two or three seconds later the animal disappeared from view in the cloudy water.

Somewhat stunned, I at once thought the animal matched the shape and size of a great white shark – I had never seen one before live, but had seen plenty of footage recorded by other divers. While thinking that the shark was most likely just passing and would not attack me, I decided it would be prudent to return to the boat to warn Steve and Marcie, so I turned the scooter round and headed back towards the Zodiac. My ascent was at a gentle angle both because I did not want to suffer an air embolism by surfacing too fast and because, recalling that many shark attacks occur on the surface, I did not want to surface too far from the boat.

I was in an alert, apprehensive state, but still calm enough to think, with my peculiar sense of humour, "Gee, I got to see it without paying for a shark diving trip." At that moment I looked below to my left and saw the massive, wide open, nearly circular, teeth-lined mouth of the shark coming at me. The mouth appeared to have a diameter of between two and three feet.

"Oh, shit," I thought, and at once felt a severe but dull pressure on my body. I do not recall being shaken by the shark nor taking any significant evasive or defensive action. But after a few seconds I appeared to be free of its hold and I thought, "It didn't bite very hard." I tried to feel if my legs were still there, and they seemed to be, so, at maximum speed, I resumed my set course, attempting not to surface too rapidly close to the boat and not thrashing around in case this encouraged the shark to bite again.

Surfacing about twenty yards from the boat, I proceeded the rest of the way on the surface. Having reached the Zodiac ... I climbed in and started to rev the engine in neutral in short bursts so as to warn Steve and Marcie. I had a dull pain in my gut, but reckoned there was probably no big loss of blood as I was still conscious. Steve surfaced after about three to five minutes ... [and] Marcie several minutes later.

We left the marker buoy in place and headed to shore. I climbed out of the Zodiac on my own, but then sat down because I felt weak. The ambulance arrived within a few minutes ...

I sustained a wound of about 1.75 inches in diameter on my left forearm (six stitches) with another one-inch scrape mark. A further eight stitches were required for a cut wound on my left upper leg. The third cut wound is on my left lower abdomen, with a bruise in the vicinity. The distance from the leg wound to the arm wound is twenty inches if my arm is down and thirty inches if my arm is held up at an angle of forty-five degrees. I do not specifically recall what position my arm was in when the shark bit, but the fact that I was using the scooter suggests it should have been up ...

My injuries from the incident are surprisingly light, considering the circumstances. One reason for this may be that the shark, for whatever reason, simply decided not to exert much force on my body. Another possibility is that, in fact, I got sandwiched between two layers of metal: the shark may have bitten on to the tank on my back and the dive tracker instrument on my front. The dive tracker instrument may well have been resting on my abdomen – its natural position. Thus, the pressure on the tank and on the dive tracker spread the force of the shark's bite over a large area and resulting in the bruise on my abdomen. If this is the case, my cut wounds may simply have been points where my body was "bulging out" between the instrument and the tank; in effect I was protected by a "sandwich" of armour ...

Marco Flagg, Internet, 2 July 1995

FLORIDA, USA, 1995
Briton James Oatley was savaged in a shark attack while on holiday in Florida.

The twenty-year-old mechanic had been surfing at Daytona Beach when the Jaws-style beast struck. It grabbed his upper thigh and pushed him out of the water as he waded through the shallows. Unsure what had happened, James struggled to the shore with blood pouring from his wounds.

When he finally managed to examine his injuries, he was horrified to find two long rows of teeth marks along his leg. A friend managed to pull him further up the shore before the shark could strike again. James is the summer's ninth victim of shark attacks along the Daytona stretch of the Atlantic coastline.

After receiving treatment for his wounds, he said: "I felt a tug like a dog biting me – it was pretty scary. I've been shark fishing before – now they are fighting back. But this will not stop me going surfing or to the beach."

His shocked parents said he had been lucky to escape

with his life. Speaking at the family home in South Warnborough, Alton, Hants, his mum Christine said: "James was taken to hospital and had lots of antibiotics and a tetanus injection. Fortunately, he is not going to lose his leg. He will be flying home at the weekend, but he'll be in a wheelchair because he can't walk."

James's relieved dad George joked: "I'm going to buy him a *Jaws* poster for his room when he gets back." The couple last saw their son about ten weeks ago when he flew off to Florida for an extended holiday.

Beach authorities in the area estimated the shark was about six feet long – slightly bigger than the beasts blamed for similar attacks this year. Experts say sharks looking for small fish are mistakenly attracted to the thrashing and bright colours of surfers and swimmers. Last month four surfers were bitten on the same beach, one receiving stitches on a four-inch gash. And ten days ago, Matt Sturgess, 12, was bitten on the leg while surfing.

Wire report, 18 August 1995

RECIFE, BRAZIL, 1995
A dramatic increase in shark attacks is threatening local surfers and the economy in Recife, a popular resort in north-east Brazil. Despite a ban on surfing, a shark claimed another life last month. International shark experts will meet in Brazil in November to study the problem.

Local surfers and fishermen say they cannot remember any shark attacks off the palm-fringed beaches of Recife before 1992. Then, suddenly, they started. In 1994 alone, there were eleven attacks along a ten-kilometre stretch of coast. The sharks go mainly for surfers, though three swimmers have also been attacked, all of them outside the coral reef which shelters most of the beaches.

Researchers believe that surfers are more susceptible

to shark attacks because of the movements they make on the surface of the water while waiting for waves, and because they spend more time in deep water.

The first response of the local government was to put up signs in Portuguese and English which said: "Surfers, be cool! Respect natural boundaries. Do not go beyond the reef." But the signs neglected to mention sharks. Local oceanographer Favio Hazin accused the government of "hiding its head in the sand". Locals began spray-painting sharks on to the signs, and surfers held a protest on the beach, complete with a bloody, mauled mannequin.

When the new state government came into power in January [1995], it promptly banned surfing and bolstered Hazin's shark research efforts at the Federal Rural University of Pernambuco. Since the crisis began, Hazin's team have caught more than 200 sharks in order to study their behaviour and life cycle. The shark meat is donated to feed hungry local children. Meanwhile, police have begun patrolling the beaches, confiscating boards from surfers who defy the ban.

"What is happening in many areas of the world is that aquatic recreation is beginning to take off, and so shark attacks are more frequent," says George Burgess, director of the International Shark Attack File at the University of Florida in Gainesville, USA. The recent spate of shark attacks off popular beaches in Hong Kong supports this view. However, Brazilian surfers have been holding championships off the beaches near Recife since the 1970s, so the increase in surfing cannot entirely explain the sudden surge of shark attacks.

In a preliminary unpublished report, Hazin and his colleagues point an accusing finger at the port of Suape, built in 1989 just south of the three beaches where most of the attacks have occurred. The port may be bringing people and sharks into closer contact, they say. The researchers found a correlation between months when there are more passing ships, and months when there are shark attacks. Sharks are known to follow big ships, especially if sailors are dumping rubbish overboard. Hazin's team has found an onion, a pineapple and a can of beer in the stomachs of local sharks.

From the imprint in a bite-shaped piece of styrofoam body-board, the biologists have identified one of the culprits as a bull shark, although there is also evidence that tiger sharks are responsible for some attacks.

The Brazilians are now seeking advice on whether to install safety nets around the beaches of Recife ... Educating local surfers to avoid going out at dawn and dusk, when the sharks are most active, to avoid water where there are birds diving and fish jumping, and to avoid channels where sharks tend to congregate may all help.

This type of advice, however, may simply be water off a surfer's back. "Those surfers who get bitten by sharks here wear their scars as a badge of honour," says Burgess. "The more dangerous they think it is, the more attractive surfing is for some people," says Hazin. "I try to emphasize that they're not only risking their lives, they're damaging the state economy."

New Scientist, 19 August 1995

ISLE OF WIGHT, UNITED KINGDOM, 1995

A recent article in *Diver* magazine reported a shark sighting in the English Channel six miles off the Isle of Wight. The report states that a wreck diver, George Hayward, of RAF Odiham BSAC was diving with his buddy Trevor Jones on the wreck of the SS *Westville* in forty metres of water.

Descending the line head first Mr Hayward received quite a shock when, at around the twenty-metre mark, "This shark of about two metres brushed against my mask as it went by, I was startled as it passed right against my nose!"

The men continued their dive despite this unexpected encounter. Mr Jones said, "The funniest thing was that, when George first saw the shark, he clung on to the shot line and pulled his arms and legs in very tight. The wrecks out there are covered with pollack and mackerel, and that attracts sharks. We reckon it was a porbeagle."

A shark encounter underwater in the UK is a rare occurrence. Among the large sharks which can be found in UK waters are blues, makos, porbeagles, threshers, basking sharks and occasionally hammerheads. This summer [1995] has been the warmest since records began, leading to many sightings of unusual visitors to these waters including loggerhead turtles and sun fish.

Reuters, September 1995

FLORIDA, USA, 1995

A marine biologist from Livonia was killed during a shark attack while scuba diving for exotic fish off the Florida Keys, police determined on Thursday. William Covert, 25, was killed by a bull shark, said the Monroe County (Fla) Sheriff's Department after reviewing the findings by marine biologists and shark experts.

"I don't think he ever saw the shark coming," said Covert's sister, Teresa Simonds of Garden City. "He was an experienced diver who had been to Brazil and around the world diving."

Covert had been missing since 13 September, when he disappeared while diving with friends for tropical fish off Alligator Reef, near Islamorada. His mother, Maryann

Fiordelis, had been working with local dive teams in Key West and the Sheriff's Department to find her son.

"We kept thinking they would find him or that a boat had picked him up," Simonds said. "Today we finally realized that he wasn't coming home."

Thomas Scaturro, a Florida boat owner and exotic fish dealer, was with Covert on his boat the night he disappeared. Scaturro said Covert was the only diver using air tanks instead of thirty-foot compressed air hoses attached to the boat. "After about an hour of diving, I saw his tanks and equipment on the bottom of the ocean," Scaturro said.

The Coast Guard searched for two days, but found nothing. Because of rough weather, it took Scaturro and other dive teams a week to find and recover Covert's equipment and shreds of his dive clothing. Scaturro said the tanks found still had air in them, which led him to believe that Covert had not drowned.

Gordon Hubbell, a shark specialist in Key Biscayne, was one of several scientists who examined Covert's clothing and equipment, and determined he was killed by a bull shark. "I was able to match the bite marks on the dive belt and tee-shirt to a ten- to twelve-foot bull shark. The attack was quick and extremely vicious." Hubbell said the attack was very rare and noted that it was the first fatal shark attack of the year in Florida.

Covert was a graduate of Stevenson High School in Livonia and received his bachelor's degree in marine biology from Michigan State University in 1993.

Mrs Fiordelis is expected to ask a Florida judge today to declare her son officially dead, said Covert's sister. "We just want this to be over. We don't want to wait seven years to have a funeral."

Detroit News, 22 September 1995

FLORIDA, USA, 1995

Florida is in the midst of a record year, a record the state would rather not have. So far this year, there have been twenty-five shark attacks in Florida waters. Experts believe there is a logical explanation for the increased number of incidents.

All summer long waves pounded Florida's east coast, driven in by one hurricane after another cruising north along the Atlantic seaboard. The larger waves have attracted more surfers and that, in turn, has led to more encounters with sharks. One surfer had his feet bitten by a shark.

CNN, 25 September 1995

CHATHAM ISLANDS, NEW ZEALAND, 1995

Diver Kina Scollay fought his way out of the jaws of death by beating off a sixteen-foot white shark with a rock. The twenty-two-year-old was close to being bitten in two by the huge predator, which clamped its jaws around his middle as he was gathering shellfish.

Horrified friends in nearby boats saw the giant shark burst to the surface with Mr Scollay in its mouth. He was thrashing at it and screaming, "Don't let it get me, don't let it get me!" Seconds later the man-eater released its grip and Mr Scollay was hauled from the water off the Chatham Islands, east of New Zealand.

"The shark was coming round to have another go at him, so we pulled him straight into the dinghy," said fisherman Richard Ennor. "As we pulled Kina up, the shark went under the dinghy. It was the scariest moment of my life."

Mr Scollay's lead diving belt was mangled by the shark's teeth and his wetsuit was shredded. But he escaped with deep gashes in his legs and chest.

From his hospital bed in Christchurch, where he was airlifted after the attack, Mr Scollay described his ordeal. He said last night: "There were a few seconds of disbelief. I felt a pretty big grip across my waist and thought 'What the hell?' Then I looked down and there was this bloody great thing. That's when I realized it was a shark. There was initial panic and I tried to kick to the surface, but, because it had me by the legs, I started hitting it with a rock I'd been bringing back to the surface to show my friends.

"It was dragging me down, but it didn't take long for it to let me go. I was thinking more about getting away from it than being scared. Now I'm just so relieved that I've still got everything – my legs and all the other important bits. And I'm pleased to be here in hospital rather than lying on a slab."

Brave Mr Scollay will not be able to dive again for at least two months, but he says the attack will not put him off, insisting, "You'd have to be pretty unlucky for it to happen twice."

Daily Star, London, 1 December 1995

1996

NEW SOUTH WALES, AUSTRALIA, 1996

A group of Australian fishermen who underwent a nine-hour ordeal yesterday after a giant shark gnawed off the bow of their twenty-one-foot boat have vowed to stick to golf in future.

The three men and one woman were fishing off the coast of New South Wales and had fed one hundred litres of shark bait – mainly offal – into the sea when a fourteen-foot mako bit into the front of their fibreglass boat, the *Mini Haa Haar* [*sic*].

Tony Barnes, one of the fishermen, said: "We had just started fishing about eight miles off shore when the shark hit us. I saw his body pass the boat, and then suddenly he ploughed straight into the bow. In three minutes the boat went down."

With room on their tiny inflatable dinghy for only one, the others had to cling to the sides with their legs dangling in the sea. Tony Green, the skipper, said: "I could see the dorsal fin going round and round, circling us for about an hour and a half. Then, eventually, the shark lost interest. That was the last we saw of it, thank God."

After nine hours the group hailed a passing tanker, but could not attract anyone's attention. "There was nobody on watch on the ship and the crew appeared not to see us," said Barnes. They had to swim towards it towing Barnes's wife, Kylin, on the inflatable before they were finally picked up, shivering from cold and shock. They were then airlifted to Wollongong hospital, near Sydney.

"We are doubly lucky to be alive," said Barnes, vowing to give up deep-sea fishing for golf. "I'm staying on land from now on and I'll buy my fish in a fish shop." The four were discharged from hospital after treatment for severe exposure and dehydration.

Sunday Times, London, 14 January 1996

FLORIDA, USA, 1996

You're a tourist splashing happily in the surf and you see a shark. You (a) run screaming on to the beach, (b) stand frozen in fear, hoping it passes you by, or (c) grab the creature by the tail. Christopher Riley picked (c), but he won't do that again.

Riley, aged thirty-three, of Kansas City, spotted the three-foot nurse shark in thigh-deep water on Tuesday.

"He grabbed it by the tail and didn't let go," said Bob Bodner, assistant manager at Bahia Honda State Park. "And it turned around and bit him on the leg."

Riley finally let go, and the shark swam away. Riley was taken to Fisherman's Hospital in Marathon with his leg wrapped in a towel. He was treated and released.

"As he said, he was being a stupid tourist," Bodner said.

Chicago Tribune, 25 January 1996

QUEENSLAND, AUSTRALIA, 1996

It seemed a perfect start to the day as Jean Hotchkiss padded across a deserted shore and waded into the clear water. Dawn was breaking over the Australian resort of Heron Island as the British holidaymaker lazily swam in the sea surrounding the Great Barrier Reef.

Then terror struck in the shape of a shark "with a mouth as wide as a chair". Before she could react, it opened its jaws and tore into her arm and leg. With blood pouring from her wounds, forty-seven-year-old Miss Hotchkiss frantically swam back to shore with her good arm, screaming for help and praying the shark would not attack again.

Yesterday, after four hours of surgery in a Brisbane hospital, the landowner from Warwickshire, England, told of her ordeal.

"I had been on the island a week and I was just enjoying my usual early morning swim, doing a gentle breast stroke, not splashing around, when I looked down to my right. A chill went through me when I saw this huge shark next to me. The only thing I could see was this big, grey head. I was horrified, but before I could do anything, I felt its teeth ripping into my arm. I thought, my God, I've been bitten, and I started shouting: 'Help,

265

help, somebody help me.' As I did that, the shark let me go.

"I was so shocked I just started swimming away as fast as I could. My biggest fear was that it would come back and take me out to sea. I looked at my arm and it was in shreds."

Despite almost fainting with fear, Miss Hotchkiss staggered 200 yards back to her hotel, banging on doors, shouting for help. She lost nearly three pints of blood.

"I managed to get to the reception and they got the nurse," she said. "Luckily there was an American doctor on holiday there and he organized a tourniquet. I was cold and shocked."

Shivering in her wet bikini and wrapped in blankets, Miss Hotchkiss was flown by helicopter to a local hospital at Rockhampton. There she was patched up and transferred to Brisbane by the Royal Flying Doctor Service. There, twelve hours after the attack, doctors repaired severed tendons and carried out skin grafts. They are confident she will regain full use of her arm.

Miss Hotchkiss, a fan of the *Jaws* movies, had swum with harmless reef sharks in Heron harbour days earlier. Experts believe her attacker was a tiger shark. She said: "I think my experience should be a warning to other people not to swim at dawn or dusk when sharks are feeding. I'm lucky to be alive.

Miss Hotchkiss, who lives off rent from the family estate near Stratford-upon-Avon, has a boyfriend, but spends a lot of time travelling alone. Her next adventure will be a cruise on the Canberra to Venice in August. "I'll need a holiday after all this," she laughed. "The streets of Venice may be under water, but at least there are no sharks."

Daily Mail, London, 9 March 1996

RED SEA, EGYPT, 1996

Three bottlenose dolphins have saved a British tourist from a shark in the Red Sea.

Mark Richardson, aged twenty-nine, from Colchester, Essex, UK, was swimming with the dolphins off the Sinai peninsula on Tuesday when friends on board a diving boat heard his scream as a shark bit his side and arm.

Dolphins encircled him, flapping their tails to scare off the shark. Although he was "very scared", he remembers punching the shark, but could not recall seeing any dolphins around him. His friends said the dolphins kept circling until he could be pulled aboard.

Mr Richardson had first seen the dolphins at the end of a diving lesson and had swum to join them.

"I didn't see anything strange, but suddenly I felt something bite my left side and it punctured my lung, and took away a part of one of my ribs," he said. "The shark went away, but came back and took a chunk from my left arm. I saw it then for the first time and managed to punch it on the nose, but it took another bite from my chest."

A statement by Israel's Recanati Centre for Maritime Studies at the University of Haifa, which monitors marine life in the area, said: "This defensive behaviour of dolphins is common when mothers are protecting their calves from predators."

Mr Richardson is recovering in an Egyptian military hospital. After a four-hour operation, the doctors told him they had stopped counting the stitches when they got to 200.

The Times, London, 25 July 1996

CALIFORNIA, USA, 1996

A thirty-five-year-old diver was bitten in the chest, shoulder and arm yesterday by what may have been a ten-foot great white shark off Tomales Point in Mann County.

The diver, Colum Tinley of Sacramento, was in stable condition and "doing fine" last night after undergoing surgery at Santa Rosa Memorial Hospital, according to a nursing supervisor.

The attack occurred in a known shark habitat. In the Tomales Point area the predatory fish have wounded at least six people since 1960. However, it has been eleven years since the last recorded attack.

Tinley was bitten in the water as he was diving for abalone with two friends from a thirteen-foot rubber inflatable boat a quarter of a mile off the Point Reyes peninsula, according to the US Coast Guard. At 11.40 a.m. Tinley called for help on his hand-held radio.

"He was screaming," said Coast Guard Petty Officer Tom Barnard. "He said he'd been attacked by a shark. He was pretty panicked."

An inflatable boat from a nearby Coast Guard cutter reached Tinley ten minutes later, and within another ten minutes a Sonoma County Sheriff's Department helicopter flew Tinley to hospital.

"He did indeed have what appeared to be bite wounds … jagged-type wounds," said Barnard. "But he was in shock. He wasn't saying much."

As a result, officials did not know exactly what bit Tinley, but he was diving in what is known as the Red Triangle, named because of the frequency of shark attacks that occur between Bodega Rock, the Farallon Islands and Santa Cruz.

San Francisco Chronicle, 14 August 1996

NORTHERN TERRITORY, AUSTRALIA, 1996

Desperate holidaymaker Brian Astin told last night how he fought off a killer shark – with his wife's false tooth!

The thirty-three-year-old electrician was struggling in the waves with missus Avril after their yacht capsized when the massive Jaws beast ploughed towards them. But in his sheer panic he remembered reading that the only way to beat off a shark was to blind it.

Said Brian: "I reached over to Avril, who was gasping for breath, grabbed one of her capped teeth and tugged it free. Then, using the pointed end, I jabbed at the shark's eye. Miraculously, it pulled its head away and swam off."

The couple, from Leeds, Yorkshire, were sailing a hire yacht off northern Australia when the horror attack happened. The boat overturned and they were flung into the sea. And the killer fish clocked them as they tried to swim ashore.

After Brian's brave rescue battle, the two crawled on top of their boat and clung on for three hours until coastguards spotted them.

Local shark expert Wilt Abraham said: "They were very lucky. They could easily have been ripped apart."

As the two recovered from shock and exposure last night, receptionist Avril said: "That tooth's going in a special display cabinet when we get home to remind us how we escaped death by the skin of our teeth."

Sunday Sport*, London, 8 September 1996

* To be taken with a pinch of salt!

1997

FLORIDA, USA, 1997

An Atlanta man was bitten in the leg by a four-foot shark while bodysurfing on Monday.

Douglas Amelio, aged thirty-three, suffered four lacerations above his left ankle. He was taken to Columbia Medical Center in Ormond Beach for treatment, but his injuries were not life threatening.

Amelio was bodysurfing with his girlfriend when he stood up on a sandbar about three feet deep and felt something grab his left leg, said Scott Petersohn, a supervisor for the Volusia County Beach Patrol. Amelio ran to shore and was helped by a lifeguard, who bandaged his leg.

It was the first reported shark bite of the year in Volusia County, Petersohn said. Two people during the weekend were treated for shark bites in Flagler County, to the north along the Atlantic Coast.

In Volusia County most shark bites occur in the Ponce Inlet, near New Smyrna Beach. "We've never had anything that's life threatening," Petersohn said. "It's usually no more severe than a bad dog bite."

Atlanta Journal-Constitution, 3 June 1997

EASTERN CAPE, SOUTH AFRICA, 1997

The father of Australian surfer Mark Penches, aged twenty-five, killed by a shark off the Transkei Wild Coast on Monday, said the sea and the environment were extremely important to his son.

Mr Tony Penches, of Narraweena, Sydney, said yesterday that his son, who graduated with a degree in coastal management last year, was killed six months into a dream tour of the world's choicest surfing spots.

The surfer's last words to his travelling companions before leaping into the surf on Monday were, "The only thing missing is my mates." But minutes later his dream trip to the rugged Wild Coast ended when he was mauled to death by a shark.

Fellow Sydney surfer Clyde Crawford, aged twenty-six, and American Terry Gibson, aged twenty-three, from Florida, had to retrieve Penches's mangled body and surfboard.

Penches took a holiday between finishing his studies and starting his career, and was due to return to Australia next month.

Eastern Cape police spokeswoman Senior Super-indendent Marinda Mills said that, on Monday, Penches went with Crawford and Gibson to a beach near the Dwesa nature reserve at the mouth of the Bashee River.

Crawford and Gibson were on the beach when the shark pulled Penches under the water. His body was washed up on to the beach about twenty minutes after the attack. His right leg had been torn off. His friends found what was left of the leg further down the beach.

"He finished his studies about eighteen months ago, worked for a year and then he wanted to do a surfing safari before he started his career," his father said.

His son held down three jobs to save enough money for the trip. Penches said his son saw the trip as good hands-on experience. "He had fixed goals, but at the same time he was an easy-going, likeable young lad."

Penches had surfed in Indonesia, Portugal and Greece. He had been in South Africa for about eight weeks.

Although the type of shark that attacked Penches has not been established, it is believed to have been a great white.

After Penches's body washed up on the beach, Gibson,

Crawford and another friend radioed police from a hotel about four kilometres away. Police then drove the forty-five kilometres from Elliotdale to the remote surf spot in a 4 × 4 off-road vehicle to retrieve the body. A post mortem will be held today before the body is flown back to Australia.

The last fatal shark attack on the Eastern Cape coast was in July 1994, when East London surfer Bruce Corby was killed by a great white. In the same attack Springbok surfer Andrew Carter was mauled severely, but survived.

Cape Times, 23 July 1997

KENT, UNITED KINGDOM, 1997

A pub landlady was attacked by a shark as she worked in the bar.

Liz Currie was badly cut when the stuffed and mounted fish, said to have been caught in the Indian Ocean in the 1820s, fell off a wall at the Wheatsheaf pub at Boughbeech, near Edenbridge, Kent.

Daily Mail, London, 29 July 1997

FLORIDA, USA, 1997

James Ogilvy, the son of Princess Alexandra and Sir Angus Ogilvy, has had to have thirty stitches in leg wounds after being attacked by a shark while swimming off a beach in Florida.

Mr Ogilvy, thirty-two, a magazine publisher, who is thirty-first in line to the Throne, had been relaxing at a private club during a break in a business trip. He was accompanied by his wife Julia and their two children: Flora, aged two, and Alexander, aged one. His wife witnessed the attack.

A spokesman for Princess Alexandra reportedly confirmed the incident. Mr Ogilvy's parents are on holiday in Africa. The former banker is expected to return to Britain with his family today.

Mr Ogilvy said that the attack occurred as he waded out for a morning swim. He said: "The water was murky. People who saw it tell me that it was not an enormous shark, but it had sharp teeth." He said he felt himself lucky that the shark had taken him on the front of his leg. It was not known late last night what type of shark had attacked Mr Ogilvy.

Mr Ogilvy, who has a Master of Business Administration degree, married Julia Rawlinson, daughter of the vice-chairman of the merchant bank Morgan Grenfell in 1988. The couple met while they were reading History of Art at St Andrew's University. They moved back to Scotland from London in 1992 when Mrs Ogilvy was promoted from her job as a press relations officer for the Crown jewellers Garrards. She became managing director of Hamilton & Inches, a jewellers and silversmiths in Edinburgh. Mr Ogilvy was formerly with brokers BZW and worked for an Edinburgh shipping agency. The pair have a home near Crail in Fife.

Last year Mr Ogilvy launched a monthly magazine called *Luxury Briefing*, a publication costing £25 per issue, which was aimed at providing news on all the top names in the "luxury industry", such as fashion house Gucci and Garrards.

Last night a marine expert at the University of Florida said that attacks by sharks were becoming increasingly rare in the state of Florida. They had, he said, fallen from a record of twenty-nine in 1995 to thirteen in 1996. In part, he said, this was because of clearer waters brought about by a less active hurricane season. He said that, although he had been in his post for more than fifteen years, he had never heard of an attack by a great white shark in coastal waters.

He said: "Fatal shark attacks are extremely rare. Although a shark may attack a swimmer or someone on a surfboard, it would normally let go because human beings are not part of the shark diet." There had been only five shark attacks in the world this year, the expert said; two of them had been in Florida.

The Times, London, 5 November 1997

WESTERN AUSTRALIA, 1997
Diver Kevin Hulkes fought off a sixteen-foot-long great white shark by whacking it in the face.

Kevin, aged 42, was being towed by an underwater scooter 130 feet down and used it to ram the monster.

He said: "I was terrified, but I drove the scooter straight into it because the best thing to do when a shark attacks is to thump it on the nose."

Kevin needed twenty stitches for an arm bite after the shark struck off Albany, Western Australia.

Daily Mirror, London, 12 November 1997

WESTERN CAPE, SOUTH AFRICA, 1997
A great white shark with a dorsal fin said to measure about a metre is believed to have been responsible for the shark attack in which avid diver Mr Ian James Hill, aged thirty-nine, of Durban, died yesterday.

According to witness accounts of the attack, Hill was spearfishing about 350–400 metres from the shore in about ten metres of water when the shark attacked him at about 2 p.m.

He leaves his wife Sandra and nine-year-old daughter Charlene. Mrs Hill and Charlene, who had been waiting on the beach for Hill to return to shore, were sedated by a Pringle Bay doctor last night.

People who saw the attack said they had spotted a

large dorsal fin in the area earlier in the day.

"They saw Hill standing in the water, then they saw the fin and then they saw a pool of blood where he had been standing," said police spokesperson Senior Superintendent John Sterrenberg. "Another witness stopped his car when he saw what appeared to be thrashing in the water. He saw a buoy and then he saw a dorsal fin measuring about a metre."

Although the circumstances of the attack are unknown, local fishermen said they suspected Hill had speared several fish and that these were hanging from his diving buoy when he was attacked. The smell of blood attracts sharks.

Sterrenberg said the South African Police Services Coastal Patrol Unit and the John Rolfe helicopter searched the area immediately after the attack was reported. He said the wind was strong and the sea became rough and the water dirty, making the search difficult. The search was called off when it became dark.

Hill's mother, Mrs Rosemary Hill, had not yet been contacted by police or family members when a Durban reporter telephoned her last night. The *Cape Times* later put her in touch with a police spokesperson. She said her son was an electrician and an avid member of the Wahoo Diving Club in Durban. She confirmed he was on holiday in the Cape with his family.

The family was due to leave Pringle Bay yesterday for Hermanus, she said, so it would appear her son may have been on a final dive at the small resort.

Shark expert Mr Triall Witthuhn of Struisbaai knew Hill and described him as "a top diver in South Africa". Witthuhn, who tags great white sharks for the Oceanographic Research Institute, said last night that south-east coast sea waters had been abnormally warm recently. Sharks had to eat substantially more as their gastric juices digested food far more quickly in warm water, he said.

"The shark moves around more and he eats more. If such a hungry great white saw a seal, he would eat it – and unfortunately a diver in a wetsuit looks like a seal," Witthuhn said. "But sharks are not aggressive – if they are hungry, they eat. When they are hungry again, they eat what they find – not necessarily a human being. The man-eater stories are rubbish."

Divers, in particular, should be aware that warmer water brings extra dangers. "Any diver will tell you our waters are full of sharks."

Cape Times, 29 December 1997

WESTERN CAPE, SOUTH AFRICA, 1997
A great white shark killed a diver, the latest in a wave of attacks in South Africa which has raised fears among surfers and tourists.

Mr Hill was spearfishing about 400 yards from the shore in about thirty feet of water when the shark attacked ... Only a speargun was retrieved and a helicopter search was called off.

The death in Pringle Bay was the first in the Cape Town area in more than a decade. It comes on the heels of a recent spate of shark attacks elsewhere in the country and has fuelled safety concerns among the thousands of British and other overseas tourists and surfers who have flocked to the sunsoaked Western Cape over the holiday season.

While surfing experts insist such incidents are isolated, they are concerned by the implications of the latest tragedy. They have given a warning that shark activity has increased because of higher sea temperatures ...

A twenty-five-year-old Australian surfer died earlier

this year when he was attacked by a shark on a remote beach in the Eastern Cape.

The Times, London, 30 December 1997

WESTERN CAPE, SOUTH AFRICA, 1997
Letter to the Editor of *The Times*, London
30 December 1997
Sir – The account of the fatal shark attack near Cape Town [see above 30 December 1997] fuels alarm about the frequency and nature of such accidents on Cape Province coasts. However, data since the 1950s confirm that there is no really discernible increase in white shark attacks off South African or indeed any other coast-lines where this rare – and increasingly protected – animal ranges.

There is no evidence to suggest that warmer conditions have affected white shark activity on Cape coasts, or that their digestive rates have thus accelerated. These are warm-bodied fish, much like mammals, and the temperature of water makes little difference to their activity levels. Any inference that they may be seeking humans as prey is sheer Hollywood fantasy. People are completely irrelevant to these versatile and ancient predators. Indeed, the rarity of white shark attacks worldwide speaks volumes in this regard.

I have been enthralled studying the predatory and social behaviour of this spectacular species off the Cape Coast and analysing, with colleagues from the shark research centre of the South African Museum, their surprisingly complex activity. The great white is only one among 400 shark species worldwide. To demonize it blindly because of sporadic attacks on humans is to do it – and its wider marine environment – a great injustice.
Yours faithfully,
Ian K. Fergusson – shark.bureau@zoo.co.uk

LIFE OF A SHARK

The Shark's Greatest Enemy

In their own environment, sharks fear few creatures. Smaller sharks may be preyed upon by larger types of shark, but the bigger sharks are generally masters of their own domain. Killer whales can put them in their place but sharks have little to fear from most other sea creatures.

Sharks are highly evolved animals with their entire anatomy designed to make them supreme hunters. They have no bones, their skeleton being composed of cartilage. This helps them to be flexible but cartilage is also lighter than bone, helping the shark to move faster while using less energy. Because it has no ribcage, if a large shark were to bask on a beach like the seals it so enjoys eating, it would "cave in" crushed by its own weight.

With its cranium, upper and lower jaws all cartilage instead of bone, the great white can dislocate its jaws from their normal position and thrust them forward, out of its mouth, to take a bigger bite of its prey – and all sharks are fantastically well equipped for biting.

Sharks' teeth come in many shapes and forms depending on the type of prey the species hunts. The tiger shark's teeth are serrated for sawing through flesh, but other sharks may have needle-like teeth for catching fish or more dense, blunter teeth for crushing crustaceans. The teeth are set in the gums rather than attached to the jaw and lie in rows, the newest teeth on the inside of the mouth moving forward in the gum like a dental conveyer belt to replace outer teeth when they are lost. A shark can count on losing thousands of teeth in the course of its lifetime.

It could be said that a shark is actually enveloped in teeth. Its skin is covered in placoid scales that are also called dermal denticles – skin teeth – because they have a pulpy core and blood supply just like teeth. The dermal denticles streamline the shark for more efficient swimming but also act a bit like armour plating. Shark attack victims often have grazes to their hands, arms and legs caused by striking out at their attacker. Shark skin can be so rough that it has been used as an abrasive and its texture also gave it superior grip for making sword handles.

While some sharks have very good eyesight, others rely more on their other senses for hunting. Sharks have an excellent sense of smell and can detect blood in water at concentrations as low as one part per million. Some sharks, such as nurse sharks or saw sharks, also have barbels drooping from their mouths or snouts that allow them to "taste" prey in murky water. The sense of hearing is also very well developed in most sharks, allowing them to hear their prey from many miles away.

The most impressive and sophisticated of a shark's senses, however, is its electroreception capability. Thousands of tiny organs (ampullae of Lorenzini) located around the shark's head can detect the electromagnetic fields produced by other living creatures, allowing sharks to find prey even if it has hidden itself in sand.

Despite its prowess as a hunter, there remains one creature that the shark should fear. Humans kill an estimated 100 million sharks every year. Around 36 million shark fins are sold annually, hacked off the shark which is then thrown back into the sea to die, because the rest of its flesh isn't marketable. Yet not all shark flesh is unpalatable to humans. Many sharks are fished to be eaten – dogfish is commonly available in British fish and chip shops as "rock salmon" and a variety of shark species are sold in Australian fish and chip shops as "flake".

We may fear the shark (although far more people are killed each year when struck by lightning than in shark attacks), but the shark has far more to fear from us.

1998

OREGON, USA, 1998

A surfer cheated death when a great white shark clamped him in its jaws – and then spat him out.

John Forse, who frenziedly punched at the shark's fin, was twice dragged under water and shaken like a doll. Recovering in hospital, he said, "I guess it didn't like the taste. I didn't have time to be scared – it was just survival."

Forse, aged fifty, was surfing off Lincoln in Oregon when the fifteen-foot shark clamped its upper jaw on his right thigh and its lower jaw on his board.

John said, "I didn't feel any pain. It pulled me under and shook me. Then, after thrashing around, it suddenly came back up and released me. Then it dived again and I was dragged under a second time as my ankle cord was caught in its mouth. The cord snapped and I popped up."

Forse – who suffered a one-foot-long gash and eight teeth punctures – was spared because his wetsuit kept in blood which could have maddened the shark. He said: "Now I want to get back in the water as soon as possible. I'm not going to let that brute ruin my hobby."

Daily Mirror, London, 24 April 1998

EASTERN CAPE, SOUTH AFRICA, 1998

A boy of fifteen told yesterday how he fought for his life against a fourteen-foot great white shark.

Marc Jucker was attacked as he bodyboarded sixty yards from shore at the South African resort of Sardinia Bay, near Port Elizabeth. Despite having one arm almost bitten off, he used his board to fend it off.

"I didn't see the shark," he said. "It came at me from the bottom and knocked me off my board. I went under and there was a lot of thrashing about, and then I suddenly felt my arm go numb. When the shark came at me again I really thought I was going to die, but I put up my board to shield myself and he bit into it."

Marc managed to clamber back on to his board and a wave carried him shorewards.

Doctors saved his arm and from hospital he vowed: "I'm determined to body-board again as soon as I can."

Daily Mail, London, 1 June 1998

SOUTH AUSTRALIA, AUSTRALIA, 1998

A fisherman died after he was savaged by a great white shark off the coast of South Australia. Douglas Chesser, aged twenty-five, bled to death from horrific injuries after snorkelling in shallow water, searching for abalone.

Mr Chesser, a professional fisherman from Port Lincoln, had been checking nets with a friend on the shark-hunting boat *Aquatur* off the barren outpost of South Neptune Island, seventy kilometres south-east of Port Lincoln, when he decided to swim and dive for abalone at about 2.30 p.m.

Mr Chesser's friend said that the great white continued to attack even after he jumped into the water to help the victim. He dragged Mr Chesser ashore to the island's lighthouse, but the shock of the attack and massive loss of blood killed him.

Mr Roger Cavanagh, lighthouse keeper on South Neptune Island – 200 nautical miles from Adelaide in the Spencer Gulf – said Mr Chesser was dead by the time he reached him. "I could see he had suffered huge blood loss. There was no pulse, no sign of life. From speaking to the lad who was with him, the attack was so fast, so quick and powerful, there was absolutely no way he could have survived."

Mr Cavanagh saw the shark circling the area after the attack and believes the huge beast responsible was a twelve-foot shark known locally as "Kong".

Great whites, which are also known as white pointers, can grow up to seven metres long and weigh up to three tonnes. The waters off South Neptune are renowned as one of the best spots in the world for viewing and hunting these sharks because of the large colonies of sea lions in the area. Professional shark fisherman Mr Chesser would have known the risks, but, after pulling up nets with his business partner, he entered the water.

Veteran diver, shark museum owner and shark attack survivor Mr Rodney Fox said later: "There's probably more great whites at South Neptune than along the whole south coast of Australia. I certainly wouldn't go for a swim there. The sharks gather there because there are about 15,000 sea lions on the Neptunes and they are one of the favourite foods of the great white."

A local charter boat operator, Mrs Irene Bennett of Seacharters, said: "Absolutely nobody would swim around the Neptunes – you'd have to be a lunatic. It's a fairly treacherous area with heavy seas."

Mr Chesser's friend, said to be in deep shock, had to wait five hours to be airlifted home to Port Lincoln.

The fatal attack is the first off the coast of South Australia in nearly seven years. In 1985, near Port Lincoln, a great white bit a woman in two and devoured the lower half of her body.

Sydney Morning Herald and
Evening Standard, London, 29 June 1998

EASTERN CAPE AND WESTERN CAPE, SOUTH AFRICA, 1998

A spate of shark attacks on surfers in South Africa's southern resorts has raised fears that a large Jaws-type predator is roaming the coastal waters.

The latest victim, Anton Devos, a twenty-year-old forestry student, died in hospital after being mauled by a great white shark while he was body-boarding off Gonubie Point, north of East London. The shark bit his hands and right calf, severing a main artery in his left thigh and causing massive blood loss.

In May Neal Stephenson, South Africa's national body-boarding champion, lost his foot and part of his right leg in an attack near Plettenberg Bay, one of the most popular resorts on the southern Cape coast.

Six other shark attacks have been reported along the coastline between East London and Saldanha Bay in recent months – the peak of the southern hemisphere's winter season, when fewer people go into the sea. The average number of shark attacks a year along the southern coast is four.

Some municipalities have closed their beaches temporarily, fearing that a solo man-eater might be on the loose. Shark researchers have dismissed the Jaws theory, but local councillors, fearing loss of tourist revenue, are demanding that they come up with an answer to the shark problem.

The surfers are philosophical. "Everyone knows there is a shark risk, but we are in greater danger of being in a car smash on the way to the beach," said Kobus du Toit, who chases the surf around South Africa's wild coastline.

The surfers know all the signs of shark activity – diving seabirds and leaping dolphins. The mid-winter sardine run along the KwaZulu-Natal coast is accompanied by thousands of marine predators. Researchers admit that a series of shark attacks during the winter months is unusual, but they are unanimous in dismissing the theory that a lone, marauding predator is responsible for all the attacks. The incidents have been some distance apart and researchers say that it is clear that different species of shark have been involved.

South Africa's coastline is usually fourth on the list of shark attack "black spots" – after America, Australia and Brazil – according to the statistics provided by the International Shark Attack File at the University of Florida. Most attacks are during the summer months when the beaches are thronged with people, so the fact that the latest spate has occurred in the winter, when the sea temperatures are low, is causing concern.

Leonard Compagno, the director of the Shark Research Centre in Cape Town, pointed out that modern, high-tech clothing and equipment enable far more people, especially divers and surfers, to enjoy the sea during winter.

The main attacker – the great white shark – is a protected species in South African waters.

Several small companies now offer tourists boat rides into shark-infested Cape waters. Thrill-seekers can enter a submerged cage while sharks are attracted by meat and blood dumped into the water. Scientists have criticized some of the operations as "an accident waiting to happen".

Sunday Telegraph, London, 5 July 1998

WESTERN CAPE, SOUTH AFRICA, 1998
Two young men were recovering in hospital yesterday after fighting for their lives against great white sharks.

Christian Lombard, aged twenty-four, was spearfishing

when the sixteen-foot shark grabbed him by the leg. But, as the shark tried to drag him away, he managed to pull out a knife and stab it, forcing it to let go.

Despite horrific leg injuries, Christian swam one hundred metres to rocks, where his terrified girlfriend pulled him ashore at Pringle Bay, Cape Town, before running for help.

Hours later and just a few miles down the coast surfer Ross Taylor, aged nineteen, was mauled by another great white shark.

The first attack happened at Pringle Bay, close to where a diver was killed by a great white last December [1997]. Rescuers on the helicopter which lifted Christian to safety minutes later said they could see the great white circling in the water below.

Last night Lombard was recovering in hospital from emergency surgery on his left leg.

Daily Record, Scotland, 3 August 1998

FLORIDA, USA, 1998

A Georgia couple was attacked off Panama City Beach, Florida, on Tuesday afternoon by a shark that is believed to have killed another man in a separate attack at the same spot fifteen minutes earlier, authorities said.

Dennis Hadden and his wife, Ann, of McDonough were swimming through the blue Florida waters in four and a half feet of water near the beach when the six-foot shark circled the couple and then swam straight at Mrs Hadden, who was on her first snorkelling expedition.

"Its head came right up out of the water, just like in the movies, just like in *Jaws*," said Mr Hadden, forty-two, who works in the training department at Delta Air Lines in Atlanta. "And I saw its teeth go right into her arm."

The McDonough couple was swimming barely twenty yards from shore as they returned from a snorkelling trip at the west end of St Andrew State Park, about one hundred miles southwest of Tallahassee.

The identity and home town of the man attacked and killed a few minutes earlier were not released.

Mrs Hadden, forty-one, was a few feet in front of her husband, who was closer to shore, when she turned around and saw the shark coming at her. "It swam right past me and I thought it was a dolphin," said Mr Hadden.

After the shark bit his wife Mr Hadden stood his ground. "That's when I kicked it," he said. "I guess it didn't like her taste, because it turned loose pretty quick."

The couple quickly moved to shore, fighting off the shark with their arms the entire time. When they hit the breakers, it turned and swam off. "If we had been in deep water and it hadn't stopped, I couldn't have held up," he said. "I was fighting a losing battle."

The couple was released from Bay Medical Center after treatment for cuts and lacerations.

Atlanta Journal-Constitution, 14 September 1998

FLORIDA, USA, 1998

Flailing his arms was the only sign of distress that nine-year-old James William Tellasmon was able to send before he disappeared under the ocean waters off Vero Beach on Saturday while on an outing with his mother and a family friend.

On Monday the Medical Examiner's office revealed the reason for the mysterious disappearance of the boy: James was killed by "a large shark" in an attack that experts say is the first such fatality on the close-in American shoreline in more than twenty years.

Twenty minutes after James, of Vero Beach, disappeared police and Coast Guard units began searching for him. It was not until 7.22 a.m. the next day that the boy's body, headless and armless, was found by fire-rescue divers.

The authorities have not yet determined what type of shark attacked the boy, and it was not clear whether the boy drowned after the shark pulled him under water or whether the decapitation occurred while he was alive.

In his report, Dr Frederick P. Hobin, the district medical examiner, said that the body was identified based on the circumstances in which it was found and because several witnesses were present at the time of the attack. James was found near where he was last seen, in shallow water, the police said.

The last recorded death attributed to a shark took place in Florida's Panhandle in 1988 and it involved a swimmer diving off a boat in deep waters far from shore. A recorded shoreline fatality like James's had not occurred in the United States since 1976, said George Burgess, the director of the International Shark Attack File at the Florida Museum of Natural History in Gainesville.

Florida leads the nation on the number of shark attacks per year, 15–25, but the state also has the highest estimated number of swimmers, so the statistical probability of getting attacked by a shark is minute, Mr Burgess said.

From 1959 to 1988, 12 people were killed in shark attacks in 23 states, compared with 1,505 who died after being struck by lightning, according to statistics compiled by the Shark Attack File. From 1984–7, there were 39 injuries inflicted by sharks in the entire country.

"Ninety-five per cent of these attacks are hit-and-run," Mr Burgess said. "The bottom line message on this is that my heart goes out to the family of this child. If you look at it from a purely detached statistical perspective, this was an amazingly unlucky event."

The attack on James came at a time of year when small fish fleeing the cooling northern waters migrate south and, in a Darwinian chain of survival, are followed by their predators, larger fish, which in turn are shadowed by several species of shark. Yet an attack this vicious is still rare, Mr Burgess said, since in most encounters between sharks and humans, the fish that bite a human limb normally release it once they find it is not their usual prey.

Two weeks ago, Andy Capak, a thirteen-year-old surfing not far from where last week's fatality occurred, was bitten on his right leg by a shark. The shark immediately released the leg, but the boy's wound still required twenty stitches, the police said.

New York Times, 25 November 1998

WESTERN CAPE AND EASTERN CAPE, SOUTH AFRICA, 1998
Shark attacks off the Cape provinces of South Africa – mostly on surfers and body-boarders, who are possibly mistaken for seals – have quadrupled this year, and the growing number of cage-diving operations is being blamed. More sharks are being attracted to the area because cage-dive operators throw chum and bait into the ocean, says Rex Hart, surfer and co-ordinator of Save Our Swimmers and Sharks. He argues that the sharks learn to associate human activity with food and he is lobbying to have the practice banned.

However, researchers at the Natal Sharks Board are sceptical. Sheldon Dudley says, "This year 5 shark attacks have occurred over a wide area from Saldanha Bay on the west coast to East London on the east coast, which is some 650 kilometres from the nearest cage-diving site."

The South African White Shark Research Institute says a more likely reason for the increase in attacks is that commercial fishing in South African waters has decimated the fish population.

The International Shark Attack File in Florida stated that the increase in shark attacks is a worldwide phenomenon, which could reflect better reporting, increasing numbers of people doing water sports or El Nino-related environmental changes affecting water temperatures and fish movements.

Sunday Times, London, 6 December 1998

1999

HAWAII, USA, 1999

It was a nightmare in Hawaii that Mark Monazzami can never forget – no matter how hard he tries.

He emerged from hospital on Thursday and planned to join the search for his bride's body in the beautiful waters off Maui. It was there, he said, that she bled to death after the shark took off her arm.

There are no eyewitnesses to the attack and no body, but there are few doubters in Hawaii, where two other shark attacks have been reported recently, and where tiger sharks were hunted earlier in the decade to reduce the threat of strikes on humans.

Most of all, there is Monazzami's story, in which a tiny kayak with the two honeymooners aboard was pitted against howling trade winds. Maui police say that at this point they have no reason to doubt the story and they hope others will pay heed.

A naturalized US citizen of Iranian descent, Manouchehr Monazzami-Taghadomi, aged thirty-nine, who goes by the name of Mark, has lived in California for twenty years. He had visited and corresponded often in recent years with Nahid Davoodabai, a twenty-nine-year-old Iranian gynaecologist. He finally asked her to marry him in December of 1997.

She accepted and the two took their vows that winter in Iran. She remained for several months to sell her clinic. He returned to Sunnyvale, where he is employed by ESG Consulting of San Francisco, under contract with United Airlines. He began the paperwork his wife would need when she emigrated.

When that finally happened last summer, they planned a spring honeymoon to the scenic shores of Lahaina, Maui. Monazzami, a frequent visitor to Hawaii, wanted to treat his wife to a week in paradise.

Genice Jacobs, a colleague of Monazzami's at ESG Consulting, said the couple were looking forward to their romantic getaway. "He's just a really sweet guy and, if you looked into his eyes, all you could see was love and passion for his wife."

On 13 March they checked into a small condominium resort just beyond the beach on the popular corridor between Kaanapali and Kapalua, north of Lahaina. In an interview from his hospital bed this week Monazzami recalled how they lounged in the sun, snorkelled and took long walks on the beach.

Others were paddling around in kayaks and it looked like fun, Monazzami said, so they decided to give it a try. They reserved a two-seat hard-plastic ocean kayak at a shop on 17 March and picked it up the next morning.

Unlike kayaks in which paddlers sit inside the shell, the seats of this version are on the exterior of the moulded plastic body. The vessel is tippy in choppy waters, but easy to manoeuvre and fast. In warm coastal waters, it is an ideal craft.

Their first paddle was fairly brief. The second was a little longer. In all, they had paddled for about three hours, Monazzami said, before taking a long rest on the beach. Monazzami's arms were weary and he was content to remain on the beach, he said, but his wife persuaded him to climb aboard the kayak one more time.

It was 4 p.m. and the water immediately beyond the beach was still relatively calm. Offshore a small-craft advisory had been issued to boaters. From the beach, a keen and knowing eye might have seen the telltale "wind line" beyond the area protected by the mountains.

Off they went, not getting very far, Monazzami said, before a big wind "came out of nowhere" and began pushing them farther from the beach. Within a short time they were more than a mile offshore. Realizing they were in trouble, they waved their paddles and screamed for help. No one saw or heard. The sun began to set.

Since their kayak was rented on an unlimited basis, payable on return, and no one was expecting them ashore, Monazzami realized that their chances of rescue that night were slim. Davoodabai asked her husband if they were going to die. He reassured her, he said, that, if they could last through the night, perhaps they could flag down someone on a boat at daybreak.

The choppy sea made it difficult to keep the kayak upright, especially with the onset of darkness. They began to capsize frequently, but soon found that it felt warmer in the water anyway. Temperatures above and below the surface were about the same, in the low to mid 70°F, but in the water they were out of the wind.

"I wanted to stay on the kayak to make it easier for someone to see us," Monazzami said, "but I was shivering and cold, and my wife begged me to come in the water, so I went in and every wave that washed over us just felt so good."

At some point during the night, however, Monazzami became concerned about the possibility of a shark attack and said so to his wife. Her response, he said, was that being warm was more important than worrying about sharks.

Moments later, he said, it was Davoodabai who cried out, "Shark!"

In an instant she was pulled under. She surfaced almost immediately, complaining with remarkable calm that her left arm was missing. He reached out to help her and clutched at the wound near her shoulder, but all he could feel was tissue and flesh. Blood rushed through his fingers.

Holding her by the right arm, he climbed back on to the kayak and pulled her aboard. He tried to stop the bleeding, using the string from his swimming trunks as a tourniquet, but the damage was too extensive.

Davoodabai drifted in and out of consciousness, at one point telling her husband that she could feel her fingers. "I said, 'No, honey, you don't have an arm,'" Monazzami said. "She said, 'I swear to God I can feel my fingers.'"

About thirty minutes passed before Davoodabai started feeling severe pain. "She started screaming from the bottom of her heart, and I was going crazy because I couldn't do anything to help her."

Suddenly the screaming stopped. Davoodabai was dead. Dizzy from grief and exhaustion, Monazzami shifted his weight and the kayak capsized again. He let go of her body and she drifted into the blackness.

Monazzami said he climbed back on to the kayak. No longer caring if he lived or died, he said, he stretched out and let the current take him where it may.

He awoke to the sound of his vessel bumping against a rocky shore. Then a wave flipped the kayak and spilled Monazzami into the water. He lost his shorts struggling to get himself on to the beach.

The current had deposited him on Kahoolawe, a small island twelve miles south-west of Maui. The island, until a few years ago used for regular target practice by the Navy, has been uninhabited for years. Live ordnance litters the island's interior.

It was the morning of 19 March when he landed. One of the first things he saw were military helicopters buzzing over the mountaintops.

Weary and feeling faint for lack of food and water, he spent most of the day resting on the beach, covering himself with trash in an attempt to get out of the wind, vowing to climb the mountain on Saturday morning.

The next day, he said, he found a pair of old sandals. "I spent five or six hours hiking ... I went all the way to the top of the mountain and – nothing."

Monazzami said he never ate, but it rained on Saturday and he drank from pools formed in the rocks. "Before that I was very close to drinking sea water."

On the way back down the mountain late on Saturday afternoon he got lost and was startled to discover a satellite dish atop an old military bunker. It was dark by the time he reached the building, but it afforded him some protection until morning. At daybreak on Sunday Monazzami fiddled with some of the equipment he came across in the bunker, but found all of it useless – until he discovered the phone.

It was concealed in a small casing on the wall. He followed the wire to a jack and plugged in the line. There was a dial tone. He dialed 911 [for emergency services].

"The guy answered and that's when I burst into tears,"

Monazzami recalled. "All the pain of not having my wife hit me."

Keith Keau, enforcement chief for the Maui division of the Department of Land and Natural Resources, was involved in the rescue effort. "When we found him, he was totally dehydrated and in shock."

Monazzami's kayak was retrieved from a nearby beach on Monday and not found to have any damage "other than scratches and dents caused by the rocks," Keau said.

On Wednesday afternoon, while searching for the body off the shore of Kahoolawe, investigators from the Maui County Police Department found a blue life jacket "similar to the one reportedly worn by Davoodabai". Asked if the vest had tooth marks or bloodstains on it, Lt Glenn Cuomo would only say, "It's still being examined."

The case is being treated as a missing person investigation by the criminal investigations division of the Police Department, according to Captain Victor Tengan. "That's just standard procedure," he explained, adding that at this point there is no reason to doubt Monazzami's story.

John Naughton, a National Marine Fisheries Service biologist and shark expert based in Honolulu, said it would not be surprising for a shark to strike a lifeless body repeatedly, thus freeing a life vest.

Monazzami was discharged from the hospital on Thursday afternoon and planned to join police in the search for his wife's body. "The sad part about it is it didn't have to happen. Nobody told us how dangerous it was out there."

Andrea Smith, manager of Extreme Sports Maui, which rented the kayak to Monazzami and his wife, said: "We tell everybody to stay inside the wind line and within the sheltered areas. And Mr Monazzami was told all this."

This was the second incident statewide this year involving kayakers getting swept out to sea, but the first such incident in at least five years in Maui, Tengan said.

The apparent attack on Davoodabai is the third shark attack this month.

On the morning of 5 March Maui resident Robin Knutson, aged twenty-nine, was bitten in the leg while swimming 300 yards off Kaanapali with her boyfriend. She remains hospitalized with extensive injuries and faces possible amputation.

Three days later an Arizona tourist, Jonathan Allen, aged eighteen, was bitten while bodyboarding off Kauai. He suffered only minor injuries and was treated and released.

The first two attacks were blamed on tiger sharks, the top predator in Hawaiian waters. Tiger sharks can measure twenty feet or longer. They feed primarily during the night or at dawn or dusk on reef fish and sea turtles. They typically move into deeper water during the day.

While shark attacks on swimmers and surfers in Hawaii average about two per year, the state hasn't had a full-blown shark scare since 1992–93, when a series of attacks within a very short span off Oahu led to the organization of a state task force and the first shark control program since the mid-1970s.

Naughton, a member of the task force, said the state, using baited hooks, removed 11 large tiger sharks amid the scare six years earlier. Freelance hunters, mostly resident surfers, are believed to have removed another 70 or so tiger sharks from near-shore waters surrounding the island of Oahu, where most of the attacks took place.

"Now we're getting calls again from people wondering what we're going to do in light of recent attacks,"

Naughton said. "They're wondering if we're going to remove any more." The answer right now is no, he said, adding that he believes Hawaii's waters remain safe for those who swim or surf responsibly – in daylight hours and away from murky areas such as river mouths, which often attract feeding sharks.

He pointed out that the two recent attacks – the swimmer and the kayaker – involved "high risk" circumstances. In the first instance, the swimmer had ventured way offshore and witnesses said she was swimming toward a small pod of humpback whales.

"I had heard there was an injured whale in the area and went up immediately after the attack, and we did see an injured whale a mile or so from where the attack took place," he said. "I recommended closing the beaches until the whale was out of the area because we know from aerial work that, if you have an injured whale, you usually have a few large tiger sharks shadowing the whale."

As for the most recent instance, Naughton, said, "We have made some recommendations to people who rent kayaks that they should certainly warn tourists about the possible dangers, and not to rent them when there are hazardous winds and large surf."

As for those who find themselves adrift in a kayak in the middle of the night, Naughton cautioned, "Stay on the vessel at all costs."

Los Angeles Times, 27 March 1999

WESTERN CAPE, SOUTH AFRICA, 1999
A grief-stricken Knysna father collapsed and wept over the body of his teenage son minutes after he was savaged by a shark in Buffels Bay yesterday.

South Western Districts rugby star and Craven week player Hercules Pretorius, aged fourteen, of Knysna was attacked and mauled on his buttocks and lower leg by a huge shark only fifty metres from the shore at about 11.15 a.m.

Despite attempts to revive the body-boarder's savaged body, Hercules died on the beach a few minutes later.

Deeply shocked, Hercules's body-boarding friend and school mate Zaack Mells, aged fifteen, described the terrifying incident. "Hercules, I and another friend, Marius van der Mescht, were in the water when suddenly I saw Hercules's board flip into the air. I looked around and saw this big shark." He then saw blood in the water.

He and Marius went to their friend's aid. "We got him to the beach and we were trying to talk to him, but he did not answer. People were trying to revive him by rubbing his hands and feet, but it was too late," he said.

When Hercules's father Harry arrived at the scene, he collapsed and wept over the body of his only son.

"Hercules was a great guy and he had a big heart," said Zaack, who befriended Hercules at Knysna High School. He said his friend had been an excellent sportsman and that he had been popular at school.

Dr Johannes Meyer, a Knysna general practitioner summoned to the scene by a witness, said Hercules must have died of rapid blood loss soon after the attack.

Later, Knysna police spokesperson Captain Michelle Lesch said that an ambulance was on the scene within eight minutes, but Pretorius, who had suffered severe injuries to his side and right leg, was already dead.

"It was a sizeable bite between his hip and ribs on the right-hand side. It was big. There is nothing left there," said Lesch. She added that it was not yet known what type of shark had killed the boy, but great whites are common along South Africa's eastern and southern coasts.

Pretorius is survived by his parents and a seventeen-year-old sister, Luczadah.

The beach at Buffels Bay has always been regarded as safe, with the last reported attack occurring about thirty years ago.

Cape Times, 16 July 1999

CORNWALL, UNITED KINGDOM, 1999
A fifteen-foot great white shark has been reported off a surfing beach in Cornwall.

If confirmed, it will be the first time the great white, which inspired the novel and film *Jaws*, has been recorded in British waters. It swam within five feet of the *Blue Fox*, a boat full of anglers, two miles off Polzeath.

Witnesses who saw the shark included Mike Turner, a former shark fisherman from South Africa. He said: "There is nothing that looks like it in the water. I am ninety-five per cent sure it was a great white. I reckon it had been following us since we were 800 yards offshore and was around for quite a while because the seagulls would not land anywhere near the boat."

Also on the *Blue Fox*, a twenty-seven-foot charter boat based at Padstow, was the angler Henry Gilbey, aged twenty-six. "It was the greatest thing I have ever seen in my life," he said. "We were fishing for porbeagle sharks when it cruised along in the water."

There have long been rumours of great white sharks circling Britain, but until now sightings have generally been dismissed as fishermen's tales. However, marine experts say that there is no reason why the sharks, which have been recorded as close as the Bay of Biscay, should not sometimes come closer.

Douglas Herdson of the National Marine Aquarium in Plymouth suspects that great whites have been living unnoticed off the coast of Britain. "A sighting is not unexpected. It is quite possible that they could come into British waters occasionally. I suspect that they have been out there for years but, for a sighting to be confirmed, there would have to be a photo or a shark expert on board the boat."

The Times, London, 26 August 1999

FLORIDA, USA, 1999

A grandmother told yesterday of the terrifying moment [on 7 September, when] she was attacked by a shark as she bathed in the sea during a family holiday in Florida.

Janet Ferguson, 61, was "testing" the water before allowing her grandchildren to go swimming. She said she was only knee-deep in the Atlantic when she felt "this excruciating pain in my thigh".

At first she thought it was a large piece of driftwood that was digging into to her, so she put her hand out to knock it away. "I made contact with something that was moving along the back of my leg, so I hit it hard and it seemed to move away," added Mrs Ferguson, who is recovering at home in Morham, East Lothian [Scotland].

"It did not even cross my mind that a shark had taken a large chunk out of my thigh." It was only when she walked out of the sea to tell her husband John that she began to realize the full horror of what had happened.

"I shouted that I had been bitten by something, but my husband just told me to stop my blathering," she added. "Blood was pouring down the back of my leg, so I put my hand there and felt pieces of flesh hanging off the back."

Mrs Ferguson collapsed from shock, and the sea off Cape Canaveral was immediately cleared by lifeguards as a sunbather with a medical kit gave her first aid.

Her daughter Gillian, who was also on the holiday

with her husband and two children, is a trained nurse and knew the wound had to be bandaged quickly. "It was really deep, about an inch all the way round," she said.

Paramedics took Mrs Ferguson to hospital, where fifty stitches were inserted. Experts in Florida think the shark involved in the attack ten days ago could have been a nurse shark.

Daily Mail, London, 17 September 1999

Pigeye Shark

The pigeye shark has a thick body and a short, blunt snout. Its fins have darker tips and it has eyes that look rather too small for its body. Also known as the Java shark, it is commonly found close to shore, in the surf and in shallow bays. It is widely sought as a game fish and its flesh is regarded as good to eat fresh, although it is also traditionally preserved by drying and salting.

Shark Facts

Length:	7 feet to 9 feet (2.1m to 2.7m)
Weight:	77 lb to 99 lb (35 kg to 45 kg)
Colouring:	Greyish green upper with white or light grey belly
Diet:	Fish, rays, squid, lobsters, cuttlefish
Pups:	Born live and up to 2 feet (61 cm)
Status:	Under threat – population declining

Pigeye Shark Range

SHARK ATTACKS
2000–09

2000

SOUTH AUSTRALIA, AUSTRALIA, 2000
A board sailor who went missing off South Australia's Yorke Peninsula last year was probably taken by a great white shark, the state's coroner found.

The coroner, Mr Wayne Chivell, said that, while the body of Mr Tony Donoghue, 22, was never found, his sailboard and his wetsuit had been discovered, and the damage to the suit was consistent with a shark attack.

Mr Chivell said that Mr Donoghue had been staying with friends at Hardwicke Bay in May last year when he decided to go board sailing. When he failed to return several hours later, his friends conducted a search along the coastline and reported his disappearance to police.

Later that night his undamaged sailboard was found washed ashore and some time later his harness and wetsuit were located.

The Age, Melbourne, 2 February 2000

NEW SOUTH WALES, AUSTRALIA, 2000
A professional shark hunter may be brought in after two shark attacks in the Parramatta river, close to

Sydney's Olympic facilities.

A shark snapped at the oars of a schoolboys' boat near suburban Gladesville. The following day a boat was punctured less than one hundred feet from shore.

Olympic officials recently gave assurances that there would be no danger from sharks.

The Times, London, 14 March 2000

QUEENSLAND, AUSTRALIA, 2000
An Australian surfer has been badly bitten in a rare shark attack in the first incident in seas off Queensland's Gold Coast in three decades.

Nets placed along beaches on the popular tourist strip had been aimed at stopping sharks getting too close to the shore. It is not yet clear how close the victim was to the shore when he was attacked.

Police identified the victim as thirty-year-old Rojcezic Andrija, who has a twelve-inch gash in his left calf. He was taken to the Gold Coast Hospital, where a spokesman described his condition as "serious".

Sydney had been placed on shark alert earlier this month after a series of attacks, sightings and nettings of sharks.

Wire report, 31 March 2000

VICTORIA, AUSTRALIA, 2000
A shark expert will examine a human foot found on a beach South-East of Melbourne.

X-rays yesterday confirmed the foot – found inside a sneaker on Koonya beach at Sorrento was human, police said. The navy blue sneaker was a size nine with Velcro fastenings, Detective Sergeant Alan Dickinson said.

He said the foot's bone structure was complete and the lower ankle bone was still attached. But pathologists were yet to remove the foot from the shoe so it was hard to judge the age, race and gender of its owner, D. S. Dickinson said.

It was unknown how long the foot had been in the water and police could not yet tell how it had become detached. Detective Sergeant Dickinson said: "There are several options, but whether it's a shark attack or human foul play or it's misadventure or whether it's the propellor of a boat is something I'll have to work out."

A man out walking found the foot at about 8.30 a.m. on Monday.

Australian Associated Press, 9 May 2000

VICTORIA, AUSTRALIA, 2000

A severed foot found on Koonya Beach in Melbourne was bitten off by a small shark close to where it was found, police say.

Tests by a shark expert and forensic scientists show the owner of the "well-manicured" left foot that was found in a blue trainer was aged between twenty and forty.

Alan Dickinson, of Rosebud police, said: "Larger sharks can digest something as big as a human foot and regurgitate it later miles down the track. But the damage to the shoe indicates it was not a larger shark that took it, so the chance it was taken miles away is far less."

He said it is unclear whether the owner of the foot was already dead when the shark attacked.

Wire report, 10 May 2000

PAPUA NEW GUINEA, 2000

A man was killed and a young boy badly injured in two separate shark attacks near a tourist resort in Papua New Guinea.

The local villager died from loss of blood following the attack, which happened when he was diving on a reef just off Long Island, near Madang, about 310 miles north of the capital, Port Moresby.

The nine-year-old boy, identified as Adam, had his left leg and ankle mauled while he was standing in knee-deep water on the island's coast.

The boy was taken to hospital by a Madang businessman who flew to the resort after hearing radio reports of the attack. The child is expected to recover, a hospital spokesman said.

Four years ago [1996] tiger sharks killed several people near Madang. It is not known what kind of sharks made the latest two attacks.

Papua New Guinea Post Courier, 10 May 2000

ALABAMA–FLORIDA, USA, 2000
Wanda Boshers and her family arrived on the sugar white sands of Pensacola Beach, Florida, after an eight-hour drive from Nashville. As the emerald-green water washed gently ashore, a wave of apprehension swept over Boshers.

"I had always got into the ocean," said the thirty-ni-ne-year-old homemaker, "but I'm not going to any more. I'm not going to get ate [*sic*] up by no shark. I'm keeping my arms and my legs.

"I'm not getting in it – and neither are my babies," she said, motioning toward her kids, two-year-old Brandon and five-year-old Amber.

Despite two nearby shark attacks within the last month, marine experts say the waters of the Gulf Coast are no more dangerous than usual – good news for beaches reliant on tourist revenue. "You have a better chance of winning the Florida Lottery than getting attacked by a shark," said George Burgess, director of the International Shark Attack File at the University of Florida.

Even Chuck Anderson agrees. He didn't hit the jackpot – but a bull shark ate part of his right arm on 9 June 2000. While training for a series of summer triathlons, the forty-four-year-old assistant principal from south Alabama bumped into a shark as he swam in the waters off the Gulf Shores near the Alabama–Florida border.

Based on teeth marks left on Anderson, biologists estimate the shark weighed 300 lbs and was more than seven feet long.

Warming up at 6.38 a.m., Anderson splashed past pier pilings destroyed by a hurricane. He bumped into something – a log, maybe a school of fish, he thought. He peered under the water.

"You see that fin coming at you and think, 'Oh, shoot,'" Anderson recounted over the weekend. "They tell you when a dog chases you to holler, 'No! No!' Well, I did that out of instinct and thought, 'Stupid, he can't hear you.'"

Anderson pushed off the shark's snout. He yelled to warn his training partner Richard Watley and another triathlete.

On the first of three passes the shark bit the fingers off Anderson's right hand. The shark pushed the former football coach to the bottom, ten feet under water. On its final attack the shark chomped down on Anderson's arm.

Then, still clamped to his arm, the bull shark pushed Anderson on to a sandbar fifteen yards from shore. Struggling in the sand and shallow water, the shark slowed its advance.

"I actually broke my own arm off," Anderson said. "I heard the snap of it. He was gnashing back and forth like in the *Jaws* movie. Once it had broken off in his mouth, I made a beeline for the shore."

The shark chased Anderson all the way to the shore and then went after his training partner, Watley, who was eighty to one hundred feet out.

Richard Watley, aged fifty-five, said he knew he had a fight on his hands when the shark bit the whole right-hand side of his body. He said, "It came up under me and I looked down and saw him staring me right in the face. I thought, 'I'm going to die,' and I decided I wasn't going to die without a fight."

So he punched the shark every five or ten seconds, while he swam to the shore. Watley said: "It bit my thigh and would have taken a chunk out of me, but I hit it again. I thought it might leave me alone, but it came at me again and again. I would punch him, he would retreat and then I would swim as fast as I could for a few seconds, but then I would have to turn round and face him again. He chased me all the way to the shore."

As for Anderson, he will have to have more surgery in two months' time, but he has kept his sense of humour. "He's got a Timex in his belly, so, when they do a commerical about it, I want my share of the royalties," said Anderson.

Four days after Anderson and Watley were attacked, another bull shark partially ripped the rear swim platform on a twenty-two-foot pleasure boat motoring west of Pensacola Beach. The boaters yelled at swimmers to leave. Another bull shark beached itself sixty miles east of Pensacola at about the same time.

Talk of the attacks has made the rounds at the beach, but tourists are undeterred. Inflatable dragons, pink water wings and silver air mattresses bob on the waves with happy passengers.

"I had heard about it, but it didn't bother me. Most shark attacks are overblown anyway," Alan Thompson, a thirty-two-year-old sales manager from Houston, said before paddling a rental kayak into the Gulf with his toddler son.

Pensacola Beach lifeguard Wes Holstman said his crew sees sharks nearly every day from their salmon-coloured wooden towers. Guards see dark shark outlines cruising forty to fifty yards from the beach. "The locals know there are sharks out there," Holstman said. "They're everywhere. Chances are real slim they'll attack."

George Burgess said bull and tiger sharks are plentiful in the Gulf. They are dangerous because their teeth "have serrations like a steak knife", so they can carve up their prey. "Remember, as we use the sea there's no guarantee that it's going to be safe. It's not like the YMCA pool in Atlanta. It's a wilderness. It's no different than going for a hike in the Rocky Mountains and considering bears or going to the Serengeti Plain and encountering a pride of lions. The ocean has its predators."

It's something Anderson considered whenever he trained for a triathlon. "Every time I got in the Gulf it still took five or ten minutes to get over the apprehension. It's like walking across the street. You do it every day of your life and you know someone could make a mistake and run you down. You just never think it's going to be you. I didn't do anything wrong. I was just out swimming in his house and he happened to bump into me."

Atlanta Journal-Constitution, 3 July 2000

Blacktip Reef Shark

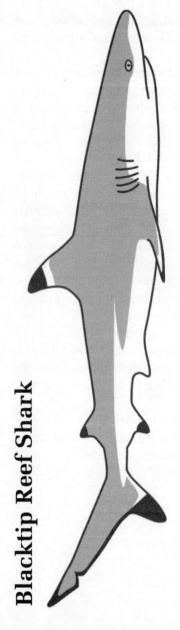

Shark Facts

Length: 5 feet to 6 feet 7 inches (1.5 m to 2 m)

Weight: Up to 30 lb (13.6 kg)

Colouring: Pale brownish grey upper with white belly

Diet: Fish such as mullet, grouper or wrasses;
             squid, shrimp, cuttlefish, seabirds

Pups: Between two and five born at a time
             up to 20 inches (50 cm) long

Status: Not seriously threatened

The blacktip is the most common shark found on tropical coral reefs in the Indian and Pacific Oceans. Although this shark has been known to attack humans, such instances are quite rare, even though the shark can be seen in large numbers in shallow water, easily identified by the black tips on its fins breaking the surface. The blacktip is fished for its meat as well as for its fins and liver oil.

312

Blacktip Reef Shark Range

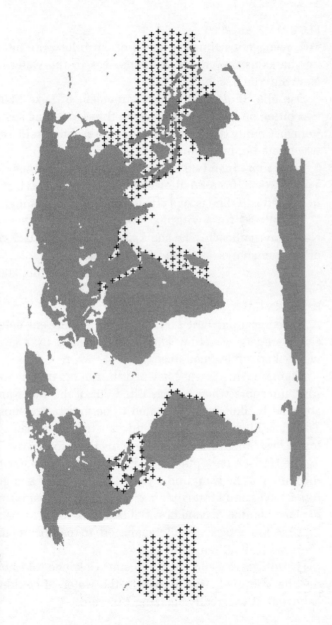

FLORIDA, USA, 2000

Two teenagers swimming in an ocean inlet were bitten by sharks as they enjoyed themselves in the water off New Smyrna Beach, Florida.

Danielle Shidemantle, aged nineteen, of Lake Mary, was bitten on her upper thigh by a three-foot-long shark, Volusia County deputy beach chief Joe Wooden said. She was treated in hospital and released.

Little more than two hours later Amber Benningfield, aged thirteen, from Bowling Green, Kentucky, was bitten in her left calf. She is in a stable condition in hospital.

The attacks were within a few yards of each other off New Smyrna Beach. The sharks were probably black tip or spinner sharks, said Joe Wooden.

Los Angeles Times, 4 July 2000

EASTERN CAPE, SOUTH AFRICA, 2000

A fifteen-year-old East London surfer underwent emergency surgery yesterday after being savaged by a great white shark off Nahoon Reef.

Shannon Ainslie was busy paddling about fifty metres from the shore when he was lifted out of the water and attacked by the shark estimated to be four metres long. The shark bit Ainslie's right hand, causing severe damage to the flesh and exposing bone on his third finger.

The Hudson Park pupil said he came face to face with the animal as he went under the water. "I looked straight into its eyes and I thought I was dreaming," he said from his East London private hospital bed.

After the attack Ainslie managed to paddle to the shore with about ten other surfers.

His fifteen-year-old friend Alistair Cokayne told how the shark flipped Ainslie over in the water. "I couldn't believe it. It was really amazing," he said.

Once on dry land, Ainslie realized he had been bitten as blood was dripping from his injured hand. His seventeen-year-old brother Brandon rushed him to Medicross, where he was treated before being transferred to East London Private Hospital. Ainslie underwent surgery on the hand to ensure the wound was clean and stitched properly.

The incident was caught on video camera by an American visitor staying at the Sugershack backpackers' hostel on the beachfront. Aquarium curator Willie Maritz, who saw the video, said: "There's absolutely no doubt it was a great white. You could actually see it grab the surfboard." He suggested the animal was returning to the Cape after following and feeding off sardines migrating to Kwazulu-Natal waters. He also felt that the shark intended to bite the teenager's surfboard, but his hand got in the way. As for Ainslie, "He was bloody lucky!"

Durban Daily News, 18 July 2000

HAWAII, USA, 2000
A windsurfer is in critical condition after being attacked by a shark off a Hawaiian island.

French holidaymaker Jean Alain Goenvec, aged fifty-three, was bitten on his lower left leg while sitting on his windsurfing board about a mile off the island of Maui.

He estimated the length of the shark at twelve to fifteen feet, said a companion.

Ananova, 16 August 2000

FLORIDA, USA, 2000
A man swimming in shallow water only feet from his Florida home was killed in a shark attack witnessed by his wife. "It was just like a Jaws situation," she said.

Thadeus Kubinski, aged sixty-nine, was dead by the

315

time emergency workers arrived following the rare shark sighting in the Intracoastal Waterway, said St Pete Beach Fire Chief Fred Golliner. The waterway runs between the barrier islands that separate the Gulf of Mexico from Florida's mainland near St Pete Beach, just across a narrow bay from St Petersburg.

Kubinski's son, Edward, said his mother, Anna, told him the couple went swimming in five feet of water about ten feet from the dock of their home in Boca Ciega Bay.

Mrs Kubinski noticed her husband struggling with a marine animal and she leaped out of the water to seek help. She told another son, Richard, that she saw a dorsal fin that was "just like the Jaws situation".

"She was pretty much in a panic," Richard Kubinski said. "She thought the best thing to do was to run and call for help."

Thadeus Kubinski suffered wounds from his armpit to his thigh. Authorities said they believe he was killed by a shark, although the medical examiner planned to consult with marine biologists for confirmation.

Edward Kubinski said his parents frequently swam in the shallow waters behind their home, where they have lived since retiring in 1984.

Authorities said they have rarely, if ever, seen sharks in the Intracoastal's waters. "I've been working with this city for twenty-five years and there has not been an incident involving an apparent shark attack in that time," Golliner said.

Atlanta Journal-Constitution, 31 August 2000

JAPAN, 2000

A Japanese surfer, twenty-one-year-old Takayuki Miura, has died from massive blood loss following a terrifying shark attack.

The man was surfing with friends off Miyako Island, near Okinawa, when he was dragged under by an eight-foot shark and bitten repeatedly in a savage mauling.

British surfer Owen Phillips, aged thirty-three, risked his own life in what proved to be a vain attempt to save Miura. He swam out to the victim, who had lost both legs and one arm. Battling against a strong current, Phillips helped bring Miura ashore with the aid of other rescuers.

Phillips, a teacher and part-time lifeguard from Barry, South Wales, said: "I only did what anybody else would have done."

Phillips and other rescuers took turns trying to resuscitate the victim until an ambulance arrived. Paramedics took him to a nearby hospital, but Miura died during the journey.

Mainichi Daily News, Japan, 18 September, and
Daily Mail, London, 23 September 2000

SOUTHERN AUSTRALIA, AUSTRALIA, 2000

No one will ever know what went through the mind of Cameron Bayes in the final moments before he was killed by a great white shark off South Australia. What is certain is that the attack lasted long enough for the young New Zealander to have been terrifyingly aware of exactly what was happening.

Bayes, aged twenty-five, from Auckland, was on a six-month working honeymoon across Australia with his wife, Tina, when he arrived at Cactus Beach.

It is a legendary but isolated surf beach, which lies on the largely unpopulated, starkly beautiful coast of the Great Australian Bight – an arc of rugged cliffs and pounding surf that extends for hundreds of miles across the base of the continent.

Having arrived at the surfers' camp site at Cactus Beach

on Saturday night, the young Kiwi was eager to catch a wave and was out on the water early the next morning.

Sunday 24 September 2000 dawned misty and overcast. The sun struggled to force its way through a thick blanket of sea fog. "It was eerie," one local surfer later recalled. The weather, he thought, "had the whiff of shark" about it.

Bayes had been surfing for less than an hour when the attack came.

Unlike most shark attacks, this one had several witnesses – surfers mostly, watching from the dunes that line the bay. They describe seeing "a vortex of water" which knocked Bayes off his surfboard – the classic "thump, bite and spit" technique of the great white shark.

Jeff Hunter, a lecturer from Port Lincoln, the nearest town of any size, has surfed at Cactus Beach for more than twenty-five years. He was walking along the beach with his son at the time when he spotted the attack. "Bayes was paddling, sitting just out the back of the breakline," he said.

He saw the shark quickly circle Bayes before knocking him into the water. "It was a ferocious attack. The shark had no hesitation. It was surrounding him – it was all over him. It took him in a circular, anti-clockwise motion."

After the initial furious assault, the shark released its victim. Bayes, incredibly, was seen to climb back on to his surfboard and start paddling frantically towards the shore. But the shark returned. This time it went in for the kill.

"It looked horrendous. There was blood and board everywhere," said Mr Hunter.

Bayes disappeared from sight amid the broiling grey water. The shark – estimated to have been 14–20 feet long and weighing up to two tonnes – then surfaced about 500 yards from the beach, where it appeared to spit out a chunk of surfboard.

Mr Hunter said he considered paddling out on his own board to help, but had had no time. "It was all over in five to six minutes."

No trace of Cameron Bayes's body has been found. His widow, who is in her mid-twenties, was taken to hospital suffering from deep shock.

Ron Gates, who runs a camping ground at the beach, said it was the first fatal attack that he knew of. He said the only other great white incident at the beach he could remember was a non-fatal attack in 1997. However, local records show that, in 1995, a local boy bled to death after a great white shark bit off his leg while he was swimming.

On average there is one fatal shark attack in Australia every year. Before this week there had been eight fatal shark attacks in South Australian waters in the past forty years, so, while not commonplace, they are by no means exceptional. The death of Cameron Bayes duly made the front pages.

What was to follow in the next twenty-four hours, though, horrified the entire nation. The next day, Monday [25 September 2000], about 130 miles down the coast, seventeen-year-old Jevan Wright was one of a group of three surfers enjoying another noted surfing beach, Black Point, just outside the tiny township of Elliston, 150 kilometres from Port Lincoln. It was early – 7.30 a.m.

Unlike Bayes, Wright never knew what hit him. Witnesses to this second attack said they saw "a large fin and a thrashing in the water". Moments later half of Wright's mangled surfboard bobbed to the surface. The churning water calmed, leaving only the sound of the surf. Jevan Wright's body has not been recovered – not so much as a shred of wetsuit.

Two surfers. Two sharks. Two fatal attacks on

consecutive days. The odds against such a double tragedy, according to experts, are incalculable.

"It's a case of tragic coincidence," said Barry Bruce, a marine scientist based in Hobart, Tasmania. He dismisses theories that a single man-eater is responsible for both attacks. Recent research, he says shows that sharks never travel more than about fifty miles a day.

"And they're not travelling in a straight line," said John West, who collates Australia's Shark Attack File at Sydney's Taronga Zoo. "They zig-zag all over the place." This week's fatalities occurred too far apart to be the work of one animal. Nevertheless, to have two fatalities in two days, said West, is "totally unprecedented".

Despite all this, in the immediate aftermath of the deaths there were calls for the sharks to be identified, tracked and killed. It was a prescription in keeping with Peter Benchley's *Jaws*, in which the stalking of the killer gives the book and film their nail-biting denouement. This version of shark behaviour casts the great white in the role of cold, calculating killer with a taste for human flesh. Failure to exterminate the predator, the thinking runs, merely invites more attacks, more deaths.

Vic Hislop hunted sharks for thirty years. He now runs his own shark museum in Hervey Bay, Queensland. Hislop is dismissed by Australia's shark academics as a renegade and a loose cannon (at least when they are being polite). This week he called for the setting up of a rapid response unit that could be flown to any beach in Australia to kill man-eaters. He branded the Australian Government "criminally negligent" for introducing legislation in 1997 to protect great white sharks.

In Elliston, though, the mood is very different. Nobody appeared to be calling for revenge. The atmosphere in the town (population 240) is one of subdued awe, mixed with sadness and sympathy for the families of the two men.

Wright's death is the biggest thing to have happened to Elliston for years. It is largely a community of the retired, who mix uneasily with a shifting population of tanned, bleached blond surfers equipped with battered four-wheel drives, stuffed with camping equipment, surfboards lashed to the roofs. There is a tiny police station, a couple of general stores and a bakery that boasts that its pies and pasties are "the best in the west".

Kevin Brooke, aged sixty-eight, is what is generally known as an outback character. Dressed in a stained singlet and shorts, and with a huge handlebar moustache, he owns a small property outside the town. He likes to shoot and skin wombats – "they taste a bit like pork, a bit like beef". As Elliston's resident ambulance driver, he was one of the first on the scene after the attack on Wright. "To me it was an accident waiting to happen. I reckon it's a rogue shark. It'll attack again for sure."

All week a steady stream of locals and curious tourists have come to the headland overlooking the spot where Wright was killed. Two sticks of driftwood have been lashed together to form a simple cross. Someone has picked out the name "Jevan" in pebbles.

Pat Clark, aged forty, a building contractor and a friend of the Wright family, who often holidays at Elliston, stood barefoot in shorts and a T-shirt on the cliff top. He and his brother Frank, aged forty-six, were on the scene of the attack within minutes in their "tinnie", the small aluminium fishing boats that are ubiquitous in the area.

"It's horrific for something like this to happen. This is a small community and everyone knows everyone," said Clark. "But to say that we should go out and kill the sharks is ridiculous. This is their environment and you enter it at your own risk. Every surfer in Australia knows that."

It is a sentiment with which Peter Benchley, the author of Jaws and now an ardent shark conservationist, agrees. "It certainly does not deserve a vigilante express out there to slaughter the sharks. The sharks responsible for these attacks were only doing what they do naturally, but they make mistakes that unfortunately cost people their lives. One of their ways of finding out if something is edible or not is to bite it. More often than not they will go off after the first bite – because we are not their normal prey. But they can still kill with just one bite."

Wright's family have been the epitome of quiet dignity in the face of their son's death. Not for them the calls for summary execution of the great white.

Jevan's father, Jeff, agrees with Benchley: "We're in their world – in their back yard. You take your chances when you go out surfing. If Jevan had had a chance to belt it in the eyes, he would have. It consoles me that he didn't know a thing when the attack happened."

The motives for the attacks might seem obvious – a shark gets hungry, runs into suitable prey and chomps it. Yet there is more to it than that. The attack on Wright, in particular, is puzzling because it occurred in such shallow water – a depth of about ten feet.

Great whites, the experts say, do not like hunting in the shallows. One suggestion is that a school of salmon was swimming near the beach and enticed the shark to swim closer to the shore than normal. Another theory is that there were seals and dolphins in the area, and they might have attracted a big shark. There are several seal colonies only a couple of miles offshore from Cactus Beach.

"These people were surfing in a particularly dangerous part of Australia because there are seal colonies around," says Benchley. "In the water a surfboard looks remarkably like a seal, especially when seen from below and behind, and sharks generally look up at their prey."

These two attacks have sent shock waves up and down the coasts of Australia, where many people base their livelihoods – and a great amount of their leisure time – on the sea. But for dedicated surfers nothing – not even the threat of a great white – can keep them from the chance of riding the perfect wave.

One Englishman newly arrived in Australia last week hired a board and headed off into the surf.

"What do we do if we see a shark?" he asked an Australian paddling out alongside him.

"Mate, whatever you do, don't tell anyone," came the reply. "These waves are so good we don't want the beach closed."

Sunday Telegraph, London, 1 October 2000

WESTERN AUSTRALIA, AUSTRALIA, 2000

An air and sea search was under way last night for a great white shark that killed one swimmer and mauled another in a terrifying early morning attack.

The water on Cottesloe Beach, near Perth, Western Australia, turned red after the twenty-foot shark lunged at forty-nine-year-old father of three Ken Crew in waist-deep water fifty yards from shore. After biting off his right leg, the shark threw him in the air and dragged him thirty yards across the sheltered bay.

Fellow swimmer Dirk Avery, aged fifty-two, who tried to help Mr Crew, was also attacked, but managed to fend off the shark with his feet and hands. One woman who saw the horror unfold had a heart attack and was taken to hospital.

The carnage happened as a group of early morning enthusiasts met for their customary swim at Cottesloe Beach, Perth's equivalent of Bondi Beach in Sydney.

Schoolteacher John Bailey had been swimming next to Mr Crew when the shark struck. "I always thought the film *Jaws* was exaggerated, but not after what I saw today," he said. "The shark took him and spun him around as if Ken was standing up in the water on a pivot.

"Seconds before that I had been carried away from him by a small wave towards the beach or it could easily have been me. Immediately afterwards the shark took off towards the beach because another swimmer had started swimming towards Ken.

"The shark attacked the second man in waist-deep water. And it was only because it was so large and the water so shallow that it was not able to grab hold of him properly and only injured his lower legs and feet."

Mr Bailey said that, when he and others helped Mr Avery out of the water, his legs and feet looked as though they had been grated.

This was the third fatal shark attack by a great white in Australian waters in less than six weeks.

A helicopter pilot sent out to look for the shark and drive it further out to sea spotted a massive great white about 500 yards from the scene. By flying low, he managed to frighten it further into the Indian Ocean, where it disappeared into the depths.

Great whites are a protected species and must not be killed. Hours later, however, the Western Australian Government agreed to overrule the law and ordered the shark to be shot on sight. With its whereabouts still unknown, police and wildlife officials put out an urgent warning to beachgoers to stay out of the water.

Mr Crew, who ran a garage which serviced school buses, was among a group of swimmers who met daily at the beach in an area known as The Basin. He was in the water with seven friends when the shark attacked.

From the balcony of the Blue Duck Café where the swimmers met for breakfast, Roman Catholic priest Brian Morrison, a friend of Mr Crew, watched in horror as the attack occurred.

"Somebody had shouted 'shark' and I and others ran to look out into The Basin," he said. "We saw Ken thrashing around and I was filled with a terrible dread. By the time I ran down to the beach, they had brought him ashore. His leg was missing and it was obvious there was nothing any of us could do for him."

Father Morrison gave Mr Crew the last rites as his life ebbed away. "We were all gathered round with our arms around him," he said. "I whispered into his ear, 'Kenny, if you can hear me, I'm going to give you the blessings of the Church, so squeeze my hand.' And he squeezed my hand just twice. It was after that point that he passed away."

Father Morrison said he had been consoling Mr Crew's wife Robyn and her three children.

Last night Adelaide shark expert Rodney Fox, an adviser on the film *Jaws* and a survivor of a shark attack thirty years ago, dismissed concerns that the great white was changing its feeding habits. "I don't think it's going after humans for any particular reason. I suspect that these last three, recent attacks are a series of sad coincidences."

In September two surfers were killed in separate attacks by great white sharks on the South Australian coast. Their bodies were never recovered.

Dr Jim Penn, a shark expert with the West Australian Fisheries Department, warned that great whites would be congregating along the coast in the next few weeks as they followed migrating whales towards the colder waters of the South.

Daily Mail, London, 7 November 2000

FLORIDA, USA, 2000

A retired British doctor holidaying in Florida narrowly escaped death when he was attacked by a shark.

Colin Shadforth managed to kick himself free of the six-foot creature after it punctured two arteries in his leg. He dragged himself back up the beach and surgeons later spent three hours repairing the damage. He had 100 stitches to his leg.

"At the very least I should have lost my foot," said Dr Shadforth, who will be seventy-four tomorrow. "I'm lucky to be alive. The pain was something shocking – the worst I've ever experienced."

For twenty-three years Dr Shadforth and his wife Margaret, aged seventy-one, from Market Rasen in Lincolnshire, have spent their holidays at the same apartment complex on the Gulf Coast. He was enjoying his daily dip, swimming parallel to the beach some forty yards offshore, when the shark struck.

"I was cruising along, admiring the palm trees and the beach, when suddenly something grabbed hold of my right leg," he recalled. "I thrashed out with my other leg at whatever was there and twisted round to try to see it – but the water was already impenetrable because of the blood – my blood.

"All I saw was this great grey shape thrashing around behind me. I gave another mighty kick and, thank God, it let go.

"I have no idea how I managed to make it to the shore. I just wanted to get out of the water. I realized I must have been attacked by a shark and I was worried the blood would attract more of them.

"I saw a friend of mine walking along the beach and waved desperately to him, but he thought I was just giving a friendly hello wave, so he carried on walking.

"The pain was so bad I couldn't speak. I tried to yell for help, but nothing came out. Finally I made it to the beach and dragged myself ashore, leaving a trail of blood behind me. There were huge puncture wounds all round my right calf and great chunks of flesh missing. The shark had punctured two main arteries and blood was spurting out. I thought I might bleed to death."

Dr Shadforth instinctively put his thumbs over the holes in his leg to stop the flow. Onlookers raised the alarm, while a friend hurried along with towels to cover his wounds.

"I must have been getting pretty weak," said Dr Shadforth, "because I just wanted to get away from the people and go back to our apartment, but then the paramedics arrived, and a helicopter landed on the beach and whisked me off to hospital."

He was well enough yesterday to return to his apartment at Bonita Springs, near Fort Myers, and phone his daughter Helen, a pharmacist in Lincolnshire, to tell her of his ordeal.

Will he venture back into the water next year? "I'm sure I'll get over it. I'm not one of those people who like swimming-pools – they're boring."

George Burgess of the International Shark Attack File said the shark was probably a sharp nose or black tip, which are seen all along the Gulf Coast beaches, though they usually go for smaller prey. "This shark probably thought Colin's leg was a medium sized fish and went after it because of the splashing."

Daily Mail, London, 20 November 2000

WORCESTERSHIRE, UNITED KINGDOM, 2000

A chef has been mauled in a shark attack at a pub sixty miles from the sea.

Horrified customers looked on as the sharks mistook Paul Smith's fingers for food when he fed one of them prawns in a 3,000-gallon tank in the pub's dining room.

Russell Allen, landlord of the Fountain in Tenbury Wells, Worcester, took Mr Smith to hospital, where the nurses logged the incident as a shark attack at a landlocked pub and gave him six stitches for deep cuts.

The forty-year-old was on a break when he decided to treat Miami, a black-tipped reef shark usually fed squid and mussels. He said that, as soon as the sharks got a whiff of the seafood, they shot across the tank.

"Within a second the water was churning like the shark attack scenes in the Jaws movie and my hand was in the middle of it," he added. "Miami did most of the damage. He was hanging off my finger and I was howling."

The pub's landlord recently installed the 15 ft by 5 ft tank and apparently diners loved watching the three sharks – especially at feeding time. "It must help them work up an appetite – seafood sales have gone up forty per cent," he said.

The unlucky chef said: "It could have been very nasty. I've learned my lesson – I'll admire them from afar from now on."

Sun, London, 14 December 2000

2001

SOUTH AUSTRALIA, AUSTRALIA, 2001

John Winslet watched in awe as a white pointer [great white] shark 4–5 metres long attacked the outboard motor of his vessel on Saturday.

"It was absolutely awesome," he said yesterday as he surveyed the teeth marks left on the motor, which was fitted to the six-metre boat four days ago.

Mr Winslet, who runs fishing trips for Glenelg Fishing Charters, said there had been no major damage to the outboard, "but you can get a perspective on how big the jaws were".

With six passengers on board, Mr Winslet was anchored off the tyre reef about ten kilometres west of the Grange jetty, when the white pointer struck.

For over ninety minutes the shark nudged the boat, lifted its head out of the water, took bites at a berley pot and latched on to the boat's anchor chain.

"It got pretty violent on the chain – it was thrashing around, shaking the boat," Mr Winslet said. At one stage the shark was so close that Mr Winslet was able to lean over the side, touch its head and grab its tail. He also radioed the Sea Rescue Squadron base just in case people were intending to dive on the reef. "I knew there had been divers out there during the week."

Mr Winslet suspects he may have "hooked up" the white pointer about a week ago. "It screamed off and bit through the trace." Mr Winslet said he wondered whether the shark was sick. "It looks like it's got some pretty nasty scratches all over its back. It seems to be missing some teeth. They all seem damaged on one side of its mouth. It may have grabbed at a propeller."

Mr Winslet said that when the shark first appeared his

passengers were very cautious. "They all stood in the middle of the boat. But after they saw my excitement, they slowly enjoyed it. It was wild!"

He had been fishing in the area for seventeen years, said Mr Winslet, and running the charter boat for the past year.

"I'm out there nearly every day and I'm seeing a lot of sharks – hammerheads and bronze whalers – every second day. It's the most sharks I've seen in seventeen years of fishing out there."

Charter operator Brad March had eleven people on his boat when the same shark circled them for an hour. He said: "It was awe inspiring, seeing something so big so close to the boat. It nudged the boat a few times and came out of the water to have a good look at us. I think it was hungry and just prowling round the boat, looking for something big to eat. It was just as well nobody fell overboard."

Adelaide Advertiser, 22 January 2001

CUBA, 2001

A man saved his wife's life by kicking and punching a shark which was trying to drag her out to sea.

The Canadian couple were celebrating their wedding anniversary with a holiday in Cuba when the shark struck fifty feet off shore.

Tarmo Hamalainen recalled: "I heard a scream. I froze and then I saw the shark trying to take my wife Soile away. It had ripped open her arm and had hold of her. I swam like crazy and, when I got to her, it was still going at her. It wanted to take her."

He described how he grabbed the shark's fin and started kicking and hitting the shark, which, he says, weighed around fourteen stone.

"It probably only lasted fifteen seconds, but it seemed like an eternity," he added.

When the shark finally retreated they were engulfed in a spreading cloud of blood, but managed to reach the shore safely.

Mrs Hamalainen was treated in hospital and is expected to make a full recovery.

Wire report, 1 February 2001

NEW SOUTH WALES, AUSTRALIA, 2001

Richard "Mark" Butler reckons sharks don't like the taste of him and that's why he's alive to tell the tale.

The forty-eight-year-old father of three was surfing off the northern New South Wales town of Brooms Head on Sunday when he was attacked eighty metres from the beach by what is believed to be a two-metre bronze whaler shark, which almost severed his leg.

Speaking from his hospital bed in Lismore after eighty stitches to repair "a hole as big as a fist", the surfer said: "It mustn't have liked the taste because he let me go."

After smacking the water several times with his hand to scare the shark "so it wouldn't come back and have a second go", Mr Butler paddled thirty-five metres towards the shore before a "beautiful wave" carried him on to the beach.

His first thought was not to allow any sand to enter the wound. Using what little strength and first-aid knowledge he had, Mr Butler used his leg rope as a makeshift tourniquet.

Noticing a chunk of his leg hanging down, he said, he held the loose muscle in place and walked 500 metres along the beach and into the village before finding help.

"I looked and saw how bad it was and I thought 'I'm going to die here on the beach, I'm not going to make it.'

Anger and partly my children kept me going," he stated. "I'm glad to be alive. It terrified me, but I will surf again if I can."

Mr Butler does not believe that the shark should be killed. "It's in its domain, doing what it does naturally," he said. But he warned other surfers away from Brooms Head, saying the water contains "a huge number of sharks".

To thank his rescuers, Mr Butler agreed to talk to television reporters only if the stations donated a "considerable amount of money" to the Lismore-based Life-Saver Rescue Helicopter Service. "It's a pittance for the television stations and I have a lot to thank the helicopter service for," he said.

The ordeal has not deterred Mr Butler's family from surfing. His eldest daughter, Emma, aged seventeen, will compete today in the Pro-Junior surfing series at Avoca.

Northern Rivers Echo, 6 February 2001

MALAYSIA, 2001

Malaysian fishermen were shocked when they caught a three-tonne shark with human bones in its mouth. The fish was caught in nets off Pulau Pangkor.

Police slit open the shark's stomach and took its internal organs and the bones out for inspection.

A police spokesman said the human bone would be sent for DNA testing.

The Star, Philippines, 13 February 2001

MALAYSIA, 2001

Human bones found inside a shark caught off Malaysia belong to a man, according to analysts. They were initially thought to have been the bones of a woman, but DNA analysis has now revealed the bones to be those of an Asian man.

A spokesman for Ipoh Hospital says the man must have died about ten days prior to the discovery last Sunday by fisherman Chia Nai Huat and three other islanders.

The Star, Philippines, 18 February 2001

WESTERN AUSTRALIA, AUSTRALIA, 2001
A large white shark has attacked a couple's fishing boat near a popular swimming beach on Western Australia's south coast.

Don and Margaret Stubbs of Perth watched in horror as the white pointer shark bit into the propeller of their fishing boat.

Mr Stubbs said the shark was as big as the five-metre-long boat, adding that they struggled to see it as the weather was over-cast and the water dark. He said they were lucky not to have been leaning over the side of the boat washing their hands or fishing.

Wire report, 1 March 2001

RECIFE, BRAZIL, 2001
The remains of a man have been washed up on a Brazilian beach two days after he went missing in an area known for its shark attacks.

The body is believed to be that of a twenty-year-old student. It was washed up on Boa Viagem beach, in the north-eastern Brazilian city of Recife.

"The front of the thorax and all internal organs were ripped out. The body was also missing a forearm, part of one of the thighs and the face," said a local doctor.

It is not known whether the man was swimming beyond coral reefs, where sharks lurk in search of food. The state government has warned swimmers not to stray beyond the coral barrier and has banned surfing in the area since a young man lost both his hands in a shark attack in 1999.

It is the thirty-third recorded shark attack and the eleventh death in the area since 1992.

Sky News, 8 March 2001

ANGUILLA, CARIBBEAN, 2001

A fisherman in Anguilla has found human remains inside a shark.

Germain Gumbs, aged nineteen, was checking his fish traps when he found the eight-foot tiger shark in one of them. The fish was alive, but he shot it with a harpoon and, when he cleaned it out, he found the bones of a left arm.

Police Superintendent Illidge Richardson suspects the remains to be those of a shipwreck victim. Nearly three weeks ago the Esperanza sank off the coast of St Martin, killing fifteen and leaving seventeen missing.

Authorities say the wooden forty-foot boat sank with an estimated thirty-six people on board while on a trip to smuggle immigrants to the US Virgin Islands.

Wire report, 2 April 2001

NEW SOUTH WALES, AUSTRALIA, 2001

A forty-year-old surfer survived a shark attack on the New South Wales north coast yesterday after his friend used a leg rope to stem the bleeding from his calf.

The shark attacked Richard Ellis's lower right leg at about 10 a.m. as he surfed at a popular spot known as the V-Wall, near the entrance to the Nambucca River.

He managed to escape from the shark and catch a wave to shore, where his friend tied a surfboard's leg rope around his leg as a tourniquet. The pair then drove to Nambucca Heads ambulance station, where he was treated by staff.

An ambulance spokeswoman said Mr Ellis hobbled

into the station, just south of Coffs Harbour, with a large open wound in his leg. The shark had torn through the calf muscle, leaving a twenty-five-centimetre wound. Ambulance officers stabilized Mr Ellis before taking him to the hospital.

A hospital spokeswoman said Mr Ellis was stable and would be treated with intravenous antibiotics. The afternoon surgery involved stitching up severe lacerations.

Richard Ellis said he did not know what type of shark was involved, as he had only seen a shadow before the attack.

Sydney Morning Herald, 3 April 2001

EASTERN CAPE, SOUTH AFRICA, 2001

A surfer had a narrow escape when he was twice attacked by a shark in South Africa. Dunstan Hogan was dragged under water by a great white or ragged tooth shark.

The forty-six-year-old South African is recovering from leg injuries in a Port Elizabeth hospital.

"The shark bit my surfboard and my body together, and took me about five to six feet under the water," he said. "I was still holding my board under the water when my feet hit the sand. I opened my eyes and saw this big fish thrashing about."

He managed to surface and pull his surfboard towards him. Once he got back on, he paddled for the shore.

"As I was paddling I saw this big thrashing of grey and then it came up from beneath and knocked me into the air."

Mr Hogan managed to cling to his board and continued paddling to the shore and safety. He said he was "very grateful and extremely lucky to be alive", and plans to go surfing again when he has recovered.

Local sports physician and general practitioner Dr

Peter Schwartz said Mr Hogan's bite wounds were the biggest he had ever seen. The East Cape beach was closed after the attack, but later re-opened.

Daily Dispatch, South Africa, 10 April 2001

FLORIDA, USA, 2001

A two-mile stretch of the Atlantic Ocean off New Smyrna Beach in Florida was closed to swimmers and surfers for about an hour on Friday after three people were bitten by sharks. They were among at least seven shark victims in the same area this week.

Swimmer Jonathan Bush, aged sixteen, told his friend he felt something bite his ankle.

Andrew Barron, aged twelve, of Longwood, was another Friday victim. Both were treated at Bert Fish Medical Center.

All of the injuries are considered minor, although twenty-year-old surfer Richard Lloyd of Orange City remains hospitalized after surgery to repair the ligament in his left foot. He was bitten on Thursday just after stepping off his surfboard.

He said the shark came at him "out of the blue, totally unexpected, not even a chance. I mean, like, I didn't see anything, no fish around – just bam!"

Lloyd added that the injury wouldn't keep him out of the water. "Maybe I'll take up shark fishing."

The story was much the same for twelve-year-old John Fazio Jr of Deltona, who was bitten on his leg and foot on Thursday while boogie-boarding. He said he felt something brush against his left foot, but didn't realise he had been bitten until he saw the bite marks after he returned to shore.

Volusia County Beach Patrol Captain Rob Horster said it is their standard operating procedure to close the water for between thirty and sixty minutes any time sharks are seen or someone is bitten. This precaution was also taken on Wednesday and Thursday after bites were reported. Patrol officers suspect the high number of bait fish swimming close to shore are attracting the hungry sharks.

Twelve people were bitten by sharks in Volusia County in 2000, more than anywhere else in Florida. None of the injuries was life threatening.

The rash of attacks occurred as sharks swam northward along the Florida coast. "Sharks are like Yankee tourists – they come south for the winter and go north for the summer," said George Burgess of the International Shark Attack File based in the University of Florida. Bites often happen in conditions of breaking surf, undertow, tidal currents and reduced visibility, Burgess added. That is when sharks are most likely to mistake the dangling feet and hands of surfers for a fish.

The sharks responsible for the nips are generally small, between four and five feet long, said Dr Bob Hueter, director of the Center for Shark Research at the Mote Marine Laboratory in Sarasota. Most incidents occur off crowded beaches around 4 July, but the week before Easter ushers in the shark attack season because of the large crowds and warm water.

Volusia County surfer and beach authorities were taking the bites in their stride. Every time a shark was sited or a bite reported swimmers within a couple of hundred yards were asked to leave the water for thirty minutes or so. The beach patrol does not post signs. "That's their turf," Horster said. "You're going into their home."

Miami Herald, 13 April 2001

River Shark

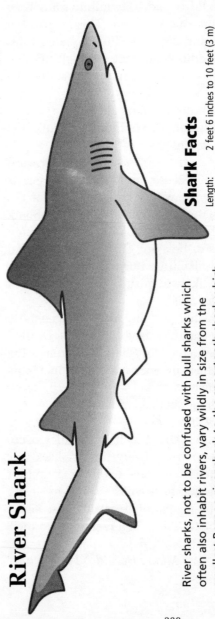

River sharks, not to be confused with bull sharks which often also inhabit rivers, vary wildly in size from the smallest Borneo river shark to the speartooth shark which may grow up to 10 feet (3 m), although no fully grown specimens have ever been caught. The Borneo river shark and the Irrawaddy river shark may be the world's rarest, few ever having been caught. Little is known about most river sharks, they do tend to have quite small eyes, relying more on their electro sensors to hunt for fish and shellfish in murky river water.

Shark Facts

Length:	2 feet 6 inches to 10 feet (3 m)
Weight:	10 lb to 350 lb (22 kg to 159 kg)
Colouring:	Grey or grey/brown upper with white or yellowish belly
Diet:	Fish, crustaceans
Pups:	Multiple pups born live and up to 2 feet (61 cm)
Status:	All types rare and endangered, most critically endangered

River Shark Range

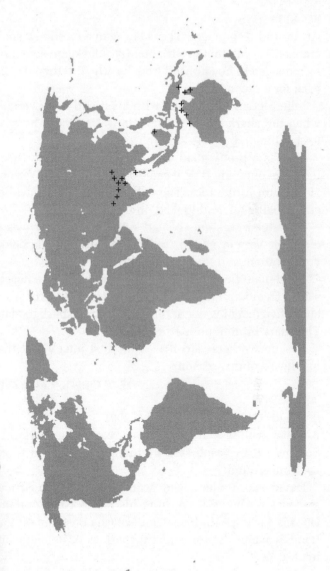

FLORIDA, USA, 2001

At around 7 p.m. on Thursday a five-foot-long shark grabbed a man's foot in a frightening attack, but somehow he managed to free himself from its grip. But then it came back for a second bite.

John McCall was surfing with his friend Ryan Vermey, when the shark attacked him. He was taken to hospital for treatment, but was later released.

"It was a pretty good bite. He said he was bit twice. It bit him once and then it came back again," said Vermey. "It bit him in the foot. The ball of his foot was swollen and hanging off, and looked pretty ugly."

The attack was unexpected because the water was so clear, Mr Vermey added. "Sharks usually see you before you see them and they are usually timid."

Lieutenant Roosevelt Prior of Jacksonville Fire Rescue said: "The victim told me he was getting off the board in about five feet of water and he spotted the shark too late. The shark bit him on his right foot."

Rescue workers said it was the first attack that they had heard of this season.

Wire report, 4 May 2001

EASTERN CAPE, SOUTH AFRICA, 2001

A surfer who was attacked by a great white shark off a South African beach said he thought it was his friend messing around.

David Van Staden, aged twenty-six, is South African and was on home leave from his job in New Zealand. He was surfing with his friend Natasha Bastenie off East London when the three-metre shark sank its teeth into his leg.

Mr Van Staden said, "At first I thought it was Natasha just fooling around, but suddenly I saw this thing

340

swimming around me and I paddled my board as fast as I could to the shore."

It was not until he reached the beach that Van Staden realized he had been bitten. He was taken to hospital, where he received ten stitches in the wound.

Marine expert Willie Maritz warned surfers to be on their guard as the water is cool and clear, and sharks have been attracted by the presence of sardines. Beaches from Gonubie to Fish River were closed after the attack.

Durban Daily News, 9 May 2001

LORD HOWE ISLAND, AUSTRALIA, 2001
A post mortem examination will be conducted this week on a human head and bones found inside a tiger shark caught off Lord Howe Island, 440 miles north-east of Sydney, last Friday night.

A skull and other bones will be examined at Glebe morgue in the hope of matching them to one of several missing people.

The remains were found by local fishermen Scott Wilson and Mark Thompson when the four-metre, 200 kg tiger shark was gutted on Saturday.

Sydney Morning Herald, 12, 13 June 2001

LORD HOWE ISLAND, AUSTRALIA, 2001
Jill and Arthur Apelt had never been to Lord Howe Island during nearly fifty years of marriage and regular annual holidays. Once they arrived there on 6 May, Mr Apelt, aged seventy-two, immediately set out for a swim at the pristine Middle Beach, but never returned.

Yesterday his family learnt that remains found inside a three-metre tiger shark hooked over the weekend belonged to the father of five. Forensic dentists matched a tooth from Mr Apelt's skull with dental records supplied by the family.

Family friend Bernie Knapp said that the identification of the remains had provided relief and closure.

"The family are relieved to know that the remains were those of Arthur because that now puts a full stop at the end of this very sad chapter," he said. "They're certain, and Lord Howe Island police believe that Arthur slipped on a rock and drowned and his body was swept out to sea and his remains obviously were picked up by a creature of the sea."

Mr Knapp said the family had been shocked and saddened when Mr Apelt disappeared, but they accepted his death with great fortitude.

The former Telstra executive retired about nine years ago and spent much time with his six grandchildren. He was an enthusiastic bushwalker and fit for his age.

Mr Apelt was last seen in the Middle Beach area – just hours after he and his wife had flown in from their Ashgrove home, in Brisbane, where they lived all their lives. The day after Mr Apelt disappeared some of his clothing was found on the beach, but searches conducted until 29 May were fruitless until two local men hooked a tiger shark containing Mr Apelt's skull and a limb bone. His remains and the shark's intestinal tract and stomach were flown to Sydney, where they were tested at the Glebe morgue.

"It's basically a team effort with the police missing persons bureau and they will point us in the right direction of people that have been reported missing," Dr Middleton said. "We will then contact the families and in turn the dentists, if that's possible."

In this case Mrs Apelt provided forensic pathologists with her husband's records and a tooth was able to be matched, avoiding the need for DNA testing and an agonizing six-week wait for results.

The Age, Melbourne, 14 June 2001

TEXAS, USA, 2001

A fourteen-year-old boy who was bitten by a shark while swimming in the Gulf of Mexico is recovering, but his father is warning others to be careful.

Ed Black said he and his wife, his nephew and his son, Jared Black, were on a beach south of Corpus Christi when his son was attacked while swimming in waist-deep water. "What scares me is that there were other people swimming in the same spot that day and they had little kids," Black said.

The attack occurred on 12 June, about ten miles south of Malaquite Beach along the Padre Island National Seashore.

"He never saw the shark," Black said. "There was just a big bite and blood all over the place."

A park ranger who saw the wound said it was from a bull shark or blacktip shark measuring at least five feet long, Black added.

The teenager was taken to Bay Area Hospital in Corpus Christi, where he received ten stitches. He has recovered from his wound without infection, his father said. A nursing supervisor at the hospital said today that no other information was available.

On 29 May a shark bit a sixteen-year-old boy swimming about fifty yards off Galveston Island. That attack was the island's third reported shark bite in twenty years.

San Antonio Express-News, 19 June 2001

FLORIDA, USA, 2001

7 JULY

The uncle of an eight-year-old boy attacked by a shark tugged on its tail to free the child, whose right arm was bitten off in the attack.

Jessie Arbogast of Ocean Springs, Mississippi remains in critical condition following the attack on 6 July in the surf at the Fort Pickens section of the Gulf Islands National Seashore, near Pensacola, in the Florida Panhandle. A National Park Service report provides details of how Jessie's uncle, Vance Flosenzier, managed to pull the shark to shore following the attack.

"Vance heard someone yell 'Shark!' and a scream," Ranger Jared Klein wrote in the report. Mr Flosenzier then saw a pool of blood in the water where the boy and other children were playing. Jessie's arm was still in the jaws of the 6 ft 6 in. bull shark when Mr Flosenzier ran into the water. He then heard Jessie cry, "He's got me – get him off me."

"Vance grabbed the base of the tail of the shark and tried to pull it away from Jessie," Mr Klein wrote. "Vance pulled a second time and the shark came free with the arm."

Jessie fell away from the shark and an unidentified bystander caught him and carried him to shore. The boy, who was initially conscious, went into convulsions and stopped breathing, his aunt, Diana Flosenzier, told Mr Klein.

Clinging to the tail, Mr Flosenzier began stepping backwards toward the beach. He described how the shark seemed to lose power as he dragged it backwards, but it kept trying to swim away. He beached the shark with the boy's arm still in its mouth about ten feet away from Jessie, witnesses said.

Ranger Jared Klein then shot the shark four times and prised its jaws open with a police baton. Volunteer firefighter Tony Thomas used a clamp to pull the boy's severed arm from the shark's gullet.

10 JULY

Jessie Arbogast has suffered harm to virtually every organ and may have brain damage. Though his reattached arm is healing well, he remains in critical condition after at least six batches of surgery to repair damage from the attack.

Dr Rex Northup said Jessie arrived at the hospital with no blood pressure, no pulse and damage to "literally his entire body". "Because of the shark injuries and loss of blood associated with these, his brain did go through a period of time with a very low amount of blood flow. If we can get another several days behind us where things don't deteriorate, we'll be happy with that."

Dr Jack Tyson, a trauma surgeon at Baptist Hospital, where the arm was reattached, said it was clear the boy was not brain dead after he and other doctors changed the dressings on his wounds and examined him. Dr Northup said a new brain wave study showed he was relatively stable.

Jessie, who has been undergoing dialysis at Sacred Heart Children's Hospital, Pensacola, since he went into kidney failure on Sunday, has not been able to talk with family members.

11 JULY

Jessie Arbogast has opened his eyes. He is still in a coma-like state, but doctors say he is showing "very promising" signs of recovery. Still threatened with brain damage after losing most of his blood during the attack, he is in a critical but stable condition at Sacred Heart Children's Hospital.

Dr Juliet de Campos, the orthopaedic surgeon who helped reattach the arm, said: "Technically, he's unconscious because he is not conversing like you and I are conversing, but he is showing very promising signs of starting to arouse somewhat. I moved his right arm – the one that was replanted. It was next to his body and I moved it away from his body to let his armpit breathe a little bit, and he immediately moved it back down."

Dr de Campos said another doctor who examined Jessie earlier reported that he responded when the physician rubbed the boy's chest and called out his name. She said: "Jessie opened his eyes and looked at the doctor, and he also moved his right foot and his left arm."

LATE JULY

Jessie Arbogast has been released from the Sacred Heart Children's Hospital, Pensacola, and was placed in an ambulance bound for his home town of Ocean Springs, Mississippi. It is not clear if he is being taken home or to another hospital.

An update on the hospital website says Jessie is still in a serious condition after his ordeal, which included eleven hours of surgery, and he is in a light coma. His kidneys have improved, though, and he no longer needs dialysis. Doctors say he has been making neurological progress.

It could be up to eighteen months before doctors know how much muscle use and sensation Jessie will regain in his arm, but they said that familiar surroundings might help his recovery.

Various news sources

FLORIDA, USA, 2001

A shark bit a forty-eight-year-old surfer on Sunday a few miles from where another shark nearly killed eight-year-old Jessie Arbogast earlier this month.

Michael Waters was surfing on Sunday afternoon off Santa Rosa Island when the shark bit him on the leg, causing puncture wounds, said Lieutenant Bob Clark of the Escambia County Sheriff's Office.

Mr Waters told witnesses that he had noticed small fish and a large shadow below him, but didn't think anything was wrong until he was bitten.

He was in good condition at a local hospital. The attack occurred about six miles from where young Jessie Arbogast was mauled on 6 July [see above].

Atlanta Journal-Constitution, 16 July 2001

FLORIDA, USA, 2001

Two shark attacks haven't deterred a summer influx of city-dwellers who have escaped to the emerald-green waters of the Panhandle beaches. Hardly anyone's staying away. And almost everyone's getting in the water. Atlanta surfer Aaron Pridgen, aged nineteen, carried his board under his right arm and across the sugar-white sand at Parking Lot 15 on Santa Rosa Island – near where local surfer Michael Waters suffered a shark bite last Sunday.

"I'm a bit concerned, yeah," Pridgen said on Tuesday, "but it's not going to stop me from having fun. This is their home and we're kind of invading it."

Charter bus driver Leonard Brand arrived on Monday with a busload of Baptists from Buford. "They're all talking about it," he said, "but I believe they're going to swim in the swimming pool at the hotel."

On the beach swimmers splashed in the warm surf of

the Gulf of Mexico. People threw balls. Others lay in the sun. It all seemed pretty normal from the lifeguard stand of Dave Greenwood.

"The sharks are there, oh yeah," Greenwood said. "We're in their environment. You can never assume the water is completely risk-free. That's why we watch the water even when it's completely calm."

Carroll Potter of Yazoo City, Mississippi, had his Pentax camera strapped around his neck as he sat in the sand and snapped shots of his three daughters swimming thirty yards into the surf. He said he picked this part of the beach because he was told it was away from the two shark attacks this month. What he didn't know was he had brought his family near to the very spot where Michael Waters was bitten last Sunday.

"At first they said they weren't going in," Potter said, "but, after about thirty minutes, they got in."

The family's first stop on their vacation was Gulf Shores, Alabama, near where an Alabama man lost part of his arm in a shark attack last year. "We talked about sharks all the way here," said Potter.

Few people have stopped by or called the Pensacola Beach Chamber to talk about sharks – except the media. "There's been no impact at all," executive director Sandy Johnston said. "In fact, we may have an increase just because of the curiosity. People want to see a shark."

Even as experts portray the life-threatening attack on Jessie Arbogast and the Sunday encounter by Waters as rare, officials are making sure that swimmers and fishermen know the rules. The Pensacola Beach Gulf Pier started strict enforcement on Tuesday of a no-shark-fishing rule that has been in place since its opening on Memorial Day weekend.

The day before, Monday, a local man used a ten-pound

bonita to hook an eleven-foot, 500-lb hammerhead shark off the pier. Earnie Polk, the man who caught the hammerhead, has been banned from the pier.

The 1,471-foot pier is about six miles east of where Arbogast had his arm bitten off. Waters, the Pensacola surfer who was bitten on the left foot last Sunday, said the pier might have contributed to his encounter. He surfed about two miles east of the pier and said fish parts may have attracted the shark.

Anglers can clean fish on the pier. They're supposed to take all the fish parts with them, but many just dump them over the side. "They say these things don't have an impact," said Waters, "but I could smell and taste it in the water. That's part of the problem at the beach."

George Burgess, director of the International Shark Attack File at the University of Florida, said banning shark fishing wouldn't cut down on encounters – but stopping fish cleaning might. "That's a no-brainer," he said. "Nothing excites a shark more than the smell of blood and bodily fluids."

Atlanta Journal-Constitution, 18 July 2001

Silky Shark

Shark Facts

Length: 8 feet 3 inches to 11 feet 6 inches (2.5 m to 3.5 m)

Weight: 554 lb to 760 lb (252 kg to 346 kg)

Colouring: Brownish grey upper with white belly

Diet: Sardines, mullet, tuna, squid, mackerel

Pups: Up to 16 pups born at between 2 feet and 2 feet 10 inches (60 cm to 85 cm)

Status: Numbers declining, vulnerable in some regions

Slim, streamlined and a powerful swimmer, the silky shark is so named after its smooth skin. While it is one of the most widely distributed sharks in the world, it is threatened by overfishing. Favouring deep water, this shark is known to hunt in groups, often "herding" fish into tight shoals near the surface and then taking it in turns to tear into the shoal. Because of its size and aggressive nature it is dangerous to humans, although few come into contact with it as it seldom strays into shallow coastal waters near beaches.

Silky Shark Range

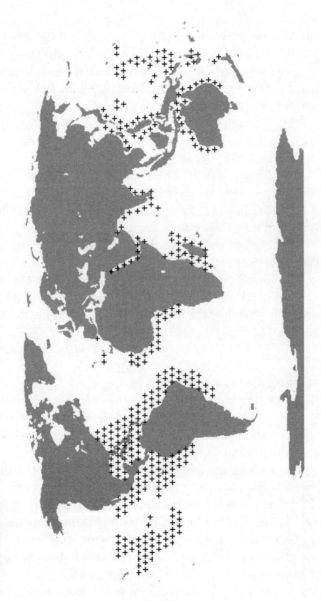

FLORIDA, USA, 2001

Three surfers have been bitten by sharks off the coast of Florida – all on the same day and on the same beach.

A twenty-year-old man has had to have surgery on a hand injury, while the others escaped with less serious wounds to their feet.

Witnesses at Daytona Beach claim so many sharks had congregated in the area that surfers had to jump over them to reach the waves.

Jeff White, aged twenty, and Dylan Feindt, aged nineteen, were competing in a Conference of the National Scholastic Surf Association event when they were bitten on their feet.

Jason Valentine was surfing near by when he was bitten on the hand.

People reported seeing eight-foot-long bull sharks and six-foot black tip sharks. Beach patrol officers closed a one-mile stretch of the beach for two hours following the attacks.

Wire report, 19 August 2001

FLORIDA, USA, 2001

Separate shark attacks on another three surfers last Sunday prompted Beach Patrol officers to ban swimming again on about one mile of the coast near the Ponce Inlet, where sharks attacked six people over the weekend.

The attacks are not cause for hysteria, but rather are multiple cases of "hit and run" bites by confused sharks, said George Burgess of the International Shark Attack File. The National Scholastic Surfing Association contest this weekend came at the same time as sharks are migrating south for the winter and following large schools of bait fish such as herring or mullet.

On Sunday a seventeen-year-old female surfer was

bitten on her left foot. She was treated and released from hospital.

Five miles to the north two other surfers were bitten within a minute of each other at New Smyrna Beach Inlet, the same area where Saturday's attacks occurred. A seventeen-year-old girl was bitten in the left calf and a thirty-two-year-old man was bitten in the right foot.

A one-mile stretch of the inlet was closed and the victims were hospitalized. The girl will undergo surgery, but was listed in good condition late on Sunday. The man was expected to be released on Sunday. Three surfers – Jeff White, Dylan Feindt and Jason Valentine – were also attacked on Saturday, the first day of the contest.

After the three attacks on Saturday and then another three on Sunday, Beach Patrol officers put signs on the sand warning surfers and sun-worshippers that "dangerous marine life" could be in the area!

Atlanta Journal-Constitution, 20 August 2001

MASSACHUSETTS, USA, 2001
A fourteen-foot-long shark repeatedly smashed into a boat carrying terrified tourists off the Massachusetts coast.

No one was hurt during the ten-minute ordeal, but the boat shook from side to side as the 700 lb shark slammed against the vessel.

The creature was believed to be a man-eating great white shark. The boat's captain, Joe Fitzback, said: "He was thrashing and banging it with his head, slapping the side with his back. We all got drenched. It shook the boat back and forth. I had to hold a couple of people's belts so they wouldn't go overboard."

Mr Fitzback, who owns Top Rod Custom Charters, and his six passengers were nearing the end of a fishing tour when the attack started near Chatham and Monomoy Island, near South Beach. Mr Fitzback alerted the Chatham harbour master to the shark, and boats have been patrolling the coastline looking for it.

Boston Herald, 23 July 2001

RIMINI, ITALY, 2001

A father and son have beaten off an eighteen-foot great white shark with a piece of wood after it started ramming their fishing boat.

They were fifteen miles off Rimini when their eighteen-foot boat was attacked.

Coastguards are monitoring the area in case the great white heads for Italy's holiday beaches. A spokesman said: "It is a man-eater. I would advise people in the sea to be careful and, if they see a fin, to get out as quickly as possible."

The men say they were lucky to escape with their lives as the shark was threatening to sink their boat. Giacomo Longhi said: "It just seemed to go on for ever. He just kept hitting the boat over and over again."

His father Tersilio added: "The shark was the length of our boat. I grabbed a piece of wood and kept hitting it. Then it disappeared."

Daily Mail, London, 4 August 2001

BAHAMAS, 2001

A Wall Street banker beat off a shark as it attacked him before swimming back to shore using only one leg.

Before Krishna Thompson passed out on the Bahamian beach he wrote his hotel room number in the sand so that he could be identified.

His wife of ten years, Ave Maria Thompson, said: "He kept punching and punching. He has cuts on his hands because of that. He is so brave to fight off a shark and then think to write the number."

Mr Thompson, who is now at Jackson Memorial Hospital, Miami, after having his left leg amputated just below the knee, was on a wedding anniversary holiday. He had been swimming alone when the shark attacked him off the coast of Freeport, Grand Bahama.

The wife of the Long Island man who lost a leg in a shark attack in the Bahamas said that his screams for help went unanswered as he swam to shore.

"When you hear a scream for help and you're a lifeguard, you're supposed to get in there," Ave Maria Thompson said at Jackson Memorial Hospital, Miami, where her husband, Krishna, is recovering. She faulted lifeguards for not doing more to help her husband after the attack.

"One of the first things he said to me when they removed the ventilator was that he was screaming and they wouldn't come. He had to swim to them," said Mrs Thompson, an assistant district attorney in Queens, New York City.

Eric Waldburger, general manager and chief executive officer of Our Lucaya Beach and Golf Resort in Freeport, Grand Bahama, said that lifeguards on duty saw Mr Thompson and immediately jumped into the water and pulled him out. "We have lifeguards who, at their own risk, jumped in there. We had him out in pretty nearly no time."

Dr Nicholas Namias said that Mr Thompson was lucky to be alive. "The injuries that he had, he should have bled to death right there in the Bahamas on the beach."

Mr Thompson, aged thirty-six, was in critical but stable condition today [7 August]. Doctors removed his left leg just above the knee after he was flown to Miami from a Bahamas hospital.

Mr Thompson, a Wall Street banker, was attacked on Saturday 4 August during what was supposed to be a quick early morning swim at the resort, where he and his wife were celebrating their tenth wedding anniversary.

Mrs Thompson said her husband used his bare hands to pound the shark and get free, reaching the shore on his own and passing out from shock and blood loss. She said that, before passing out, he was able to scrawl his hotel room number in the sand, so the staff could find her.

But hotel officials gave a contradictory account. In a statement released this afternoon, they said that two lifeguards had seen the shark's fin in the water and jumped in after Mr Thompson, who was between fifteen and eighteen feet from shore. As they neared Mr Thompson, the lifeguards saw blood in the water and used a hand-to-hand rescue method to pull him out. Once ashore, the lifeguards applied towels and a tourniquet to stop the bleeding.

Earlier accounts of the rescue given by Mrs Thompson and doctors in Miami credited a doctor who happened by as the one who placed the tourniquet on Mr Thompson.

Asked why Mr Thompson told his wife that no one helped him get to shore, Mr Waldburger suggested that he was probably in shock. Mr Waldburger said the hotel had prepared a report of the incident, but was not investigating the matter.

New York Times, 6, 8 August 2001

BAHAMAS, 2001

A shark bit the leg of an American man who was snorkelling with his wife near the island of Grand Bahama, hospital officials said.

The shark attack on Thursday was the second this

month off the island, about 120 miles north-west of Nassau, the capital on the main island.

The man was being treated for injuries to his left leg at Rand Memorial Hospital, said Dr Jerold Forbes. He would not say whether the injuries were life threatening, adding only that the man's leg was not severed.

The hospital did not release the name of the couple involved. Dr Forbes would not provide further details on the attack.

Wire report, 16 August 2001

VIRGINIA, USA, 2001

A ten-year-old boy has died after being attacked by a shark while swimming off the coast of Virginia. It was the first fatality after a summer of shark attacks off the east coast of the United States.

David Peltier from Richmond, Virginia, was surfing and swimming about fifty yards from the shore in water only about four feet deep when he was bitten by the eight-foot shark.

His father, Richard, who was surfing near by, wrestled with the shark, punched it on the head, and managed to free the boy from its jaws.

The boy was treated on the shore by lifeguards and paramedics before being taken to three different hospitals in a bid to save his life. However, the attack had severed an artery in one of the boy's legs and he had lost a large amount of blood. David, whose two brothers had been surfing near by, died early yesterday morning at the Children's Hospital of the King's Daughters in Norfolk.

Rex Carter, a witness to the attack, said: "There were shark bites all along his leg. It also looked like maybe the shark got him right inside the thigh. He lost a lot of blood."

The attack, which took place off Sandridge Beach,

just south of Virginia Beach, was believed to be by a sandbar shark. It was the first reported attack in the area for thirty years, according to Ed Brazle, chief of the local emergency medical services.

Meyera Oberndorf, the mayor of Virginia Beach, said: "I speak for the entire city of Virginia Beach when I say how terribly saddened I am by this horrible accident."

Helicopters later carried out surveillance of the area before declaring it shark free. The beaches were open yesterday and people were fishing in the waters.

Of the 40 shark attacks reported worldwide so far this year none had been fatal, according to the International Shark Attack File; 28 have occurred in Florida waters. In the year 2000 there were 79 shark attacks worldwide, of which 51 were in the US. The ISAF estimates that there are, on average, between 5 and 15 fatal attacks annually, but that those in Third World countries are often not reported internationally.

Guardian, London, 3 September 2001

GEORGIA, USA, 2001
Sharks feed and school in the murky green waters off Georgia's beaches, but rarely do they bother swimmers.

A Milledgeville man said he was the exception this summer while floating face down in knee-deep water off Jekyll Island. It happened around 6.30 p.m. in late July, he said.

"I was floating on my belly, feeling for sea shells on the bottom," recalled John Davis, aged thirty-six, a school custodian in Milledgeville. Davis said he felt something push his foot hard. "I slapped at it, turned around and saw blood in the water. I knew something got me, but didn't know what it was. I thought it might have been a stingray."

Davis said a doctor at the South-East Georgia Regional

Medical Centre in Brunswick said he might have been bitten by a small shark.

"It made a two-inch gash that took six stitches to close," he said. "I also got a little cut on my thumb when I slapped at it."

Because Davis never saw what injured him, it was not recorded as a shark attack, said hospital spokeswoman Susan Bates.

There have been only nine confirmed shark attacks in Georgia waters since 1918, according to the International Shark Attack File. None of the attacks was fatal.

Coastal fishermen have long claimed that St Andrew's Sound between Jekyll and Little Cumberland Islands is a gathering area for large sharks. Several state records have been caught in the sound. But fisheries biologist Carolyn Belcher said her studies indicate Georgia's most prevalent shark species are Atlantic sharpnose and bonnethead [*sic*] sharks, both small species.

Belcher, with the University of Georgia's Marine Extension Service in Brunswick, is conducting a three-year study of shark nursery grounds in Georgia.

Because of shark attacks elsewhere in the United States this year, Tybee Island officials are trying to close their municipal pier and beaches to shark fishing, said city manager Tom Cannon. "We've passed the first reading of an ordinance and will have the second reading on 13 September," he said.

Cannon said city officials believe the ban on shark fishing will reduce the likelihood of attacks. "We were having people throwing chum off the pier, right in the center of one of our most popular swimming beaches."

Atlanta Journal-Constitution, 5 September 2001

Sleeper Shark

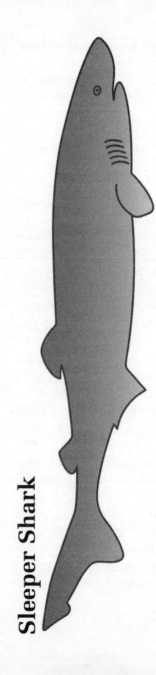

Shark Facts

Length: 12 feet to 23 feet (3.65 m to 7.6 m)

Weight: 700 lb to 800 lb (22 kg to 159 kg)

Colouring: Mottled grey or grey/brown

Diet: Fish, crustaceans, squid, octopus, horses, reindeer

Pups: Up to 10 pups born live and up to 3 feet (90 cm)

Status: Some types known to be under threat

Sleeper sharks are so called because of their sluggish movement in the water which makes it seem like they are asleep. Species like the Greenland shark or Pacific sleeper can be found as deep as 6,600 feet (2,000 m) or more but they feed nearer the surface in winter, looking for warmer water. Greenland sharks have been found with the remains of whole deer and horses, which were clearly floating dead in the water and scavenged, in their stomachs. The flesh of the Greenland shark is considered a delicacy in Greenland after it has been left to rot and ferment to rid it of the natural chemicals that stop the shark from freezing. Eaten fresh, it is toxic and makes you feel like you are extremely drunk.

Sleeper Shark Range

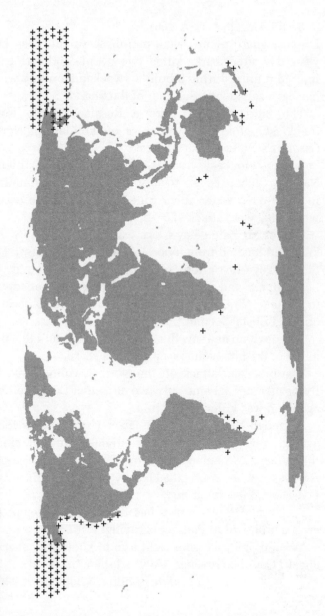

NORTH CAROLINA, USA, 2001

US coastguard planes were patrolling Atlantic beaches yesterday after sharks killed two people and seriously injured a third during a holiday weekend, ending what has been called "the Summer of the Shark".

The latest victims were a Russian couple from the Washington area who were on holiday on North Carolina's Outer Banks islands.

Serge Zaloukaev, twenty-eight, and his girlfriend Natalia Slobonskaya, twenty-three, were swimming in waist-deep water about nine metres from the beach when they were attacked.

One of Mr Zaloukaev's legs was bitten off below the knee and he died from blood loss and cardiac arrest. Ms Slobonskaya lost a foot and suffered severe wounds to her buttocks and hip. She was evacuated by helicopter to Norfolk, Virginia, where she was reported to be in a critical but stable condition.

Although no one saw the fish, the severity and the diameter of the bite wounds suggested a shark.

The first fatal attack off the North Carolina coast in living memory, it came only two days after David Peltier, aged ten, was killed in Virginia.

Although there have been fewer shark attacks than average this year, they have attracted interest since the struggle to reattach the arm of eight-year-old Jessie Arbogast, who was attacked by a bull shark near Pensacola, Florida, in July.

An animal rights group has dropped its attempt to erect a billboard in Pensacola saying:

"Would you give your right arm to know why sharks attack? Could be revenge. Go vegetarian."

Guardian, London, 5 September 2001

CORNWALL, UNITED KINGDOM, 2001

Darren Smith, a chef, needed seventeen stitches after he was savaged by a dead shark. Smith, of Newquay, Cornwall, was driving the seven-foot porbeagle shark to a restaurant when he had to brake sharply.

The 110-lb monster shot from its icebox and, when Smith tried to shove it back, he caught his right hand in its mouth, severing an artery.

"The nurses at the hospital couldn't stop laughing," he said. "I must be the first person in history to be attacked by a shark on dry land."

Sunday Times, London, 9 September 2001

FLORIDA, USA, 2001

An angler who hooked a shark and hauled it into his boat was bitten on his legs and hand.

The forty-four-year-old man caught the shark near Florida's Everglades National Park. He is said to be in good condition in Miami's Jackson Memorial Hospital on Sunday with bite wounds and lacerations.

After hauling the shark aboard the boat, the man was spraying himself with insect repellent when he slipped – falling into the water with the shark.

More than forty shark attacks have been reported along the Atlantic and Gulf coasts in recent months, two of them fatal, according to the International Shark Attack File, which is based at the University of Florida.

The file counts only unprovoked attacks, such as those on swimmers and surfers. It does not consider bites suffered by fishermen as shark attacks because they involve direct handling of the shark.

Los Angeles Times and Wire report,
10 September 2001

QUEENSLAND, AUSTRALIA, 2001

An Australian man has survived an attack by a great white shark whilst he was paddling in an inflatable boat. Matt George said the shark had attacked his boat for over half an hour just off Sovereign Beach at Moreton Island, north-east of Brisbane.

The shark's bite caused one side of the boat to deflate, but the thirty-one-year-old managed to paddle to safety as he clung to the side of the wrecked boat.

Mr George said: "The whole side of my boat exploded and the shark was pushing the boat back in towards the beach. It blew up and that just wrecked my day. Every now and then I'd stop and look around, then I'd give myself enough time to have a paddle and enough time for a shark to come in, then I'd have another look."

Wire report, 5 October 2001

NEW SOUTH WALES, AUSTRALIA, 2001

An Australian surfer was launched two metres into the air when he was attacked by a large shark.

Roger Frankland's board was hit by the bronze whaler shark, propelling it out of the water. It happened while he was surfing off Flat Rock Beach, near Lennox Head in New South Wales.

The forty-nine-year-old was unhurt, but his board now has some impressive souvenir teeth marks.

"I've been surfing for forty years and I've been nudged by sharks, and had dolphins around me and stuff like that, but I've never been boosted out of the water," he said. "Whatever hit me didn't have any good intent. It was a full-on attack. I was really lucky because I was lying flat on the board and the way it hit me, I stayed on the board until right at the end, when I slid off the back.

"Surfboards are quite tough, but, from the teeth marks on the board, if it had hit me just as a person, it would have killed me. I just felt totally at risk. I thought I was going to get hit again at any time.

"I've always felt that sharks aren't that bad, but, after feeling the power that I got hit by, I just don't feel good about it. When I got to the beach, I was pretty happy."

Sydney Morning Herald, 23 November 2001

2002

HAWAII, USA, 2002

A snorkeller has survived after being bitten on his bottom by a tiger shark.

Tommy Holmes, from Los Angeles, says he is ecstatic to be alive after the attack off the Hawaiian island of Maui. He was in the water with his girlfriend Monica Boggs, admiring a group of twelve to fifteen turtles, when they saw the shark approaching.

"We were just watching the turtles for about ten minutes when Monica spotted the shark about twenty-five feet away and grabbed my hand," said Mr Holmes.

Miss Boggs told our reporter: "It was swimming right at us at an alarming speed. It didn't look curious – it looked like it knew what it wanted. I thought we were going to die."

Mr Holmes added: "I put my mask back in the water to see where he was and he was around four feet away. I saw his open mouth and teeth, and a very big head."

The shark bit Mr Holmes on the backside and swam off. The couple swam to shore and Mr Holmes was taken to hospital.

"We were quite happy once we were on the shoreline. We were both ecstatic. I had all my limbs, and we knew it was in the butt and that we had gotten off easy. I'm a lucky guy," he said.

Honolulu Advertiser, 3 January 2002

KWAZULU-NATAL, SOUTH AFRICA, 2002

A teenager's leg was amputated after a shark attacked him as he stood fishing in shallow water.

Sixteen-year-old Adrian Sheik kicked and punched at the fish as it attacked him during the night-time fishing expedition with friends.

It happened on the sandbanks of the Royal Natal Yacht Club in South Africa's Durban Harbour. Adrian believes the shark was a Zambezi [bull shark].

He finally escaped by stabbing at the shark with his fishing rod, and then he was rushed to Addington Hospital, where his leg was amputated.

The attack is the second in KwaZulu-Natal waters in less than a week, and the Natal Sharks Board is warning beachgoers to stay out of the water at night.

Adrian's best friend, Kevin Moonsamy, says the actual attack was quick, but helping his friend swim back to land took about half an hour. When they approached the shore, another fisherman, Jack Potgieter, came to the boys' assistance.

"I heard screaming and turned to see what was happening," Mr Potgieter said. He quickly put a towel around Sheik's leg and helped drag him to the shore.

"We believe it to have been quite a large shark," said Natal Sharks Board biologist Sheldon Dudley.

Ananova, 25 January 2002

TURKS AND CAICOS ISLANDS, CARIBBEAN, 2002

The scene could have come straight out of *Jaws*, but this one was real – two men clinging to the keel of a capsized fishing boat encircled by sharks.

The horror of the pair, and their friends who tried to swim for help but never returned, was described by retired British policeman Philip Harding.

The former head of CID in Derby told how a simple fishing trip off an island in a paradise setting turned to tragedy. One friend was devoured by sharks and another disappeared, apparently meeting the same fate, while Mr Harding and a colleague clung to the wreckage of their boat for thirty-one hours as man-eating tiger sharks circled them.

Mr Harding, aged fifty-one, was on a fishing trip with three local policemen in the Turks and Caicos Islands, a British Crown colony in the Caribbean, when their boat began to sink after a water pump broke and then capsized in high seas.

"I have had some hairy times as a policeman, but nothing like this, when common sense says you won't make it and all the odds are stacked against you," said Mr Harding yesterday.

He and a fellow survivor were finally rescued by a Cuban tugboat when the wind changed and blew the wreck of their vessel towards shore after more than a day spent fearing for their lives as they drifted three miles out to sea.

They were rescued about half a mile off the coast after being spotted by a group of workmen building on the normally deserted West Caicos Island. The former Detective Superintendent – who left his Derbyshire force in March 1999 to take up an eighteen-month contract with the Royal Turks and Caicos Islands Police and then stayed to work as a consultant – was recovering at a hotel on the island of Providenciales yesterday.

He had gone fishing with Inspector John Sutton, Sergeant Cromwell Warrican and Detective Sergeant Kingsley Laborde off the north-east coast of West Caicos on Saturday morning. But they were barely two hours into the trip when the boat's stern began to sink and then they were thrown into the water as freak waves capsized the vessel about a mile off West Caicos, near a spot called Silly Creek, close to Princess Alexandra Marine Park.

Knowing that they would not be missed until that evening, when they were due back in dock, Inspector Sutton and Sergeant Warrican decided to swim for help.

Inspector Sutton's shark-devoured body was found two days later. Sergeant Warrican is still missing.

Mr Harding and Detective Sergeant Laborde were left clinging to the keel and to the faint hope that they would be spotted in the gathering gloom.

The Briton, who was treated in hospital for shock and exposure, revealed: "I said to Kingsley, 'This is a nasty situation. Set off and swim if you think you can make it back to the shore.' But ten minutes later he came back, saying he couldn't leave me on my own. It's a good job he came back – he saved my life five times in the next twenty-four hours. It was a nightmare. In the night we could see sharks swimming around the boat. I couldn't grip, but luckily Kingsley gave me the courage to hang on."

Exhausted, Mr Harding, suffering from dehydration and sunburn, was hauled back on to the boat by Sergeant Laborde every time he slipped into the water. He added: "We were constantly being washed over by waves, and the sharks were all around us. It was the longest night I have ever experienced."

Mr Harding, whose wife Rosemary and son Jack,

seven, were visiting him from their home in Heage, Derbyshire, said: "I'm not a strong swimmer, so I'm extremely relieved. I was just so grateful. You wouldn't believe the thoughts that are going all through your head when you think you are not going to make it. Now my thoughts are with the families of my lost friends. Those brave men tried to swim to get help and didn't make it. My feelings are all over the place."

The Turks and Caicos Islands group is made up of some forty islands and has a population of about 20,000. It is known for its fishing and diving sites, and the sharks most commonly found around the islands are the nurse and reef sharks, neither of which is considered to be particularly dangerous. But tiger sharks, which have been known to eat humans, are also found around the islands. They can grow to twenty feet in length and have distinctive tiger-like markings. The islands have long recruited British policemen to oversee the archipelago.

Daily Express, London, 28 February 2002

FLORIDA AND HAWAII, USA, 2002

A shark bit an eleven-year-old tourist on Monday as she waded in shallow water on an Atlantic Ocean beach, officials said.

"She had a serious injury to her left foot, but it was not life threatening," said Cocoa Beach Fire Captain Rod Donhoff.

Tori Lawrence of Sterling, Illinois, was standing in knee-deep water when she screamed and began to crawl to the beach, witnesses said.

Lawrence was taken by helicopter to Orlando Regional Medical Center's pediatric trauma unit, where she was listed in fair condition on Monday afternoon.

Meanwhile, a two-mile stretch of beach remained

closed in Hawaii after a shark bit off the foot and ankle of a teenager. Harmon Aki, father of seventeen-year-old Hoku, said his son is "doing quite well" despite his injuries. Hoku lost his left foot and ankle in the attack on Monday afternoon as he was body boarding in murky water off Kauai. The teenager told rescuers he "was being thrashed around under water". The shark released him when he poked it in the eye.

There were more than fifty shark attacks in US coastal waters last year, including more than thirty-five in Florida.

Atlanta Journal-Constitution, 26 March 2002

HAWAII, USA, 2002

The seventeen-year-old Kauai boy, who survived a shark attack, but lost a foot, described the terrifying experience. The attack happened at Brennecke Beach in the Poipu area of Kauai, where the beach is still closed because of shark sightings. Hoku Aki told the story of his survival from his hospital bed: "I opened my eyes and I could see the shark. It was just tossing me all over the place. I remember hearing my leg break. I heard the bones snap."

One day after the vicious shark attack tore off his foot, Aki, a high school senior, was feeling well enough to show off his musical talents by playing his ukulele as he recovered in Wilcox Medical Center.

"I remember I tried to open its mouth and trying to get it off me. That didn't work either. So I just grabbed the shark's eye and ripped it out, and then it let me go," he recalled.

Aki said he thought he was going to die, but found the strength to make it to shore. "I had a look at my leg and I just noticed the skin was all torn up and all my flesh was ripped. I didn't notice my foot was gone until I was in the ambulance."

A family on holiday saw Aki just after the attack. Mrs Mona Schantz said: "I saw a pool of blood and the boy yelling for help. There were other people on the beach and I saw they were getting up and walking towards him."

Unaware, at this stage, how bad his injuries were, Aki said, "I was with my brother at the time and he told me that my foot wasn't there, but I was just in shock and couldn't believe it. I still can't believe it."

Mrs Schantz ran for help, while a vacationing nurse pulled Aki to shore and stopped the bleeding from his leg. Aki said: "I'd like to thank that nurse who was on the beach yesterday. She saved my life."

Family members said Aki should be out of the hospital in ten days. Doctors want him up and walking around as soon as possible.

Aki is a high school track athlete and fire-knife dancer besides being a body-boarder. Despite the loss of his foot, he remains upbeat. However, he said he does not plan on any fire-knife dancing any time soon and he doesn't plan to go back in the water. "I'll just sit on the beach and watch the waves or something," he said. And he hopes to work on his music.

Brennecke Beach remained closed because of shark sightings; lifeguards will decide later if it is safe to re-open it.

State officials said it appears that Aki was attacked by a tiger shark.

TheHawaiiChannel.com, 26 March 2002

FLORIDA, USA, 2002
A shark bit an Ohio swimming coach on the arm on Monday as he swam in the Atlantic Ocean.

Matthew May, of Coldwater, Ohio, was in town with a group of children for a swimming tournament at the International Swimming Hall of Fame.

May, aged twenty-nine, was bitten twice on his left arm. Doctors at North Ridge Medical Center, where May received eleven stitches, said the bite appeared to come from a shark.

"I thought, at first, it was probably a jellyfish," May said at a news conference, wearing a large bandage on his left arm above the elbow. "Then I saw there was blood in the water and blood running down my arm, and I realized it was serious."

George Burgess, director of the International Shark Attack File, said that the incident was typical of Florida shark attacks – a quick bite followed by release and an injury that was not life threatening.

South Florida Sun-Sentinel, 1 April 2002

BAHAMAS, 2002
A shark expert known for his unusual research methods and "pushing the envelope" in his studies has been badly bitten by a shark in the Bahamas.

Dr Erich Ritter, chief scientist for the Global Shark Attack File, based in Princeton, New Jersey, was bitten in the calf by a 350-lb bull shark during filming of a Discovery Channel programme off Walker's Cay, in the Bahamas, on Tuesday.

"It was a serious injury," said Marie Levine, executive director of the Shark Research Institute in Princeton. "he's going to be in the hospital for four or five more weeks."

A series of particularly gruesome shark attacks, including one in which a boy [Jessie Arbogast] lost an arm to a shark in Florida, were widely reported last summer. But experts say shark attacks are rare and might be increasing only because more people are using the oceans for recreation.

Mr Ritter, aged forty-three, was bitten in murky, waist-deep water as he worked with lemon, black-tip and bull sharks, Ms Levine said.

The bull shark was chasing a remora fish and bit Mr Ritter by accident. "There was food in the water about fifteen yards from Erich. A bull shark closed on the remora, but in the low visibility bit Erich instead."

The shark's teeth went to the bone and Mr Ritter was rushed to a hospital in Florida, where he underwent an arterial graft.

"They were really pushing the envelope," said Ms Levine. "This is one of those things that can happen when you're working with big animals."

But Sam Gruber, a University of Miami shark expert who worked with Mr Ritter in the 1990s, said his methods were scorned and called him "an accident waiting to happen". "He has been getting more and more fearless, or some would say bold. This method is basically to titillate television cameras. He wants to impress people that he can control these sharks and they will never bite him."

Scotsman, Scotland, 12 April 2002

FLORIDA, USA, 2002

A shark bit a Volusia County surfer, Nolan Sutliff, in the foot on Thursday morning. Authorities said Sutliff, aged twenty-eight, was surfing near the south jetty at Ponce de Leon Inlet, some twenty yards offshore, when he started screaming for help.

Marc Latore, a nearby surfer, was leaving the water when he saw Sutliff paddling in the surf – and then he heard his screams. "I ran into the water and helped him out," said Latore. "He was bleeding badly and in a lot of pain."

Sutliff of Port Orange was listed in good condition at Bert Fish Medical Center. A hospital spokeswoman said that Sutliff was scheduled for surgery to repair tendons in his left foot.

Last year 20 of Florida's 37 reported shark attacks were in the waters near the jetty. There are no plans to close the beach, according to Captain Rob Horster of Volusia County Beach Patrol.

"It's that time of year," Horster said. "We know the sharks are there and we know they bite."

There were 62 unprovoked shark attacks reported in the United States last year. Three were fatal: one each in Florida, North Carolina and Virginia.

Associated Press, 18 April 2002

NEW SOUTH WALES, AUSTRALIA, 2002
A shark boat skipper slit the belly of an 800 lb monster his crew caught – and recoiled in horror when a human head rolled out. Bob van Lawick and shipmates also found a pelvis and an arm inside the ten-foot tiger shark. Captain Bob said: "We were shocked. The skull was pretty well preserved and still had all its teeth. I reckon the remains were no more than a fortnight old."

The fishermen had fought the animal for two and a half hours before landing it. Back on shore, they decided to cut open its stomach to see what it had eaten.

"The first thing we found was a whale bone," said Bob. "Suddenly the head rolled out, then the rest. We realized we'd caught a man-eater and called the police. You don't expect to fillet a fish and see human body parts fall out."

Crewman Andrew Pattie added: "Everyone was sick. We said, 'We're not touching it any more.' It was very scary."

The beast was hooked in a shark fishing contest off

Newcastle, New South Wales.

Aussie cops are now trawling DNA files and dental records in hundreds of unsolved murder and missing persons cases. Detective Sergeant Murray Lundberg of Newcastle police said: "We can't establish the sex or if the person was killed intentionally or died of natural causes."

Fatal shark attacks are rare in Australia, though there were three in 2000. The find has revived memories of Sydney's infamous Shark Arm Murders in 1935, when a tiger shark placed in an aquarium spat out a tattooed arm which had been chopped off by killers and hurled into the sea. Cops knew the victim, who was connected to a smuggling gang, but no one was ever charged as the only potential witness was murdered the night before the inquest.

Sun, London, 23 April 2002

NEW SOUTH WALES, AUSTRALIA, 2002

Human remains found inside a ten-foot tiger shark caught off eastern Australia belong to a missing fisherman, police said yesterday.

A skull, arm and pelvis were found on Sunday, when fishermen cut open the shark after catching it about sixty miles north of Sydney.

Kang Suk Lee, aged fifty-two, disappeared on 2 April.

Independent, London, late April 2002

SOUTH AUSTRALIA, AUSTRALIA, 2002

Deckhand Shannon Jenzen will never forget how close he came to saving a mate whose leg was bitten off by a great white shark as he was hauling him on board their scallop boat.

Mr Jenzen tried desperately to pull Paul Buckland out of the water as the six-metre shark tore at his body.

Mr Buckland, aged twenty-three, a professional diver from Port Lincoln, was attacked as he dived for scallops off Smoky Bay, in the Great Australian Bight, on Tuesday. He surfaced in distress, yelling to Mr Jenzen to get him out of the water.

"He was in the shark's mouth," said Chief Inspector Malcolm Schluter, of Port Lincoln police. "His partner rammed the boat against the shark to make it let him go, which it did."

Mr Buckland was hauled from the water, but the shark had bitten off his leg and part of his torso, and he bled to death in his friend's arms on board the boat. "He died doing something he loved," said Mr Jenzen.

The shark had been harassing boats in the area for two months and was so aggressive that it ignored a shark repellent device. Mr Buckland was wearing an activated SharkPOD – a South African-made device – which failed to protect him.

Chief Inspector Schluter said it appeared that a hungry white pointer [great white] intent on a target was not deterred by the device.

A local fisherman said that Mr Buckland had been warned about the shark by another fisherman only a few days earlier, but had assured him he was using a SharkPOD.

Mr Jenzen escaped injury, but was taken to his local hospital to be treated for shock. Yesterday he spoke of his friend, saying: "Diving and sailing were his two passions. He's a guy that lived every day to the fullest. He was an awesome guy. It's a great loss to everyone that knew him."

A decision on the fate of the shark has divided Smoky Bay. Local fishermen have called for it to be killed.

Allan Suter, who heads the West Coast Professional

Fishermen's Association, said the shark had approached his boat while he was line fishing two weeks ago and was easily identified by its fearlessness, size and girth. "I have had a very good look at it. It swam right up to the boat and I could have patted it on the head," he said.

But the South Australian Fisheries Department said the shark would only be destroyed if it threatened human life again. The department's policy director, Will Zacharin, said there had been several sightings. He said the bay would be monitored to determine if the shark was still a threat.

"There are other options to killing it. We can harass it from the area," he said. "It would be a last resort to capture the shark and destroy it. It's a protected species."

Gail Dodd, from the Smoky Bay general store, said the town was divided. "Some people think it should be killed. Others, like myself, think that, when you enter the water, you enter the food chain and that's the risk you have to take."

SeaChange, the Australian manufacturers of Shark Shield shark repellent technology, said Mr Buckland was wearing a device no longer in production and they were seeking further information about the attack. SeaChange has adapted the South African technology for the Australian market.

Sydney Morning Herald, 2 May 2002

CALIFORNIA, USA, 2002

A 12–14-foot shark bolted out of the water near Stinson Beach on Friday afternoon and clenched a screaming surfer in its razorsharp jaws as fellow surfers watched in disbelief.

The attack, which prompted National Park Service officials to bar anyone from entering the water at Stinson

Beach for five days, occurred inside the so-called Red Triangle – the stretch of Northern California coast where more shark attacks have taken place than anywhere else in the world.

Lee Fontan, aged twenty-four, a Bolinas landscaper and life-long surfer, needed 100 stitches to close four bite wounds after Friday's attack.

"We were out there kidding around, talking, waiting for the next wave. Then, all of a sudden, we heard a scream," said John Gilbert, aged thirty-three, an avid surfer who lives in Stinson Beach and owns the town's Parkside Café. "I looked over and this guy was about three or four feet out of the water in the shark's mouth. You could see its teeth, its gums. Its eyes were shut. Its gills were wide open, like shutters. The whole dorsal fin on its back was out of the water."

When the shark crashed back into the ocean, it released the surfer and disappeared. Fontan was left clinging desperately to his board. A dozen surfers pulled him to shore and then tended to his wounds – including an eight-inch gash in his left thigh and tooth holes below his ribs.

"You could see all the way to the bone," said Paul Fontan, the surfer's father, who was on his way to the beach when the attack happened. "It made me sick."

Paramedics from the Stinson Beach Fire Department arrived soon after the attack was reported at 2.17 p.m., followed by National Park Service lifeguards, Marin County Fire Department ambulance crews, the Marin County Sheriff's Department and security officers from the nearby Seadrift residential development.

Fontan was taken by helicopter to Eden Hospital in Castro Valley, where he underwent an hour and a half of surgery to repair skin and deep tissue wounds to his left leg and left shoulder and arm.

Dr Scott Snyder, a trauma surgeon, said that Fontan remained in critical condition, but that his injuries were not life threatening. He said he found no whole teeth inside the wounds, but removed some white matter that will be tested.

Fontan was alert and in good spirits, even joking with hospital workers, Snyder said, recounting the surfer's response when he was asked what the shark looked like: "He said it was a large white shark with large white teeth."

The attack took place as a group of 12–15 surfers sat on their boards about fifty yards offshore from the Seadrift residential enclave, near the channel between Stinson Beach and Bolinas Lagoon.

The surfers were enjoying a southerly swell breaking right toward Bolinas Beach, making for excellent surfing. Fontan, who had been riding the waves for a couple of hours, was about ten feet farther out to sea than anyone else, Gilbert said.

The attack, recalled Gilbert, was surreal in its swiftness, more unbelievable than horrifying. "You see sharks on television, where seals are attacked. It was just like that – straight up like a missile. The shark hit him and launched him out of the water."

Witnesses said the shark thrashed wildly as it clamped down. But the surfer, who is described by relatives as athletic and muscular, fought back, striking the shark soundly at least once on the snout, according to witnesses.

The shark left a huge arching bite mark – about thirteen inches wide – in Fontan's six-foot yellow surfboard. On the bottom of the board Fontan had affixed a locally popular "no sharks" decal depicting an open-jawed shark beneath a circle and a slash.

"Obviously the sticker didn't work," said his father, "or maybe it made him mad."

Most likely the shark mistook Fontan, who was wearing a wetsuit, for a seal or sea lion, said John McCosker, one of the world's foremost shark experts and a senior scientist at the California Academy of Sciences, in San Francisco's Golden Gate Park. In McCosker's opinion the attack sounded like the work of a great white shark, but he added that he would have to talk to witnesses and doctors before he could make that determination.

If it was a great white – and all the perpetrators of attacks off the Northern California coast have been great whites – it would be the thirteenth such attack since 1952 in Mann County and the forty-third in the Red Triangle, which stretches from southern Monterey County to the Farallon Islands and to Tomales Bay. Only 7 of the 79 attacks off California between 1950 and 1998 were fatal.

The zone has the highest concentration of shark attacks in the world, McCosker said, because of its large seal and sea lion populations and the large number of beachgoers, boaters and anglers. "It amazes me there are not more attacks," he said. "I wouldn't be surprised to learn that there are sharks swimming along Stinson Beach all summer long."

The last Bay Area shark attack occurred in August 1998, when Jonathan Kathrein, then aged sixteen, of Lucas Valley, on the north edge of San Rafael, was bitten while boogie-boarding at the southern end of Stinson Beach.

On Friday, Kathrein was skim-boarding at Rodeo Beach, near Stinson, but was home by the time he heard about the latest attack.

"I was hoping that no one would have to go through it again," Kathrein said.

It took him a year to recover from the bite, which extended from his right knee to his hip, and he still does not have full power in that leg.

"I'd like to be able to surf more, but it's been harder to get into the water," Kathrein, now aged twenty, said ruefully. "I've realized the reality of sharks in the area. It's pretty serious."

But the sixteen surfers riding the waves at sunset near the scene of the attack, outside park boundaries, had no such qualms.

"Denial is a very good thing," said one surfer who didn't want to give her name. "Sharks are always here, but the waves aren't."

San Francisco Chronicle, 31 May 2002

FLORIDA, USA, 2002

A shark bit a ten-year-old boy in the leg on Sunday as he played in shallow surf off the Atlantic Coast of Florida, authorities said. Corey Brooks was in stable condition after receiving 125 stitches to close the eight-inch wound on his right calf, said Connie Brigg, a spokeswoman for St Mary's Hospital in West Palm Beach.

Corey, his baby-sitter and her children were at the beach on Hutchinson Island, about thirty-nine miles north of West Palm Beach. After he was bitten, Corey ran out of the water crying, said Lieutenant John Recca of Martin County Fire-Rescue: "The boy said he thought someone had pinched him."

The gash went to the bone, but Corey was able to move his leg and toes, Recca said. Beachgoers were ordered out of the water for a couple of hours, but no one else saw the shark.

There were seventy-six unprovoked shark attacks in the United States last year – thirty-seven in Florida – according to the International Shark Attack File at the Florida Museum of Natural History in Gainesville.

Boston Globe, 9 June 2002

Tiger Shark

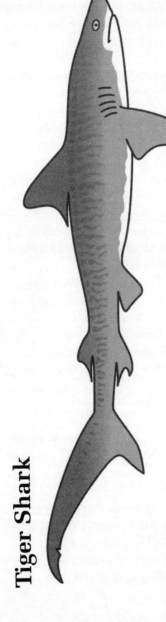

Shark Facts

Length: 10 feet to 14 feet (3 m to 4.2 m)

Weight: 850 lb to 1,400 lb (385 kg to 635 kg)

Colouring: Blue or light green upper with white or yellowish belly

Diet: Fish, sea birds, dolphins, seals, turtles, rays, other sharks

Pups: Between 10 and 80 born at a time each up to 2 feet (61 cm)

Status: Under threat – population declining

Known as the second most dangerous shark to humans (after the great white), the tiger shark – not to be confused with the far smaller sand tiger – can often be found in shallow coastal areas or harbours searching for prey. They tend to hunt alone and are recognized as being under threat because of over fishing and "finning". Young tiger sharks have stripes on their bodies, hence the name, which tend to fade as the shark gets older.

Tiger Shark Range

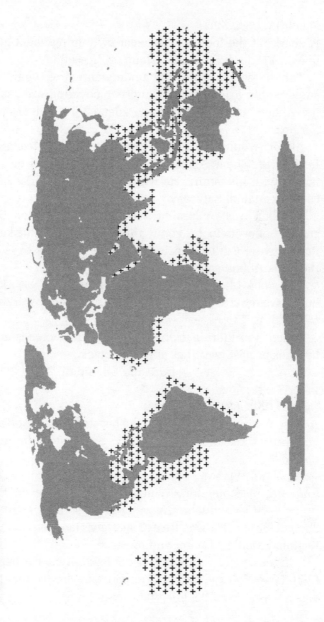

FLORIDA, USA, 2002

A shark bit the foot of a teenager swimming about 200 feet off Florida's St George Island, police said.

The sixteen-year-old boy underwent three hours of surgery after Friday's attack and is recovering well, said Jay Abbott, chief of St George Island Fire and Rescue Service.

Abbott would not release the name of the teenager from Birmingham, Alabama, who was vacationing on the island with his family. He was released from a Panama City hospital on Saturday.

The boy was swimming with his brother when the shark, believed to be about three feet long, attacked. People were fishing and feeding gulls near the boys at the time, Abbott said.

The shark bite left a deep gash on the boy's left foot, but he was able to get to shore, where emergency workers treated him.

Officials in Florida did not close the St George Island beaches or post warnings after the attack.

Daily Mail, London, 2 July 2002

NORTH CAROLINA, USA, 2002

A Wisconsin teenager visiting the beach for the first time had thirty-three stitches and staples after a shark bit him on the leg.

At about 11 a.m. on Monday Robert Pollan, aged fourteen, of Stoughton, Winconsin, was bitten on the upper right leg while in the water at the southern end of Topsail Beach. He was treated at New Hanover County Regional Medical Center and released.

"He took a big chunk out of my leg, but after it heals I will be ready to go back in," Robert said shortly after he was released from the hospital.

Topsail Beach police chief Ricky Smith said the bite was the first reported shark attack on the beach in his eighteen years with the department.

Robert, who is about 5 ft 4 in., said he was standing in waist-deep water playing with other family members and a dog when he felt something nick his leg. He thought the dog had clawed him until he saw blood in the water, flesh hanging from his leg and holes in his swimming trunks, he said. He walked to the shore to family members.

A paediatric doctor, Tom Kayrouz, who happened to be vacationing on the beach, examined the wound and identified it as a shark bite. Chief Smith said the bite was about six to seven inches in circumference and he believed the shark to be about four or five feet long.

Wire report, 6 August 2002

FLORIDA, USA, 2002

A teenage surfer was attacked by a shark in waist-deep water, becoming Volusia County's sixth shark-bite victim this year.

Brennan Smith, aged fifteen, of Riviera Beach, said he was coming in after riding his last wave on Wednesday when he felt a "pinch" just above his left ankle.

The teenager alerted a lifeguard and was taken to Bert Fish Medical Center, where doctors sutured a four-inch wound. He was released on Wednesday afternoon.

Of the thirty-seven attacks last year in Florida, twenty-two occurred in Volusia County.

Associated Press, 8 August 2002

RECIFE, BRAZIL, 2002

Recife is a huge conurbation on the north eastern coast of Brazil. With almost 4 million people living in the area, it is the country's fifth-largest population centre and in the sunshine on the beaches that line its Atlantic coast, the people love to get into the water. Jaboatão dos Guararapes is one of the cities that make up the Recife metropolitan area and the long stretch of sand on Piedade Beach is one of the region's most popular. It was here that Fabrício José de Carvalho was swimming when a bull shark clamped its jaws around his left thigh. The bite was so serious and the damage so great that surgeons were left with no choice but to amputate the leg.

Piedade Beach, 16 September, 2002

RECIFE, BRAZIL, 2002
A month after the attack on 19-year-old de Carvalho, 46-year-old Luiz Soares de Arruda was swimming off the same beach at around the same time in the afternoon when he was taken by what was thought to have been a bull shark, one of the most common types in the area. His body was never recovered.

Piedade Beach, 13 October, 2002

RECIFE, BRAZIL, 2002
Boa Viagem is a 5-mile stretch of sand where the wide beach is flanked by some of the finest hotels in Brazil and the night life in the many bars and clubs of Recife keeps the area as busy after dark as the beach is during the day. In fact, the beach is lit up at night so that beachgoers and swimmers can enjoy the ocean, although it is cooler in the evening than during the day when the water remains at a pleasant 25 °C all year round. It was on this beach that 19-year-old Aylson Gadelha met his end on the first day of December, sustaining injuries that were unsurvivable.

Boa Viagem Beach, 1 December, 2002

QUEENSLAND, AUSTRALIA, 2002

The same type of shark known to feed in the shallow waters off Recife is also responsible for some vicious attacks in Australia, not only in the ocean but also in the country's inland waterways. Miami Lake is linked to the series of rivers, canals and stretches of open water that criss-cross the countryside inland from Australia's Gold. Coast. In December 2002, 23-year-old Beau Martin went missing while taking a late-night swim across Miami Lake. His body was found by his father several days later with a horrific leg wound. A post mortem revealed that he had been attacked before he died.

Miami Lake, Gold Coast, 16 December, 2002

2003

QUEENSLAND, AUSTRALIA, 2003

Gold Coast residents were warned not to swim in any of the area's lakes or canals after kayakers discovered the body of 84-year-old Bob Purcell in Burleigh lake. The former Commonwealth Games bowler had disappeared after his regular early morning swim in the lake and when his body was discovered it was found to have injuries consistent with an attack by a bull shark probably measuring around seven feet. Anyone using the Gold Coast waterways was urged to take great care as it was estimated that several hundred bull sharks inhabited the lakes and canal system.

Burleigh Lake, Gold Coast, 8 February 2003

VENEZUELA, 2003

Margarita Island lies 25 miles off the northern coast of Venezuela, so close to the equator that the daytime temperature never varies much from around 29 °C and the sea temperature is just a couple of degrees cooler. This, and the fairly constant wind of between 20 and 30 knots make Margarita a haven for watersports enthusiasts, with the island hosting professional windsurfing contests each year. The water off the beach at Playa El Yaque is such a Mecca for windsurfers that it often looks like there's as much traffic manouevring as a busy street in central New York. In amongst that wind-blown traffic in April 2003 was 28-year-old Frenchman Yann Perras, having the holiday of a lifetime. Dropping into the water for a few moments to make some adjustments to his rigging, he suddenly felt a vice-like grip fasten around his foot and looked down into the clear water to see a shark attached to his leg. Shocked and panicked, Yann fought off the animal, but the damage was done. He lost his leg.

Years later, still learning to cope with his disability, Yann showed no hard feelings towards the world's shark population when he joined a campaign urging the United Nations to take steps to save the lives of sharks, many species falling into the endangered category and their dwindling numbers threatening to upset the delicately balanced food chains – and hence the entire ecosystem – of our oceans.

Playa El Yaque, Margarita Island, 11 April 2003

RECIFE, BRAZIL, 2003

Towards the early evening, around 5.00pm, 17-year-old Tiago Augosto de Silva Machado was surfing off the beach at Pau Amarelo, about 10 miles from Recife, when he was attacked by a bull shark. He was bitten repeatedly on his hand and foot and the injuries to his left leg were so severe that it later had to be amputated by surgeons.

Pau Amarelo, 23 April 2003

NORTHERN TERRITORY, AUSTRALIA, 2003
Surf ski enthusiast Martin Gunda was about a mile offshore at Nhulunbuy in Australia's Northern Territory, training for a charity event when he was suddenly catapulted out of his ski into the water. The surf ski looks like an elongated kayak but is very stable and very fast when in the hands of a trained paddler and the impact was such that at first 37-year-old Gunda thought his friend must have rammed him. Then he saw a dark grey shape in the water and he hauled himself back aboard his ski as fast as he could. He "paddled like hell" back to shore and then noticed that the ski had been taking on water through a series of bitemark holes in its hull and on its rudder.

Gunda counted himself lucky but was quickly back in the water as part of the regime that saw him training five times a week with his team.

Nhulunbuy, 24 July 2003

CALIFORNIA, USA, 2003
Four lifeguards risked their lives to save a woman in trouble in the water off Avila Beach in San Luis Obispo County, California, little realizing that Deborah Franzman had been attacked by a shark. Franzman was a regular swimmer in the area, often exercising in the water with friends, swimming amongst the local sea lions. On this particular Tuesday morning, however, the 50-year-old college lecturer was alone. A dedicated athlete and triathlon competitor, she had put on her wetsuit and fins and slipped into the water for her early morning swim.

She was about 75 yards from shore when the great white attacked her from below.

The lifeguards who came to her aid were on a nearby pier, watching colleagues testing their skills in the water below when they heard the screams. They immediately ran down the pier and dived into the water to swim to Franzman, finding her floating face down in a spreading stain of blood. Turning her over, they supported her head and body, floating her to shore while casting anxiously around for the shark. Their efforts, however, were to no avail, Franzman's left thigh had been stripped of flesh and her femoral artery severed. She was dead in the water before the lifeguards reached her.

Avila Beach, 19 August 2003

FIJI, 2003
Fisherman Epeli Mate was wading between his boat and the shore near the Welagi reef at Drekeniwai when he was attacked by a shark. The fatal attack happened at night and when his body was recovered the 40-year-old was discovered to have bites to his abdomen.

Drekeniwai, Taveuni, 29 September 2003

HAWAII, USA, 2003
Champion surfer Bethany Hamilton was just 13 years old and surfing with her best friend Alana Blanchard, along with Alana's father and brother, early in the morning at Tunnels Beach in Kauai, Hawaii. A local girl, she was lying on her board with her left hand in the water when a tiger shark rose from the depths and bit off her arm. Blanchard immediately came to her aid, helping her to paddle back to shore where her father tied a tourniquet using a surfboard rope before they rushed Hamilton to Wilcox Memorial Hospital. By the time she got there she had lost more than

half the blood in her body but, by strange coincidence, her father was about to go into the operating room for knee surgery. His daughter took his place.

Having lost an arm might be enough to put most people off surfing but Hamilton was back in the water within a month of the attack. At first she used an adapted board that was longer and thicker for better stability and which had a handle to help her climb aboard. She learned a new paddling technique, taught herself to surf again on a normal board and entered a competition in January 2004. She would go on to become a professional surfer, winning many more competitions both at home and abroad, inspiring the 2011 Hollywood movie about her experiences, *Soul Surfer*.

Kauai, 31 October 2003

KWAZULU-NATAL, SOUTH AFRICA, 2003
Diving instructor Sheldon Jee was spear-fishing off the reef near Sodwana Bay on the KwaZulu-Natal coast when his friends and the dive boat lost track of him. Because of its coral reef and 1200 species of fish, Sodwana Bay National Park is a popular destination for scuba divers from all over the world. Sharks tend to leave scuba divers alone, their metal tanks and strange shape confusing the shark's senses, but Jee was free diving with his spear gun well away from the areas used by scuba divers. A search was mounted but all that was found was his severed left hand. The search party also spotted a 13-foot tiger shark in the area.

Sodwana Bay, 27 November 2003

COOK ISLANDS, 2003
Two fishermen found themselves in trouble when their boat overturned on a Saturday night trip several miles

out from Pukapuka Atoll. When they failed to return, a search was mounted for them the following morning but only 50-year-old Punavi Tamiti Peua was found. He had no idea what had happened to his friend, 45-year-old Teta Vaotiare. Police and rescue services widened the search area and on Monday they discovered some badly mauled human remains floating in the sea. Although it was not possible to tell if the remains were actually those of Vaotiare, fisherman had reported seeing mako and tiger sharks in the general area and the search was called off.

Pukapuka Atoll, 13 December 2003

2004

EGYPT, 2004

Shark spotting is one of the attractions that bring holidaymakers to the luxurious hotels and beautiful beaches around the Sharm el-Sheikh region of Egypt's Red Sea coast. Swimming in water where sharks are known to feed, however, is always dangerous. An Egyptian man snorkelling in the Coral Bay area on Valentine's Day, accompanied by a number of other holidaymakers, was attacked by a shark but, despite suffering severe bite wounds, he made it back to shore. He was immediately rushed to hospital where he died from blood loss.

Coral Bay, Sharm el-Sheikh, 14 February 2004

QUEENSLAND, AUSTRALIA, 2004

Spear fisherman Mark Bryant disappeared while spear fishing with two friends at Tweed Heads, near Cook Island off Australia's Gold Coast. Bryant, using a snorkel, not scuba gear, surfaced with his friends and then took one last dive on his own. He never resurfaced and when his friends raised the alarm a search was mounted. Only his spear gun, with a fish attached, was found but the presence of several large tiger sharks in the area led to the obvious conclusion that the bleeding, injured fish, thrashing about on the spear, had attracted the sharks to Bryant.

Tweed Heads, Gold Coast, 17 February 2004

RECIFE, BRAZIL, 2004

The infamous waters off Recife claimed another victim when 29-year-old Edimilson Henrique dos Santos was attacked while swimming just ten yards from the beach. Dos Santos suffered numerous deep bites and mauling to his legs and hips and was helped to the beach where emergency services provided first aid before he was rushed to hospital. He died from shock and loss of blood shortly after reaching the hospital.

Piedade Beach, 29 February 2004

RECIFE, BRAZIL, 2004

Alcindo de Souza Leão was body boarding off the beach at Boa Viagem when he felt something latch onto his left leg. Others nearby heard his screams for help as he battled with the shark and by the time they reached him the 22-year-old had an open fracture between the knee and the ankle. Two swimmers and two fire fighters from the local surf rescue supported de Souza in the water until they reached the beach where they tended to his injuries. He was then whisked off to hospital where surgeons were forced to amputate the leg.

Boa Viagem, 29 March 2004

HAWAII, USA, 2004

Courtney Marcher was a young woman pursuing her dream. The 22-year-old had been living in Hawaii for two months, having moved there from Florida in a bid to become a professional surfer. In Velzyland on Oahu, she shared a house with two Australians just five minutes from the beach and went surfing with them one morning just before 7.00 a.m. After almost two hours, she said she was heading for shore, but that was the last anyone ever saw of her. Marcher disappeared without her purse, her cell phone or her medication – she suffered from epilepsy – but her surfboard went with her.

Her friends alerted the police later that day when she failed to show up and a search was mounted. Four days later her surfboard was found by fishermen about 18 miles away from the beach at Velzyland. The leg rope was severed but the length still attached to the board showed no clear signs of a shark attack. Neither could police find any traces of shark attack when they examined the board. It was suggested that Marcher may have drowned, having had some kind of seizure in the water after leaving her friends, but if that had been the case her body would most likely have been found, either washed ashore or floating in the ocean. Her disappearance remains a mystery, with a shark attack providing the most obvious explanation.

Velzyland, Oahu, 4 April 2004

WESTERN CAPE, SOUTH AFRICA, 2004

John Paul Andrew was surfing with his friend Jay Mitchell at around 2.00 p.m. off the beach at Muizenberg in Cape Town's False Bay when the two youngsters were horrified to see a great white breach the surface right next to them. The shark knocked Andrew off his board but, as far as Mitchell could see, made no attempt to bite him. The 16-year-old quickly climbed back aboard and both surfers started paddling frantically for the shore. Andrew was just a yard or so behind Mitchell when he saw the shark rise out of the water again, this time clamping Andrew in its jaws. Mitchell watched helplessly as Andrew was lifted clear of the water before being smashed back down in a spray of red and white foam. Then he vanished from sight.

Mitchell looked around, made towards the shore and teamed up with another surfer, Grant Kirkland, the two then paddling around together looking for any sign of Andrew. Kirkland spotted Andrew floating in the water and paddled towards him. Andrew was alive, conscious and able to tell Kirkland that the shark had bitten off his right leg. Kirkland hauled Andrew onto his board and paddled for the beach.

On the beach lifeguards were quickly on the scene as were paramedics who restarted Andrew's heart when he "died" for several minutes. His heart also stopped beating when he reached Constantiaberg Medi-Clinic and it took surgeons and doctors four days to stabilize him. Around the same time that Andrew was showing the first signs of surviving his ordeal, police found his severed leg, still with the mangled surf board attached by the leg leash, on a beach at Gordon's Bay, which lies on the other side of False Bay from Muizenberg.

Muizenberg, Cape Town, 5 April 2004

HAWAII, USA, 2004
When retired Los Angeles police officer Rodger Coomds paddled out to join his friend Willis McInnis surfing about 300 yards offshore from Pohaku Park in Kahana, he was surprised to hear 57-year-old McInnis yelling for help. Then he spotted the huge chunk that had been

bitten out of McInnis's right thigh. Tina Cooper, who had paddled out with Coomds, immediately headed back to shore to raise the alarm while Coomds slipped into the water to try to push McInnis, who was lying on his own board, towards the beach.

Although McInnis was fully conscious when Coomds started to push him to shore, even admitting to his friend that he reckoned he would lose his leg, he quickly grew weaker and, by the time others had arrived to help them ashore, he had died from loss of blood.

Kahana, 11 April 2004

TONGA, 2004

Four men were left clinging to floats and debris for seven hours in rough seas when their fishing boat sank off the coast of Tonga. The men were rescued by the Tongan Navy after the New Zealand authorities passed on a message from an overflying Air New Zealand aircraft which had picked up signals from a rescue beacon. Locating the men in heavy seas in the dark had proved extremely problematic and by the time the rescuers reached them at around 10.00 p.m., one of the four was dead. They had been repeatedly attacked by small sharks, probably hungry juveniles, and the dead man had suffered several bites, despite his friends' efforts to protect him. Another of the group had also been bitten and was later treated in hospital.

South Pacific, 13 April 2004

RECIFE, BRAZIL, 2004

Recife beachgoers continued to risk life and limb in the water off Piedade Beach, with 22-year-old Orlando Oscar da Silva suffering fatal shark bites while swimming on 1 May and Naiane Barbosa Bringel was wading in the same area when she too was attacked three weeks later.

The 24-year-old sustained several bite wounds to her legs and buttocks, causing enormous pain and distress but she fared better than 17-year-old Valmir Pereira Silva the following day when he was bitten on the left arm and calf before having his left foot severed.

Piedade Beach, 1–23 May 2004

WESTERN CAPE, SOUTH AFRICA, 2004

Nkosinathi Mayaba was on a fishing expedition, poaching the valuable perlemoen [also known as abalone] around Dyer Island, and was swimming back through the water towards Pearly Beach with his two friends when their lookout on shore saw a large shark rise up out of the water with 21-year-old Mayaba in its jaws. Having grabbed Mayaba around the torso, the shark then ripped off his leg and disappeared beneath the waves with the body. Mayaba's two friends swam for their lives and waited on shore with the lookout for any sign of him, but two hours later the young man had still not reappeared.

Anglers discovered Mayaba's badly mutilated body when it washed ashore four days later about six miles from Pearly Beach.

Pearly Beach, Gansbaai, 2 June 2004

EGYPT, 2004

Dahab, an old Bedouin fishing village on Egypt's Red Sea coast about 50 miles north of Sharm el-Sheikh, has enjoyed a new lease of life in recent years as a tourist destination. It is especially popular with divers, although Swiss holidaymaker Mirjam Buser would surely no longer count it as one of her top vacation destinations. Buser was snorkelling off the beach at Dahab when a black tip shark appeared from nowhere and bit off her hand.

Dahab, Red Sea, 2 July 2004

WESTERN AUSTRALIA, AUSTRALIA, 2004
A shark hunt was launched off Western Australia after two sharks, thought to be either great whites or bronze whalers, attacked 29-year-old surfer Bradley Adrian Smith. There were a number of people enjoying the sand and the surf on Sunday afternoon at Left Handers Beach, near Gracetown, south of Perth, when a shark that witnesses described as being as big as a car, rose from the water, biting Smith's surfboard in half. The second shark then attacked him, biting him repeatedly in an encounter that lasted for around 20 seconds, witnesses reporting that Smith punched and battered the shark while trying to escape.

Smith suffered appalling injuries to his abdomen, pelvis and legs and, while two other surfers bravely helped him to shore, he died before they got him to the beach.

Left Handers Beach, Gracetown, 10 July 2004

CALIFORNIA, USA, 2004
Randy Fry and Cliff Zimmerman had dived together for 30 years and were seeking out abalone about 50 yards from the California's Mendocino coast a little way north of Fort Bragg on a clear, calm and sunny Sunday when disaster struck. Zimmerman was within arm's reach of 50-year-old Fry, the pair diving wearing wetsuits, snorkels and fins but without tanks, when he felt something rush past him. He caught a glimpse of a dorsal fin and the water filled with blood. Although they were in water only about 20 feet deep, the shark disappeared as suddenly as it had come, taking Fry along with it.

Zimmerman never saw his old friend again. The Coast Guard mounted a search and his body was discovered the following morning, another diver identifying Fry by the distinctive wetsuit that he always wore.

Fort Bragg, 15 August 2004

RECIFE, BRAZIL, 2004

The Recife coastline was the scene of another gruesome attack when an unidentified woman was taken by a shark while swimming off Pina Beach, the third fatal attack on this stretch of coastline this year.

Pina Beach, 8 September 2004

RÉUNION, 2004

Vincent Motais de Narbonne was in the water at Ti'Paris, near the Pointe du Daible at Saint-Pierre on Réunion island at around 4.30 p.m., with his coach and a couple of fellow body-boarders. The 15-year-old French Junior Champion was training for the forthcoming French Championships at Royan in only three weeks' time. Two other competitors, both girls, were about to join the group when they saw something very strange happening out on the water. Vincent let out a yell and his coach, just a few yards from the youngster, described how he turned to see a shark's fin and Vincent fighting for his life.

Onlookers who saw what was happening from a nearby clifftop immediately alerted the emergency services as Vincent's companions quickly floated him forty yards to shore on his board. The shark had bitten off his right leg and he was losing a lot of blood. On the beach, they tied a tourniquet around his leg and paramedics, along with doctors, were quickly on the scene. They spent an hour trying to stabilize Vincent's condition, beachgoers building a wall of sand to help keep the advancing tide from swamping the site, before moving him to hospital where he underwent surgery. Vincent later participated in a conservation campaign urging the United Nations to take action to protect sharks around the world.

Saint-Pierre, 6 October 2004

WESTERN CAPE, SOUTH AFRICA, 2004

At dawn every day, except on Sundays when she would walk to church, 77-year-old Tyna Webb went for a swim to keep fit. Slim and athletic, the grandmother had been taking her early morning dip off Fish Hoek beach for 17 years, generally with a group of friends. The morning of 15 October, however, was to be Webb's last swim.

Witnesses saw a large great white, estimated at around 22 feet long, attack the swimmer in a sudden burst of violence before circling round her, grabbing the stricken swimmer in its huge jaws and disappearing beneath the red-stained waves. A search was mounted to try to locate Webb's body, but all that was ever found was her familiar red swimming cap.

Fish Hoek Beach, Cape Town, 15 November 2004

QUEENSLAND, AUSTRALIA 2004

When 38-year-old Mark Thompson took time off from his upholstery business in Cairns, he liked nothing better than to go out on the water with friends for a spot of spear fishing. He was doing just that, swimming from the sports fishing boat *Espresso* with two companions around lunchtime at Opal Reef, a little under 50 miles north of Cairns, when his friends heard him cry out. They looked round to see the water around Thompson turning red. A shark had ripped into his upper left leg causing massive damage and severing his femoral artery.

Thompson's friends got him out of the water and called the emergency services but by the time the Queensland Rescue Helicopter Service arrived on the scene Thompson had gone into cardiac arrest due to loss of blood and was dead.

Opal Reef, 11 December 2004

SOUTH AUSTRALIA, AUSTRALIA, 2004

On the first really hot day of the Australian summer, four teenagers from Adelaide were messing about on the water, riding on a surfboard towed behind a dinghy equipped with an outboard motor. Nick Petersen had recently left Adelaide's Sacred Heart College, where the four had become best mates, and was an experienced surfer. He jumped into the water and called for the others to throw the board in for him. It was then that a huge great white appeared and grabbed him by the left arm. As his friends looked on in horror, Petersen was dragged around the boat by the shark. They tried to fight it off using the boat's oars but the shark paid no attention. Then a second shark appeared and the two fish tore Petersen apart, disappearing into the deep with his dismembered body.

The youngsters circled round, looking for Petersen, but he was gone and all they could do was head for shore and warn others about the menace lurking in the ocean off West Beach. Two of the boys later went back out on the water with rescue services hoping to find Petersen's body but they found nothing. Petersen's surf board was eventually washed ashore and some human remains were recovered from the water.

West Beach, Adelaide, 16 December 2004

2005

CUBA, 2005

Hurdenis Jérez was swimming off the village of Uvero on Cuba's south coast when he was attacked by a shark estimated at 10 feet in length. The 19-year-old had his right foot bitten off.

Uvero, Santiago de Cuba, 20 January 2005

WESTERN AUSTRALIA, AUSTRALIA, 2005

The Abrolhos Islands and the coral reef that surrounds the 122 specs of atoll that form the island chain, is an area of natural beauty teeming with wildlife where tourists can visit on charter boats from Geraldton, some 38 miles east on the coast of Western Australia. *The Matrix* was one such boat, its passengers looking forward to spotting bottlenose dolphins, white chested sea eagles and the huge Sampson fish, some of which are so friendly they can be fed by hand. Anchored off Pelseart, one of the three island clusters that make up the 62-mile long Abrolhos group, this was the catamaran's maiden voyage, with everyone on board looking forward to the next leg of the trip north towards Kimberley.

For now, however, there was time to enjoy some Saturday afternoon snorkelling on the reef and one of the crew, 26-year-old Geoffrey Brazier, joined the passengers in the water. They had been bobbing around in the calm, clear water for some time when suddenly a shark reported to be almost 20 feet long appeared out of nowhere and slammed into Brazier. Witnesses said that the giant shark almost bit its victim in two, such was the ferocity of the attack. Brazier was killed almost instantly and the shark, either a tiger or a great white, made off with his body. Police and the Western Australia Fisheries authority were called in and searched the area around the islands for hours, but no trace of Brazier's remains was ever found.

Abrolhos Islands, 19 March 2005

QUEENSLAND, AUSTRALIA, 2005

Each year it is estimated that in any given year between two and three thousand yachtsmen are somewhere along the way to sailing solo around the world. In May 2005, Ben Edelstein was halfway through his trip. The estate agent from Austin in Texas had set sail from the United States in December in his 42-foot yacht, *Gypsy Soul*, heading across the Gulf of Mexico to Cuba, then through the Panama Canal for a spot of island hopping across the South Pacific. He was in no real hurry and even took some time off to head home in December 2004, leaving the *Gypsy Soul* in Australia and returning to her after spending a while exploring the country. He also picked up six backpackers who were touring Australia, offering them a 10-day sailing trip along the Great Barrier Reef.

Edelstein had been spear fishing off Whitsunday Island and, having just bagged a large snapper for lunch, he was heading for the surface to tell his backpacker friends that there were no sharks around when a six-foot black tip reef shark came straight towards him. Edelstein backpedalled fast, kicking his flippers at the shark and pulling himself through the water with his hands. It was then that another shark clamped on to his right hand. Edelstein smacked it hard with his free hand and the shark let him go, but not before it had mangled his hand. Streaming blood from his badly mauled hand, Edelstein struck out for the surface and yelled "Shark!" as soon as he got his head into the fresh air.

One of his friends jumped into the *Gypsy Soul*'s dinghy and sped towards him, hauling him out of the water and taking him back to the boat. Edelstein's first aid procedure involved cleaning the gashes on his hand with purified water and smothering it with iodine while administering straight tequila orally. They then set sail for Townsville, over 40 miles away. When a doctor was eventually able to treat his injuries, they found that, despite the flesh being flayed open to the bone, there was no serious nerve or tendon damage. After three hours and 75 stitches, the wounds were closed but his hand remained immobile.

Edelstein had no option but to rest until he was able to use his hand again. The *Gypsy Soul* stayed tied up in the marina at Townsville for several weeks until Edelstein was once more able to haul ropes and furl sails. He then resumed his round-the-world odyssey.

Whitsunday Island, 15 May 2005

WESTERN CAPE, SOUTH AFRICA, 2005
Medical student Henri Murray was spear fishing with his friend Piet van Niekerk on a sunny Saturday afternoon about 200 yards from shore at Miller's Point not far from Cape Town when he spotted a large shark nearby. Murray yelled to van Niekerk to get out of the water, then the 22-year-old watched the massive great white, thought to be at least 20 feet long, circle around him.

As the shark closed in, Murray managed to scare it off while desperately making for the beach. Again it came for him and again Murray frightened it away. A yachtsman who witnessed the drama described how the shark then lunged at Murray for a third time, rising from below and taking him in its jaws, feet first, swallowing him almost up to the armpits. Van Niekerk tried to go to Murray's aid, shooting the shark with his spear gun, but the creature vanished into the depths, taking Murray with him.

A search was mounted to try to recover Murray's body, van Niekerk joining the hunt for his friend, but all that was recovered was his spear gun, dive belt, goggles and a flipper. The jacket of his wetsuit was later washed ashore at Muizenberg on the other side of False Bay.

Miller's Point, Cape Town, 4 June 2005

VANUATU, 2005
Tragedy struck a New Zealand family on a yachting holiday when they visited Vanuatu, the South Pacific

island nation situated east of Australia between New Caledonia and Fiji. The Websters sailed to Malekula island from Vanuatu's capital, Port Vila, and seeing local children swimming off the beach, they naturally assumed it to be safe.

Alysha Webster was just a month from her eighth birthday and a good swimmer, but there was nothing that she or her parents, Grant and Sheree, could do when the shark attacked her. The little girl's left leg was bitten off at the thigh and, despite being rushed to a local hospital, she died from shock and blood loss.

Malekula, 22 June 2005

FLORIDA, USA, 2005

Jamie Diagle, from Louisiana, was on holiday in Florida with her family and swimming with her friend Felicia Venable about 200 yards off Miramar Beach on the Gulf of Mexico coast. The two 14-year-olds were using boogie boards for bodysurfing just after 11.00 a.m. in the morning when they saw a shark. Terrified, they both immediately headed for shore but the shark latched on to Daigle and dragged her under the water.

Surfer Tim Dicus heard the girls screaming and paddled over to help. Daigle was floating unconscious in a cloud of blood when Dicus reached her, pulling her onto his board as the six-foot bull shark came back for a second attack, continuing to harass them as Dicus struck out for the beach. He punched it when it stuck its nose out of the water, trying to scare it off, but it followed them almost all the way in. Daigle had been bitten on her left leg and Dicus thought that the injuries were so bad that she would probably lose the leg. In fact, she appeared to have stopped bleeding by the time two other swimmers with a raft came to help get the injured girl out of the water. She had probably bled to death before reaching the beach and was pronounced dead on arrival at hospital.

Miramar Beach, 25 June 2005

FLORIDA, USA, 2005

Craig Hutto was fishing with his brother in waist deep surf on a sand bar about 60 yards off Cape San Blas on Florida's Gulf of Mexico coast when he was attacked by a shark. At first, passers-by on the shore thought that the brothers, struggling through the waves, were simply larking around. Then they spotted the trail of blood in the water.

Hutto's right leg had been horribly savaged and he was losing a great deal of blood but, while others called for the emergency services, two holidaymakers – one of them a doctor – administered first aid and applied a tourniquet. Hutto was taken to a local hospital and then airlifted to Panama City by helicopter but even there he was not out of danger, with medical teams working hard to resuscitate the 16-year-old who was in shock and suffering from massive blood loss. Surgeons were later forced to amputate his leg and credited his survival to the timely aid he received on the beach.

Cape San Blas, 27 June 2005

LIBERIA, 2005

In April 2005, Senior Warrant Officer Valentyn Onuk from the Ukraine was posted to Liberia as part of a United Nations peacekeeping force. The 29-year-old was a driver-mechanic, part of an aviation engineering team and, four months after his arrival in the country, he took some time off from his duties to go swimming in the Atlantic surf. He was never seen alive again. His body was washed ashore two weeks later, having sustained numerous shark bites.

James Beach, Marshall, 17 July 2005

WESTERN CAPE, SOUTH AFRICA, 2005
A man out for a Sunday stroll found a severed foot floating in Milnerton Lagoon, Cape Town. The foot had been bitten off above the ankle and police believed that it was the remains of a shark attack victim, although no positive identification could be made.

Milnerton Lagoon, Cape Town, 14 August 2005

SOUTH AUSTRALIA, AUSTRALIA, 2005
Two University of Adelaide research students, diving as part of a four-man team off Glenelg Beach, were attacked by a great white shark while they were collecting cuttlefish eggs. Justin Rowntree described how he felt something nudge his side, thinking at first that it was a dolphin. He quickly realized that it was a shark and both men headed for the surface. The shark continued to circle round them, repeatedly approaching Rowntree's dive partner, 23-year-old Jarrod Stehbens, who kept it at bay as Rowntree was helped aboard the dive boat. Then, the shark lunged at Stehbens once again, grabbing him by the leg and taking him down into deep water. The dive team watched in horror as Stehbens tried to extricate himself from the shark's jaws but could do nothing to help him. Elements of Stehben's diving equipment were later found during a search but his body was never recovered. This was to have been Stehbens last dive in Australia before he left to live in Germany.

Glenelg Tyre Reef, 24 August 2005

THAILAND, 2005
A Cambodian fisherman working on the deck of a trawler 100 miles offshore was attempting to sort out a problem with the boat's drag net when he was attacked by a large shark that was tangled in the netting. The shark bit the 21-year-old, known only as Ham, on the arm and the leg causing such severe wounds that the young man bled to death before the rest of the crew could get proper medical attention for him.

Gulf of Thailand, 2 September 2005

SOUTH CAROLINA, USA, 2005
Greg Norton was surfing with friends about 60 yards out from Folly Beach in South Carolina when he simply disappeared. Although other surfers had reported seeing sharks in the area, no one actually saw the 18-year-old student being attacked. An extensive search of the area, hampered by deteriorating weather conditions, failed to find any trace of him. His surf board was recovered – he was not using a leg rope – but showed no evidence of an attack.

Folly Beach, 11 September 2005

CANARY ISLANDS, 2005
Competing in a transatlantic rowing race is a tough undertaking that requires fitness, stamina and a great deal of courage, which is why the image of New Zealanders Tara Remington and Iain Rudkin hiding in the well of their boat staying as quiet as two church mice seems a little bizarre. The couple were more than three weeks out from the Canary Islands, heading for the West Indies when their specially built rowing boat was attacked by a large shark. Hoping that the creature would lose interest and leave them alone, Remington and Rudkin

decided to pretend that no one was home. The shark spent quarter of an hour butting and biting the hull of the boat, threatening at any moment to capsize the craft, then vanished.

The damage caused to the hull was exacerbated by bad weather over the next few days, the boat beginning to take on water. They called for help just before a huge wave flipped the boat over and they were tipped out. With thoughts of the shark preying on their minds, they scrambled into their life raft and were later picked up by a rescue boat, with Remington having sustained a cut to her head that required several stitches.

Atlantic Ocean, 21 December 2005

2006

QUEENSLAND, AUSTRALIA, 2006

Friends on Amity Beach – the same name as the beach in the movie *Jaws* – thought that 21-year-old Sarah Whiley was joking when they heard her yell "Shark!"... until they saw the blood in the water. Whiley was swimming at Stradbroke Island at the mouth of Moreton Bay about 40 miles east of Brisbane when she was attacked by as many as three bull sharks. She was dragged under and screamed for help when she resurfaced a few seconds later. Two fishermen dragged her to the shore, shocked by the ferocity of the attack. Whiley had several vicious bites to her legs and body, the sharks also having bitten off both of her arms. Beachgoers tried to stem the blood flow with towels and comfort her as she lay on the beach, still conscious, before Whiley was flown to hospital in Brisbane where she died from shock and loss of blood.

Amity Beach, 6 January 2006

Whale Shark

The whale shark is the largest species of shark and the world's biggest fish, yet it is a docile creature which, like the basing shark and megamouth shark, feeds by filtering small organisms out of the water that it sucks in through its five feet-wide, (1.5 m) mouth. It is thought that these creatures can live to be 100 years old and young whale sharks, like their parents, appear unthreatened by humans, even playing with divers. Although only one pup is born at a time, pregnant females are known to carry inside them up to 300 young at various stages of development.

Shark Facts

Length:	31 feet to 41 feet (9.4 m to 12.7 m)
Weight:	20,000 lb to 47,000 lb (95 kg to 315 kg)
Colouring:	Grey upper marked with stripes and spots, white belly
Diet:	Plankton, krill, small squid
Pups:	Single pups of up to 2 feet (60 cm) are born at regular intervals
Status:	Vulnerable, a protected species in most regions

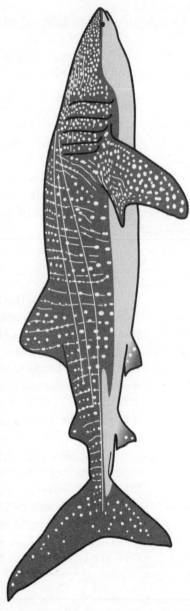

Whale Shark Range

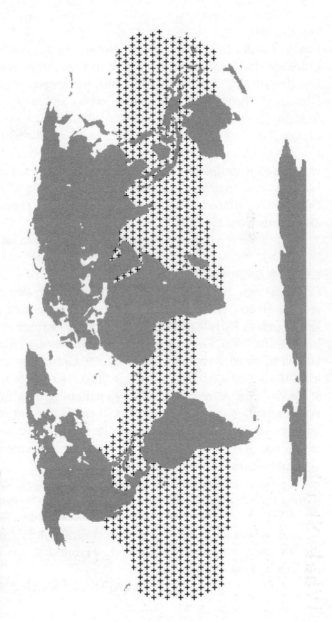

TONGA, 2006

Peace Corps volunteer Tessa Horan from Aspen, Colorado, USA was enjoying a spot of relaxation while working on the island of Vava'u lahi, the largest of the islands in Tonga's Vava'u group, when she and her friends decided to take a swim to cool off after a game of football. The 24-year-old hadn't been in the water long, swimming off the beach at Tu'anuku, when she was dragged under by a tiger shark. When she fought her way to the surface, most of her right leg was gone. Despite the efforts of her friends, Horan died shortly afterwards from blood loss.

Vava'u lahi, 1 February 2006

EASTERN CAPE, SOUTH AFRICA, 2006

Grahamstown in South Africa's Eastern Cape attracts around 50,000 visitors when it hosts SciFest Africa in late March or early April each year. Lorenzo Kroutz and his friends from Colesberg High in Philipstown were among those who visited in March 2006, taking time out from the science fiction extravaganza to visit the beach at nearby Port Alfred for a spot of swimming on a fine Wednesday afternoon. Kroutz was in the water not too far from shore off West Beach when he disappeared, one of his teachers describing it as though he had simply been pulled under the water.

The National Sea Rescue Institute were on the scene within minutes but could find no trace of the 17-year-old. His body was washed ashore the following day, not far from where he disappeared, with several shark bites, the teacher who identified the body saying that one of his legs had been bitten off.

Port Alfred, 22 March 2006

SIERRA LEONE, 2006

Fisherman Riad Hassan knew that he'd hooked a big one while fishing from his boat off Lumley Beach in Freetown. The jeweller was in for a shock, however, when, after he and a companion spent an hour trying to reel in the fish, he realized that he had caught a 10 foot shark. The shark was too big to haul aboard his boat, but Hassan towed the fish back to harbour where local fishermen identified it as having been responsible for the deaths of four of their number over the previous few weeks. Hassan gave the shark to the locals to eat.

Lumley Beach, Freetown, 28 March 2006

RECIFE, BRAZIL, 2006

The beach at Punta del Chifre in the town of Olinda, north of Recife, had been cleared for watersports, with no shark sightings having been reported for some time, when Humberto Pessoa Batista was enjoying a Sunday afternoon in the waves. There were about 30 surfers in the water only 50 feet from the beach when Batista was attacked. He sustained severe bites to his leg and died from loss of blood.

Olinda, 18 June 2006

CALIFORNIA, USA, 2006

A 60-year-old man messing about in the water off Malibu Beach in California became the "accidental" victim of a shark attack that left him totally paralysed.

Bruce Lurie was boogie boarding with his 13-year-old son when a huge shark, thought to have been chasing a sea lion, slammed into him. Lurie suffered a broken neck and damage to his spinal cord that left him completely paralysed from the neck down. His son hauled him out of the water, where he had almost drowned, and other surfers on the beach helped to resuscitate him.

Lurie underwent surgery and was in intensive care for a month, unable at first to speak, breathe or even swallow unaided. He was prone to infections that hampered his recovery but, after many months of intensive rehabilitation therapy and a special diet that helped him to fight the infections, he began to show signs of recovery, although it was to be a long three years before he began the painful struggle to learn to walk again.

Malibu Beach, 29 July 2006

WESTERN CAPE, SOUTH AFRICA, 2006

Achmat Hassiem and his younger brother Taariq were training to sit lifesaving exams off the beach at Muizenberg in False Bay when Achmat spotted a large great white in the water nearby. He yelled at friends in a nearby boat to get Taariq out of the water then started slapping the surface to lure the shark away from his brother. Taarriq was pulled safely onto the boat as the shark headed for 24-year-old Achmat. It latched onto his leg and dragged him 50 yards through the water until Achmat felt one final blow followed by a loud snapping sound and he was free. The boat reached him before the shark could return and he looked down as he was being hauled out of the water to see that his right foot was gone.

Achmat underwent surgery to amputate the lower part of his right leg, but it didn't keep him out of the water. Just two years after his accident he was in Beijing, competing for South Africa in the Paralympics. In 2012, he won bronze in the men's 100 m butterfly at the London Paralympics. He claimed he could motivate himself to swim fast by imagining a great white racing up behind him.

Muizenberg, Cape Town, 13 August 2006

RÉUNION, 2006

Sebastien Emond was surfing with his family and two friends when the 34-year-old was attacked at Pointe du Diable near Saint-Pierre. The two friends that he was with at the time reported that the shark lunged at Emond time after time before they could get to him and drag him to shore. Emond suffered serious bite wounds and lost an arm in the attack. Paramedics treated him on the beach and rushed him to hospital but he later died from his injuries.

Saint-Pierre, 20 August 2006

YEMEN, 2006

A statement from the United Nations reported that more than 100 refugees from East Africa had died while crossing the shark-infested waters of the Gulf of Aden to seek sanctuary in Yemen. Refugees aboard one boat claimed that at least five Ethiopians had been beaten by the smugglers they had paid to help them escape the country and had then been thrown overboard to be attacked by sharks. In another incident, 25 Ethiopian refugees were held captive aboard one boat when it reached Yemen and were not allowed to go ashore. The boat had developed problems and they were required as "ballast" to keep the craft balanced on an even keel for the return journey. They were never seen again and their fate can only be imagined.

Gulf of Aden, October 2006

WESTERN AUSTRALIA, AUSTRALIA, 2006

Brothers Zac and Sam Golebiowski were surfing together off Wharton Beach on Western Australia's south coast early in the morning when Zac felt something cannon into him. He remembers a sharp tug on his leg and seeing a tail and a fin in the water, the 15-year-old immediately realizing that the lower part of his right leg had gone. Sam was close at hand, the 26-year-old grabbing hold of his brother and dragging him towards the shore, yelling out to a couple who were about to start fishing. The couple, on holiday from New Zealand, tied a tourniquet around Zac's leg to stop the bleeding then accompanied the brothers by car on the road from the remote beach towards the town of Esperance, meeting the ambulance they had called.

Zac was flown to the Royal Perth Hospital, spending almost two months there recovering, having lost his right leg above the knee and had a chunk taken out of his left calf. One of the first things he did on leaving hospital was to hobble down to the beach on his crutches where he met with 16-year-old Bethany Hamilton, who was in the area while competing on the professional surfing tour. The two discussed their love of surfing and how unlucky they had been to fall victim to shark attacks, Bethany having lost her left arm to a shark three years before. Inspired by Bethany's courage, Zac was back in the water again as soon as his injuries would allow.

Wharton Beach, 2 December 2006

2007

EASTERN CAPE, SOUTH AFRICA, 2007

Having survived a shark attack in 2004 that left him with scars on his legs as a souvenir of his encounter, lifeguard Sibulele Masiza was well aware of the risks when he went swimming off Second Beach at Port St Johns, but considered them negligible, believing that this was a safe beach. He was never seen again. One of his flippers was washed up on the beach bearing marks that experts maintained could only have been caused by a tiger shark. His body was never recovered.

Second Beach, Port St Johns, January 2007

NEW SOUTH WALES, AUSTRALIA, 2007

Fisherman Eric Nerhus was diving for abalone, as he regularly did off the coast of Cape Howe in New South Wales, when he came face to face with a great white shark. Having spent years on and under the water, Nerhus has seen sharks many times, the big fish often coming up close to take a look at him before swimming away. This time it was different.

Diving in around 25 feet of water from a boat manned by his son, Mark, 41-year-old Nerhus was searching the sea bed for abalone, breathing via an air line that went all the way back up to the boat. A lead-weighted dive vest helped him to stay down in water where, on this particular day, visibility was not too good. Nerhus had his head down, peering through the murky water to try to spot the shellfish when suddenly everything went black and he felt a tightening across his chest and shoulders. Without even knowing it, he had swum straight into the jaws of a great white and it had swallowed his head! In an instant, as soon as the shark shook him from side to side, Nerhus realized to his utter horror what had happened.

The shark had his head, shoulders and right arm inside its mouth. Only the lead vest that Nerhus was wearing was stopping the shark from tearing him to pieces. He frantically reached up with his left hand, groping around the tough exterior of the shark's head until he found something that he described as feeling like a slimy tennis ball. He knew he had the shark's eye, digging his fingers in as hard as he could to claw, twist and gouge. The shark loosened its grip, allowing Nerhus to wriggle backwards, freeing himself a little before it clamped down on him again. The force of the second bite buckled Nerhus's face mask, breaking his nose and the shark's teeth starting to sink into his face until he ripped at the eye again. Suddenly the pressure was released and Nerhus was able to push backwards out of the shark's mouth.

Streaming blood from deep gashes on his chest, back and shoulder as well as his face, Nerhus tried not to panic, heading for the surface as calmly as possible while holding his bag of abalone out in front of him. He knew that all the blood in the water would make the shark very excited and hoped that if it came back for another bite at him it might just take his catch instead of himself. When he broke the surface in the middle of a pool of blood, he yelled to his son that there was a shark in the water and 16-year-old Mark brought the boat straight to him, grabbing his father by the back of his wetsuit and hauling him aboard. They radioed for help and Nerhus was airlifted to hospital where he was treated for shock and loss of blood, having bled out almost 80 per cent of the blood in his body. He survived to tell the tale of the day a great white swallowed his head.

Cape Howe, 23 January 2007

COSTA RICA, 2007
Having moved from Brighton, England, to Costa Rica in 2004, Jason Holmes was living an idyllic lifestyle. The 36-year-old musician and DJ, who lived with his wife and ten-month-old daughter in the capital city, San Jose, went missing after going swimming off the coast. His remains were later washed ashore bearing bite marks from a shark attack. Although the cause of death was drowning, it may have been that Holmes drowned as

a result of being attacked, although the possibility of a shark scavenging on his body after he drowned could not be ruled out.

Costa Rica, 5 February 2007

YEMEN, 2007

At least 29 refugees died and 71 others were reported as missing when up to 450 Somali and Ethiopian refugees being smuggled across the Gulf of Aden to Yemen were thrown overboard. The United Nations High Commission for Refugees said that the 293 survivors, who had paid up to $150 to bribe former fishermen to take them across the gulf to find a better life in Yemen, reported that passengers crammed onto the four boats were forced overboard when the boats were spotted by Yemeni security forces. In order to make a quick getaway, the boats' owners needed to lighten the load. The defenceless refugees were forced overboard by the crew at knifepoint. Those who refused to jump were beaten with clubs and stabbed before being hurled into the water. Survivors reported that many were taken by circling sharks in the stormy seas off the coast at Ras-Alkalb.

Ras-Alkalb, Gulf of Aden, 22 March 2007

TURKS AND CAICOS ISLANDS, 2007

Illegal immigrants headed for the United States crammed aboard a small sailing boat got into trouble off the Turks and Caicos Islands in the middle of the night. With high winds and rough seas threatening to sink the boat, with almost 100 Haitian refugees aboard, was taken in tow by a Turks and Caicos police launch. They were about half a mile from Providenciales, in the west of the Turks and Caicos group, when the sailing boat finally capsized. Although 73 were pulled from the water by rescue boats, it is thought that at least 22 died in the shark-infested waters. News reporters on Providenciales said that they saw bodies being brought ashore with severe bite wounds and missing limbs.

Providenciales, 4 May 2007

NEW SOUTH WALES, AUSTRALIA, 2007
Human remains washed ashore at Kingscliff Beach in New South Wales indicated that an unidentified 45-year-old man who went missing two days earlier while swimming in heavy surf off the beach had been taken by a shark. An extensive search involving the coast guard, police, life guards and a helicopter had failed to find any trace of the man after his brother, who was on the beach while the man was in the water, completely lost sight of him. A shark attack seemed like the most likely explanation for his disappearance.

Kingscliff Beach, 8 May 2007

KENT, UNITED KINGDOM, 2007
The owner of a local tackle shop was out fishing from Folkestone Pier in Kent when he landed a large dogfish which he held up to show off to a friend. The fish, however, not best pleased at being caught, squirmed and leapt out of Phil Tanner's hands, clamping its jaws around his nose. Tanner was in agony and terrified that the fish, with its teeth gnawing at his nostrils, might chomp off the end of his nose, but passers-by were of little help because they all fell about laughing as soon as they saw him. With the help of his giggling friend, Tanner eventually freed himself from the mini shark but, even though his badly bleeding nose probably needed stitches, he refused to go to hospital for fear that doctors there would laugh at him too.

Folkestone, Kent, 17 May 2007

VIRGINIA, USA, 2007
It was a bad day at the office for Beth Firchau when the 40-year-old Curator of Fishes at the Virginia Aquarium was assisting her veterinary team in giving Tidbit, a black tip reef shark resident at the aquarium, an annual medical. Tidbit had been sedated and was slow in coming round, so Firchau was in the tank helping to pass water over the 10-year-old shark's gills. Eventually, it seemed to feel better and started to swim off, only to turn round, sink its teeth into Firchau's leg and refuse to let go. When they eventually persuaded Tidbit to relinquish the curator's leg, Firchau had to be rushed to the local hospital for emergency treatment where she remained in good cheer as her wounds were stitched up.

Virginia Beach, 24 May 2007

FLORIDA, USA, 2007
A beautiful day out on a boat in the sunshine off the Florida Keys was one of the highlights of Ashley Silverman's holiday with her boyfriend, Christopher Wood, until she decided to jump in the Bud 'n' Mary's marina at Islamorada to cool off. Immediately she felt something bite into her arm and looked down to see bare bone on her arm, chunks of her flesh floating away and the water filled with blood. She screamed to Wood, still on the boat, for help and he immediately jumped overboard, lifting her up so that she could be hauled aboard. He then helped fasten a tourniquet around her arm before she could be airlifted to hospital.

Silverman had a large chunk missing from her arm and needed many hours of reconstructive surgery to repair the damage before she could begin to regain the use of that limb. While a small bull shark was thought

421

likely have been responsible for her injury, a barracuda could also have been the culprit.

Islamorada, 7 August 2007

FLORIDA, USA, 2007

Marine biologist Chris Olstad was taking his usual evening swim at about 9.15 p.m. from the beach at Founders Park on Plantation Key, heading about quarter of a mile out to a boat anchored offshore. When he reached the boat, he turned for the return journey using a leisurely back stroke. It was then that the 52-year-old felt himself being bumped in the side. Then came a terrible pain and he reached down to feel a large flap of skin, realizing to his horror that he had been attacked by a shark. Holding one hand over his wound to try to stem the flow of blood that was turning the water red around him, he swam for the closest stretch of shore.

By the time he reached the shallows, near some mangroves some way from the beach where he had started out, Olstad was exhausted from lack of blood and didn't think that he would be able to walk back to the beach, so he carried on swimming, finding it easier than trying to stand up. When he reached the beach, he hauled himself out of the water to head for his Jeep, parked well within sight just thirty yards away. He passed out several times trying to reach the car, collapsing onto the beach, cutting his face and mouth. When he finally dragged himself to the car, he climbed inside and drove just 200 yards to a Sheriff Department sub-office where two officers had a paramedic on the scene within minutes.

Olstad's injury ran from just under his arm down to his waist, with a big lump of flesh missing. He had lost a lot of blood, but the paramedics worked to stabilize him as best they could before an ambulance rushed him to the Mariners Hospital in nearby Tavernier. He was later whisked off by helicopter for treatment in Miami.

Olstad had been living and working in the Florida Keys for a number of years and didn't blame the shark for attacking him, believing that it had just taken a bite to see if he was worth eating which explains why no bones were broken and no greater damage done. He planned to swim off the Keys again as soon as he was able.

Plantation Key, 19 August 2007

NEW CALEDONIA, 2007

A French nurse who had been working in a hospital in Nouméa, the capital of the French territory of New Caledonia, was relaxing on a beach holiday with a friend before heading home to France. The pair were swimming off the beach at Lifou early in the morning and 23-year-old Stephanie Bellard was about 200 yards offshore when she was attacked by a shark. Her leg was ripped open from the hip to the knee and by the time her friend could summon help from locals on the beach, she had bled to death.

Lifou, 29 September 2007

2008

FLORIDA, USA, 2008

Surfer Jordan Marsden was looking to catch one final wave before the beach at Playalinda closed for the evening. He reached down with his left leg, immediately realizing that he was in slightly too deep to push off the bottom and was pulling his leg up when he felt something latch onto his foot. He described the pressure on his foot as like being run over by a car and yanked his leg up onto his board. It was then that he saw his foot streaming blood.

Marsden made straight for the shore, not daring to look back for fear that whatever had bitten him was still on his tail. His friend helped him out of the water and they bandaged his foot as best they could before heading for hospital. Marsden needed surgery to close his wounds and to remove shark tooth fragments from his foot. It was unclear exactly what kind of shark had bitten him, although Marsden counts himself lucky that it was a small one and that it lost interest in him before he could reach the beach.

Playalinda Beach, 10 January 2008

BAHAMAS, 2008

The M/V *Shear Water* had nine Austrian tourists on board when she left Florida heading for the northern tip of the Bahamas on a week-long trip where they would be introduced to the delights of diving in the open ocean with some of the most dangerous sharks known to man. They would not enjoy the reassuring safety of descending into the sharks' domain inside a steel cage, but would be able to get far better underwater photographs scuba diving with no more than a wetsuit for protection.

Markus Groh, a 49-year-old lawyer from Vienna and an experienced scuba diver, was one of the dive party and on the morning of their first dive with the sharks, crates of dead and mushed-up fish having been anchored to the ocean floor, he swam down to the bottom, 80 feet below the surface, lying still in his vantage point ready to see some close-up shark action. The divers hoped that the bait would attract tiger, lemon, hammerhead or bull sharks and it was the bull sharks who showed up first for the feast.

Dive master Grey O'Hara went into the ocean just after

9.00am with fresh bait, looking down through the clear water to where his clients had positioned themselves. He saw a large bull shark nudge one of the bait crates towards Groh and an instant later the Austrian had disappeared in a cloud of sand, the shark thrashing with its tail as it latched onto his leg. O'Hara was with Groh in seconds, grabbing hold of his client and kicking out at the shark, slamming his foot into the creature's head again and again until it released the injured man.

The dive master headed for the surface fast, blood pumping from Groh's leg. Once on board Groh passed out and the crew worked on him furiously, using coagulant powder to stop the bleeding and employing highly professional first aid skills to keep the Austrian alive until a helicopter could evacuate him to hospital in Florida. The helicopter located the Shear Water in less than an hour, its crew winching the injured man aboard and flying him straight to the Ryder Trauma Center in Miami. Their efforts, however, were to no avail. Markus Groh, on the adventure holiday of a lifetime, was pronounced dead in the hospital at 11.33 a.m.

"The End of the Map", 24 February 2008

NEW SOUTH WALES, AUSTRALIA, 2008
Brock Curtis showed a hero's disregard for his own safety when he went to the rescue of his friend Peter Edmonds after spotting him apparently in difficulties off Lighthouse Beach at Ballina in New South Wales. The two 16-year-olds were at school together and were taking advantage of a day off to go body boarding when Curtis realized that Edmonds was in trouble. He paddled towards his friend and, despite seeing a large, grey shadow pass by him in the murky water, pressed on to find that Edmonds was unconscious on his board with deep lacerations to his left

leg. He had, in fact, been bitten twice by a bull shark.

Curtis grabbed hold of Edmonds and dragged him to the beach where he desperately tried to resuscitate him, but his friend died from loss of blood.

Lighthouse Beach, 8 April 2008

FIJI, 2008

When fisherman Rutu Meli picked a fight with three sharks that were after the fish he had just speared, punching one of them right in the snout, they retaliated by ripping open his left arm. It might not have seemed like it at the time, but this was Meli's lucky day.

The big Fijian soon had help from locals on his remote island, but he was bleeding badly and seeking any kind of special medical help meant taking a boat to the mainland and then a four-hour car journey. That was easily time enough for him to bleed to death.

Meli's friends sought the help of a Californian who had sought out the island on the advice of friends who told him it was a surfers' paradise. Tom Rolfes, a dentist by profession, could see that Meli's arm, with muscle and sinew spilling out of the many lacerations and blood flowing freely, was in a bad way and, knowing how far they were from any other help, he told his 17-year-old son to fetch the emergency kit they carried with them and they set to work. Although he was more used to stitching gums, Rolfes put Meli's arm back together as best he could, inserting some 200 stitches in the process. The bleeding was stopped. When Meli eventually did get to hospital, the doctors there were so impressed with the dentist's work that they decided to leave it just as it was, commenting that, had Rolfes not intervened, Meli might never have made it to see them alive. It had, indeed, been his lucky day.

South Pacific, 9 April 2008

MEXICO, 2008
Joram Galleros Villanueva went missing while swimming off the beach at Quintana Roo in what were described as rough seas. The 32-year-old was reported missing by his pregnant wife and was not seen again until his body washed ashore three days later with serious shark bites to the feet and face, and both arms missing.

Quintana Roo, Cancun, 18 April 2008

MEXICO, 2008
A bartender from San Francisco, who saved all his money to travel the world surfing, was bitten on the thigh by a tiger shark while in the water off the village of Troncones in Mexico. Adrian Ruiz had his thigh torn open to the bone from hip to knee and although his surfing partner and locals got him ashore at the remote holiday spot and even took him in a phone company van to a nearby naval hospital – a regular ambulance taking too long to reach them – the 24-year-old was dead when he arrived at the military base.

Troncones, Guerrero, 28 April 2008

FIJI, 2008
A night diving expedition turned to tragedy when a group of men from Yasawa took to the water off Turtle Island at around 9.00 p.m., later realizing that one of their number was missing. They found 28-year-old Aisake Sadole on the sea bed with shark bite injuries to his face and left leg. Sadole's friends got him ashore and took him to Lautoka Hospital where he was pronounced dead on arrival.

Turtle Island, Yasawa Islands, 15 May 2008

MEXICO, 2008
Just six miles away from where Adrian Ruiz had been

attacked only a month before, a 21-year-old Mexican student, Osvaldo Mat Valdovinos, fell prey to a shark while surfing at Pantla Beach in the resort of Zihuatenejo on Mexico's Pacific coast. Valdovinos was surfing with friends when they saw a seven-foot shark grab him and pull him under the water. When he struggled back to the surface, Valdovinos had no left hand and his thigh was badly lacerated, the shark having bitten so hard and deep into it that it broke his leg. His friends helped him to the beach but he had lost so much blood that he died before paramedics could reach him.

Pantla Beach, Zihuatenejo, 23 May 2008

RECIFE, BRAZIL, 2008

The notorious Piedade Beach claimed yet another victim when 14-year-old Wellington dos Santos ventured out beyond the reef that marks the limit of the area that is designated as safe for swimmers. Lifeguards came to the teenager's rescue when he was spotted in trouble in the water to find that a shark had bitten off his right hand. The shark had also taken a huge bite out of his backside, removing a large proportion of both buttocks. Dos Santos was rushed to hospital in a critical condition but survived his appalling injuries.

Piedade Beach, 1 June 2008

HAWAII, USA, 2008

The opihi is a limpet-like shellfish found clinging to the rocks along much of Hawaii's shoreline, although they have proved so popular over the years, with people downing them straight from the rocks, swallowing them like oysters, that opihi pickers have to venture to remote areas to find good crops. Nathan Labarios, from Kona on Hawaii's Big Island, had been camping with friends in the wild and remote Kau area in the south of the island when he decided to go looking for opihi.

When he failed to return, his friends reported him missing and a search was mounted in the area into which the 58-year-old had headed. Divers eventually discovered his opihi bag and some human remains that showed all the hallmarks of a vicious shark attack.

Kau, 28 June 2008

US VIRGIN ISLANDS, 2008

Elizabeth Riggs had enjoyed an afternoon swimming and snorkelling off Buck Island in the US Virgin Islands and was still cooling off in the water in the early evening, dangling off the side of their sailing boat, when she saw the dark shape of a shark cruise past. Riggs had seen sharks before elsewhere without them ever posing any apparent threat, but decided she was better off out of the water. As she climbed aboard the boat she felt a bite on her left foot that didn't feel too serious until she pulled her leg out of the water and saw her foot flayed open to the bone.

Riggs' friends wrapped the wound tightly to help stem the flow of blood and set sail for Cheney Bay, where they had parked their cars, with Riggs in increasing pain and an increasingly distressed state. Once ashore, they raced to Luis Hospital where it took 175 stitches to close the gaping wounds in her foot.

Buck Island, 17 August

DEVON, UNITED KINGDOM, 2008

Angler Stephen Perkins had caught sharks before and was particularly pleased with the 5-foot blue shark that he struggled to land on his boat, *Serenity*, while fishing with friends off Lundy Island in Devon. The anglers never kept sharks when they hooked them, they just took a quick picture then released them back into the sea. Unfortunately, no one told the shark that. He clearly thought that he was on that evening's menu, wriggled free from Perkins' grasp and sank his teeth into the 52-year-old's right wrist. Perkins' friends didn't realize quite how serious the bite was as they laughed and dropped the shark back into the water, but the injured angler was losing so much blood that it quickly became clear he needed proper medical aid. They called for help and an RAF Sea King helicopter was quickly on the scene, winching Perkins on board, an experience that he claimed was more frightening than being bitten by a shark. Perkins required surgery for his wound and counted himself lucky to have escaped so lightly as the only recorded case of a man attacked by a blue shark in British waters.

Lundy Island, 30 August 2008

PHILIPPINES, 2008

Fisherman Joel Bacud and his son, Louie, had left their home village of Callaguip at around 5.00 a.m. in their bacud, a long, slim boat with outriggers for stabilisation and were still out fishing five hours later when 39-year-old Joel jumped overboard to sort out a problem with their nets. He was attacked by a shark which bit him in the back, ribcage, chest and on his right arm.

Louie, just 17, yelled to other fishermen working near-by for help, but by the time they got his father out of the water, he was already dead.

Paoay, 6 November 2008

TAIWAN, 2008

When the Taiwanese fishing vessel *Fu Chi Hsiang 767* was hit by massive waves 50 miles off Kaohsiung, the boat was swamped and the crew sent out a distress signal. Help was on its way when the 993-tonne boat capsized and its 28-man crew found themselves in the water. The men, a mixture of Chinese, Taiwanese, Vietnamese and Filipinos, clung to life rafts and debris in the raging seas, praying for a rescue ship or helicopter to come to their aid.

By the time a helicopter did find the first group of survivors, 45-year-old Chen Te-hsing was dead. His friends described how he had been attacked by a shark and badly bitten on his legs. They had clung on to him in the water, supporting him, until he went into shock from loss of blood and passed away. When the group was hit by a huge wave, the injured man sank out of sight. The men spent 16 hours in the water and, as well as Chen Te-hsing, 18 were listed as missing.

Kaohsiung, 10 November 2008

MOZAMBIQUE, 2008

Chidenguele is a small holiday resort in unspoilt southern Mozambique known especially for its game fishing. Darryl Kriel was spear fishing off the long sandy beach in shallow water when he was attacked by a shark that savaged his thigh. He died from his injuries.

Chidenguele, 8 December 2008

WESTERN AUSTRALIA, AUSTRALIA, 2008

Early in the morning, around 7.00 a.m., 51-year-old Brian Guest and his son, Daniel, were snorkelling off their local beach near Rockingham, south of Perth, enjoying a relaxing Saturday looking for crabs. Daniel was about 20 feet away from his father, concentrating on spotting crabs, when he noticed the water turning red and looked round to find no trace of his father. The 24-year-old swam quickly to shore to raise the alarm, only to find that beachgoers had already done so.

One witness described seeing a commotion in the water and a thrashing of fins before a great white rolled over with Guest clamped firmly in his jaws. Rescue boats and helicopters were quickly on the scene but, despite an extensive search, Guest's body was never recovered. The only trace of him that was found were a few scraps of his wetsuit. From the way witnesses described the attack, the coroner later reported that Guest must have been killed almost instantly.

Rockingham, 27 December 2008

2009

ECUADOR, 2009

Surfer Gonzalo Vasquez Alcivar was paddling to catch a wave off a popular beach on Isabela Island in the Galapagos group when he felt something grab his leg. He looked down to see a large shark gnawing and shaking his leg. The terrified 20-year-old screamed, alerting friends in the water nearby, and reached down to try to push the shark away. The shark then snapped at his hand, biting one of his fingers off.

Biting at his hand, however, had released the shark's grip on Alcivar's leg, and the surfer paddled desperately for shore. He was taken to hospital on the neighbouring island of Santa Cruz before being transferred to Guayaquil on the mainland where he needed surgery on his hand, and his foot, part of which had been bitten off. Surgeons also operated to try to save the use of his leg, the shark having taken a large bite out of his calf, severing muscles and tendons.

Isabela Island, Galapagos Islands, 10 January 2009

EASTERN CAPE, SOUTH AFRICA, 2009

Life guards at Second Beach in Port St Johns were horrified to see one of their colleagues, 25-year-old Sikhanyiso
Bangilizwe, falling prey to a huge tiger shark while they
remained powerless to help him. The attack was over
in an instant, the off-duty life guard falling prey to the
shark while he was swimming with a colleague, who
saw the shark tearing his friend apart, biting off his right
arm and leaving his body in three pieces.

Other lifeguards launched a boat when they realized
there was a problem, but there was nothing for them to
do but recover Bangilizwe's remains.

Second Beach, Port St Johns, 24 January 2008

SYDNEY, AUSTRALIA, 2009

The Adelaide class guided missile frigate HMAS *Darwin*
was docked at the Royal Australian Navy baseat Garden
Island in Sydney Harbour, and navy diver Able Seaman
Paul de Gelder was testing equipment in a routine
exercise close by. With the *Darwin* and several other
ships in dock, the naval base was a busy place, even at
seven o'clock in the morning. De Gelder was swimming
on his back, on the surface, heading for shore when he
was suddenly attacked by a nine-foot bull shark. The
shark grabbed his right hand and leg, its teeth easily
slashing through de Gelder's wetsuit. He punched and
hammered at the shark until it let him go, but not before
it had bitten off his hand.

Help was close by and de Gelder was quickly hauled
out of the water, navy medics providing first aid until
they could get him to hospital. It was there that surgeons
evaluated the damage to de Gelder's leg, deciding that it
had to be amputated.

At 31 years of age, de Gelder was extremely fit and within

a few weeks of his operation he was learning to walk with the use of a prosthetic leg as well as learning how to use a mechanical hand. Within eighteen months, he was back in a wetsuit doing the job he loved – navy diver. De Gelder stayed in the navy, training new divers to work in the same waters where he was attacked by the shark.

Garden Island, 11 February 2009

NEW CALEDONIA, 2009

Kevin Harrecart, from Cherbourg in France was studying in Nouméa, the capital of New Caledonia, and taking time out to go surfing with his lifelong friend Amaury Lafage. The beaches of the Bourail region are very popular with surfers, and it was from the sands of Roche Percée, famous for the turtles that lay their eggs there, that 19-year-old Harrecart headed out in a boat with Lafage. They decided to try the waves at a point 20 minutes from shore, on a reef half a mile or so to the south of Green Island.

Harrecart was in the water, paddling to catch a wave, while Lafage kept an eye on him from the boat. Suddenly a shark rose out of the depths and lunged at Harrecart, biting off his right arm. Horrified, Lafage immediately sped towards his friend in the boat, but before he could help him out of the water the shark, a great white, had attacked again, inflicting horrendous bite wounds to Harrecart's legs.

Having dragged Harrecart onto the boat, and tended his injuries as best he could, Lafage headed for shore. By the time they reached the beach at Roche Percee, Harrecart was very weak from loss of blood and, despite the efforts of paramedics to resuscitate him, he died on the beach.

Roche Percée, Bourail, 6 March 2009

EASTERN CAPE, SOUTH AFRICA, 2009
Luyolo Magele was learning to surf and when the 16-year-old took to the water off Second Beach with a bunch of his fellow board students from the Iliza Surf Academy, the waves were running high and it was a perfect day for surfing.

All went well with the practice session until a scream filled the air and Magele's fellow surfers, as well as the manager of the surf school, saw a spreading patch of red around Magele's board. He paddled towards the beach but was losing a lot of blood from a massive bite wound to his leg. He passed out as he made it to the shallow water and all efforts to revive him failed.

Second Beach, Port St Johns, 21 March 2009

BAHAMAS, 2009
A couple from Deerfield Beach in Florida, enjoying a romantic break in the Bahamas, rented a boat to try their luck with a spot of fishing. Living close to the ocean at home, 48-year-old Louis Hernandez and his wife Marlene (46) were happy to be out in the small boat off the Exuma Islands and Louis, an experienced spear fisherman hoped to be able to catch something tasty for supper.

Hernandez knew, of course, that spear fishing, spilling blood in the water with an injured fish convulsing in its death throes on the end of the spear, was a good way to attract sharks, whether you wanted to try some shark spotting or not. Sharks, however, had never troubled him in the past, so when a 7-foot bull shark arrived to investigate, his first reaction was to admire the creature. Expecting the fish to swim off, he gave it a prod with his spear gun to move it out of his way, which was when the shark flew at him and savaged his right arm.

When the shark let go of his arm, Hernandez could

435

see muscle and flesh hanging off the bone and blood clouding the water all around him. Fortunately for him, his wife had also seen what happened and was ready in the boat to help him aboard when he reached the surface. Then, although she normally can't stand the sight of blood, she made a tourniquet for his arm and took the boat to shore. Hernandez underwent several rounds of surgery to save his arm but knew that he had his wife to thank for saving his life.

Exuma Islands, 6 May 2009

EGYPT, 2009

A French holidaymaker, snorkelling from a tour boat off Marsa Alam on Egypt's Red Sea coast, was one of a group of twenty swimmers watching an oceanic white tip shark swimming nearby. Katrina Tipio dived towards the shark to take a closer look and was on her way back to the surface when the shark attacked her.

The shark bit her on the legs but she made it to the boat and was helped back on board, with the shark still holding on, gnawing at her legs as she was hauled out of the water. When it let go and she was safely aboard, it became clear that she had lost a significant amount of blood and she lapsed into unconsciousness, dying soon afterwards.

Marsa Alam, Red Sea, 1 June 2009

WESTERN CAPE, SOUTH AFRICA, 2009

Glentana Bay, on South Africa's Western Cape, has a beautiful stretch of beach for surfers, as 25-year-old Gerhard van Zyl knew only too well. He lived close by at Mossel Bay and was surfing at Glentana with a friend on a perfect Saturday when tragedy struck.

Van Zyl was attacked by a shark that ripped off the

lower part of his right leg. His friend dragged him out of the water and applied a tourniquet to his leg but van Zyl had lost a lot of blood by the time the emergency services arrived. He was in a critical condition when he was airlifted to hospital in the nearby town of George where, despite strenuous efforts to resuscitate him, he later died.

Glentana Bay, 29 August 2009

ST KITTS AND NEVIS, 2009

When Brian Mills, his wife and two children set out from home in Charlestown on the Caribbean island of Nevis for a day at the beach, they headed slightly off the beaten track, away from the beaches that are used by holiday-makers, making for the south of the island and Indian Castle Beach.

Although the beach at Indian Castle doesn't boast as much in the way of amenities as the more popular tourist beaches, it makes up for it with its rugged beauty and a regular procession of waves that make it a magnet for surfers. Mills was an excellent swimmer, so it was a complete mystery to his family how he managed to disappear while swimming with his daughter. When they reported him missing, the coast guard mounted a search but could find no trace of him.

Two days later a dead tiger shark measuring almost 10 feet was spotted floating in Indian Castle Bay and towed ashore using a jet ski. The tiger had wounds to its head and gills indicating that it had been in a fight with another shark, the damage to its gills suggesting that it had drowned. Its stomach was also extremely distended. When it was cut open it was found to contain a plastic bag, the remains of a turtle and the head and torso of Brian Mills.

Indian Castle Beach, Nevis, 2 September 2009

RECIFE, BRAZIL, 2009

When his girlfriend decided to play in the surf on Piedade Beach, even though she couldn't swim, and appeared to be getting into trouble, 15-year-old Giovanni Tiago Barbosa de Freitas thought that she was drowning and ran into the water to save her. He didn't stop to think that he couldn't swim either. His girlfriend made it back to the beach, but Giovanni, whose grandmother later said that he didn't much like the sea and never went in more than waist deep, appeared to be caught by a wave, disappearing beneath the surface. He never came back up.

Local emergency services were quickly on the scene to search the area but found nothing until the following day when brave Giovanni's body was discovered with shark bites to his legs, back and buttocks. A post mortem revealed that he had bled to death rather than having drowned.

Piedade Beach, 7 September 2009

NORTH CAROLINA, USA, 2009

Richard Snead was a highly active 60-year-old who enjoyed hill walking and climbing as well as being a keen swimmer. On holiday from Pennsylvania in Corolla, North Carolina, with 20 members of his extensive family, it came as no surprise to Snead's wife when he told her he was off to take a swim at the beach at nine o'clock in the evening. When he hadn't returned to their holiday home by midnight, the family raised the alarm.

Despite an extensive search, nothing was found of Snead until his body was washed ashore several days later and found by a tourist out for an early morning stroll. Snead's body showed extensive bite marks and the local medical examiner's office ruled that he had died as the result of a shark attack. This opinion was later revised to "death by accidental drowning" and then changed back again to the original conclusion, creating lasting confusion about how Richard Snead actually met his end.

Corolla, 12 September 2009

RECIFE, BRAZIL, 2009

Bricklayer's assistant Mauricio da Silva Montiero went missing around four o'clock in the afternoon while the 34-year-old was swimming off Boa Viagem beach. His body was washed ashore near the same spot a day later with bite marks to his arms, back, buttocks, chest, face and with one leg almost torn off. The body was too badly damaged to determine for certain whether he drowned and the sharks scavenged on his body or whether a shark killed him, although the stretch of coastline around Recife has a notorious reputation for shark attacks.

Boa Viagem, 13 September 2009

NEW ZEALAND, 2009

When the tools that Maurice Philips and his friend, Norm, needed for the work that they were doing on an irrigation system at Whangamata on the east coast of North Island were stolen, they found themselves at something of a loose end and decided to go fishing. From the beach at Whangamata you can look out on several offshore islands including Hauturu, or Clark Island. At low tide you can wade out to Clark Island and it is popular with tourists exploring its rock pools during the summer months.

The workmen got hold of a two-man kayak and paddled out of the harbour at Whangamata at around 4.00p.m., heading for Clark Island. They were wearing heavy work clothes and had no lifejackets, so when the kayak started taking on water and capsized, they had a tough job swimming to the island. In the end, only Norm made it. He pulled himself out of the water expecting to see Philips close behind him, but there was no sign of him.

Once Norm managed to summon help, he joined the search for his friend but surf rescue squads and police divers covered the whole of Whangamata Bay and the surrounding coastline without spotting him. When Philips' body was eventually discovered there were bite marks on his legs with a huge gouge of flesh having been taken from his upper thigh. Loss of blood from this wound would have led to his death within minutes but it was still difficult for the coroner to say whether the shark bites were inflicted before or after Philips died.

Whangamata, North Island, 15 December 2009

EASTERN CAPE, SOUTH AFRICA, 2009

Lifeguard Abongile Maza was paddling on a paddle board behind the board of fellow lifeguard Tshintshekile Nduva in the water off Second Beach at Port St Johns when the unthinkable happened right in front of his eyes. A huge shark rose out of the water, lunging at 22-year-old Nduva and knocking him into the sea. An instant later, the shark appeared again, grabbing Nduva and dragging him under. The whole horrific attack had taken only a moment leaving behind on the surface just a spreading cloud of blood in the water around Nduva's paddle board.

The body of the young lifeguard was not found until several days later when lifeguards spotted a human skeleton on the shoreline. Intact save for an arm and the skull, the skeleton still had some flesh on one of the legs and, from marks on the foot, Nduva's family were convinced that these were his remains.

Second Beach, Port St Johns, 18 December 2009

Cookie Cutter Shark

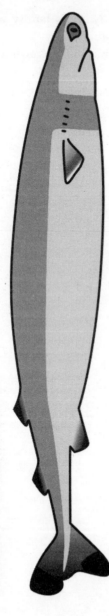

Shark Facts

Length: 1 feet 5 inches to 1 foot 10 inches
(42 cm to 56 cm)

Weight: 7 lb to 10 lb (3.2 kg to 4.5 kg)

Colouring: Dark brown with lighter belly

Diet: Great white sharks, dolphins, sperm whales,
elephant seals

Pups: Up to 12 pups born at 6 inches (15 cm)

Status: Not under threat

The little cookie cutter shark takes its name from the round bites that it takes out of its prey. During the day it lives in water over 2 miles deep but at dusk it heads to shallower water, camouflaged against the surface light by its own light-emitting cells, where it picks on the really big guys, including great white sharks. Its lips form a kind of sucker that anchors it to its victim, then its teeth inflict a bite more than 2 inches (5 cm) wide and almost 3 inches (7.5 cm) deep. Although its bite is not fatal, some beached whales have suffered hundreds of cookie cutter bites, inflicted while the whale was in trouble at sea.

Cookie Cutter Shark Range

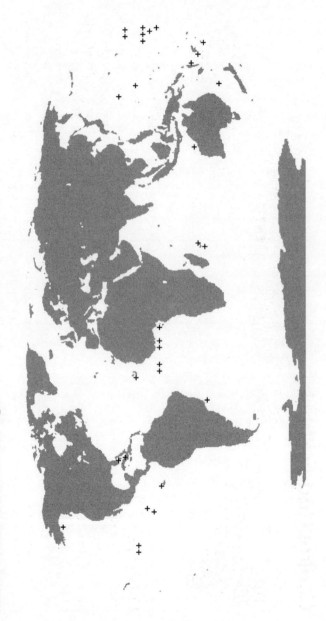

SHARK ATTACKS
2010–13

2010

WESTERN CAPE, SOUTH AFRICA, 2010

A Zimbabwean tourist visiting South Africa to attend a wedding was snorkeling off Cape Town's Fish Hoek Beach when he was taken by the dreaded great white shark. Lloyd Skinner was standing chest deep in the water, with other swimmers close by, adjusting his face mask, when the shark, described by one witness as being as big as a minibus, made its first attack. People on shore desperately began waving towels and shouting to warn the other swimmers, who looked round in time to see the shark pounce once more, disappearing beneath the surface with 37-year-old Skinner's body. Only the face mask was left behind. Skinner's body was never recovered.

> Fish Hoek Beach, Cape Town, 12 January 2010

FLORIDA, USA, 2010

A life guard spotted kite surfer Stephen Shafer apparently in difficulties about 500 yards offshore at Stuart Beach on the Atlantic coast of Florida and when he paddled out on his own board to try to help he saw several sharks circling the stricken Shafer. The life guard used his paddle to frighten the sharks away, then got Shafer ashore as fast as he could. Shafer, 38 years old and a local Florida resident, had suffered severe bite wounds to his legs and buttocks as well as lesser wounds and bruising to his hands and arms that were probably caused as he tried to fight off the sharks. Although he was alive when the life guard brought him ashore, he later died in hospital from his injuries.

Martin County, 3 February 2010

FIJI, 2010

The captain of a fishing boat whose divers were hunting for sea cucumbers on the reef about an hour from the island of Yadua, one of more than 300 islands that comprise the Republic of Fiji, looked on in horror as one of his young crew came to the surface just a few yards from the boat, struggling to fight off a shark attack. Henry Usimewa was just 19, but an experienced diver and extremely fit, when his friends spotted him battling with the unseen shark on the morning of 15 February. The others had no chance to go to his aid as the shark dragged Henry under and disappeared with him. Four other divers were in the water at the time but, despite spending the next two days scouring the area, all they ever found of Henry were a few battered elements of his diving gear and his sack of "sucu walu" sea cucumbers.

Yadua, 15 February 2010

EGYPT, 2010

Intended to be a holiday to remember, a trip to the Sharm el-Sheik resort with his parents to celebrate their 25th wedding anniversary instead became something British tourist James Elliott wishes he could forget. James was enjoying the sunshine, treading water alongside his dad, when he felt something grab his left leg. He felt an intense pain and looked down to see a five-foot shark with its jaws clamped around his lower leg. He kicked out with his free leg and the shark let go, having caused severe lacerations and having severed Elliott's Achilles tendon. The shark circled round and sped back towards the terrified swimmer, its dorsal fin and half of its body breaking the surface, then it swerved, dived and was gone. Elliott was rescued by a passing boat and rushed to shore to receive medical attention.

Sharm el-Sheik, 4 April 2010

VIETNAM, 2010

Local fishermen were encouraged to embark on a shark hunt, even though they knew it was almost impossible to identify the creature responsible for an attack on two women in Quy Nhon on 19 May. Nguyen Thi Tanh and Nguyen Thi Thu Thao were swimming around 6.00 a.m. when Tanh was mauled on her left foot. The two women were less than 20 yards from shore and Thao immediately came to Tanh's aid. They had made it to just five yards from the shore when Thao was also bitten on the leg. Witnesses on the beach helped both women from the water and took them to a nearby military hospital where both received medical attention and Tanh required surgery for her wounds.

Binh Dinh Province, 19 May 2010

NORTH CAROLINA, USA, 2010

Carley Schlentz was swimming with friends off the beach at Topsail Island in North Carolina when she felt something grab hold of her foot. At first the 13-year-old thought it was her friend's sister, larking around in the water, but then she felt the pain and realized that whatever it was that had got hold of her didn't want to let go. Schlentz managed to pull her leg free and could immediately see how bad the damage was as blood poured from the wound and the flesh was flayed open to the bone. She made it back to the beach with the help of her friends and her friend's stepfather bound his shirt around her lower leg to try to stem the blood loss, also wrapping her foot in a towel to try to close the wounds and stop the bleeding. Emergency services were on the scene within minutes, rushing Schlentz to hospital where she needed 60 stitches.

Topsail Island, 25 June 2010

KWAZULU-NATAL, SOUTH AFRICA, 2010

Student Sarah Haiden had a very lucky escape when she was dragged underwater by a shark while snorkeling near Sodwana Bay close to the Mozambique border on 4 July. The 21-year-old was swimming on a reef about a mile offshore when she felt something bump against her and then grab her leg. Haiden at first thought that one of her companions, who were scuba diving on the reef, was teasing her but when she realized it was a shark, she screamed for help and kicked it in the face to try to fend it off. As suddenly as it had appeared, the shark released her leg and was gone. The crew of the boat that had taken the diving party out to the reef dragged her aboard and rushed her to shore where she was treated in hospital for severe lacerations to her leg.

Sodwana Bay, 4 July 2010

FLORIDA, USA, 2010

Kimberly Presser was better equipped than most to figure out the odds of her surviving when she spotted a shark in calm, clear water, just five feet away from her. The

37-year-old Professor of Mathematics at Shippensburg University in Pennsylvania was on holiday with her family, standing chest-deep in the water off the beach at Mickler's Landing near Jacksonville, at around 11.00 a.m., having just watched her mother and nephew swoosh past her on boogie boards. In the car on the way to the beach, she had reassured her 6-year-old son when he had asked about sharks, telling him that he needn't be frightened, because sharks weren't really interested in people. This one, however, was definitely interested in her. Presser watched as the five-foot shark flicked its tail and shot towards her. She put up her left arm to protect herself and the shark tore a chunk out of her forearm. With blood pouring from the wound, Presser screamed a warning to everyone else swimming nearby and began running towards the beach. A lifeguard tended to her wound on the beach before she was whisked off to the Mayo Clinic hospital in Jacksonville for surgery that included 150 stitches. Doctors who treated her there said that shark attacks on that stretch of coast were rare and that hers was the first such injury they had ever dealt with. Even though she knew that the odds on her ever coming face to face with a shark again were pretty small, Presser then displayed some real courage. Bitten on a Monday, released from hospital on a Tuesday, she was back at the beach and paddling in the water again on Friday, determined that her children should not become frightened of being in the sea.

St Johns County, 2 August 2010

BAHAMAS, 2010

A fishing trip for an investment banker and his friends turned into a nightmare when they uncovered evidence of another fishing expedition that had gone disastrously wrong. On the morning of 4 September Humphrey Simmons hooked a 12-foot tiger shark about 40 miles south of Nassau, the shark having apparently been after the same grouper as the fisherman, but when he and his companions hauled the shark aboard they discovered evidence of another meal. The shark regurgitated a partially decomposed human leg, complete from the knee down. The dead shark stank horribly and, by the look of its distended stomach, it clearly had more gruesome evidence inside. Out of radio range, the fishermen decided to tow the shark's body behind their boat and head back towards Nassau.

The men contacted the authorities once they were a bit closer to the port and they were met by a ship of the Royal Bahamas Defence Force, which took charge of the shark and the human remains. When they reached shore, the shark was opened up, revealing another severed leg, two severed arms and a man's torso in two pieces. There was no head. Fingerprints identified the remains as those of Judson Newton.

Newton was a 43-year-old Bahamian who worked on cargo ships or as a chef in local restaurants. A keen fisherman, he never passed up an opportunity to take a boat out with friends and had done just that on 29 August. Five men were in the boat fishing off New Providence, but only three ever made it back to dry land. The boat developed engine trouble and, while they waited for help to arrive, Judson Newton and another man decided to jump overboard and swim to shore. Neither ever made it to the beach and no trace was ever found of Newton's fellow swimmer. Newton was said by his friends to have been an excellent swimmer and they refused to believe that he could have drowned, convinced that he had been taken by the shark before he could reach the beach. The ill-fated fishing party's boat got into trouble off Jaws Beach, where sequences for the 1987 shark attack movie, *Jaws: The Revenge*, were filmed.

Jaws Beach, 29 August 2010

WESTERN CAPE, SOUTH AFRICA, 2010

Fishing for perlemoen shellfish, a type of abalone, is strictly controlled in South Africa after over fishing led to fears that the species was in danger of extinction. The perlemoen is now off the endangered list, but one of the conservation measures adopted by the South African Government is to ban fishing for the perlemoen except with a special license. Perlemoen, however, is regarded as a delicacy and can fetch up to £25 per kilo, making it a tempting target for poverty-stricken, unlicensed poachers – yet they often risk more than being arrested and fined. Khanyisile Momoza was a fisherman who set out with a group of 12 friends to harvest perlemoen at Dyer Island, east of Cape Town. The men had set out very early in the morning, wading and swimming for two hours to reach the island which lies around three miles off shore. Once there they gathered as many perlemoen shells as they could find before heading back towards Pearly Beach on the mainland. The swimmers stuck together in a large group when they saw a great white shark cricling them, but 29-year-old Momoza had fallen slightly behind when his friends heard a horrific scream. They turned to see the shark rising out of the water with Momoza in its jaws. It dived beneath the water, taking their friend with it. He was never seen again and no remains were ever found.

Dyer Island, 21 September 2010

CALIFORNIA, USA, 2010

Matthew Garcia was enjoying the early morning waves off Surf Beach at Vandenberg Airforce Base along with his college roommate, 19-year-old Lucas Ransom, the two UCSB students having decided to take advantage of the perfect conditions to do a spot of boogie boarding before classes. Garcia, just a few months older than Ransom, was about 100 yards offshore with his friend only a couple of feet away when he heard Ransom yell for help before he suddenly disappeared beneath a wave. The water turned red and Garcia was left in little doubt about what had happened. Ransom and Garcia had been through high school together, competing on the same water polo and swimming teams. They both loved water sports and both loved swimming in the sea, fully aware of the risks that could entail. They had previously discussed the possibility of becoming caught up in a shark attack but, with the invincibility of youth dismissing any thought that they might ever come to harm and with the conviction that such tragedies were things that happened to other people, they couldn't believe they would ever fall victim to a shark. Now, however, the unthinkable was actually happening.

The brief glimpse that Garcia had of the shark was enough for him to realize that it was a great white, apparently almost 20 feet in length. Garcia struggled through the waves, searching for Ransom under the water. He found him, grabbed hold and dragged him to the surface, the shark seemingly having lost interest. Supporting Ransom's body, Garcia swam his friend to the beach, performing chest compressions in a desperate attempt to save his life. Sadly, it was to no avail. Ransom's left leg had been almost severed in the attack and he had lost a huge amount of blood. He died on the beach.

Santa Barbara, 22 October 2010

DOMINICAN REPUBLIC, 2010

Pinales Pedro Zapata was diving with friends off the Las Malena Beach at Boca Chica, about 35 miles from Santo Domingo, on 15 November when they spotted sharks in the water and wisely decided to head for shore. Zapata, however, opted to linger a little longer and the 21-year-old was never seen alive again. A Dominican Navy unit recovered his badly mutilated body.

Las Malena Beach, Boca Chica,15 November 2010

PALMYRA ATOLL, 2010

Palmyra Atoll is a reef on which sit around 50 small islands, lying due south of the Hawaiian Islands towards American Samoa. The area falls under US jurisdiction and was declared a National Wildlife Refuge in 2001. There is no permanent population on the islands but a handful of scientists and conservation workers are regular visitors. Kydd Pollock, a New Zealander now based in Honolulu, was one such visitor, the 33-year-old scientist spending between four and six months at Palmyra each year working for The Nature Conservancy. Pollock was highly experienced in dealing with ocean wildlife, having worked with his father in the family's sports fishing charter boat business, qualified for his own skippers license when he was only 18, helped to build an offshore fish farm and having captained his own fishing boat. That shark that attacked him, however, clearly had no respect for Pollock's qualifications.

Pollock was working with a team of divers, laying wide nets in the water to catch and tag giant humpheaded Maori wrasse when a seven-foot reef shark became entangled in one of the nets. Divers working on that net cut the shark free but it immediately turned, and swam towards the net on which Pollock was working.

Realizing that the fish was extremely agitated, Pollock took his net down to the sea bed, lowering the obstruction to let the shark swim free. The shark swam straight past him, then turned and bit the back of Pollock's head. Pollock spun round and the shark lunged again biting him in the face, the full force of the attack being absorbed by Pollock's mask. The glass shattered and the frame was mangled during the struggle. The shark then attacked for a third time, sinking its teeth into Pollock's head and forehead before it turned and fled. Pollock's fellow divers rushed him to shore where, although there was no doctor, his girlfriend, who was also part of the research team, cleaned and stitched his wounds. He was lucky not to have sustained injuries that would have been immediately life threatening as it would have taken up to a full day to get him to hospital. Instead, he will carry scars on his face and head to remind him of the day he tried to be kind to an angry shark.

Pacific Ocean, 19 November 2010

EGYPT, 2010

Towards the end of the year, the popular Egyptian Red Sea resort of Sharm el-Sheik became the scene of series of shark attacks that rocked the country's tourist industry. On October 20, a Russian holidaymaker, Elena Rubanovich was snorkeling when she was bitten on both legs by a shark, suffering severe lacerations. All was quiet for just over a month but anyone who thought that the horrific attack on Rubanovich was an isolated incident could not have been more wrong. On November 30, Lyudmilla Stolyarova was snorkeling in shallow water when her husband, Vladimir, heard the 70-year-old yelling "Shark!" She managed to push the shark away from her and make for the shore, but not before it bit off her arm. Before she could get out of the water, it attacked again and severed her foot.

Minutes later, before word of the Stolyarova attack could spread to other areas of the South Sinai beaches, 19-year-old Elena Martynenko was swimming with her mother, Olga, when a shark struck. Elena heard her mother scream at her to stay back as she fought the shark. She lost part of her hand and managed to swim to a jetty where she was pulled from the water with the shark still clinging on to her upper thigh. Rescuers battered the shark's head, desperately trying to make it release its grip, but it ripped off Martynenko's buttock before disappearing. The 48-year-old Russian sustained severe lacerations to her legs and arms as well as a serious spinal injury.

Within only quarter of an hour two men, one Russian and one Ukrainian, were also attacked. Both sustained serious leg injuries, one requiring surgery and partial amputation of his foot. The Egyptian authorities closed the beaches, suspended all watersports and instigated a shark hunt. An oceanic whitetip measuring over seven feet was caught along with an eight-foot mako. Some doubted that these two were responsible for all of the attacks, but on 4 December the beaches were re-opened and holidaymakers were back in the water.

On 5 December, a 70-year-old German tourist who loved the Sharm el-Sheik resort at Naama Bay so much that she had been coming there for the past 11 years, was swimming around noon when she was dragged under the water. The shark tore off her arm and by the time rescuers could get her to shore she was dead.

Sharm el-Sheik, 20 October to 5 December 2010

Great White Shark

Shark Facts

Length: 13 feet to 20 feet (4 m to 6 m)

Weight: Up to 4,200 lb (1,900 kg)

Colouring: Brownish or blue/grey upper with white belly

Diet: Seals, tuna, dolphins, turtles, rays, whales, sea otters, sea birds, other sharks

Pups: Up to 10 pups born at 5 feet (1.5m)

Status: Listed as vulnerable, protected in most regions

The most feared fish in the ocean, its reputation due in no small part to the 1975 movie *Jaws*, the great white shark is an "apex" predator – top of the food chain – although killer whales have been known to attack and eat great whites in areas where they compete for food. The great white can swim at speeds of up to 25 mph (40 km/h) and can leap completely clear of the water. They regularly hunt in shallow water and are infamous for attacking humans although, overall, we are actually more dangerous to them than they are to us.

The species has been hunted as a game fish for many years and its numbers are now low enough worldwide for it to be classed as vulnerable and protected in most regions.

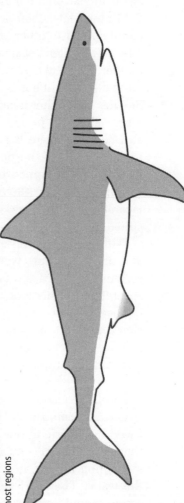

Great White Shark Range

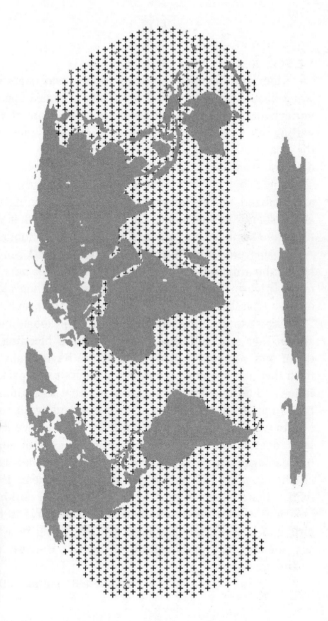

2011

Canadian holidaymaker Nicole Moore was standing waist-deep in the water, rinsing off after a game of beach volleyball when she heard a couple of men on jet-skis yelling at her. The 38-year-old nurse was enjoying the beach at Cancun with friends and her two young daughters and was confused by what the men were shouting. Then she felt something bump against her leg and realized to her horror that they were warning her about sharks in the water. One shark bit into her left thigh and removed a chunk of flesh the size of a football. As she staggered towards the shore, another shark caught her by the arm and she pounded it with her free hand to make it let go. One of the jet-ski riders was then close enough to grab hold of her and drag her to the beach.

There, Moore directed helpers to tie tourniquets around her arm and leg to stop her from bleeding to death and someone actually found the huge chunk of flesh that had been taken out of her thigh. It was packed in ice and followed her to hospital where it was stitched back in place. Infections set in, however, and by the time Moore was flown home to hospital in Toronto five days later, doctors were left with no option but to amputate her damaged arm and remove the flesh that had been stitched in place in Mexico. Tissue rejections meant that, by the time Moore returned to Cancun with her children ten months after the attack, determined to prove to her girls and herself that they need not fear going into the sea, she still had open wounds on her leg. Bravely, she swam anyway.

Cancun, 31 January 2011

SOUTH AUSTRALIA, AUSTRALIA, 2011

Peter Clarkson described how he had a close encounter with a great white while diving off Kalbarri in Western Australia in 2010. He was slowly swimming towards the surface when he became aware that he was not alone. The giant shark was ascending vertically, keeping pace with him, about thirty feet away. Clarkson was wearing a shark deterrent that emitted signals that interfered with the shark's electrical receptors, causing it to have muscle spasms, encouraging it to keep its distance. The 50-year-old diver had been diving for half his life but had never come across such a shark before, believing that the deterrent system had probably saved his life. Six months later he was diving for abalone near Perforated Island, South Australia when the captain of the dive boat saw him break the surface only to disappear again in a frothing cauldron of blood as two great whites attacked him. The sharks took Clarkson's body out to sea and nothing was ever recovered. It is not known whether he was wearing the shark repellent system at the time.

Eyre Peninsula, 17 February 2011

NEW SOUTH WALES, AUSTRALIA, 2011

Lisa Mondy was enjoying a day wakeboarding off the beach at Port Stephens, known as the "blue water paradise", in New South Wales when she had a brush with a great white. The 24-year-old had just fallen off her wakeboard and was waiting for the boat to come back for her when the shark struck. Rising from the deep without warning, the shark clamped its jaws around her face tearing open her chin and neck before suddenly releasing her. Mondy barely had time to appreciate what was happening and snatch a breath of air before the shark was back and ripping into her left arm. Again, it released her and she was dragged to safety aboard the boat. Despite her horrific injuries and the extensive surgery she had to endure to repair her face and save her arm, which was so badly shredded that doctors at first believed they would have to amputate it, Mondy bore no ill will towards the shark, saying that it wasn't his fault and her ordeal was "just one of those things".

Port Stephens, 16 March 2011

NEW SOUTH WALES, AUSTRALIA, 2011
Dave Pearson was trying out his brand new surf board, having joined friends in the water at around 6.30 p.m. off Headland Beach in New South Wales. He had only been on his board for around ten minutes when what is thought to have been a bull shark bit straight through it. Pearson was knocked into the water by the force of the attack, suffering lacerations to his face and losing a chunk of his forearm. When the 49-year-old surfer's friends saw he was in trouble, and clearly saw the blood in the water, Pearson yelled at them to stay away because he could see the shark was still swimming around below him. Ignoring his friend's warnings, 30-year-old Aaron Wallis quickly paddled over. He grabbed hold of Pearson and struck out for the shore, catching a wave that helped push them towards the beach. Pearson received immediate first aid and oxygen from a lifeguard on the beach while Wallis shouted at other beachgoers to call for an ambulance, holding Pearson's arm aloft to help stop the blood loss while another surfer used his leg rope to apply a tourniquet. The injured surfer was airlifted to hospital for emergency surgery and survived his injuries.

Crowdy Head, 23 March 2011

KWAZULU-NATAL, SOUTH AFRICA, 2011
It had been pretty much a perfect Saturday for 28-year-old Warren Smart. His girlfriend of eight years had recently come out of hospital after recovering from an accident and they were about to become engaged. As one of the founder members of the Zululand Spearfishing Club, Smart liked to get out on the water almost every day and was enjoying himself fishing with three friends. They had set out at around 7.00 a.m. and, five hours later, Smart was 12 metres below the surface off Leven Point, about 14 miles north of Cape Vidal. He had just speared a king mackerel when a shark suddenly appeared, sinking its teeth into his left leg. Smart's friends got him to the surface and dragged him aboard their boat but Cape Vidal was still 40 minutes away and Smart had already lost a great deal of blood from a severed artery. They called ahead to make sure that emergency services were waiting, applying a tourniquet to Smart's leg as he explained to them that he believed the Zambesi shark, also known as a bull shark, had been after his speared fish, not him. The attack was simply a case of mistaken identity. Paramedics were waiting on the beach at Cape Vidal where they fought to save Smart's life but he had lost so much blood by then that his veins had collapsed, making it difficult even to insert an intravenous drip. Smart faded in and out of consciousness as they frantically worked on him but, despite all the efforts of the medics, he died on the beach.

Cape Vidal, 21 May 2011

NEW CALEDONIA, 2011
A 15-year-old boy, known only as Nathan, was enjoying the first day of a holiday with family and friends, having spent the morning fishing with his father, a friend and

two other teenagers near the village of Koumac. In the afternoon, the boys decided to make the most of the strong breeze by doing a bit of kite surfing. Nathan fell off his board and was partly swimming, partly using his kite to drag him through the water to get back to it when the shark struck. He was badly mauled on the leg by what is thought to have been a tiger shark and died from blood loss.

Koumac, 23 May 2011

COSTA RICA, 2011

Five young friends enjoying surfing around noon on a peaceful Sunday at Playa Grande near Santa Cruz decied to ride just three more waves before getting out of the water. Suddenly, 15-year-old Kevin Moraga Jesus Rodriguez was knocked off his board by what is believed to have been a five-foot bull shark. The surfer's four companions looked on in horror as the sea turned red, the shark having taken a huge chunk out of Kevin's right leg. Only a few metres from the beach, the boys dragged their friend to the shore and used a surf board as a stretcher to carry him out of the water. Within 15 minutes he was in an ambulance on the way to hospital where doctors battled to save his life as he suffered a heart attack due to massive blood loss. Kevin sank into a coma and died as a result of his injuries five days later.

Playa Grande, Santa Cruz, 19 June 2011

COLUMBIA, 2011

The Gulf of Morrosquillo coastline is particularly picturesque in the San Onofre area, a perfect place to paddle a kayak in the Caribbean. That's exactly what 17-year-old Tulio Andres Amaya Vidal was doing, enjoying the peace and quiet – no motor revving, no sails flapping, just the sound of the waves lapping against the kayak and the splash of his paddles dipping into the water. Then, as he pushed forward with his right hand, a shark rose from the depths and sank its teeth into his arm. Screaming with pain, Hulio punched and pounded the creature with his left hand, struggling to keep his balance in the fragile kayak. As quickly as it had appeared, the shark gave up his prize and dived back down into the deep water. Tulio battled his way to the beach and relatives rushed him to hospital in Sincelejo where he underwent surgery for his injuries.

San Onofre, 5 July 2011

TEXAS, USA, 2011

Nicholas Vossler was enjoying swimming in the surf with his family and friends at the Texas wildlife reserve of Matagorda Island, standing in water less than 4 feet deep, when a shark tore into his foot. The 12-year-old was rescued from the jaws of the bull shark by a family friend who carried him towards the shore where Nicholas's father wrapped his shirt around his son's badly mauled foot to try to stem the blood flow. His mother then flagged down a passing motor boat and, calling ahead to the emergency services, they were whisked off to meet a waiting helicopter. Cradled by his father in the boat, Nicholas, bleeding heavily, told his mother to pray for him. Airlifted to hospital, Nicholas underwent a series of operations to save his foot and was expected to make a full recovery.

Matagorda Island, Texas Gulf, 7 July 2011

NORTH CAROLINA, USA, 2011

Few things can be more fun for a six-year-old than playing in the water on a boogie board with your parents and your sister. Lucy Mangum from North Carolina loved the water and visiting the beach at Ocracoke Island was a real treat – until a shark tore into her right leg as she played in just 18 inches of water. Hearing her daughter scream, Jordan Mangum turned to see the shark right next to Lucy. She snatched the little girl into her arms and called to her husband, Craig, who was just a few yards away in deeper water. He ran over and could immediately tell that the wounds were serious – he is an emergency room doctor – and that there was arterial bleeding. Jordan and Craig got both of their girls out of the water and did their best to minimize Lucy's blood loss until she was rushed to hospital where doctors used so many stitches to repair her wounds that they lost count. She later said that she understood that the shark had mistaken her for food and forgave him for biting her, although she still preferred dolphins.

Ocracoke Island, 19 July 2011

SEYCHELLES, 2011

A dip in the sea after enjoying lunch at the Bonbon Plume restaurant on the idyllic beach at Anse Lazio is what scores of holidaymakers look forward to each day on the island of Praslin. French tourist Nicholas Virolle was no different. The 36-year-old, who taught English in Rodez, was holidaying on the nearby island of Mahé, visiting Praslin to enjoy a delightful change of scenery. He was swimming about 50 yards offshore when sunbathers on the beach heard him call out. At first they thought he was larking around, but then they heard the word "Shark" and Virolle was dragged beneath the surface, the water turning red with blood. There were few people in the water at the time and they made quickly to shore while two locals raced towards Virolle when he resurfaced.

They dragged him aboard and raced towards the beach where witnesses described the swimmer's badly mauled body as having had most of its stomach ripped away. It is believed that he died from trauma and blood loss before the two men in the boat had brought him ashore, there being no chance that he could have survived his injuries.

Anse Lazio, Praslin, 1 August 2011

RECIFE, BRAZIL, 2011
Gabriel Alves dos Santos was just 14 years old when he was reported missing while swimming off Pina, one of the popular beaches of the Recife stretch of coastline. The following day, his body was recovered by lifeguards. The Recife area has become notorious for shark attacks and, while the sands remain popular for sunbathing and beach sports, few venture more than ankle deep in the water, watersports are discouraged and no one swims out beyond the reef after which the area is named. Dos Santos's disappearance was at first attributed to drowning but when his body was pulled from the water it had numerous bite marks and both legs were missing. Because of the injuries having contributed to rapid decomposition of the body, the coroner was not able to come to a definite conclusion about whether the cause of death was drowning or shark attack.

Pina Beach, 1 August 2011

SEYCHELLES, 2011
A dream honeymoon for a Lancashire couple turned into a nightmare on the beach at Anse Lazio less than a fortnight after their wedding day. Gemma and Ian Redmond had been together for eight years and had spent two years renovating a cottage that they were due to move into when they returned from the Seychelles.

Teacher Gemma, just 27, was sunbathing on the beach following lunch at the Bonbon Plume while her 30-year-old husband went snorkeling just 20 yards offshore, hoping to spot turtles. The peace and quiet of the beach were shattered when Ian's screams filled the air. Locals who had been working at the beach two weeks before knew immediately what had happened. This was the same beach where French holidaymaker Nicholas Virolle had lost his life in a shark attack just two weeks before. A tourist in a dinghy dragged Redmond aboard and people on the beach rushed to help him out of the water. A doctor who was also on holiday at the resort tried to administer first aid as others comforted the victim's wife, trying to keep her away from the disturbing sight of her husband's mutilated body. Reports indicated that he had lost an arm, his left leg was open to the bone and there were shark bites to his chest and stomach. He died on the beach. Scandalously, there had been no official warnings posted on the beach about the fatal shark attack on Virolle just a fortnight previously, otherwise Ian Redmond might have thought twice about going turtle spotting.

Anse Lazio, Praslin, 1 August 2011

RUSSIA, 2011

In what was described by local experts as unprecedented events, with no attacks on humans having been known for more than fifty years, two young men suffered appalling injuries after encountering sharks on Russia's Pacific coastline. Denis Udovenko and his wife, Polina, had been swimming from an island about 100 yards offshore in Telyakovsky Bay near Vladivostok when Udovenko yelled to his wife to swim faster because there was a shark in the water. Determined to save his wife, the 25-year-old grabbed the shark's nose, punching and pounding it to try to scare it off. The shark flipped him up in the air and then dragged him under. Moments later he reappeared on the surface and was hauled out of the water by two men in a boat. Both of his hands had been bitten off. Udovenko was rushed to hospital for emergency surgery, with surgeons having to perform partial amputations of his arms up to the elbows. The following day, a 16-year-old was mauled in much the same stretch of water where Udovenko and his wife had been swimming. Valerija Sidorovich was attacked while diving not far from shore. When they heard his cries for help, locals raced to his aid in a small boat, lifting him out of the water and calling for an ambulance which rushed him to hospital. Sidorovich had sustained serious bites to both legs but his wetsuit had afforded him enough protection that surgeons believed they would be able to repair the damage and avoid amputation.

The authorities banned swimming in the area and instigated a shark hunt to try to catch the culprits.

Telyakovsky Bay, Sea of Japan, 17 and 18 August 2011

WESTERN CAPE, SOUTH AFRICA, 2011

After seeing a whale rise from the water close to where they were waiting to catch a wave, local Plettenberg Bay surfers, accompanied by a couple of Australian visitors, joked that they had better watch out for sharks. Tim "Boots" van Heerden, a 49-year-old local carpenter and leatherworker whose famous hand-made moccasin shoes had earned him his nickname, had surfed the bay for years, never having known any danger of shark attacks. But as he paddled back out at around 9.00 a.m., heading to take up station and wait for another wave, he heard one of the Australians yell "Shark!" The next thing anyone knew, van Heerden had been tipped off his board by the fish. Climbing back on, he was caught by the shark once more, dragging him under the water. A few seconds later he bobbed back up to the surface and the water around him was completely red. A friend who had known van Heerden for twenty years, saw what was happening and, as the surfer drifted towards the mouth of the Keurtbooms River, he swam out to pull him ashore. Emergency services were on the scene within minutes but van Heerden had lost so much blood from bites to his legs that had severed his femoral artery that, even when he was transferred to the Plettenberg Bay Medi-Clinic, they stood no chance of saving his life.

Plettenberg Bay, 23 August 2011

WESTERN AUSTRALIA, AUSTRALIA, 2011

Overcast skies, dark water, whale activity, seals in the area and a little light rain created what were described by experts as the perfect conditions for a shark attack in Bunker Bay. Kyle Burden wasn't too concerned. The 21-year-old had been living in the area for the past four years, originally having come from Sydney on the east coast, and enjoyed the open-air lifestyle out west, especially body-boarding with friends in the surf off an area of beach known as "The Boneyards". He was swimming on his board a few yards from shore with his friends close by when a shark, which none of them had seen coming, rose from the depths, clamped its jaws around Burden and cut him in half. The others dragged Burden's remains to shore, realizing beyond a shadow of a doubt that their friend was already dead, and screamed at everyone else nearby to get out of the water. A great white or possibly a bronze whaler – also known as the copper shark, a species of requiem shark – was thought to be responsible for the attack.

Bunker Bay, 4 September 2011

KENYA, 2011

A young man, reported to be only 16 years old, was attacked while swimming off Mama Ngina Beach near Mombasa, by a bull shark that ripped off his right leg and partially severed his left. Although the youth was quickly pulled out of the water and rushed to the Coast Provincial General Hospital where medical staff fought to save him, he died three hours after the attack.

Mama Ngina Beach, Indian Ocean, 8 September 2011

FLORIDA, USA, 2011

Seven friends from Florida set out for a day's fishing off Ana Maria Island, something they had done many times before, enjoying the sunshine, filming dolphins riding the bow wave of their boat and taking pictures of each other spearing hogfish and king mackerel. Having already bagged a healthy catch for the day, 21-year-old Charles Wickersham was bobbing in the water next to the boat, with two girls from the fishing party lounging in floating chairs nearby, when he looked down to see a nine-foot bull shark tearing into his leg. Wickersham yelled a warning to his friends before he was momentarily dragged under. The girls abandoned their floating chairs and swam for the boat as Wickersham battled the shark, hammering at it with his unloaded spear gun until it released his leg, although the flesh on his thigh had been sliced open to the bone.

With scant regard for his own safety, one of Wickersham's friends, Connor Bystrom, jumped into the water and helped those on the boat heave Wickersham aboard as one of the girls called the emergency services. They tied a rope around Wickersham's leg as a tourniquet to try to stop the bleeding, comforting the injured man by telling him that his injuries weren't as bad as they looked, while the boat sped back to shore. Wickersham, however, was under no illusions about his predicament. He had seen his own thigh bone and the back of the boat was awash with blood yet, despite losing half the blood in his body, he remained conscious, very much aware that his friends were racing to save his life.

Paramedics were waiting at the dockside when the friends arrived and Wickersham was loaded onto a helicopter to rush him to hospital. Wickersham was hugely fortunate that the emergency room doctor who was waiting at the hospital had recently returned from military duty in Afghanistan and was well acquainted with the problems involved in major injuries such as this. He was able to deal with the immediate problems and prepare Wickersham for immediate surgery. After two operations and around 800 stitches, the medical team managed to repair Wickersham's wounds and save his leg. Interviewed some time later as he recovered at home, Wickersham acknowledged his huge debt to his friends without whose bravery, calm attitude and swift actions he would never have lived to reach the hospital.

Gulf of Mexico, 24 September 2011

WESTERN CAPE, SOUTH AFRICA, 2011
Accountant Michael Cohen lived to regret ignoring the warnings of shark spotters when he dived into the waves off Fish Hoek Beach in Cape Town's False Bay – but only just. The 42-year-old was an enthusiastic swimmer who knew the risks he was taking when he was advised that great white sharks had been seen close to shore. They are so common in the area that shark spotters are employed to raise signal flags telling beach users that the water is out of bounds. The spotters also warn those on the beach in person when it is dangerous to go into the water but

Cohen, who was British but had lived in South Africa for many years, was determined to enjoy his lunchtime swim. He paid a terrible price for his few minutes of exercise. He was repeatedly bitten by a great white that tore off his right leg and caused serious damage to his left. When they saw that he was in trouble in the water, two passers-by waded in to drag him out and a shark spotter used his own belt and part of his wetsuit to tie tourniquets around Cohen's legs. A helicopter was called to fly him from the beach to the Constantiaberg MediClinic. Cohen needed extensive surgery that included removing part of his badly damaged left foot. He was not expected ever to be able to walk again.

False Bay, Cape Town, 28 September 2011

PUERTO RICO, 2011

Rafael Colón Casanova was enjoying the prospect of a morning's surfing with a friend in the Atlantic waves off the beach at Hatillo on the northern coast of Puerto Rico. A little before 10.00 a.m., he was sitting on his board when he felt something tugging at his lower leg, and then a searing pain shot through his body. The two surfers immediately headed for shore, Casanova leaving a trail of blood behind him in the water. Once on dry land they could see that the cause of the excruciating pain was a series of deep lacerations between his knee and his ankle, the flesh on his leg gaping open. They bound the wound as best they could and headed for hospital where Casanova's injuries required more than 80 stitches. Experts were unsure whether the injuries were caused by a small shark or a large barracuda. Either way, Casanova counted himself lucky to have escaped without even more serious injury.

Hatillo, 30 September 2011

WESTERN AUSTRALIA, AUSTRALIA, 2011

Anyone who regularly walked along Cottesloe Beach in Perth in the morning could not fail to recognize Bryn Martin. The popular local businessman made it his habit to take a swim early every morning and on Sunday mornings at 8.00 a.m., he took to the ocean with the Freemantle Master's Swimming Club's Freo Fins group. The 64-year-old had always been keen on watersports and was an excellent swimmer, the oldest competitor in the local Rottnest Island race. On this particular day, a Monday, he was seen going into the sea near a water-front café and heading for a yellow buoy anchored about 300 yards offshore. That was the last time anyone saw him alive. Martin's wife called the police when he didn't show up for breakfast with the family as planned and a search was launched but his body was never found. Police divers did recover his shredded swimming trunks from the sea bed, the damage to the swimsuit indicating that Martin had been taken by a shark.

On the following Sunday morning, an emotional group of Freo Fins went into the water, swimming to pay their respects to the late Bryn Martin.

Cottesloe Beach, 10 October 2011

WESTERN AUSTRALIA, AUSTRALIA, 2011

Texan George Thomas Wainwright – Tom to his friends – was living his dream, having worked in Australia on a visa for six months staying in Perth with a job as a project manager for a marine company that allowed him plenty of time to indulge his passions for diving and fishing. It was on one such trip to Rottnest Island, diving with friends from a boat anchored about 500 yards off an area called Little Armstrong Bay, that Wainright was attacked by a great white shark. His friends didn't realize that there was anything wrong until they saw a turbulence of bubbles rise to the surface followed by a spreading stain of blood and then the badly mauled body of the diver. Wainright's injuries were described by local fishermen as horrific and he was dead before his friends could get to him.

This third death from shark attacks in the same general area in just a few weeks sparked a shark hunt to try to track down what some believed to be a rogue man-eater, although shark experts maintained that the attacks were highly unlikely to have been perpetrated by just one fish.

Rottnest Island, 22 October 2011

CALIFORNIA, USA, 2011

Pigeon Point, about 50 miles south of San Francisco, boasts the tallest lighthouse on America's west coast and an unenviable reputation amongst kayak anglers for shark attacks. Angler Harry Pali counts himself extremely lucky to have survived a tussle with a great white while out fishing with his friend, Ted Akizuki, on a reef just north of the famous lighthouse. Weather conditions were becoming gradually less conducive to a pleasant day's fishing, the sea turning ever more choppy, and the friends were considering heading for shore when Pali was suddenly catapulted into the air when something slammed into his kayak from below. He described the impact as like being hit by a car. Akizuki quickly came to his friend's aid as Pali clambered back aboard his upturned kayak. Both men could clearly see a set of teeth marks on the bottom of Pali's boat, immediately below where he had been sitting. They had no doubt a shark was responsible – and it had to be a big one.

Akizuki attempted to tow Pali's kayak back to shore, but could make little headway with the boat still upside down. They had to right the stricken kayak, Pali shuffling onto the bow of his friend's boat in order to do so. Akizuki's boat was then in danger of swamping in the rough sea, so Pali had to get back into his own leaking kayak. That meant jumping back into the water, knowing that the shark was almost certainly still lurking in the murky depths. Pali broke all records for remounting his kayak from the water and within moments both men were pulling for shore, water streaming into Pali's boat through the holes made by the shark's teeth.

When they reached shore and dragged their boats out of the water, they were able to survey the damage to Pali's kayak more extensively. Experts later confirmed that the bite marks indicated an attack by a great white, probably around 18 feet long. It was the third such attack in the area in five years, with kayak anglers also having reported various "bumps" and investigative swim-past encounters by sharks that will see the outline of a 14-foot long kayak from below as some kind of competitor muscling in on their feeding grounds. In a way, of course, the shark is absolutely right.

Pigeon Point, 22 November 2011

2012

EASTERN CAPE, SOUTH AFRICA, 2012

Surfer Lungisani Msungubana was enjoying himself in the sunshine off Second Beach at Port St Johns when he fell victim to a bull shark while in water that was only waist deep. According to his friends, the shark reared up out of the water and sank its teeth into Msungubana who yelled at them to get out of the water and fought with the creature for almost five minutes, the water turning red around him. He suffered multiple bites before rescuers could drag him to the beach. A doctor who happened to be on hand tried to treat him but Msungubana had suffered severe bite injuries to both of his arms and his legs as well as his stomach. He died before he could be transferred to hospital.

Second Beach, Port St Johns, 15 January 2012

WESTERN AUSTRALIA, AUSTRALIA, 2012

Peter Kurmann was diving from a boat on a reef off Stratham Beach around 15 miles south of Perth, enjoying the early morning trip with his brother, Gian. It was 34-year-old Gian, a year older than his brother, who later described how a shark about 14 feet long appeared from nowhere, tearing into Peter and ripping him apart. Kurmann died instantly and his brother helped to recover some of his remains to the boat. Parts of his body were washed ashore on Preston Beach in Peel, more than 60 miles away, a week later.

Stratham Beach, 31 March 2012

WESTERN CAPE, SOUTH AFRICA, 2012

Bodyboarder David Lilienfield took his watersports seriously. He had been South African junior bodyboard champion in 2009 and had represented his country at the World Games in the Canary Islands towards the end of 2011. He loved nothing better than being in the waves and was enjoying practicing in the surf with his brother, Gustav, in the noon sunshine in Kogel Bay, just East of Cape Town, when he was taken by a great white. A family of tourists who had stopped on the clifftop road to take in the view told how they saw the two bodyboarders having fun in the waves when the 15-foot great white rose out of the water and attacked Lilienfield. The 20-year-old was knocked off his board as the shark relentlessly slammed into him several times in just a few seconds. Lilienfield fought back, fending the shark off with his board before it finally took him in its jaws and disappeared beneath the surface.

While their parents dashed off to raise the alarm and summon help, the two brothers who had witnessed the tragedy climbed down to the rocks at the water's edge to see if they could help Lilienfield ashore. They were soon joined by Gustav, who had been desperately trying to get to his brother, the shark having carried him out of reach. They first found Lilienfield's board and then his body. His right leg had been torn off at the hip and he had died in the water.

Kogel Bay, 19 April 2012

FLORIDA, USA, 2012

Karin Stei was enjoying a holiday in the Florida sunshine, far from the chilly water of Lake Constance and her home town of Konstanz in southern Germany, swimming and wading with her friend, Brigitte Schmid, in the warm, tranquil Atlantic at Vero Beach in Florida. Stei was a little behind her friend when the 47-year-old started screaming and Schmid turned to see her surrounded by blood. A shark had clamped its jaws around her left thigh, paring the flesh away down to the bone. A lifeguard was quickly in the water as were passers-by anxious to help, none of them knowing for sure if the shark had actually abandoned its attack, and as they brought Stei to the beach an emergency helicopter that had been flying overhead landed nearby. One of the flight paramedics had spotted the blood in the water and had signaled to the pilot to set down.

Stei was flown to the Lawnwood Regional Medical

Center in Fort Pierce where she received emergency surgery to her leg. Her injuries suggested that either a bull or tiger shark had been responsible.

Vero Beach, 9 May 2012

MEXICO, 2012

Fisherman Benigno Medina Navarrete was diving with his friend Juan Mendoza off the beach at Boca de la Lena, in Guerrerro on Mexico's Pacific coast, using spear guns at around 9.00 a.m. when he was attacked by a 13-foot bull shark. The shark clamped its jaws around his left forearm and bit off his hand and wrist. The two men were only a few yards from shore in about 15 feet of water when the attack happened and Mendoza was able to help his friend ashore and get him first aid before he was taken to hospital where he immediately underwent three hours of surgery.

Boca de la Lena, Guerrerro, 29 May 2012

WESTERN AUSTRALIA, AUSTRALIA, 2012

Surfer Ben Linden was attacked by a 15-foot great white shark off Wedge Island, about 100 miles north of Perth, on 14 July, the shark biting the 24-year-old in half. A jet-ski rider towing another surfer led his friend to safety before racing back out to the scene of the attack, but Linden was already dead. The jet-skier attempted to recover Linden's remains but the shark returned, nudging the jet-ski to try to knock the rider off, then making off with the rest of Linden's body.

Wedge Island, 14 July 2012

RÉUNION, 2012

Fabien Bujon loves the sea. The 41-year-old had surfed all over the world for more than thirty years and painted marine wildlife – sharks were one of his favourite subjects. Over the years he had met hundreds of sharks and he knew that one day he was likely to come face to face with one, unexpectedly, somewhere in the ocean. He never dreamed that it would happen off the beautiful beach at Saint-Leu. On 5 August 2012, towards the end of the afternoon, Fabien was sitting on his board with his legs dangling in the water, waiting for a wave, when the 10-foot bull shark struck. He saw the shark rise out of the water and clamp its jaws around his leg. He was tipped off the board into the sea, and through the water that was already stained red with his own blood, he could see the shark's head shaking from side to side with his leg in its jaws. He felt no pain, shock, adrenalin and terror working together to spare him the agony and desperately fought the shark, raining blows on its head, even though he knew that they were softened to a featherlight uselessness by the water. Fabien grabbed the shark by the gills with his left hand pulling and tearing violently at the creature while trying to twist himself free.

Suddenly, the shark no longer had hold of him. Fabien grabbed his board and only then realized that his right hand was missing, bitten off by the shark. His lower right leg he knew was badly mauled and he suspected that his foot, too, had gone. Using his left hand, he hauled himself onto the board and, growing ever weaker from loss of blood, Fabien paddled towards the shore. He was spotted in the shallows by holidaymakers, including his brother, Emmanuel, who used a lace from his shoe to make a tourniquet for his brother's arm. The leg rope from his board was used as a tourniquet on his leg before he was rushed to Saint-Pierre Hospital.

Despite his ordeal, Fabien must count himself as lucky. Over the previous couple of years, several swimmers and surfers who encountered sharks in the waters off Réunion had not lived to tell the tale. Alexandre Rassica was surfing off the beach at Trois-Bassins when the 22-year-old was attacked by a shark which bit off his leg. Despite his friends helping him to shore and administering first aid, Rassica died on the beach before paramedics could reach him.

On 13 October 2011 the remains of an unidentified woman were discovered in the water near La Possession in the north of the island. Only a leg and torso remained, the body, estimated to have been in the water for only a day, clearly having been attacked by sharks.

Former bodyboarding champion and surf school manager Matthieu Schiller was surfing with friends off Boucan Canot beach on 19 September 2011 when they spotted a shark circling them. The shark suddenly moved in with incredible speed, dragging Schiller off his board into the water. Sea conditions were rough but the others then managed to drag 32-year-old Schiller, who had sustained horrific injuries to his leg, back onto his board. It is unclear whether a wave or the returning shark then knocked the badly wounded surfer back into the water. He was never seen again.

Only three months earlier, on 15 June 2011, off Saint Giles in the same area of the island where Schiller lost his life, 31-year-old surfer Eddy Auber was the victim of what witnesses described as a frenzied attack by a number of sharks. He was seen struggling in the water but no one could get near to him as several sharks were circling. Auber's right arm was bitten off, he had bites to his thigh and hip and one of his legs was severely mutilated. He died before rescuers could get him out of the water.

On 19 February 2011, Saint Gilles was again the scene

of a horrific attack. Towards the end of the afternoon, several surfers were enjoying the waves when they heard a scream and saw 32-year-old Eric Dargent struggling as the water turned red around him. A shark had bitten off his leg at the knee. Dargent was helped ashore and rushed to hospital, fortunate to have escaped with his life.

Indian Ocean, 2011–2012

RECIFE, BRAZIL, 2012

A trip to the beach with his sister and brother-in-law ended in tragedy for 18-year-old Jose de Oliviera da Silva. The teenager was swimming alone off a beach on the Pernambuco coast in the north east of Brazil when he simply disappeared. His body was washed ashore at Itapuama Beach two days later with massive shark attack injuries, much of the flesh having been stripped from his right leg. The coroner ultimately established the cause of death as being from loss of blood, not drowning.

Pernambuco, 26 August 2012

INNER HEBRIDES, UNITED KINGDOM, 2012

Fisherman Hamish Currie got more than he bargained for when he caught a seven-foot porbeagle shark off the island of Islay in the Inner Hebrides. Currie had gone after sharks in the area when he heard that they had been attacking seals as he was involved in a "tag-and-release" programme intended to help learn more about these sharks' habits in the wild. No one, however, told the shark that it was to be safely released and when Currie hauled it aboard it sank its teeth into his boot. Currie kicked out at the shark, scrambling towards the cabin of his fishing boat while his friend grabbed the shark by the tail, beginning a deadly tug-of-war that ended only when Currie's boot came off in the animal's mouth. Although the boot was shredded, its steel toecap had saved the fisherman's foot.

Islay, Scotland, 31 August 2012

TONGA, 2012

Australian "treasure hunter" Kylie Maguire worked with a team investigating shipwrecks off the Tongan coast and co-operating with the Tongan authorities in uncovering the island's maritime history as well as involving themselves in a number of conservation projects. On 10 September she was swimming behind a kayak with another female member of the team when she was attacked by what is thought to have been a bull shark. Even though she was an experienced professional diver and fully aware of the risks involved in swimming in the area, Kylie never saw the shark coming. Bitten on the thighs and buttocks, she somehow managed to avoid any serious injuries to nerves or arteries and swiftly received medical attention in hospital in Tonga before being transferred by air ambulance for further treatment to infected wounds in Brisbane.

Eueiki Island, 10 September 2012

CALIFORNIA, USA, 2012

Windsurfer Gunnar Proppe was thinking about calling it a day, cruising on a dying breeze about quarter of a mile off the beach at Davenport Landing at around 6.30 p.m. when a tremendous impact suddenly hurled him into the air. At first he thought he must have hit something in the water but, as he splashed into the sea he was convinced that he hadn't been going fast enough for a massive collision like this to happen. Then he felt something brush past his right foot and saw a grey fin slicing through the water. Proppe scrambled back onto his board only to discover that the shark had snapped his mast. Frantically, he struggled to free the board from the mast and sail so that he could try to paddle ashore before the shark returned. Glancing left and right to check for the tell-tale fin in the water, he released the rigging and struck out for shore. He tried yelling to a couple of other windsurfers and boarders still in the water to warn them about the shark but they couldn't hear him. Expecting at any moment to feel the shark's teeth gouging his flesh, Proppe paddled desperately towards the beach, eventually catching the other boarders' attention as he drew closer and then catching a wave himself that took him all the way to the beach. There he discovered he had a cut on his toe but had no idea whether it had been caused by the shark, his board or a rock in the water – he simply counted himself as lucky to be alive.

Davenport Landing, 7 October 2012

CALIFORNIA, USA, 2012
Surf Beach near Vandenberg Air Force Base in California had been the spot where 39-year-old Francisco Javier Solorio Jr had surfed since he was a boy, but on the morning of 23 October the expert surfer's favourite beach turned from paradise into a nightmare. Solorio's friend watched in horror as a great white shark estimated at around 16 feet long clamped its jaws around his companion's torso. The shark released Solorio and his friend dragged him to shore, providing first aid until paramedics arrived on the scene. Unfortunately, Solorio died on the beach.

Surf Beach, 23 October 2012

MEXICO, 2012

Sinaloa is a state in the north west of Mexico lying on the Gulf of California roughly opposite the tail of the Baja peninsula. Nuevo Altata is a developing beach resort where Fernando Cardenas Garcia worked as a lifeguard. On the morning of 22 November at 11.30, Garcia dived overboard from his dinghy when it became tangled up in a length of rope. No sooner had he cut the rope free of the boat when he was attacked by a shark. The creature inflicted massive damage from his lower leg all the way up to his buttock and, although rescued by friends and rushed to hospital, Garcia died from his wounds.

Nuevo Altata, Sinaloa, 22 November 2012

HAWAII, USA, 2012

Thomas Kennedy from Oregon will be reminded of his trip to Hawaii every time he looks at the scars on his left leg. Kennedy was snorkeling with friends about 200 yards offshore when what is thought to have been a 10-foot tiger shark clamped its jaws around his left leg. Kennedy had no warning of the attack and hadn't seen the shark coming but no sooner had the 61-year-old realized what was happening than the shark simply spat him out. Although in excruciating pain, Kennedy swam for shore as fast as he could, daring to glance back now and again to check that the tiger wasn't coming back for more and worrying about the swirling clouds of blood that were trailing in his wake. Fortunately, one of Kennedy's fellow snorkelers was a nurse who was able to give him first aid until he could get to hospital. Even more fortuitous was the fact that the shark had somehow managed to miss damaging any major blood vessels, otherwise Kennedy might well have bled to death in the water.

Kihei, 30 November 2012

EASTERN CAPE, SOUTH AFRICA, 2012

Despite its reputation as the most dangerous beach in the world, where shark attacks are common, the picturesque Second Beach near Port St Johns on South Africa's Eastern Cape was thronging with revelers enjoying the sunshine on Christmas Day. Barbecues were in full swing, there was music and laughter, with scores of people cooling off in the water. Avuyile Ndamase was playing volleyball on the beach – he never went into the water there – when he spotted the tail of a large shark weaving between swimmers and waders. Then there was a sudden commotion, a violent thrashing in the water and people scrambled for the beach as the ocean turned red. The shark, thought to be a tiger shark, had grabbed 20-year-old Liya Sibili of Gauteng and dragged him under. His body was never found.

Ndamase had good reason to stay clear of the water at Second Beach. Less than two years before, on 15 January 2011, he was surfing with his 16-year-old brother, Zama, in the bay. Both boys were talented surfers and had been selected to represent the region in a series of competitions, scoring some commendable victories. As they waited together for a wave just after noon, Zama suddenly disappeared into the water. Ndamase thought nothing of it as all of the boys who surfed in the bay used to sneak up on each other and pull each other off their boards while larking around. But this time it was different – Zama had been taken by a shark. He managed to haul himself back onto his board and make for the beach, his brother screaming for someone to help and he was hauled ashore by lifeguards who did their best to tend to the deep wounds in his legs. The trail of blood Zama had left behind him in the water, however, was from a severed femoral artery and he had lost too much blood to survive for long. He died on Second Beach.

Exactly a year later, 25-year-old Lungisani Msungubana was relaxing with a group of friends in waist-deep shallow water off Second Beach when he was attacked by a shark. He suffered shocking wounds to his arms, legs and torso and was dead before lifeguards could drag him ashore. Zambesi sharks, also known as bull sharks have been responsible for seven fatal attacks at Second Beach in seven years, yet the area remains a prime destination for local beachgoers and tourists. On Boxing Day, 2012, less than 24 hours after the death of Liya Sibili, the beach parties were back in full swing with surfers and swimmers splashing about in the water.

Second Beach, Port St Johns, 25 December 2012

NEW SOUTH WALES, AUSTRALIA, 2012

A bull shark was thought to be responsible for the attack on 29-year-old surfer Luke Allen near Diamond Head in New South Wales. Allen was surfing with friends around 10.45 a.m. when the attack happened and they spotted him getting into trouble. He was bitten on the thigh and groin, and also lost two fingers from his left hand as he tried to fight off the shark. His friends dragged him to safety on the beach and applied basic first aid, using the leg ropes from their surf boards as tourniquets to stem the flow of blood until help arrived. Allen was airlifted to hospital, his friends' swift actions having undoubtedly saved his life.

Diamond Head, 28 December 2012

NEW SOUTH WALES, AUSTRALIA, 2012

Sydney lifeguard Danny Sheather counts himself as one of the luckiest surfers in the world following an encounter with an eight-foot shark while he was surfing with friends off a beach north of the city. Concentrating on riding a wave, Sheather suddenly felt the board buck as it was hit from below and he was thrown off into the water. A large slice was carved out of the bottom of the board, but 23-year-old Sheather was left completely unscathed and didn't even see the shark that caused the damage. With the beaches closed, the shark was spotted cruising off the beach by lifeguards and a rescue helicopter. Sheather had been surfing for eighteen years and never before suffered any kind of shark attack.

Sydney, 30 December 2012

FLORIDA, USA, 2012

The dubious honour of being the final shark victim of 2012 went to a male swimmer who was attacked off Jensen Beach in Martin County, Florida on New Year's Eve. Lifeguards raised red flags, meaning "no swimming" after the man was bitten on the lower leg and ankle by the shark. Although shocked and in great pain, the bather's injuries were, for a shark attack, relatively minor and not thought to be life threatening. The type of shark involved in the attack could not be confirmed.

Jensen Beach, 31 December 2012

2013

HAWAII, USA, 2013

The rocky Hawiian beaches of picturesque Kiholo Bay on Big Island's north west coast, where the mixture of salt and fresh water famously turns the ocean a thousand different shades of blue, had been a favourite surfing spot for friends Steve Macres and Paul Santos for as long as they could remember. The sound of the waves was suddenly drowned out when 65-year-old Macres heard Santos screaming in pain. He turned in time to see a 15-foot tiger shark leap from the water then disappear again beneath the surface. At this point there was no sign of 43-year-old Santos and, convinced that his friend was dead, Macres began to paddle for shore. He had gone only a few feet when he turned for another look and saw Santos desperately paddling towards him.

Santos had sustained a serious bite to his right leg below the knee and a horrendous injury to his right arm. Although Macres could see that the arm appeared to be intact, his hand had been all but severed, hanging on by just a few tattered strips of flesh. Macres helped his friend ashore where local residents bound his wounds and applied a tourniquet to stop the bleeding while Santos described how he had punched and pounded the shark with his free hand to make it release him. He was rushed to hospital by the emergency services where he required immediate surgery to successfully re-attach his badly mauled hand.

Kiholo Bay, 16 January 2013

QUEENSLAND, AUSTRALIA, 2013
French surfer Matthieu Cassaigne narrowly escaped with his life when he was attacked by a shark at Noosa, north of Brisbane on Australia's Sunshine Coast. Cassaigne, a 22-year-old sky diving instructor, was resting on his surf board, lying on his back, when the shark clamped its jaws around the board, its upper teeth sinking into the Frenchman's neck and shoulder. The shark immediately released its grip and Cassaigne swam for shore, abandoning his board. The attack happened in an area where two shark nets and three drumlines – baited shark hooks designed to attract and catch the

creatures – are deployed to keep the beach safe.

Noosa, 25 January 2013

NEW ZEALAND, 2013

Adam Strange loved living by the ocean and swimming in the ocean whenever he could. The flim maker, whose work on art movies and advertisements had won awards all over the world, was a keen surfer, bodyboarder and swimmer. Strange's mid-week swim on Wednesday lunchtime was part of the 46-year-old's training regime for a forthcoming race. He was trying out new goggles and planned to swim about one-and-a-half miles in preparation for the annual Auckland to Rangitoto endurance swim. The weather was fine during the southern hemisphere summer and there were upwards of 200 people on Muriwai Beach near Auckland when Strange dived into the water. He had been swimming just a few minutes when a great white estimated at 14 feet long attacked him about 200 yards from the shore. A group of fishermen on nearby rocks saw what was happening and yelled at Strange to make for the rocks, but it was too late. They immediately called the police and the beach's lifeguards were already in the water, speeding towards Strange in an inflatable dinghy. They rammed the shark but couldn't drive it away from Strange who, by that time, was already dead.

Police officers quickly arrived, launching their own boat and firing shots at the shark, although it is now believed that more than one was involved in the attack, in order to recover Strange's body.

Muriwai Beach, Auckland, 27 February 2013

Avoiding a Shark Attack

The chances of an unwelcome encounter with a shark can be reduced by following a few simple guidelines courtesy of The Shark Trust, UK:

- Avoid swimming, diving, kayaking or surfing alone.
- Avoid areas where dangerous sharks are known to congregate, for example sandbars, steep drop-offs, near channels and particularly river mouths.
- Avoid the water at dawn and dusk, when many sharks are more active and approach the shore to feed.
- Avoid water where visibility is poor.
- If diving, do not hang around on the surface any longer than strictly necessary.
- Avoid uneven tanning, wearing contrasting/brightly coloured clothing and jewellery, which may resemble the glinting scales or shiny flesh of a prey fish.
- Avoid excessive splashing and noise. Keep pets and other domestic animals out of the water as their erratic movements may attract sharks.
- Don't swim near people who are fishing/spearfishing or cleaning fish.
- Avoid seal and sea lion colonies, and schooling fish in large numbers, especially if they begin to behave erratically.
- If a shark is considered to be a threat, leave the water promptly and calmly.
- Never provoke or harass a shark, or approach too closely, even if it is small.
- If a shark is swimming in a jerky or rigid manner, hunches its back or drops its pectoral fins, retreat slowly and calmly as any of these may be a threat display.

To which fairly comprehensive advice could only be added: before entering unknown waters, ask the locals what sharks are around – there are bound to be some, even if only relatively harmless ones.

Surviving a Shark Attack

The vast majority of shark attacks are not fatal, but if you want to be a survivor you have to keep your wits about you and follow some basic rules:

- If you see a shark, stay calm. If you panic and start splashing about swimming for shore, you will attract its attention.
- Call out to anyone nearby to let them know that there is a shark danger.
- Swim smoothly and calmly towards the shore or a boat but if the shark takes an interest, stay still.
- If you are diving and can't get out of the water, get your back to a rock outcrop or other solid surface to reduce the shark's attack options.
- If you are swimming with a friend, get back to back so that you can see the shark coming from any direction and try to defend each other.
- If the shark grabs you, fight back. Poke, claw or gouge at its eyes and gills or batter it around the snout until it lets go.
- Use anything you can reach as a weapon – surf board, paddle, rock or shell.
- If the shark lets you go, don't hang about – it will be back. Swim for the shore or get into a boat as quickly as you can.
- Once safe, concentrate on stopping the bleeding. If blood is pumping from a severed artery, you can bleed to death in less than 15 minutes. Use pressure on the wound to reduce bleeding or a tourniquet tied around the limb above the wound to cut off the blood supply.
- Seek medical attention even for a minor injury. Infections can easily set in.

Having survived your encounter with the shark, you should also make sure that the local authorities know what has happened, if they don't already know, so that they can take steps to protect others.

Select Bibliography

Allen, Thomas, B., *Shark Attacks: Their Causes and Avoidance*, Constable & Robinson, London, and Lyons Press, New York, 2001.

—— *The Shark Almanac*, Lyons Press, New York, 1999.

—— and MacCormick and Young, *Shadows in the Sea*, Lyons Press, New York, 1996.

Baidridge. H. D., *Shark Attack*, Berkley Publishing Corp., New York, 1974; Everest Books, UK, 1976.

Brown, Theo W., *Sharks: The Silent Savages*, Little, Brown, Boston, 1973.

Compagno, Leonard, *Sharks of the World*, FAO Species Catalogue, Rome, 1984.

Coppleson, Victor M., *Shark Attack*, Angus & Robertson, London, 1959.

Davies, David H., *About Sharks and Shark Attacks*, Shuter & Shooter, Pietermaritzburg, 1964.

Ellis, Richard, *The Book of Sharks*, Grosset & Dunlap, New York, 1976.

—— and McCosker, John E., *Great White Shark*, HarperCollins, London and New York, 1991.

Klimley, A. P., and Ainley, D. G. (eds), *Great White Sharks*, Academic Press, San Diego, 1996.

Lineaweaver, Thomas H., and Backus, Richard H., *The Natural History of Sharks*, Lippincott, Philadelphia, 1969; Deutsch, London, 1970.

Maniguet, Xavier, *The Jaws of Death: Shark as Predator, Man as Prey*, HarperCollins, London, 1992.

Sharks: Silent Hunters of the Deep, Reader's Digest, Sydney, Australia.

Springer, V. G., and Gold, Joy P., *Sharks in Question: The Smithsonian Answer Book*, Smithsonian Institute Press, Washington DC, 1989.

Stafford-Deitsch, Jeremy, *Shark: A Photographer's Story*, Sierra Club Books, San Francisco, 1988.

Steel, R., *Sharks of the World*, Blandford Press, 1985.

Stevens, J. D. (ed.), *Sharks*, Facts on File Publications, New York, 1987.

Wallett, T. S., *Shark Attack in Southern African Waters and Treatment of Victims*, Struik, Cape Town, 1983.

Young, Captain William E., *Shark! Shark! The Thirty-Year Odyssey of a Pioneer Shark Hunter*, Gotham House, USA, 1934.

Acknowledgements

The authors would like to acknowledge, with grateful thanks, the help of the following individuals and organizations in this revised edition: George Burgess and the staff of the International Shark Attack File (www. flmnh.ufl.edu/fish/Sharks/ISAF/ISAF.htm); Clive James and Ali of the Shark Trust, Plymouth, UK (enquiries@ sharktrust.org); Ian Fergusson at shark.bureau@zoo. co.uk; the staff of the British Library Newspaper Library at Colindale; the staff of Battersea Reference Library, London; Bill Curtsinger and National Geographic; Vinay C. Patel of Jeffrey's News, Battersea; Barbara Guthrie and Charles, William, Katherine and John Jennings; Nick Robinson, Josephine McGurk, Duncan Proudfoot, Pete Duncan and all their enthusiastic colleagues at Constable & Robinson.

List of Illustrations

Photo Credits

'Watson and the Shark' original oil painting by
John Singleton Copely, 1778

Great white off Dyer Island, South Africa –
photograph by Alban
https://creativecommons.org/licenses/by-sa/3.0/deed.en

Tiger shark hanging up – United States National Oceanic and
Atmospheric Administration

Great white off Isla Guadalupe, Mexico –
photograph by Terry Goss
https://creativecommons.org/licenses/by-sa/3.0/deed.en

Hammerhead shark off Cocos Island, Costa Rica –
photograph by Barry Peters
https://creativecommons.org/licenses/by/2.0/deed.en

Grey reef shark – Untied States National Oceanic and
Atmospheric Administration

Male whale shark, Georgia Aquarium –
photograph by Zac Wolf
https://creativecommons.org/licenses/by-sa/2.5/deed.en

Bamboo shark courtesy or Merlin Entertainments National
Sea Life Centre, Birmingham

Great white shark, False Bay, South Africa, courtesy of
Vnoucek, F/DPA/Press Association Images

Bethany Hamilton courtesy of Matt Sayles/AP/Press
Association Images